To Detain *or* To Punish

States, People, and the History of Social Change

SERIES EDITORS ROSALIND CRONE AND STEVEN KING

The States, People, and the History of Social Change series brings together cutting-edge books written by academic historians on criminal justice, welfare, education, health, and other areas of social change and social policy. The ways in which states, governments, and local communities have responded to "social problems" can be seen across many different temporal and geographical contexts. From the early modern period to contemporary times, states have attempted to shape the lives of their inhabitants in important ways. Books in this series explore how groups and individuals have negotiated the use of state power and policy to regulate, change, control, or improve people's lives and the consequences of these processes. The series welcomes international scholars whose research explores social policy (and its earlier equivalents) as well as other responses to social need, in historical perspective.

4 Indentured Servitude
Unfree Labour and Citizenship in the British Colonies
Anna Suranyi

5 Penal Servitude
Convicts and Long-Term Imprisonment, 1853–1948
Helen Johnston, Barry Godfrey, and David J. Cox

6 In Their Own Write
Contesting the New Poor Law, 1834–1900
Steven King, Paul Carter, Natalie Carter, Peter Jones, and Carol Beardmore

7 Looking After Miss Alexander
Care, Mental Capacity, and the Court of Protection in Mid-Twentieth-Century England
Janet Weston

8 Friendless or Forsaken?
Child Emigration from Britain to Canada, 1860–1935
Ruth Lamont, Eloise Moss, and Charlotte Wildman

9 Fraudulent Lives
Imagining Welfare Cheats from the Poor Law to the Present
Steven King

10 Slow Train to Arcadia
A History of Railway Commuting into London
Duncan Gager

11 Prisoners' Bodies
Activism, Health, and the Prisoners' Rights Movement in Ireland, 1972–1985
Oisín Wall

12 To Detain or to Punish
Magistrates and the Making of the London Prison System, 1750–1840
Kiran Mehta

To Detain *or* To Punish

Magistrates and the Making of the London Prison System, 1750–1840

KIRAN MEHTA

McGill-Queen's University Press
MONTREAL & KINGSTON • LONDON • CHICAGO

© McGill-Queen's University Press 2025

ISBN 978-0-2280-2408-8 (paper)
ISBN 978-0-2280-2409-5 (ePDF)
ISBN 978-0-2280-2410-1 (ePUB)

Legal deposit first quarter 2025
Bibliothèque nationale du Québec

Printed in Canada on acid-free paper that is 100% ancient forest free (100% post-consumer recycled), processed chlorine free

McGill-Queen's University Press in Montreal is on land which long served as a site of meeting and exchange amongst Indigenous Peoples, including the Haudenosaunee and Anishinabeg nations. In Kingston it is situated on the territory of the Haudenosaunee and Anishinaabek. We acknowledge and thank the diverse Indigenous Peoples whose footsteps have marked these territories on which peoples of the world now gather.

LIBRARY AND ARCHIVES CANADA CATALOGUING IN PUBLICATION

Title: To detain or to punish : magistrates and the making of the London prison system, 1750–1840 / Kiran Mehta.
Names: Mehta, Kiran (Kiran A.), author.
Series: States, people, and the history of social change ; 12.
Description: Series statement: States, people, and the history of social change ; 12 | Includes bibliographical references and index.
Identifiers: Canadiana (print) 20240509331 | Canadiana (ebook) 20240509366 | ISBN 9780228024088 (paper) | ISBN 9780228024095 (PDF) | ISBN 9780228024101 (EPUB)
Subjects: LCSH: Prisons—England—London—History—18th century. | LCSH: Prisons—England—London—History—19th century. | LCSH: Imprisonment—England—London—History—18th century. | LCSH: Imprisonment—England—London—History—19th century.
Classification: LCC HV9650.L7 M44 2025 | DDC 365.9421/209033—dc23

This book was designed and typeset by Lara Minja in Adobe Jenson Pro 11 pt /14.5 pt with Warnock Pro for headings and subheadings. Copyediting by Grace Seybold.

Contents

Tables and Figures

TABLES

FIGURES

Acknowledgments

I first started thinking about London prisons, especially houses of correction, in 2013, when I was an undergraduate at Cornell University. My adviser and course professor at the time, Rachel Weil, supported and encouraged my interest, and she helped me to develop a plan for an honours thesis exploring the controversies that surrounded the Middlesex bridewell in the eighteenth and early nineteenth centuries. That initial project spawned first a master's dissertation, then a doctoral dissertation, and now a monograph on London's prison system. My greatest thanks go to those who have supervised these works. Not only did Rachel get me interested in bridewells and provide essential advice as I was first starting to navigate archival research, but she has continued to offer support and friendship over the years, for which I am grateful. This work could not have been completed without Joanna Innes, who supervised my master's and doctoral dissertations. I know few people more generous with their time and their insight than Joanna. Her feedback and support have been invaluable, not just in the years that I was completing my degrees, but in the years following. Thank you for everything, Joanna.

Various people have enriched this work by reading draft chapters or commenting on seminar papers. I would especially like to thank my doctoral thesis examiners, Deborah Oxley and Brodie Waddell, who provided fulsome feedback and early steering. Deb, in particular, has been a source of intellectual and professional support in recent years. Thank you also to the four anonymous reviewers who read my book manuscript.

When writing first the doctorate and then this book, I benefited immensely from the lively academic community at the University of Oxford, where I spent eight years studying and later teaching. My thanks to attendees of the Graduate Seminar in British History (1660–1850) and its stalwart convenors. Key friends who have offered advice, support, and consolation through the years include Emma Day, Drew Holland, Tim Wade, Richard Bell, and Hunter Harris. In addition, I am immensely grateful to Kathryn Gleadle, whose impressive scholarship is matched by her exceptional teaching; it has been a privilege to learn from you, Kathryn. Finally, I would like to thank Worcester College, where I held my first teaching post after completing my doctorate. Particular thanks go to my colleagues and friends there, especially Conrad Leyser and Bob Harris, and to the History students.

Several other institutions and funding bodies have supported me as I completed this book. I was lucky to spend six months in Frankfurt, Germany, in 2023–24 as a visiting research fellow at the Max Planck Institute of Legal History and Legal Theory, during which time I completed and submitted my manuscript. Thanks to Stefan Vogenauer, a director of the Institute and head of the European and Comparative Legal History Department, for inviting me; to members of the Common Law Research Seminar, who made my time in Frankfurt so lovely; and especially to Matilde Cazzola and Nina Cozzi. In April 2024, I started a Leverhulme Early Career Fellowship at the University of Leicester under the mentorship of Clare Anderson. This position has allowed me to complete the edits for this manuscript and the Leverhulme research funding has enabled me to visit other English county archives, permitting me to say something (however limited) about practice outside London. Thank you, Clare, for helping me to navigate the transition to my new position and thank you to Leicester and my new colleagues for being so welcoming.

I also want to thank the archivists and librarians who helped me to access and granted me permission to reproduce materials: the London Metropolitan Archives, the Surrey History Centre, the Bodleian Libraries, the Wellcome Collection, the Metropolitan Museum of Art, the Widener Library at Harvard University, Norfolk Record Office, the National Archives at Kew, the British Library, the Wiltshire and Swindon History Centre, and the Buckinghamshire Archives.

The team at McGill-Queen's University Press have been wonderful. Thank you to Kyla Madden, Richard Baggaley, Grace Rosalie Seybold, Kathleen Fraser, and Catherine Bienvenu. I am also grateful to the series editors of *States, People, and the History of Social Change*, Rosalind Crone and Steven King, for their interest in my project.

Last but not least, I must thank my family. I could only follow this path because my mom and dad, Barbara and Rai, supported and encouraged me. My sister, Sarah, has been a model whom I have strived to emulate, as well as my closest friend. And finally, Tim: thank you for living and writing alongside me. This book is dedicated to you.

Abbreviations

BCGM	Bridewell Court of Governors Minutes
BL	British Library
BPCM	Bridewell Prison Committee Minutes
BPSCM	Bridewell Prison Sub-Committee Minutes
CAGCP	Court of Aldermen Gaol Committee Papers
CAGCM	Court of Aldermen Gaol Committee Minutes
LL	London Lives (www.londonlives.org)
LMA	London Metropolitan Archives
MGOC	Middlesex General Orders of the Court
MPCM	Middlesex Prison Committee Minutes
MPCR	Middlesex Prison Committee Reports
MSP	Middlesex Sessions Papers
OBO	Old Bailey Online (www.oldbaileyonline.org)
PP	Parliamentary Papers
SHC	Surrey Historical Centre
SIPD	Society for the Improvement of Prison Discipline
SSP	Surrey Sessions Papers

Original spelling has been preserved in all quotations.

To Detain *or* To Punish

INTRODUCTION

Imprisonment in the "Nation of Liberty"

There are in London, and the far extended bounds … notwithstanding we are a nation of liberty, more publick and private prisons, and houses of confinement, than any city in Europe, perhaps as many as in all the capital cities of Europe put together.[1]

London, as the writer Daniel Defoe found when touring Great Britain in the 1720s, was a city crowded with prisons. By Defoe's count there were at least twenty-seven 'public' prisons and dozens of 'private' ones in England's largest city, most of which, at least the public ones, were still open in the 1750s, when this study begins. London's penal landscape was not just vast, but also varied. Its collection of confining institutions included gaols, compters, lock-ups, roundhouses, debtor's prisons, state prisons, houses of correction or bridewells, and, from the end of the century, hulks and penitentiaries. Londoners were deeply acquainted with these institutions. The buildings dotted the city landscape, abutting private houses, inns and pubs, sites of worship, and places of work. The smells and sounds of prisons permeated the neighbourhoods in which they were based, much to the occasional disgust of surrounding homeowners. Crucially, a great many spent time in these prisons. Some would have entered as traders, selling goods to prisoners; others as prison officers or servants; yet more as visitors to friends or family confined; some went in an official capacity, as magistrates, sheriffs, or members

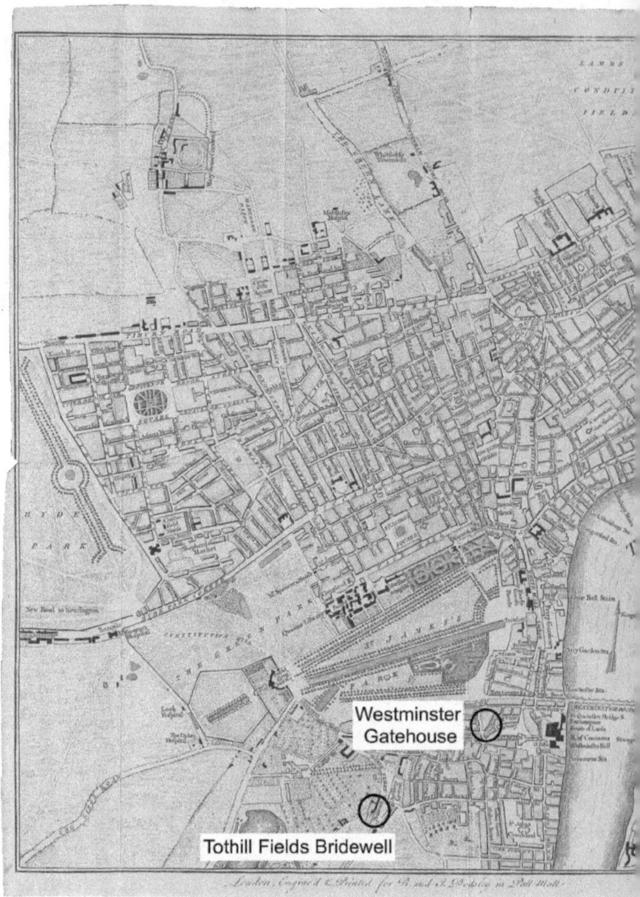

Figure 0.1 • Map of London's prisons, c. 1770. Labels added by author.

of parliamentary committees or royal commissions. And of course, thousands spent some time as inmates in London's prisons each year in the eighteenth century. In short, incarceration was exceedingly familiar to Londoners, embedded into everyday life.

Imprisonment fulfilled three main purposes in eighteenth-century England: to safely detain offenders accused of unlawful acts, to hold debtors while creditors pursued civil suits for debt, and to punish convicted offenders. The variety of prisons related in part to the sundry functions that imprisonment served. Yet although particular prisons had usually been founded with specific purposes in mind, by the eighteenth century, most had long served an assortment of roles, so institutions generally held a diverse range of inmates

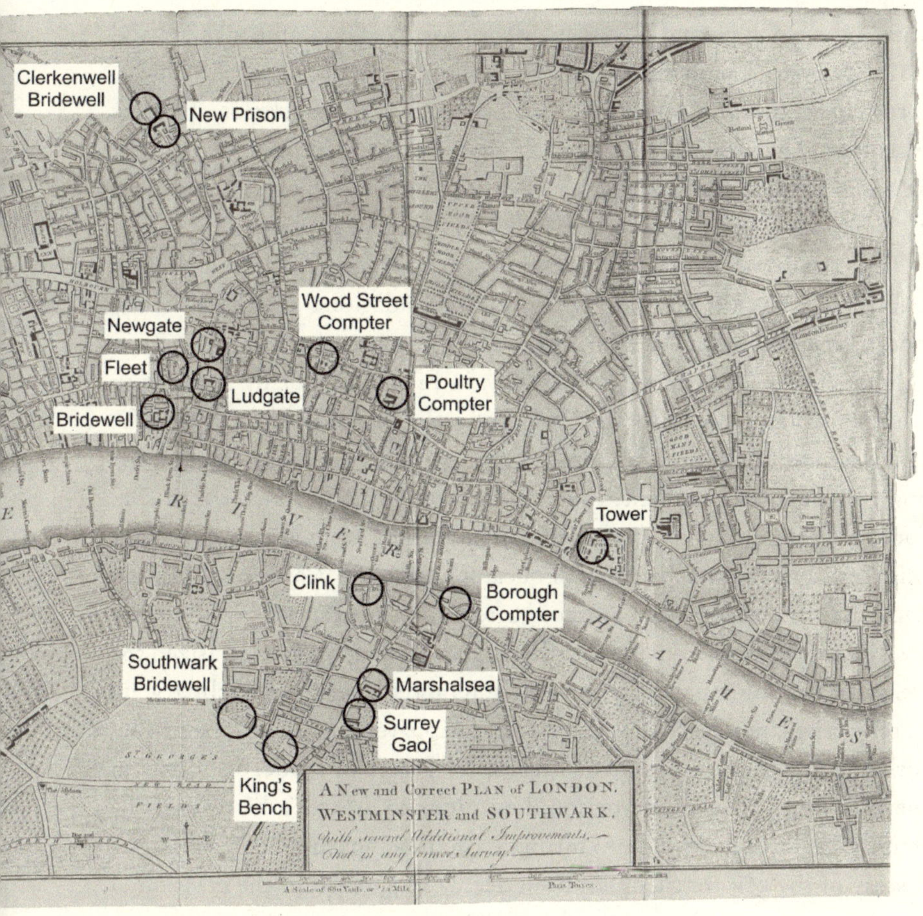

incarcerated for a multitude of reasons. Over the course of the eighteenth century, this changed.

This work aims to rewrite the story of the rise of criminal imprisonment and the so-called 'birth' of the modern prison. As the tale commonly goes, before the end of the eighteenth century, imprisonment was used only rarely as a punishment, at least for serious offences; yet, by the middle of the nineteenth century, it had become, by far, the most common punishment handed out by the courts. Scholars have long been fascinated by the sudden and overwhelming embrace of imprisonment and have offered an array of explanations for the prison's rapid ascent. Until the 1970s, progressive narratives of history, often known as 'Whig histories' in the British context, were dominant. In such accounts, a change in mentalities, namely the growth of humanitarianism and sensibility, associated with the spread of Enlightenment and Evangelical ideas, prompted contemporaries to embrace the prison.[2] For these scholars, reforms to the criminal law represented one facet of modernizing projects that swept Britain and Europe in the long eighteenth century and which saw the "barbaric cruelty," ignorance, and corruption of previous centuries replaced.[3]

The field was transformed by the intervention of Michel Foucault, who in 1975 published *Surveiller et Punir*, perhaps the foundational text in the study of modern imprisonment's origins.[4] Foucault's account charted the shift in punishment in the late eighteenth century, in France especially but also in the Western world more generally, away from the brutal practices of public execution, torture, and corporal punishment towards the development of the seemingly milder, more humane, and more 'civilized' institution of the prison. For Foucault, the revolution in punishment stemmed from an ambition "not to punish less, but to punish better."[5] Foucault and other Western scholars in the 1970s and early 1980s who embraced a 'revisionist' perspective did not see the new systems as more humane or enlightened. Rather, they emphasized the austere, authoritarian aspect of the new prisons and the severe disciplinary nature of reformist language.[6] Though Foucault's apparent focus was the prison, his work is really an account of the exercise of power in modern society. In considering the history of the prison, he sought to create "a history of the different modes by which, in our culture, human beings are made subjects."[7] The history of the prison, then, has been deeply implicated in the creation of various modernities, not least that of the self.[8]

In the wake of Foucault's intervention and the findings of revisionist historians, scholars have continued to debate the reasons behind the turn to imprisonment as well as the character of penal confinement. Some, for instance, stress the importance of changes in economic structures and modes of production. Dario Melossi and Massimo Pavarini, writing in the 1970s and drawing on work published in the 1930s by Georg Rusche and Otto Kirchheimer, took a Marxist approach, linking the 'birth' of the prison to the spread of capitalism. For these Italian criminologists, the prison was ancillary to the factory. It was used by capitalists, supported by states, to create and discipline a proletariat class.[9] Similarly, in accounting for the advent of the penitentiary in England, Michael Ignatieff pointed to the changes wrought in the fabric of English society by the industrial revolution.[10] Others have continued to stress the importance of changes in mentalities. John Beattie maintained that Enlightenment ideas, especially rationalism but also perhaps humanitarianism, played a role in changing contemporary attitudes towards punishment.[11] Randal McGowen, meanwhile, spotlighted changes in attitudes towards the body in shaping the evolution of punishment.[12] Pieter Spirenburg, drawing on the German sociologist Norbert Elias, understood changes in the forms of punishment to be part of a "civilising process," linked to state formation.[13]

What this scholarship makes clear is that there was no single reason that prompted authorities across England to embrace imprisonment. Instead, imprisonment spread because it appealed to many different groups of authorities for several reasons. In particular, as this book will explore, it could be sold not only as a more humane punishment, but also as a more rational, efficient, and effective one. As we shall see, a desire to punish with greater mercy was not incompatible with a desire to punish better. Yet these studies have notable limitations which mean that our understanding of imprisonment – its use by the courts, its management by local authorities, and its daily operation – is incomplete.

First, most studies of imprisonment are partial, in that they tend to focus *either* on court sentencing practice *or* on the administration and experience of confinement. While court studies invaluably chart how courts came to adopt imprisonment, they say little about how the punishment was actually carried out or what it entailed. Prison studies, meanwhile, address the nature of incarceration, but typically they do not consider the sorts of individuals subjected to the confinement. This study, by contrast, integrates an examination of the process of becoming a prisoner – arrest, interrogation, trial, and sentencing – with a study of prison reform, administration, and discipline.[14] Such an approach is more onerous than focusing on only one element of imprisonment, and therefore it is rarely done, but it has several advantages. Not only does it allow us to consider how the growth of imprisonment fitted into larger patterns in the evolution of criminal punishment and of prison systems, but this approach also shows how patterns in the commitment of offenders crucially shaped, and in turn were shaped by, changes in the organization of confinement.[15]

Second, most imprisonment histories, whether they focus on courts or on prisons, deal almost exclusively with the use of imprisonment to punish serious felonies. The shift away from execution and transportation and towards imprisonment in punishing these felonies was undoubtedly a monumental one, with important consequences for modern Britain;

nonetheless, it should be remembered that most crimes committed and tried in eighteenth- and nineteenth-century Britain were of a less serious nature. This work, in recognition of the patterns of law-breaking and prosecution, takes a broader approach. It looks at the use and experience of imprisonment as a punishment not only for felonious offences, but also for misdemeanours and summary offences. To do this, this study considers the sentencing and prison commitment practices of a variety of courts, including the Old Bailey, the Surrey assizes, the various London quarter sessions, and the summary courts. It pays particular attention to summary courts, which have received less scholarly attention, especially as regards their punishment practices. In this respect, this work follows the groundbreaking work of scholars such as Peter King, Robert Shoemaker, Doug Hay, and Drew Gray, who called our attention to the treatment of less serious offences and the petty courts that dealt with them. Crucially, however, this study is not just about punishment. It additionally considers incarceration as a means of criminal detention: that is, the use of prisons to temporarily detain offenders while they awaited examination, trial, or sentencing, until they provided sureties to the relevant authorities, or to give evidence in court.

Third, most imprisonment histories insufficiently attend to the differences between carceral institutions. Scholars have been generally uninterested in the specific institutions in which prisoners were confined. Studies often focus primarily on one type of prison (usually a gaol), or if more prison types are discussed, these are treated as largely interchangeable or not substantially different. The house of correction has been especially neglected.[16] By contrast, this work closely considers each of the three main kinds of criminal prisons that operated in London in the eighteenth and nineteenth centuries: gaols, compters, and houses of correction. Doing so allows us to ask whether London authorities used their different prisons in distinct ways, and, if so, to explore exactly how.

This study is not comprehensive, however. It is principally concerned with *criminal* rather than civil imprisonment, so confinement for debt, a very common – and well-studied – use of imprisonment in this period, is largely excluded from this work.[17] Additionally, I touch only briefly on those carceral institutions (penitentiaries and convict prisons) that were established in the nineteenth century by central authorities to hold serious convicts who had been sentenced to a long term of imprisonment or whose sentence of transportation included a prior period of imprisonment. Not only have these prisons been well served by other scholars, but they stand apart from my main focus, the prison commitment practices of and prison management by London authorities. Those who ended up in these institutions did so primarily at the initiative of Home Office officials rather than through local decision-making, and the institutions themselves were run by Westminster appointees.[18] There is also good methodological reason to shift the focus away from the penitentiaries, Millbank and Pentonville: only a very small proportion of prisoners ordered to be imprisoned ever spent time in these institutions. Instead, the vast majority of prisoners were incarcerated in gaols, compters, and houses of correction – institutions which, as noted already, have been insufficiently studied.[19]

For many decades, local studies of the prison have fallen from favour, castigated as overly parochial and particular. However, a local perspective is vital to understanding changes in penal policy, court practice, and prison operation in this period. Indeed, it is key to telling the broader story about punishment and government in eighteenth- and nineteenth-century England. This work is indebted to an earlier generation of scholars who, working in county archives in the 1970s and 1980s, closely attended to the actual practice in and management of English prisons. Their efforts made a strong case for reconsidering the role and character of imprisonment in the period before the late eighteenth century, which, they argued, was not as chaotic, mismanaged, or one-dimensional as reformers and early scholars had suggested. W.J. Sheehan's 1975 doctoral thesis, "The London Prisons System, 1666–1795," a study of the management and regulation of prisons in the City of London, has been especially influential in shaping my view of City imprisonment.[20] Still, the account of incarceration presented by these studies is quite partial. Not only do they cover only a handful of counties, but most concentrate on the final third of the eighteenth century onwards. A new group of scholars is tackling this chronological limitation, providing us with a fuller and more nuanced understanding of prison management and experience in the seventeenth and early eighteenth centuries. Mostly, however, these studies focus on London, and so our knowledge of incarceration in England and Britain more broadly remains limited.[21] In spite of these serious difficulties, this volume will try when possible to place London developments in a wider, national framework.

In deviating methodologically and conceptually from earlier studies, this work aims to provide a more holistic perspective of the rise of imprisonment and the development of the modern prison. In particular, it offers a radical reappraisal of the prison system in the London metropolis. It makes a case for the wider and deeper appeal of imprisonment in the eighteenth century, and for the specialized nature of London's prison system. I argue that, as the use of imprisonment expanded and the number of offenders incarcerated grew, committing bodies across London, led by the local justices of the peace, assigned specialized roles to the prisons under their jurisdiction. Prison specialization was not a new idea or practice in the late eighteenth century; indeed, London prisons had filled highly specialized roles at the start of the eighteenth century. However, from 1720, the purposes of the different prisons became somewhat mixed, as changes in statute law made it increasingly possible to blur the distinctions between prisons and to use them interchangeably. In London, with its plethora of prisons, committing bodies had a range of options regarding where they sent offenders. While authorities in the mid-eighteenth century took advantage of this flexibility, using their prisons as multi-function custodial institutions, by the 1780s this policy was under fire. Increasingly, magistrates, both as a bench making policy decisions and as individuals in their commitment practice, used their stock of prisons to target commitments and create distinctive penal regimes.

Crucially, this period saw the crystallization of two distinct forms of confinement: custodial detention and punitive imprisonment. Across London, local authorities came to treat prisons as *either* custodial *or* punitive, and with increasing regularity, they directed prisoners confined for punishment to prisons – namely, houses of correction – distinct from those where prisoners held for safe custody were detained – primarily, gaols and compters. This period, then, saw the consolidation of the 'modern' conviction that individuals who had not been convicted of a crime or who had not been sentenced to imprisonment as a punishment should be held separate from and treated differently from those incarcerated for punishment. This book traces the genesis of this idea for the first time and charts how it revolutionized London's prison system.

These shifts in attitude, and specifically the commitment practices that they inspired, provide a crucial context for understanding changes in the administration and internal operation of London prisons. At the end of the eighteenth century, local magistrates across England, undirected and uncoordinated but dealing with similar problems (gaol fever, crumbling prisons, and severe overcrowding, for example), took up the cause of penal reform. In the London metropolis, every prison was either rebuilt or substantially reconstructed.

Historians have repeatedly charted this process, but they have focused primarily on the ideology of reformers and on the substantive reforms enacted, seeking primarily to resolve the debate over whether reformers were driven more by humanitarianism or by a desire to impose a more severe discipline. What they have not done is to relate changes in commitment practices to the chronology and character of change in prison regimes. These changes, however, provided the matrix within which prison reform took place and crucially shaped its character. In short, we cannot understand the form a prison took without understanding the role that it played in the justice system.

Reform at gaols and compters, the main sites of custodial detention, differed markedly from reform at houses of correction, the main prisons for punishment. At the former, local authorities designed a regime of "mere detention," while, at the latter, they instituted a regime that was punitive and reformative. Struggles to define the meaning of 'mere detention' and the appropriate conditions to ensure punishment and reformation consumed local and central governments, reformers, prison authorities, and prisoners in the late eighteenth and early nineteenth centuries. In London, the obligation to labour, more than anything, came to define punitive confinement and to separate convicted and non-convicted prisoners. As a result of the reforms, by the start of the nineteenth century, prisoners confined in houses of correction were experiencing a vastly different regime of confinement from those in gaols – and this remained the case throughout the first half of the nineteenth century.

This work, then, presents a very different view of English imprisonment from that which is typically presented. Historians have generally concluded that although there were different kinds of imprisonment, these were hardly distinct, and moreover that from the late seventeenth century, the different prisons effectively merged in form and function. This convergence, it has been assumed, stemmed from contemporaries' lack of faith in imprisonment as an effective punishment. Consequently, by the start of the eighteenth century, the prison appealed more as a place to hold unwanted people, to get them off the streets, than as a place of punishment or rehabilitation. As a result, houses of correction lost their specific purpose and regime, and they became, like gaols and compters, just another site of detention.

This view originated with Sidney and Beatrice Webb. In *English Prisons under Local Governance*, first published in 1922, the Webbs noted that houses of correction were founded in the sixteenth century to confine and put to work vagrants and idle and disorderly persons, but claimed that by the end of the seventeenth century these distinctive features had almost totally disappeared. Magistrates had abandoned their commitment to disciplinary labour, and they were sending a greater variety of offenders, not just vagrants, to the bridewell for detention as well as punishment. The Webbs concluded that, in most counties, by the early part of the eighteenth century, it was "difficult to discover any practical distinction between the house of correction and the common gaol, whether in administration, discipline or the character of the inmates."[22]

The historiography of English prisons has moved on considerably since the Webbs; nevertheless, their conclusions as to the condition of English bridewells and their relationship to gaols have regularly been repeated.[23] Some historians have pushed back against this interpretation, most notably Joanna Innes and John Beattie, both of whom argued that bridewells did not lose their distinctive identity or purpose in the eighteenth century.[24] However, despite these important interventions, the view has not been integrated more widely into the historiography. Generally, gaols, compters, and houses of correction are either treated as interchangeable or, at least, not sufficiently distinguished and differentiated. Attending to the distinctions between prisons, however, reveals that differences existed between these institutions at the start of the period, and that, over the course of the late eighteenth and early nineteenth centuries, these differences developed further.

PARAMETERS AND STRUCTURE OF THE STUDY

England's capital was by far its most populous city, home to roughly 10 per cent of the population by 1750. Its geography was also expansive. What we understand today as London was historically made up of four discrete areas, the Cities of London and Westminster and the urban parishes of the counties of Middlesex and Surrey. This study is concerned with court practice and prison operation in all these areas except the City of Westminster, which is largely excluded. Few records for the Westminster prisons survive for the period under study, so it is difficult to study them in any detail.[25] It is also not evident that including Westminster would change the picture presented here. By the middle of the eighteenth century, responsibility for justice in this area rested primarily

– and increasingly – with the Middlesex sessions, so we can get a sense of commitment practice and prison use in Westminster by studying Middlesex.[26]

This work is structured chronologically and thematically. The first four chapters focus roughly on the years 1755 to 1815, the period which saw the rise of the first prison reform movement. The final chapters focus on the period from 1815, when the Napoleonic Wars ended and agitation for prison reform resumed, to the 1840s, when penal policy was increasingly centralized.

Chapter 1 examines prison commitment practice in the City, Middlesex, and Surrey, proceeding from the lowest levels of justice to the highest. It draws on a wide range of archival and manuscript sources, including: court books; prisoner lists, books, and rolls; criminal registers; police records; parliamentary papers; professional manuals; justices' working papers; and newspaper articles. By drawing on such an unusually broad range and unprecedented number of records, this chapter shines a light on London's local prison system, so often deemed impenetrable by scholars, and provides coherence to the previously opaque and seemingly random sentencing decisions of local authorities. In particular, it charts the specialization of London's prisons and offers a new interpretation of the growing use of imprisonment as a punishment.

Local interest in setting certain kinds of prisoners to work principally drove and shaped prison specialization, as chapter 2 charts. Contemporary interest in prison labour has usually been overlooked by historians, who have assumed that inmates rarely if ever worked in the eighteenth century. This view stands in need of radical reassessment. In London, magistrates could reasonably expect that, when sending a convicted prisoner to a period of confinement in a bridewell, that prisoner would be put to work. At the end of the century, prison labour took on renewed importance, assuming a critical role in shaping commitment decisions and prison discipline. Greatly concerned about the state of contemporary morals, especially the poor's, but confident in the human potential for reform, magistrates looked to institutionalized labour, combined with religious instruction and some isolation, as a means to suppress vice and improve morals.

Chapters 3 and 4 revisit the late-eighteenth-century prison reform movement. Chapter 3 focuses on the ideologies of prison reform, especially that of the pre-eminent reformer John Howard, and on the nature of the pre-reform prison. It aims to contextualize Howard's complaints about prisons and his recommendations for reform by considering the extent to which his objections reflected the reality of confinement in London. This chapter pushes back against three common tendencies: to see the proposals of prison reformers as totally new; to emphasize a clear break between pre-reform and reform prisons; and to suggest there was one single model of prison reform. Reform, we shall see, was a vibrant movement with a great many proponents and contributors, and there was not total agreement amongst them regarding priorities and policies. Unsurprisingly, therefore, reform projects, even within a single county, took various forms. This last point will be taken up in chapter 4, which aims to markedly revise our understanding of the 'reformed prison.' It traces how local authorities tailored reform projects according to the type of prison and the sorts of prisoners held within it. One effect of this policy was to make the system of imprisonment in houses of correction ever more distinct from that at gaols and compters. Chapter 4 concludes with a coda, which reflects on the ideological and practical reasons that drove magistrates at the end of the eighteenth century to pursue policies that allowed them to keep apart and treat differently tried and untried prisoners.

As imprisonment became a more popular sanction in the nineteenth century, the uses of imprisonment expanded and altered, and the numbers incarcerated soared. Chapter 5 traces these expansions and their consequences. As we shall see, changes in sentencing practice forced local authorities to adapt their prisons and their commitment practices. Although London's jurisdictions responded differently to sentencing shifts, there was a clear trend across the metropolis towards increasing prison specialization: authorities stepped up efforts to enforce a separation between custodial detention and punitive imprisonment.

Chapter 6, the final substantive chapter, explores the nature of discipline at London prisons in the first half of the nineteenth century. Historians have taken different views on this period of prison history. While many have highlighted the ongoing commitment to reformative philosophies of confinement, others have noted a hardening of attitudes towards the poor and criminal offenders, which they say prompted the introduction of tougher measures within prisons. This chapter revisits these debates by considering why and where harsher measures were introduced and the impact these measures had in practice. It focuses especially on one measure: prison labour.

This work ends with a conclusion which, first, considers the fate of London's specialized prison system as the capacity for local authorities to shape prison policy diminished in the face of greater centralization and bureaucratization in the nineteenth century, and second, reiterates this work's major contributions to the history of imprisonment.

The remainder of this introduction now provides an overview of the development of imprisonment in England, the origin of the different prison types, and the laws that governed the application of imprisonment. As we shall see, prisons were founded to serve distinct purposes, but as legislation and court practice extended the uses to which imprisonment could be put, the traditional divisions between the prison types were largely erased, in principle if not in practice.

IMPRISONMENT IN ENGLAND

Imprisonment has been used in England as far back as the Anglo-Saxon period. In this context, imprisonment encompassed the confinement of the body in any manner, whether in a building specified for that purpose, or in the pillory or stocks. Imprisonment served custodial as well as coercive and punitive purposes. Although it is sometimes asserted that the use of imprisonment as a punishment is a modern phenomenon, Ralph Pugh proved definitively that imprisonment was a punishment from at least the ninth century and probably earlier.[27] Over the ensuing centuries, as imprisonment came to be used with more regularity, the number of prisons expanded, and the kinds of prisons diversified.

In the twelfth century, certain prisons, known as gaols, were established across England under the jurisdiction of the king's sheriffs. Sheriffs were royal appointees responsible for bringing suspects to trial. For this role, a number had begun to provide special buildings, gaols, to keep prisoners safely until trial – an arrangement which received royal approval and new impetus in 1166 when Henry II ordered sheriffs to build or provide gaols in counties that lacked them. The sheriffs responded swiftly. In 1166, at least seventeen counties and one city spent money on building or repairing gaols, and by 1216, only five counties lacked one.[28] From the thirteenth century, accused offenders found it increasingly difficult to stay out of prison while awaiting trial, and consequently, custodial imprisonment became more common.[29] By an act of 1403, prisoners held for safe custody could be committed to the common gaol only "and not elsewhere."[30]

Table 0.1 Main types of criminal prison in England

Gaols	Compters or Counters	Bridewells or Houses of Correction
Foundation: 12th century	Foundation: 14th century	Foundation: 16th century
1166 Assizes of Clarendon	Jurisdiction: Sheriffs	Bridewell, City of London, 1553–55
Jurisdiction: Sheriff	Unique to City of London?	Jurisdiction: Justices of the Peace
Original function: Custodial	Original function: Custodial	Original function: Punitive
Debtors held here	Constructed specially to accommodate the sheriffs' offices, prisoners, and courtrooms	Penal arm of the poor laws
	Sheriffs' debtors held here	

From the twelfth century, the City of London had two gaols, the Fleet and Newgate.[31] The latter served as a common gaol for both the City and Middlesex. In 1685, the Middlesex magistrates built an additional gaol, New Prison, in Clerkenwell, and from then on, Middlesex prisoners could be held in either Newgate or New Prison.[32] In Surrey, the county gaol was based originally at Guildford Castle, a royal residence built shortly after the Norman conquest. The existence of a gaol there was first mentioned in 1202, and it continued to be used as such until some point in the mid-fifteenth or early sixteenth century.[33] From at least 1580, the Surrey gaol came to be based in the White Lion in Southwark.[34]

Soon after the gaols were founded, the sheriffs of London and Middlesex established another type of prison, the counter or compter. From the last quarter of the thirteenth century, each sheriff exercised jurisdiction in his own court, and compters were established to serve as offices, prisons, and sometimes additional courts for the sheriffs.[35] The location of the compters shifted regularly at first, as they were frequently based in the sheriff's house, but from the 1390s, they started to have fixed locations.[36] In 1393, a large mansion was converted into Poultry Compter, and in 1412, a second compter was set up on Bread Street, replaced in 1555 by Wood Street Compter.[37] A third compter was established in Southwark in 1550–51. The City had long exercised some authority over Southwark, but in 1550, a royal charter made Southwark a borough of the City of London, which among other things made the inhabitants subject to city law. Swiftly, the Corporation ordered

St Margaret's church in Southwark to be adapted into a "Justice house" with a compter attached.[38]

The house of correction was the first institution purposely designed, as opposed to ad-hoc co-opted, to use imprisonment as a punishment. Houses of correction originated in London in 1553 with the conversion of the disused royal palace of Bridewell following intensive petitioning by City notables. Bridewell's Charter envisioned an institution that would educate poor children, provide refuge and employment for hospital convalescents and recently discharged prisoners, and also correct and set to work the disorderly poor.[39] This last objective was enshrined in parliamentary legislation that aimed to spread houses of correction throughout England at the end of the sixteenth and start of the seventeenth centuries. Conceived of as the penal arm of the poor laws, houses of correction were intended to detain at hard labour the workless poor who wandered idly, perhaps begging or pilfering, and refused to work on public stocks of raw materials. Similar institutions subsequently appeared in cities across Europe, including Amsterdam, Copenhagen, Hamburg, Lyon, Madrid, and Brussels.[40]

Elizabethan acts placed the responsibility for establishing, organizing, and supervising houses of correction upon the local justices of the peace and authorized justices to use the county rates to build and stock them.[41] By an act of 1609–10, every county was required to erect at least one house of correction; in counties that failed to do so, each justice was liable to be fined five pounds, which would go towards building the bridewell.[42] Justices acted relatively swiftly, whether as a result of parliamentary pressure, legal obligation, or general endorsement of the bridewell's objectives. By 1630, there was at least one bridewell in every English county for which records survive.[43]

These different prisons, then, were established in specific contexts; they were linked to particular jurisdictions or officers and had specific functions relating to these roles. However, from the medieval to the early modern period, legislation and court practice extended the uses to which imprisonment could be put, and in so doing, largely eroded the original divisions between the prison types.

Almost as soon as a network of gaols was established in England, primarily to help sheriffs safely detain offenders awaiting trial, various authorities began to see benefits to using gaols as sites of punishment as well. Between 1274 and 1529, at least 180 statutes were passed that included the imposition of imprisonment as a punishment, threat, or means of coercion, while various kings ordered that specific offences be punished by imprisonment. In London, casebooks attest to the application of these laws by sheriffs, mayors, and aldermen, and they show that such sentences were served in gaols. For example, in 1328, a City court ordered a man convicted of stealing a tunic, valued at 10*d.*, to Newgate for forty days, and in 1388, the Lord Mayor and alderman ordered that butcher Richard Bole should be imprisoned in Newgate for six months for overcharging for his meat and insulting an alderman.[44] Newgate was still being used as a site of punishment for convicted offenders sentenced by the quarter and assize sessions in the eighteenth century. The offences punished by imprisonment were minor, though felons might also be imprisoned in gaols as a punishment through benefit of clergy or the use of pardons (see below).[45]

The appeal of imprisonment as a punishment grew larger in the context of successive crackdowns on petty crime and increased interest in monitoring and dictating the behaviour of the lower orders. Early modern authorities adopted new laws and altered their sentencing practices to target such groups and offences more effectively. In doing so, they expanded the house of correction beyond its traditional role in correcting the disorderly poor to additionally encompass the punishment of petty criminals. One device for doing this, employed regularly from the mid-sixteenth century, was to reimagine criminal offences as vagrancy, with the result that those convicted were directed to houses of correction. Other statutes extended the offences that could be punished by summary procedure and prescribed that violators be sent to houses of correction. Under summary jurisdiction, magistrates acting outside of quarter sessions – either alone, as a small group, or as part of a petty sessions bench – were empowered to resolve cases immediately before them without indictment or trial by jury.[46] The scope of summary jurisdiction expanded considerably in the eighteenth century and even more in the nineteenth.[47]

Most statutes of this kind specified that offenders be imprisoned in a house of correction, often at labour or even hard labour, the latter a nebulous term which presumably referred to work of a more painstaking or laborious kind but whose meaning was not further elucidated in parliamentary statutes or legal handbooks and whose specifics were apparently left to each county's justices to determine.[48] Yet, a handful authorized justices to imprison convicted offenders in any prison. Justices might imprison individuals summarily convicted of unlawfully pawning goods in "the house of correction, or some other publick prison," for example, and similarly, they could send silk throwers convicted of purloining, embezzling, or pawning silk to "prison or to the house of correction" for punishment.[49]

A 1719–20 act was especially significant in blurring the traditional divisions between prison types. This act explicitly allowed justices to commit "vagrants and other criminals, offenders and persons charged with small offences" to a common gaol or a house of correction either for those offences or for want of sureties to answer the offences. It enabled justices to use the house of correction for detention, a function previously reserved to gaols and a clear shift away from the bridewell's punitive purpose. Moreover, it gave justices a general authority to commit petty offenders, including vagrants, to *either* the house of correction *or* the gaol for punishment. Gaols therefore were specifically allocated a role in the punishment of the poor and of minor criminal offences. These broad powers of commitment were subsequently clarified and reaffirmed in 1783.[50]

The act was passed in trying circumstances. The 1710s saw a surge of indictments and prosecutions in London, animated by the onset of peace in 1713 and the accompanying demobilization of soldiers and sailors; by socioeconomic difficulties related to poor harvests; and by the controversial accession of George I in 1714.[51] Commitments to London gaols and houses of correction grew markedly.[52] Moreover, 1720 saw the return of plague to English shores, prompting concern amongst London officials about the cleanliness of prisons and the health of prisoners, both closely linked to the fullness of prisons.[53] This legislation was probably an attempt to embed greater flexibility within the law, reflecting the practical need to abandon temporarily the legal distinction between gaols and houses of correction as some prisons filled beyond capacity. As the statute's preamble stresses, the inability of justices to use the prisons at their disposal as they saw fit had "by experience … been found to be very prejudicial and expensive."[54]

In London, the legislation likely legitimized, rather than initiated, a practice already common. Possibly authorities sought greater alignment between practice and legislation during this challenging time to remove a possible basis for challenging a prison commitment. The act did not make gaols and bridewells interchangeable: the bridewell's custodial role was specifically limited to "small offences." Its passage nonetheless highlights the degree to which the perceived functions of bridewells and gaols had changed, and it paved the way for further confluence, including the use of bridewells as sites of safe custody for felons from 1783.[55]

Bridewells and gaols were also impacted by an expansion in the use of imprisonment to punish felonies. Following the establishment of bridewells in the early seventeenth century, some assize judges experimented with sending individuals convicted of lesser felonies, especially petty larceny, to houses of correction for punishment.[56] This practice was not widely taken up, but the number of felons imprisoned nevertheless grew as the courts' use of benefit of clergy evolved. Under English common law, all felonies were capital offences. However, from the twelfth century, a privilege, namely benefit of clergy, developed through which some convicted felons, by pleading the benefit, could save themselves from capital punishment. This privilege initially extended to clerics only, but from the late sixteenth century, it applied to all literate men convicted of certain categories of crime, and in the 1690s, it was extended to women. In 1706 the literacy requirement was abolished by statute.[57] By the early eighteenth century, then, felonies were either clergyable or they were not. In seventeenth-century London, most of those released by benefit of clergy were branded on the thumb and discharged, but growing dissatisfaction with the punishment and a widespread desire for a better punishment between "hanging and acquitting" prompted courts at end of the century to experiment with alternatives. In the City, various groups – members of Parliament, aldermen, juries, tradesmen, and shopkeepers – pushed to replace branding with imprisonment at hard labour, which was seen as a greater deterrent.[58] This was not a new idea: earlier legislation had empowered courts to imprison, for up to one year, clergyable male felons as well as first-time female offenders convicted of small felonies. These acts, however, had been used only irregularly.[59] In 1706, as a result of City pressure, Parliament passed the *Hard Labour Act*, which affirmed, publicized, and broadened the use of imprisonment to punish clergyable felonies. The act gave judges a general authority to sentence clergied felons, male or female, to imprisonment at hard labour in either a house of correction or a workhouse for between six months and two years.[60] London and Middlesex courts initially employed this statute with enthusiasm, and there is some evidence to suggest that the courts and the prison authorities closely monitored the application of hard labour.[61]

Generally, however, most London courts preferred to sentence minor felons to transportation, especially as that punishment developed after 1718, so in the following decades, imprisonment was again used only infrequently to punish felons.[62] Labour, then, was clearly central to English penal policy from the end of the seventeenth century, but authorities typically preferred such labour to be carried out in the colonies. The changed circumstances of the 1770s, namely the indefinite suspension of transportation following Britain's war with America, prompted a revival of interest in imprisonment at hard labour. Parliament passed two further statutes authorizing the quarter and assize sessions to substitute imprisonment at hard labour for transportation. The first of these, the 1776 *Hard Labour Act,* directed that prison sentences be served in either a house of correction or a prison hulk, but the 1779 *Penitentiary Act* allowed the courts to send convicts to gaols as well as houses of correction.[63]

These statutes responded to a variety of sometimes transient circumstances. They show people juggling a fairly consistent set of options and repeatedly establishing some version of these but balancing their use in different ways in different circumstances. Taken together, they allowed a growing range and number of offenders to be imprisoned and gave committing authorities greater flexibility about where and how to incarcerate, whether their object was detention or punishment. In this sense, the legislation embraced the notion that local elites were best placed to make decisions about local policy and the uses of local taxes. In London, with its plentiful supply of prisons, the courts had an especially wide range of options when confining offenders. In the early eighteenth century, committing bodies took advantage of statutes that allowed them to use their prisons for multiple purposes, blending to a certain (but clearly limited) extent the different sorts of prisons. This blending, however, was ultimately rejected by local elites. As the following chapter will show, in the late eighteenth century, justices of the peace, as individuals in their commitment practices and as a body designing commitment policy, increasingly assigned (or perhaps we should say reassigned) specialized roles to the prisons under their jurisdiction. In doing so, they gradually separated custodial from punitive confinement.

CHAPTER ONE

Becoming Prisoners

Locking People Up in Eighteenth- and Early-Nineteenth-Century London

How and why did local authorities in London use imprisonment? Who did they choose to incarcerate? Where were inmates locked up? These questions are at the heart of this chapter, which seeks to illuminate London's prison system and its use in the eighteenth and early nineteenth centuries. To recover the decisions of local authorities, we will follow the path that an individual accused of a crime within each of the several metropolitan jurisdictions would take through the criminal justice system. We begin with a suspected offender's first interaction with the system – picked up for an offence and taken to a justice of the peace, sitting outside of formal sessions, for examination. We move on to follow the course of those formally charged with an offence. Finally, we trace the path of the small portion of accused offenders who were tried, and in some cases convicted, at the quarter and assize sessions.

This approach reveals how individuals, moving through the levels of the criminal justice system – arrest, judicial examination, trial, sentencing, and punishment – were generally conveyed sequentially through the various stages within the prison system. These practices, evident in all metropolitan jurisdictions, were driven by the desire of local authorities to impose greater order and regularity on their prisons at a time when criminal courts were using imprisonment with greater frequency and for an expanding range of purposes.

Ultimately, these practices led to the crystallization of at least two distinct and separate forms of confinement in London: custodial imprisonment, for individuals held for safe custody, and punitive imprisonment, for those sentenced to incarceration as a punishment.

I. INITIAL CONFINEMENT: PRE-TRIAL EXAMINATION

In July 1834, Frederick Cunningham, a wholesale ironmonger in Borough, Southwark, travelled to Herne Bay to sea-bathe following bouts of ill-health. With his entire family accompanying him, Cunningham left his servant, Elizabeth McKensey, in charge of the house. On his early return a fortnight later, he found the beds stripped of sheeting, the pillowcases missing, and the table linen gone.[1] Cunningham accused McKensey of the robbery and handed her into the custody of a police constable, who subsequently brought her to the Borough Compter to await examination before the justice at Southwark Town Hall.[2]

For most people in eighteenth-century London, their first experience of imprisonment followed either directly on from their arrest, as it did for Elizabeth, or after an examination by a justice of the peace sitting outside sessions. Since extra-sessional hearings functioned partly as a context for preparing cases for trial at the higher courts, suspected offenders were frequently examined by a justice multiple times, and in between these examinations, the offender was kept imprisoned.[3] Mary Wood, for example, was detained in custody "upwards of a fortnight" on suspicion of felony, during which time she was examined "several times" by the sitting magistrate at Guildhall "in the expectation of procuring sufficient evidence against her."[4] In this instance, Wood, with the assistance of her solicitor, gained release from custody, the charge dismissed, after the magistrate acknowledged – "unwillingly," he claimed – that the evidence for the felony had not materialized.[5]

Whether the accused was taken directly to a justice for examination or to a local prison to await such examination depended on the time of day and the location of the arrest. During the day, they were typically brought to the magistrate directly, thereby avoiding detention, at least temporarily. Explaining his reasons for bringing offenders to the magistrate in 1828, a constable from Hanover Square noted, "the two gentlemen having just preferred charges against each other at the watchouse, he thought it better, as he knew the

Figure 1.1 · A parson and constables visiting a parish lock-up.

magistrate was then sitting, to bring them at once before him, and have the case heard, rather than keep them locked up all night, as he must otherwise have done."[6] With constables and watchmen enjoined to arrest "all disturbers of the peace in the night," the number of "night charges," those arrested after judicial hours had concluded, could be considerable.[7] This system applied alike in the City, Southwark, and Middlesex, though with different consequences.

In committing night charges to prison, London police officers – to use a generic term for the wide range of policing authorities active in the period – had a variety of institutions from which to choose.[8] Indeed, officers need not use prisons at all. Some statutes allowed them, "if the time be unseasonable, as in or near the night," to keep their arrestees in the stocks or, ambiguously, "in an house."[9] Location played an important role in determining these decisions: when James Davis, a City constable, found Elizabeth Gurney, sick and begging, in Cheapside in the 1780s, he took her to the Poultry Compter because it was nearer than the workhouse and his orders prevented him from going "above half an hour from the watch house."[10]

Generally, officers in the City of London and its borough of Southwark committed such offenders to a compter, usually after a brief stay in a watch-house or local lock-up. The latter were ubiquitous throughout England, but unfortunately we still know relatively little about them.[11] An incident from 31 January 1809 illustrates this process clearly. In the early hours of the morning, William Arkinstaff, yelling that money had been stolen from his person, chased Mary Powell, Mary Smith, and Mary Brown, the alleged culprits, through the streets of London. With the assistance of two passers-by, Arkinstaff captured the three women and brought them to a local watchhouse, where the night constable "took charge of them and sent them to the [Giltspur] Compter."[12]

Some of those held in a watchhouse overnight were simply released in the morning rather than transferred to compters. In this way, policing bodies fulfilled their obligation to clear the streets at night without assuming any additional responsibilities. Surviving watchbooks show that this was common practice. For example, on 21 June 1774, a beadle for St. James's parish reported, "the constable and Lantern Bearer went to the Castle in Swallow Street after twelve o clock and brought out of the house twelve disorderly girls and in the morning at four let them all go without going before the Justice which is often."[13] Many of those released the next day had probably been brought to the compters drunk, perhaps unruly, and then let go after sobering up. For a later period, Metropolitan Police records report that 76 per cent of the 31,355 persons arrested for drunkenness in 1831 were discharged by police superintendents once they sobered without ever seeing a magistrate.[14] In recognition of the considerable discretion exercised by them in deciding how to deal with night charges, officers came to be known popularly as "midnight magistrates" in the nineteenth century.[15]

City of London and Borough of Southwark

In the City, police officers committed, on average, 2,300 "night-charges" to the Wood Street Compter and 1,669 to the Poultry Compter each year between 1770 and 1783. Annual commitments increased in the years leading up to the war with America, primarily due to night charges, perhaps reflecting more intensive policing of London's streets. Committal records to Southwark's Borough Compter do not survive for the eighteenth century, but evidence from the nineteenth century shows that it too was used, in the words of the Prison Inspectors, "as a watch-house for persons apprehended in the streets by day and by night."[16] As this comment implies, compters were seen by many officials as extensions of the watchhouse system. Indeed, night charges accounted for an overwhelming

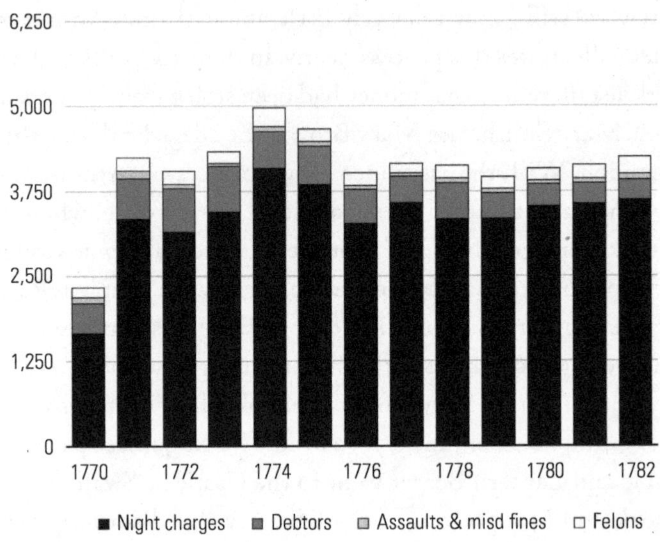

Figure 1.2 • Wood Street and Poultry Committals, 1770–82. Note: 1770 only includes commitment figures for Wood Street.

majority of annual commitments at both institutions – 85.5 per cent at Poultry and 80.2 per cent at Wood Street – in the late eighteenth century (figure 1.2).

The compters had been used to detain night charges since their foundation in the fourteenth century, so, by using them for this purpose in the eighteenth century, officers were following long-established practice.[17] Though compters had been established to serve as holding centres for those waiting to be examined or tried by the London sheriffs, they quickly came to hold all sorts of accused offenders awaiting examination, regardless of whether their hearing was before the sheriff. In the mid-eighteenth century, when regularly sitting summary courts were established at Mansion House and Guildhall, it became convention that prisoners intended to be examined by the Lord Mayor at Mansion House would be taken to the Poultry while those for examination by the aldermen at Guildhall would be confined in Bread (later Wood) Street.[18]

These customary practices received official articulation at the end of the century, when officers' freedom to choose the prison to which they brought charges was curtailed. In 1785, the governors of London's Bridewell directed the porter to allow entry only to officers carrying a warrant of commitment signed by a magistrate – a policy reiterated in 1802.[19] By specifying that commitment decisions be made by magistrates after a hearing, this policy closed Bridewell to just-arrested offenders. This may have forced officers to rely more completely on the compters, though it is more likely that it formalized a more generally observed convention.

As initial holding places for suspected offenders, the compters brought together individuals accused of a wide variety of offences, from crimes as serious as murder to those as minor as begging on the streets. In 1791, Giltspur Compter took over the functions of the compters at Wood Street and Poultry, though the latter continued to accept prisoners until the mid-1810s. Giltspur's commitment records, the earliest of which start in 1807, show that prisoners confined for examination were accused of felony, fraud, assault, military desertion, offences against one's master, and vagrancy; others were held to give evidence in court. No single offence predominated among commitments, but at both Giltspur (1807–09) and Borough (1815–17), the most common offence was vagrancy.[20]

Most of those imprisoned in this manner saw the charges against them dismissed when they were brought before a justice, usually after one examination but sometimes after several. At Giltspur, nearly two-thirds of prisoners were discharged following a pre-trial hearing between 1807 and 1809, while at Borough roughly three-fourths of prisoners committed between 1815 and 1817 were subsequently discharged.[21] Most supposed offenders arrested and imprisoned in London, then, exited both the criminal justice and prison systems at this early stage.

Even this brief contact could be expensive: before such fees were abolished in 1815–16, the keepers of Giltspur and Poultry Compters reported taking a fee of 3*s*.6*d*. from each prisoner discharged by a magistrate before they could leave the prison. These amounts were established in 1732; before this, fees were considerably greater.[22] Many were unable to pay and some left without doing so, but gaolers nevertheless collected around £150 annually through such discharge fees.[23] On top of admission and discharge fees, prisoners also paid for their own food, drink, bedding, copies of legal documents, and other necessities, and at many prisons, they were required to pay garnish (fees) to their wardmates on commitment too.[24] Even those who saw the charges against them dismissed could spent days or weeks languishing in prison for failure to pay fees.

In the compters, where inmate turnover was so high, the populations fluctuated in size and composition constantly. Although compters saw some of the highest numbers of annual committals in the eighteenth century, "stocks" of inmates in prison at any one moment were comparatively small. Moreover, the constant ferrying of prisoners between the compters and the summary courts meant that inmates often spent much of their "confinement" either in a courtroom or en route to one. One's experience of incarceration varied greatly depending on the time actually spent in prison, the size of the inmate population, and, of course, socio-economic status. Mostly, the compters held debtors whose cases were being dealt with at sheriffs' courts.[25] Since debtors were typically imprisoned for longer periods than prisoners confined for examination or trial, they generally made up the most stable element of compter populations.[26] The preponderance of debtors probably benefited criminal prisoners, helping to ensure that regulations remained fairly lax.

Non-debtor terms of imprisonment were usually short because such prisoners were confined only while the justice assessed the veracity of the charge, the strength of the evidence, and the willingness of the prosecutor to prosecute. Once a decision was made, whether to dismiss the charge, pass the case on for trial, or convict the offender summarily, the prisoner was usually removed. At the Poultry, between 1 June and 31 December 1800, nearly every prisoner who, after examination by the Lord Mayor, was subsequently committed for trial was at that point either bailed or removed into Newgate.[27] Only nine of seventy-nine prisoners committed for trial were kept in the Poultry, and of the nine, four were never tried but instead discharged by proclamation at the City Sessions.[28] As a result of this practice, the City compters catered almost exclusively to prisoners accused of but not formally charged with an offence, on the one hand, and debtors, on the other.

Middlesex and Surrey

No such specialization characterized the corresponding pre-trial prisons in Southwark and Middlesex – largely because that was scarcely an option, given the number of prisons in these jurisdictions. The prisons in Southwark included a compter, county gaol, and house of correction, but as a consequence of its odd jurisdictional position, as both a City ward and part of Surrey county, most Southwark authorities could not commit offenders to all three prisons. The gaol and house of correction were Surrey prisons, so only a handful of City justices could commit individuals there, with most relying instead on the

Borough Compter. Conversely, the Surrey justices in general could not commit individuals to the Borough Compter, so they sent the accused to the gaol or house of correction. As a result of this arrangement, the Borough Compter acted as a compter, gaol, and house of correction. Principally, it served as a pre-trial site. 90 per cent of criminal commitments were for examination between 1815 and 1818. Additionally, it admitted prisoners held for want of sureties or security, for want of evidence, to await trial, and for punishment after conviction.[29]

In the case of Middlesex, though the county was well-supplied with a gaol and bridewell, it did not possess any equivalent to the City's compters. Therefore, Middlesex justices confined together all custodial prisoners, whether held for examination, trial, or want of surety, and for many decades in the eighteenth century, they used both their gaol and house of correction to confine them.[30] They received explicit permission to use their bridewell for this purpose in 1719–20, but the practice became common only from the mid-1740s.[31] As in the City, officers in Middlesex frequently brought accused offenders and witnesses, typically referred to as 'evidences,' to hyperlocal places of confinement such as a watchhouse or roundhouse first and from there to the county's prisons of New Prison or Clerkenwell.[32] These prisons were next door to one another, so there was nothing to distinguish them in terms of locational convenience (figure 0.1). Occasionally, magistrates divided the parties involved in a dispute between the prisons specifically to keep them apart, thereby preventing collusion or disagreements.[33]

From the late eighteenth century, some Middlesex authorities pushed to adopt more specialized practices. They consequently moved to limit the traditional discretion afforded to committing bodies, with important effects on pre-trial custody and the prisons more generally. First, in 1796, the bridewell governor complained to the magistrates about "great inconveniences having arisen in the management of the prison in respect to persons being brought in as night charges."[34] By this point, the Middlesex house of correction had become almost exclusively a prison for punishment, and as a result, the governor felt keenly the intrusion of a few offenders who were brought into the prison after hours and likely would leave again in the morning. The magistrates apparently sympathized, for they ordered the governor to refuse entry to charges and directed officers to commit them to New Prison, "the proper place of confinement for such persons."[35]

The magistrates on the prison committee, those most knowledgeable about the internal state of the county prisons and those most active in trying to shape prison policy, also tried to stop the commitment of accused offenders, confined to await judicial examination or re-examination, to the bridewell, but with less success. The bench issued recommendatory orders to its justices to commit inmates before trial to New Prison in 1796, 1799, and 1802.[36] Some magistrates ignored these pleas, so into the nineteenth century, the numbers committed for examination remained considerable: 276 in 1800, 503 in 1816, and 504 in 1818.[37] Perhaps justices saw this practice as convenient, or they were loath to change their ways. Some possibly missed the bench's orders. How long pre-trial inmates remained in prison varied considerably: some were held for a handful of days while others were confined for a month or more, but most stayed for between ten days and a fortnight.[38]

By the end of the eighteenth century, then, individuals upon first entering the criminal justice system were generally imprisoned in compters, if arrested in the City or the City's borough of Southwark, or in common gaols, if arrested in Middlesex or other parts of Surrey. The unofficial policies that shaped these patterns of practice were driven primarily by justices of the peace, as collective bodies making policy decisions about where accused offenders should be imprisoned and as individuals processing prisoners. While not every individual justice followed in every instance the philosophy that developed during the period of separating prisoners based on their type of committal, many if not most did, suggesting that they supported these specializing trends. To bring the wayward into line, the county benches and the City Corporation moved at the end of the century to make these unofficial practices mandatory.

II. IMPRISONMENT AT SUMMARY PROCEEDINGS

In 1836 two officers from the Mendicity Society brought three males, aged fourteen to twenty, to the Magistrate's Office at Hatton Garden and accused them of being vagrants. Though the officers did not witness the youths receiving money, they observed them "singing glees and touching their hats to passengers."[39] The *Morning Post* angrily reported that, though "the manner and demeanour of the prisoners while at the bar were superior to the common order," the magistrate, a Mr Liang, nevertheless convicted all three and committed them to a house of correction for hard labour – in the newspaper's scathing view, for "offending the 'ears polite' of the mendicity officers." The men were given sentences ranging from fourteen days to one month; James Hurd, whom Liang accused in court of being an "impudent fellow," received the longest sentence.[40]

Justices acting summarily, like Liang, decisively shaped the pattern of commitments to London prisons and the composition of inmate populations. The vast majority of people who encountered the law in eighteenth- and nineteenth-century England did so at the summary level. Though most histories of crime and justice in England focus on the jury trials at the assize sessions and, to a lesser extent, the quarter sessions, interest in the summary process has been growing since the early 2000s.[41] This section adds to these studies, focusing particularly on the use of imprisonment as an outcome of summary processes, a topic that has not been studied in detail. Drawing on newspaper reports, prison registers, and surviving court records, it shows how justices at the summary level shaped prison function and composition.

This section traces how justices increasingly separated prisoners for trial from prisoners for punishment. Before 1720, these kinds of prisoner had usually been held separately, with those incarcerated to await trial held in gaols and those sentenced to punishment in houses of correction, but growth in the numbers prosecuted and convicted in mid-eighteenth-century London prompted magistrates to use their prisons more flexibly. This changed in the 1780s as magistrates sought to restrict gaols and compters to custodial purposes and houses of correction to punitive roles. Ultimately, these practices ensured that houses of correction became ever more distinct from gaols and compters.

Though thousands of individuals were imprisoned annually in late-eighteenth- and early-nineteenth-century London, it was relatively uncommon for an offender to be sentenced, as the young singers were, to punitive imprisonment. Instead, most of those who, having been accused of a crime, came before the justices at the summary level saw the accusations against them either dismissed outright or resolved informally. As is suggested by the shock of the newspaper reporter in 1836 – "the decision of the Magistrate is most extraordinary and unprecedented" – contemporaries expected this to be the case when the offence was minor. Contemporary legal commentators and handbooks urged magistrates to work as mediators between the disputants and as filters for the higher courts. Not only were magistrates tasked with acting "as a peacemaker" by reconciling disputants, but they were also responsible for curbing vexatious prosecutions.[42] This approach towards legal settlement was both less expensive and less divisive within communities, and as a result, it appealed widely. Into the nineteenth century, the flexibility of magistrates and the emphasis on negotiation and mediation were viewed not only as hallmarks but also as strengths of summary justice. As a magistrate at the Union Hall public office expounded in 1833,

> The value of his police does not consist more in the strict legal performance of his judicial and administrative duties, than in the exercise of a sound discretion, and in the considerate application of the principles and feelings of humanity, as an adviser, an arbitrator and a mediator.[43]

On occasion, however, informal methods of resolution broke down or else proved insufficient, and in such cases, the offender was either committed for jury trial or convicted summarily.

The following subsections focus on the instances when formal action was taken, first, in the City of London and Southwark, and second, in the counties of Middlesex and Surrey. Each section begins by discussing the organization of summary justice in the specific jurisdiction and the sorts of records that survive before diving into the details of court practice.

City and Southwark

From the middle of the eighteenth century, the City operated three public courts, purpose-built for summary hearings: at Guildhall (from 1737), Mansion House (1753), and Southwark Town Hall (c. 1606). All were open five days a week and had set working hours.[44] At these courts, informal negotiation was the norm with the justices primarily playing an arbitrational role. The Justice of the Bridge-Yard, the City's judicial agent in Southwark who held court at Town Hall, represented one extreme in that he resolved around 90 per cent of examinations informally, without recourse to the higher courts, and dismissed nearly 79 per cent of cases between 1776 and 1781, the only years for which court records survive.[45]

Table 1.1 Outcomes at city summary courts, c. 1776–89

	Southwark Town Hall	% S	Guildhall	% G	Mansion House	% MH
Settled and discharged	1,400	78.5%	214	59.0%	455	48.9%
Summarily punished	131	7.3%	69	19.0%	208	22.3%
Sent on for trial	124	7.0%	36	9.9%	143	15.4%
Unknown	70	3.9%	44	12.1%	125	13.4%
Other	58	3.3%	—	—	—	—
	1783	**100.0%**	**363**	**100.0%**	**931**	**100.0%**

Source: Southwark Justice Book, LMA, CLA/031/001; Drew Gray, "Summary Proceedings and Social Relations in the City of London, c. 1750–1800" (PhD diss., University of Northampton, 2006), 45.

Note: Gray's sample covered the periods from Nov. 1784 to March 1785 and Nov. 1788 to March 1789. Kettibly's notebook, from which the data for Southwark has been compiled, covered 20 Apr. 1776 to 23 May 1781. "Other" encompasses those discharged on recognizance, passed to settlement, and passed to military commissioners for impressment into armed forces.

By comparison, the justices at Guildhall and Mansion House proved more willing to formally charge offenders, though there too, the courts overwhelmingly preferred informal resolutions (table 1.1). As the individuals examined were only rarely ordered for jury trial or summarily convicted, only a small portion remained in the prison system following their initial examination. In this way, the justices indirectly kept in check the numbers imprisoned, whether for trial or punishment. Generally, City justices followed specialized commitment practices: defendants imprisoned for trial, most of whom were male, were held in either Newgate or the compters, while those who were convicted and sentenced to imprisonment, defendants who as in other urban contexts were overwhelmingly female, were sent almost exclusively to Bridewell.[46]

Commitment for Trial

Across all City summary courts in this period, roughly 7 to 15 per cent of individuals examined were passed on to jury trial, making commitment for trial a relatively uncommon outcome. Once committed for trial, accused offenders were generally removed from the prison (usually a compter) in which they had been held during pre-trial examination and either bailed (mostly in cases of misdemeanour) or transferred to another prison (especially for felony charges) to await trial. Overwhelmingly, City prisoners were moved to Newgate, the common gaol for London and Middlesex.

In the eighteenth century, Newgate's primary function was to hold individuals awaiting trial at the quarter or Old Bailey sessions: 85 per cent of prisoners annually committed to Newgate between 1747 and 1764 were incarcerated on this basis. Since men were sent to trial in greater numbers than women, a majority of commitments were male (figure 1.3). These commitment patterns made Newgate into an overwhelmingly male space. In the 1810s, when surveys of the inmate population were taken, male prisoners accounted on average for 79 per cent of those held.[47] Though these annual commitment patterns might suggest that Newgate had a relatively homogenous population, in actuality the gaol served as a catch-all institution. On a daily basis, it confined together pre-trial inmates, transports, misdemeanants sentenced to imprisonment, debtors, and convicts awaiting execution. Indeed, the Old Bailey judges and the justices at the City and Middlesex sessions regularly used Newgate to punish individuals convicted of offences including theft, riot and assault, coining, bigamy, and sodomy, who might serve sentences of one month to three years there.[48]

A small number of prisoners committed to await trial were kept confined in a compter. Those remaining had been accused of minor offences and were to be tried at the local quarter sessions. Those who remained in the Poultry Compter for trial in 1800, for example, were charged with breaches of peace, mainly assaults, which in this period were treated more as civil than as criminal offences.[49] Similarly, those who remained in Giltspur were to be tried at the City quarter sessions.[50] Through these practices, City justices separated prisoners for trial according to seriousness of offence, sending those accused of major crimes to Newgate while sometimes leaving those accused of petty offences in compters to await trial. Significantly, if a prisoner had not been committed to a compter in the first instance, he or she would not be moved there at a later stage to await trial.

The City's general practice of removing prisoners formally charged with an offence from a compter into a gaol was not customary in Southwark. The Southwark justice, as a City official, could send offenders to await trial in Newgate, and as a magistrate of Surrey, he could move them to the Surrey

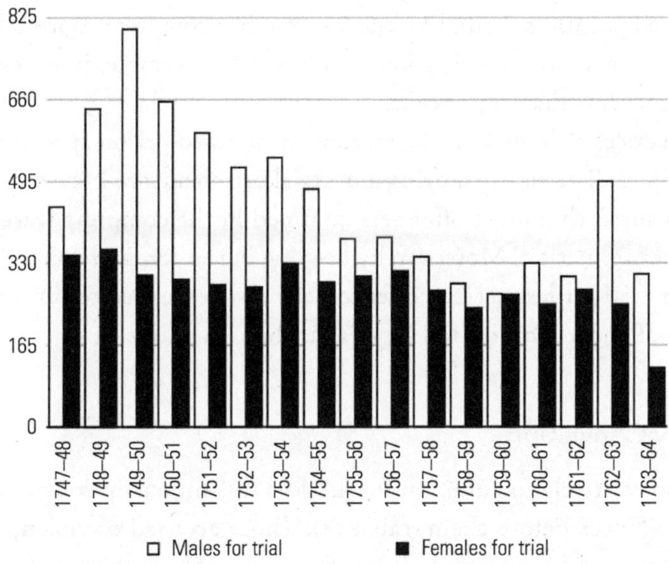

Figure 1.3 Commitments to Newgate for trial by sex, 1747–64. The years run from Michaelmas to Michaelmas.

county gaol.[51] In the 1770s and the 1810s, the years for which records survive, the men who acted as Southwark justice rarely took either option. Instead, when a suspected offender held in the Borough Compter was ordered for trial, he or she typically stayed there. Between 1815 and 1817, at least 224 people imprisoned therein for examination were subsequently committed for trial. Of these, only thirteen (less than 6 per cent) were removed to another prison for trial.[52]

Such decisions were probably linked to the time and expense of transferring prisoners committed for trial. In July 1824, for example, the Borough Compter keeper, John Law, recorded paying 1*s*.6*d*. to hire a coach to move a prisoner, William Mocock, to the Surrey county gaol preparatory to his trial at the Surrey assizes. In the same month, he also paid three shillings to convey Catherine Wilson to Brixton, where she had been sentenced for one month.[53] When prisoners were to be tried at the Old Bailey or Surrey assizes, transferring them to Newgate or the Surrey gaol was worth the expense as such prisoners would need to be moved regardless, but when the prisoners were to be tried locally, for example at the Lord Mayor's sessions in Southwark Town Hall, which was adjacent to the compter, transfer to a more distant prison must have seemed pointless. Still, like the City's other compters, Borough mainly received prisoners for examination. In 1815–17, for example, inmates for trial accounted for less than 11 per cent.[54]

The practices sketched in this section encouraged prison specialization in the bigger jurisdictions. By moving most trial prisoners into Newgate, the City justices ensured that most offenders confined in the compters were held for summary examination. Moreover, by keeping in the compters offenders committed for trial for less serious offences, the justices served to limit Newgate to serious offenders committed for trial at the Old Bailey.

Summary Conviction

It was also relatively uncommon for justices to summarily convict those accused of offences before them (table 1.1). Those accused of violent offences, including assault or threatening speech, were rarely convicted, while those accused of property offences, including acts of theft, fraud, extortion, or property damage, were slightly more likely to be summarily convicted, but such an outcome was still uncommon (table 1.2). The alleged offences were generally minor. John Harding, for example, was summarily convicted and imprisoned for a month as a disorderly person for picking pockets; Ann Hudson was imprisoned for fourteen days for purloining a quantity of fur.[55] Court practice suggests that in cases where the justices believed a violent or property offence had been committed and the offence was serious enough to warrant punishment if proved, justices preferred to send the offender for jury trial. Summary conviction offered only one possible way, and overall a slightly less preferred way, of dealing with significant charges of this nature.

The courts mainly used their powers of summary conviction to punish behaviour of which they disapproved but which they did not believe merited jury trial or serious punishment: vagrancy and other 'regulatory offences,' a category that encompasses acts affecting London's streets and communities by transgressing, for example, regulations on trade, employment relations, morality, public space, and poor relief. While the overall rate of discharge was 79 per cent at Southwark (1776–81) and 52 per cent at Guildhall and Mansion House (c. 1784–96), the percentage discharged for those accused of vagrancy was only 37 per cent at Southwark and 34 per cent at Guildhall and Mansion House.[56] Consequently, of the 131 individuals summarily convicted by the Southwark

Table 1.2 Punishments for violent and property offences at city summary courts

	Guildhall and Mansion House, 1784–96			Southwark, 1776–81		
	Imprisonment	Fine	Total charged	Imprisonment	Fine	Total charged
Assault	2	2	693	1	1	278
Property	149	0	859	11	1	247

Source: Table 1.1; Gray, "Proceedings," 139–40.

Table 1.3 Punishments at Southwark Town Hall, 1776–81

	Imprisonment	Fine	Total	%
Vagrancy Acts	93	0	93	71.0%
Property	12	1	13	9.9%
Regulatory	1	9	10	7.6%
Violence	1	1	2	1.5%
Not Specified	13	0	13	9.9%
	120	11	131	100.0%

Source: LMA, CLA/031/03/001.

justice in 1776–81, 71 per cent were convicted of a vagrancy offence and another 7.6 per cent of a different type of regulatory offence.

The governors responsible for managing Bridewell convened a separate summary court in their house of correction, until they lost their *ex-officio* commitment powers in 1781. They likewise used their powers of summary conviction mainly to punish vagrancy and regulatory offences: 64.5 per cent of the 504 individuals convicted by the court in 1778–88 were charged with vagrancy or a regulatory act (table 1.4).[57] Most of the 'vagrants' confined had in fact been accused of prostitution or petty theft. At all these courts, women were convicted in greater numbers than men, evidence that points to the gendered nature of policing vagrancy in eighteenth-century London.

Summary convicts were either fined or imprisoned, and the specific punishment was shaped by the offence committed (tables 1.2 and 1.3). Those

Table 1.4 Bridewell Court of Governors commitments, 1778–88

	Total	%
Vagrancy acts	334	66.3%
Regulatory	108	21.4%
Property	57	11.3%
Violence	5	1.0%
	504	100.0%

Source: BCGM, 22 Jan. 1778 to 25 Apr. 1788, *LL*, BBBRMG202080642–BBRMG202090324.

summarily convicted of assault were as likely, if not more likely, to be fined than imprisoned, whereas offenders convicted of a property offence were almost always imprisoned. In punishing vagrancy, the courts relied primarily on imprisonment, but for other regulatory offences, they frequently used fines. Because so many vagrants – and at some courts property offenders – were summarily convicted in London, large numbers of such offenders were funnelled into London prisons for punishment.

Justices proceeding summarily sent nearly all convicts sentenced to imprisonment to a house of correction, regardless of offence. The City magistrates sent their summary convicts primarily to Bridewell.[58] This prison, perhaps uniquely, served exclusively as a site of punishment throughout the eighteenth century. By the early nineteenth century, Bridewell's role and composition were shaped decisively by City magistrates, who were responsible for the overwhelming majority of commitments. Their attitude towards idleness and disorderliness shaped the nature of commitments and the daily population. Between 1809 and 1816, between 84 and 92 per cent of prisoners annually committed were convicted under the *Vagrancy Acts*; women accounted for nearly half of all commitments.[59] Between 1787 and 1805, women made up about 60 per cent of the prison's daily population.[60]

At Southwark Town Hall, all but two sentenced to imprisonment were confined in a house of correction. In the two exceptional cases, men convicted of assault were imprisoned in the Borough Compter not as part of their sentence but because, having been fined for the assault, they had failed to pay.[61] The compter was probably thought the most appropriate place for individuals not strictly sentenced to imprisonment because of its less severe discipline, given that it was a prison that mainly held offenders awaiting examination and debtors.

At the end of the eighteenth century, justices in Middlesex and Surrey developed patterns of committal practice similar to those witnessed in the City and Southwark. In these counties, justices more and more sent individuals imprisoned for safe custody to await trial exclusively to the common gaol, while they more and more directed offenders sentenced to imprisonment to a house of correction.

Middlesex and Surrey

Outside of the City and Southwark, records of summary proceedings are scarce, so this section relies instead on prisoner lists to trace the committal patterns of justices acting summarily.[62] By comparison with summary court records, prisoner lists have several shortcomings. The first relates to their method of counting. The Southwark calendars, for example, are printed lists which were drawn up by prison keepers for the quarter sessions and which listed the individuals who had been committed between the sessions and still remained in the bridewell at the calendar's printing. Any inmates who were committed and discharged between the sessions, either because they had served their summary sentence or because the case against them had not materialized and so they were dismissed, were not included. Individuals committed for trial who were later bailed, however, were usually noted.[63] These lists, then, underestimate the incidence of summary conviction and imprisonment. Middlesex authorities produced similarly partial, "gaol delivery" calendars, which listed only the inmates still in the prisons at the time of the sessions and what happened to them.[64] In addition, authorities produced several kinds of fuller lists, which recorded all individuals committed between the sessions. The commitment books, one such set, were drawn up by gaolers in preparation for the sessions; these were then roughly copied by the clerk of the peace and stored with the sessions rolls; finally, authorities, probably the clerk of the peace, also kept registers of those committed to prison by magistrates between the sessions.[65]

The second limitation relates to the information recorded. The Southwark calendars are probably the most revealing: they give the prisoner's name, commitment date, committing authority, name(s) of prosecutor(s), offence, and usually the legal reason for confinement. If the prisoner was incarcerated for punishment, the calendar usually specified the sentence. The Middlesex gaol delivery calendars, conversely, tell us in general terms what happened to prisoners at the sessions – whether they were discharged, continued, or tried, and if tried and punished, their sentence. However, unless the individual was tried, the calendar did not consistently specify the offence or reason for the prisoner's confinement. The other Middlesex calendars are more detailed as they give the prisoner's name, commitment details, and offence. However, they do not always specify the basis of the commitment; this is especially true for calendars from the 1770s onwards.

Finally, many lists do not survive. For New Prison, for example, only one commitment book survives for the period before 1755; the earliest roll dates from 1771; and the two registers cover, respectively, February 1747–February 1748 and January 1778–October 1780. The gaol delivery papers date from 1690, but the vast majority of early records are unfit for consultation. Generally, then, lists of prisoners committed to New Prison, especially commitment books, survive in greater number from the 1760s, but there remain considerable gaps. For the house of correction, by contrast, only eight commitment books survive for the entirety of the eighteenth century; no eighteenth-century registers survive. Luckily, however, many rolls, dating from 1740 onward, survive, though several are unfit and cannot be consulted. We noted above that the Surrey calendars are exceptionally fulsome; yet, many dating from before 1780 are missing. Our assessment of survival thereafter is complicated by the fact that the number of calendars produced each year varied.

The shortcomings of the surviving records mean that, for Middlesex and Surrey, we do not know what proportion of those brought before justices were sent on to trial or summarily convicted. Still, the surviving calendars record the commitment of thousands of prisoners, and these give us a sense of how justices used the prisons in their jurisdiction.

Middlesex

Just as justices in Middlesex used both their house of correction and their gaol to confine prisoners for summary examination, so too did they use both institutions to detain prisoners who were subsequently committed for jury trial. While the gaol had been used for this purpose since its foundation, the house of correction began to receive pre-trial prisoners only after 1720. Yet, justices did not treat these prisons interchangeably. Justices throughout the eighteenth century used the gaol as the primary site of custodial confinement. The house of correction was used for this purpose only when necessary, either because prosecution levels were especially high or because the gaol was unfit.

It is generally believed that pre-trial commitments quickly came to dominate the Middlesex bridewell after 1720. However, a detailed examination of surviving prisoner lists from the succeeding decades suggests that this was not the case. Accounts of Middlesex prisoners tried at quarter and assize sessions in the 1720s and 1730s show that most were held in New Prison or Newgate; comparatively few were detained in the house of correction.[66] Justices began using the bridewell more regularly for custodial purposes from the mid-1740s. Mainly, those sent were accused of a violent offence and were confined until they provided sureties, but a considerable portion, almost all charged with a property offence, were held specifically to await jury trial. Commitments for safe custody may have grown especially from the late 1750s. At this point, they may have made up around half of all commitments.[67] For the 1760s and 1770s, Innes and Shoemaker both found that prisoners awaiting trial accounted for over three-quarters of commitments to the Middlesex and Westminster houses of correction.[68] Yet, a more extensive survey of calendars from these years suggests this picture is not entirely representative. 75 per cent probably marked the high point of custodial committals rather than the average. In the period 1769–83, they probably accounted for anywhere between one-third and three-quarters of commitments.[69]

At New Prison, custodial commitments were more dominant. A sample of 842 commitments to the gaol between May 1739 and October 1764 shows that, on average, 88 per cent of commitments were for detention (including for want of sureties, trial, examination, and evidence), less than 1 per cent were for punishment, and 11 per cent were not specified.[70] The type of offences for which individuals were confined likewise points to the mainly custodial role of New Prison, with over 94 per cent committed for a violent or property offence. As with the bridewell, later New Prison calendars record the basis of commitment only irregularly. So, for 1772–73, we know that at least 35 per cent of commitments, on average, were for custody and less than 1 per cent for punishment, with 64 per cent not specified. Looking at the offences charged, however, suggests that on average 95 per cent of commitments between 1769 and 1773 were custodial.[71] Similarly, a complete run of calendars for September 1772 to December 1774 shows that 95 per cent of commitments were custodial and a little over 1 percent were definitely for punishment (table 1.5).

Table 1.5 Commitments to New Prison: Custodial and punitive, 1772–74

	For punishment				
	Convicted and imprisoned by quarter sessions	Convicted and imprisoned summarily	Possibly convicted and imprisoned summarily	Custodial	Total committed
September to December sessions 1772	1	1	7	499	508
January to December sessions 1773	8	6	58	942	1,014
January to December sessions 1774	7	8	22	585	622
	16	**15**	**87**	**2,026**	**2,144**
	0.7%	**0.7%**	**4.1%**	**94.5%**	**100.0%**

Source: LMA, MJ/CC/B/016–032.

Note: The 87 possible summary convictions were individuals confined for offences that could be and often were punished summarily – namely, idle or disorderly behaviour, evil fame, being disorderly apprentices, or (for men) deserting their families. However, it is impossible to be sure on what basis these prisoners were confined because the calendar entries relating to them did not list a term of imprisonment.

Magistrates, then, called upon both the gaol and the bridewell to hold the hundreds, if not thousands, incarcerated for safe custody in eighteenth-century Middlesex. They took a different approach with respect to prisoners after conviction. Magistrates sent offenders for summary punishment to the gaol only exceptionally, preferring instead to commit them to the house of correction. The gaol, in short, was not widely perceived by magistrates or judges as a prison for punishment.

Even as the bridewell was receiving considerable numbers of inmates for safe custody, it remained the prison for vagrants. In this sense, the bridewell continued to fill its traditional role. Thus, between October 1769 and September 1772, 1,268 "disorderly" persons or vagrants were committed to the Middlesex prisons, most of whom were probably committed by summary conviction; 90 per cent were imprisoned in the house of correction.[72] This practice of confining vagrants primarily in the house of correction received legislative backing and was extended to the rest of the country by the 1823 *Gaol Act*. The act pronounced the house of correction "the only legal Place of Commitment" for vagrants, in an attempt to resolve "the Inconvenience to the classification of prisoners" and the impossibility of instituting "a Uniformity of Practice in the Management of Prisons" when vagrants were committed to common gaols.[73] By this point, then, some parliamentary authorities likewise sought specialized prisons where like offenders were grouped together.

As we have seen already, magistrates on the prison committee launched an assault against purely custodial commitments to the house of correction in the late eighteenth century. Between the 1770s and early 1800s, they issued a series of orders encouraging justices acting for the county to commit to the gaol all prisoners for safe custody, i.e. those for trial and for examination. Such practice would allow the house of correction to be "solely appropriated to the punishment of the idle and disorderly," as they believed the law intended.[74] As a result of this pressure, the numbers and proportions confined for trial fell drastically. In 1786, for example, eighty of 1,580 prisoners committed to the bridewell (5 per cent) were sent for trial at the quarter or Old Bailey sessions, whereas in 1815, only sixteen of 2,100 committals to the bridewell (less than 1 per cent) were so sent.[75] As magistrates fell into line with county policy, especially from the 1810s, offenders convicted under summary jurisdiction came to constitute an outright majority of yearly committals.[76]

By the start of the nineteenth century, therefore, nearly all accused offenders incarcerated to await jury trial were sent to the gaol at New Prison. This was not the fate of all Middlesex's prisoners for trial, however. In the early eighteenth century, Middlesex justices developed, reluctantly at first, a two-tier system of custodial imprisonment.

Lawfully, all Middlesex prisoners committed for trial for felony at the Old Bailey could have been sent to Newgate, but Middlesex justices generally preferred to commit such offenders to New Prison.[77] In 1726 the judges at the Old Bailey moved to change this, for organizational purposes, by ordering that all felons for trial at the Old Bailey be moved into Newgate six days before each sessions to allow the prison keeper to create a "perfect calendar" of trial prisoners.[78] There was no 'hard and fast' rule governing which felonies were tried at the Old Bailey as opposed to the quarter sessions, but generally, the most serious were tried at the Old Bailey.[79] By transferring felons from New Prison to Newgate, the magistrates removed the most serious offenders from their gaol for their final days in custody and concentrated them in Newgate in expectation of their upcoming trials.

Initially, many Middlesex justices resisted the change in policy. In May 1727 a committee convened to consider the matter argued against complying, contending that the inconveniences attending the policy outweighed the benefits.[80] They particularly highlighted the dreadful state and organization of Newgate. Gaol distemper was rampant and the prisoners "highly oppressed" by the gaol's "exorbitant" fees, which together were "in effect almost as bad as an Imprisonment for life."[81] "Many Innocent Persons," they warned, "will [lose] their Lives from the Hardships and Severity of the said Gaol" if the order was followed.[82] Despite this vociferous opposition from the county magistrates, by the middle of the century at the latest, serious felons were regularly moved from New Prison to Newgate for trial at the Old Bailey.[83] Yet, the magistrates' concerns regarding Newgate remained unresolved. A prison committee in 1772 claimed that inmates held in Newgate to await trial were brought to court in "a most deplorable[,] languid[,] and dangerous state" and expressed a wish for county prisoners to be "brought to tryal without being lodged in Newgate at all."[84] To restrict the numbers subjected to Newgate confinement, the magistrates subsequently forbade the keepers of New Prison, Clerkenwell house of correction, and Westminster's Tothill Fields bridewell from removing prisoners, except those charged with capital offences, to Newgate until future order.[85]

From the mid-1770s, the views of the bench changed. For the first time, at their own instigation, they proposed keeping inmates for trial for serious offences totally separate from those charged with misdemeanours and lesser felonies by hardening the division between New Prison and Newgate. By transferring serious felons for trial out of New Prison, following the 1726 order, the bench started to curtail New Prison's role in holding serious felons.[86] Deviation from this general practice was rare: in 1765 the county noted that "if perhaps once in Fifty Times, the County Magistrates find it necessary to deviate from it, by committing Offenders [for felonies and other offences properly triable at the Old Bailey] originally and immediately to Newgate, rather than to the other Gaols, the exceptions are hardly worth opposing to the general Rule."[87] The bench took aim at this uncommon practice in 1775 when they urged fellow magistrates to "commit such persons as are guilty of smaller offences to New Prison" and send those for "grander offences" or "capital Felonies" to Newgate.[88] In a December 1799 order the magistrates called explicitly for serious felons to be committed directly to Newgate: "felons, when committed for Trial be sent in first instance, to the County Gaol of Newgate."[89] Without noting why, the prison committee declared this policy "absolutely necessary."[90]

In Middlesex, then, the late eighteenth century saw dramatic shifts in sentencing practices and prison use. The new policy of using bridewells as sites of custodial detention was severely rolled back, a significant development that has gone unnoticed within the historiography. Opting to pursue a policy of prison specialization rather than amalgamation, Middlesex authorities divided their pre-trial and post-conviction prisoners into totally distinct prisons. Moreover, by this point, the magistrates were starting to separate pre-trial prisoners into different gaols according to the magnitude of their offences. These moves suggest a developing view that prisoners should be separated not only according to their commitment type but also by the nature of their crimes. Such separation would prevent convicted offenders and those charged with serious felonies from 'contaminating' those charged with minor offences, and it would also allow local authorities to tailor prison discipline to the type of offender held within.

Surrey

The changes in commitment practice traced in Middlesex were also evident in those parts of Southwark beyond the boundaries of the City's Bridge Ward Without. Given the striking similarities, I will discuss the Surrey pattern only briefly.

In Surrey, as in Middlesex, the county gaol and the house of correction had served a variety of functions in the eighteenth century. Surviving records, less voluminous for Surrey, show that both institutions received prisoners for trial as well as prisoners for punishment. Mainly, though, justices sent prisoners for custody to the gaol, and prisoners for punishment to the house of correction.[91] In this sense, commitment practices were already fairly specialized by the 1770s, at the latest. In the following decades, these patterns of commitment solidified such that it became rare for prisoners for punishment to be sent to the gaol, and conversely, for custodial prisoners to be sent to the house of correction. The Surrey justices said even less than their counterparts in Middlesex about why they were using their prisons in this way, but the overwhelming consistency in their patterns of practice clearly shows that it was a deliberate policy.

The general adoption of these commitment practices in various parts of London at the end of the eighteenth century points to the widespread desire for greater coherence in prison use. Although many justices had long treated the range of prisons available to them as distinct rather than interchangeable institutions, there was nevertheless some blurring in prison function over the course of the century. From the 1780s, magistrates, especially those on prison committees, were increasingly frustrated with this blurring, and they pushed instead for more specialized commitment practices. More and more, when sending offenders to prison following summary procedures, justices in the City, Middlesex, and Surrey distinguished between those held for safe custody and those confined for punishment. It is to the fate of those few offenders who were committed for trial at the quarter and assize sessions, and the smaller numbers who were convicted, that we turn next.

III. IMPRISONMENT AT ASSIZE AND QUARTER SESSIONS

In December 1822, a young man, "Rogers," was indicted at the Westminster Sessions accused of having stolen a bundle of unfilled tickets from the Old White Horse Cellar, a well-known coaching inn, where he worked as a porter. The man was found guilty, but because of his youth, the court opted against imposing the "utmost punishment." Rather, the newspaper reported, "he should have an opportunity of again entering into society, and that he might be prepared for it by an industrious course, the sentence of the Court was, that he should be imprisoned in the House of Correction for three months, and kept to hard labour at the tread-mill."[92]

If an offender was unlucky enough to progress through the various pre-trial stages to reach and be convicted at the higher courts, that offender was, for most of the eighteenth century, unlikely to be imprisoned. This was especially true if the offender was accused of a felony, all of which were capital offences under English common law. Even for non-capital felonies and misdemeanours, imprisonment was not a widely popular sanction, with courts often preferring forms of corporal punishment, such as whipping or branding, or fines.

While England's criminal law was exceptionally "bloody," in practice this severity was mitigated in several ways. The issuance of partial verdicts by juries saw defendants convicted of reduced offences, rather than the capital felonies with which they had been charged. Legal fictions, such as benefit of clergy, allowed offenders convicted of certain felonies to escape execution and instead be punished more lightly, typically with branding on the thumb, while juries engaging in pious perjury deliberately undervalued stolen goods to allow capital offences to be treated as non-capital ones. The routinized granting of royal pardons to the capitally convicted further reduced the numbers sent to the gallows.[93] Finally, over the course of the eighteenth century, the impossibility – and gruesomeness – of executing the vast numbers sentenced to death combined with growing concerns about the unpredictable, unequal, and possibly ineffective nature of existing punishments prompted authorities to develop and rely increasingly on 'secondary' punishments. The two main such punishments in this period, transportation and imprisonment, offered authorities an alternative to death that nonetheless seemed to punish offenders more harshly than the existing options.

From 1718, transportation to America, commonly for seven or fourteen years, was the most popular option open to London authorities, both as a sentence for those convicted of non-capital offences and as a condition of pardon for capital offenders sentenced to death. Not only did transportation allow authorities to push some of the responsibility and cost of problem individuals onto others, but it also seemed a harsher punishment, feared more by convicts, than imprisonment or corporal punishment. The preference for transportation was overwhelming at the Old Bailey, where, between 1714 and 1750, 75 per cent of defendants convicted of non-capital property crimes and nearly all capital convicts granted conditional pardons were ordered to be transported.[94] Elsewhere in England, transportation was somewhat less popular.[95] Its adoption, in short, was highly uneven, underscoring the highly localized nature of penal policy in this period as well as the comparative severity of punishment in London. In total, between 1718 and 1776, at least 36,000 convicts were ordered by English courts to be forcibly removed from Britain and sent to work in America; around 13,000 further convicts were probably transported from Ireland in this period and around 700 from Scotland.[96]

From its peak in the 1750s and 1760s, transportation to America came under increasing criticism, and in the years preceding the American war, the numbers so sentenced declined across England. In searching for a replacement for transportation (however temporary), the courts had a series of established options: clergyable discharge, which transportation itself had replaced; corporal punishment such as whipping or branding; capital punishment; or imprisonment. They might also have developed a new punishment.[97] In the short term, many courts turned to corporal punishment, especially whipping.[98] Yet, by the end of the eighteenth century, the general preference was for imprisonment.

As noted in the introduction, common law practice had long allowed for the penal imprisonment of offenders found guilty of misdemeanours, and from 1706, judges at the quarter and assize sessions had a general authority to sentence clergied felons to imprisonment at hard labour in either a house of correction or a workhouse for between six months and two years.[99] London courts made great use of this legislation initially, during a period when war made transportation difficult, but the attractions of transportation, as that punishment redeveloped after 1718, meant that few felony convicts were imprisoned at hard labour during the middle years of the eighteenth century.[100] Still, the experiment had longer-term impacts on some bridewells, including Middlesex's, which was restocked with work tools and hemp and supplied with handcuffs and other irons for securing convicts sent from the Old Bailey, and whose structure was made more sound and permanent through work such as paving the yards in the late 1710s.[101]

In the following decades, hard labour as a punishment was not entirely forgotten, but it found little support: the mid-century saw a failed proposal by a lord of the Admiralty to substitute hard labour on the dockyards for male felons liable to be transported.[102] Imprisonment saw a revival in the 1770s, aided by the American War and the promotion of the punishment through Parliament's passage of two additional acts, in 1776 and 1779 respectively, which authorized the courts to substitute long terms of hard labour for transportation.[103] Certain government officials, notably William Eden, actively championed the new punishment, but in general, the government did not order the localities to use prisons. Understanding its role to be "loosely directive" rather than regulatory, the government developed a framework of options, then left the judges and justices to determine criminal justice policy and to administer it as they saw fit.[104]

In seeking to explain the shift from transportation to imprisonment, historians have suggested several motivations, the majority of which rest on contemporary views on transportation. As scholars have charted, contemporary concerns about transportation "almost cease[ing] to be a punishment" took hold at a time when fears about violent crime and social disorder, especially in London, were on the rise.[105] In this context, elites desperately sought a punishment that would instill fear in the hearts of potential criminals. Worries about depopulation in the wake of a wave of emigration to North America in the early 1770s led to further scrutiny of transportation. And of course, worsening relations with America undoubtedly played a role, as transportation ultimately depended on the existence of colonies or penal settlements able and willing to accept the convicts.[106] Some contemporaries saw transportation as too inflexible and the courts' reliance on it as too extreme. Influenced by the European and British Enlightenments, such men looked to establish a more rational and equitable system of punishments and to ensure the equality of its application.[107] Finally, it was not only officials who influenced court practice. Scholars have also spotlighted the role played by accused and convicted offenders in transportation's downfall. For example, Hitchcock and Shoemaker posit that offenders' contempt for transportation and their ability to subvert the punishment accelerated judges' loss of faith in it.[108] Relatedly, historians have recently sought to uncover the role of victims in shaping penal outcomes, and they have shown how the status of the victim and the involvement of police in trials influenced the punishments handed out.[109]

In explaining the growth of imprisonment for felony, historians have generally assigned a much smaller role to new arguments made in favour of imprisonment as a means of reforming criminals. Peter King's interpretation of the motive forces behind the growth of imprisonment, based on his magisterial study of the administration of justice in Essex, is instructive. In his view, the increasing importance of imprisonment after the resumption of transportation in 1787 resulted from the inability of the new Australian settlements and remaining hulks to absorb the larger number of convicts sentenced to transportation by the courts. As transportation became necessarily restricted to more serious offenders, imprisonment was relied upon by default to deal with those convicted of less serious offences who, King suggests, might have been transported had numbers allowed.[110] Additionally, King stresses the appeal of imprisonment in giving courts "much greater flexibility in attuning the level of sanction to the nature of both offence and offender." Sentence length could be adjusted easily, and prison terms could be used in conjunction with sanctions such as fines, a requirement to provide surety, or corporal punishment. Finally, King downplays the role played by a new belief in the "reformatory qualities" of imprisonment in shaping sentencing patterns.[111] More generally, while many scholars agree that some prison reformers were increasingly convinced of the superiority of reformative imprisonment, they stress that this was a small group, confined mainly to dissenters and utilitarians, whose ideological views were not widely shared by county justices.[112]

In seeking to refine these explanations for the expansion of imprisonment, I do not wish to discount the role played by contemporary thinking on transportation. Across the London metropolis, judges and justices remained firmly convinced, well into the mid-nineteenth century, that transportation was indispensable to the criminal justice system – not least because it allowed them to dispose of serious offenders in the longer term. The continued faith in transportation considerably affected the frequency with which imprisonment was used and the types of offences punished by imprisonment (generally, less serious ones). Nevertheless, from the mid-eighteenth century, those same groups who embraced transportation for the most serious categories of offenders not executed also sought a punishment, complementary to transportation, for less serious felons that would "attack the root of crime rather than simply terrorizing offenders into obedience."[113] For this purpose, they embraced imprisonment at hard labour, the instrument through which criminals were to be reformed. A widespread belief, then, in the potential of moral reform, and a conviction that reform could and should be done at home, specifically through setting convicted offenders to work, helped transform the philosophy and practice of punishment in late-eighteenth-century England.

Sentencing Practices

The pace at which quarter and assize courts in England moved away from transportation, the motivations behind the changing practice, and the solutions adopted in lieu of transportation differed by county. King has demonstrated, for example, that Essex courts moved away from transportation, especially in punishing property offences, in the early 1760s, though at this point, they mainly adopted whipping as a replacement. The courts turned decisively to imprisonment in 1772, largely through the efforts of one judge, Lord Mansfield.[114] The jurisdictions under study here moved more slowly, reflecting the particular nature of the crime problem – both more serious and more extensive – in London and its urban environs. In Surrey, the expansion in the number and proportion of prison sentences preceded the outbreak of war with America, with hostilities quickening rather than initiating the shift in sentencing practices, whereas in Middlesex and the City, the growth of imprisonment as punishment for felony came only after war began.

Surrey

At the assizes, as John Beattie has shown, practice began to change in 1772. Up to this year, transportation had accounted for over 63 per cent of non-capital punishments for property crimes (the most common offence tried) before Surrey courts, but in the four years that followed, this fell to under 40 per cent.[115] In place of transportation, the assizes sentenced a growing proportion of offenders to imprisonment at hard labour. The court's embrace of this punishment during the war years was overwhelming: in 1776–82, hard labour, in either houses of correction or hulks, accounted for nearly 90 per cent of sentences handed down by the assizes for defendants convicted of non-capital property crimes.[116] By comparison, transportation as a condition of pardon for capital convicts remained popular right up to the war with America, and after it ended, the sanction regained its popularity.[117] So, while Surrey judges were starting to move away from transportation when punishing the less serious offences that came before them, they continued to prefer that punishment over other available options when dealing with offenders accused of more serious offences whom they wished to save from the gallows.

At the quarter sessions, the magistrates embraced imprisonment earlier, in the 1760s, but to a lesser degree than at the assizes. Whereas, in 1763–67, an average 73 per cent of convicted property offenders were transported, compared to 4.5 per cent imprisoned, during the period 1769–75, the percentage transported dropped to 49 per cent while the percentage imprisoned grew to 22 per cent.[118] The reliance on imprisonment grew during the American War, but following the conclusion of hostilities the quarter sessions retreated somewhat from imprisonment and began again sentencing prisoners to periods of transportation, suggesting the war-time reliance on confinement was largely a consequence of the inability to transport convicts rather than a general embrace of incarceration. Nonetheless, by the period 1799–1802 imprisonment was again, and would remain, dominant, accounting in these years for 75 per cent of all non-capital punishments for property offenders.[119] As these sentencing patterns suggest, views towards imprisonment were highly malleable as magistrates continually weighed the benefits of different punishments in shifting circumstances.

The quarter and assize sessions used imprisonment in distinct ways. Whereas the vast majority of property defendants sentenced to imprisonment at the assizes were confined for hard labour, those sentenced to imprisonment at quarter sessions were confined mainly as "a way of adding further pain to a sentence of whipping."[120] The prison, then, did not "bury the whip"; it operated alongside traditional, corporal punishments.[121] Therefore, of the defendants sentenced to imprisonment at the quarter sessions between 1776 and 1782, 57 per cent were imprisoned without hard labour.[122] As these distinct patterns suggest, imprisonment was a highly flexible punishment whose terms and conditions could easily be adjusted by courts to better fit the offender's crime and with reference to their character, gender, or age. This was clearly an important part of the punishment's appeal.

Because the courts used imprisonment differently, they relied on different prisons to confine those they incarcerated. The Surrey assizes preferred overwhelmingly to send convicted property offenders sentenced to imprisonment to a house of correction. The hulks were another popular option during the war with America, but after hostilities ended, as the hulks' shockingly poor conditions and astoundingly high mortality rates were publicized, the court's reliance on them declined appreciably.[123] The county gaol, by contrast, does not seem to have been popular with the assizes at any point from the mid-eighteenth century onwards. Only four of 105 offenders (3.8 per cent) sentenced to imprisonment were confined in the gaol between 1776 and 1782, for example.[124]

By contrast, the magistrates at the quarter sessions, who mainly used imprisonment as a supplement to whipping, sent property offenders primarily to the gaol, the site deemed most appropriate by the magistrates for individuals imprisoned without hard labour. The small number of offenders who were sentenced to imprisonment at hard labour were directed to either the house of correction or the hulks – generally magistrates preferred the hulks.[125]

This pattern – using the house of correction for offenders sentenced to hard labour and the gaol for those sentenced to imprisonment without hard labour – was also common in the Northeast, in Durham, Newcastle, and Northumberland, in the mid-to-late eighteenth century.[126] Such patterns evidence an impulse to distinguish between prisons when sentencing offenders which went beyond London. They also underscore the longstanding association between houses of correction and labour discipline. Just as most offenders sentenced to hard labour in the early eighteenth century were directed to houses of correction, so too were offenders so sentenced at the end of the century.

Quarter session practice changed dramatically after 1799. In this year the magistrates' new county gaol and house of correction at Newington opened. John Beattie has argued that the construction of Newington, which not only allowed prisoners to be classified and separated but which made hard labour a "central element of the discipline," symbolized the Surrey magistrates' "conversion" to imprisonment at hard labour.[127] This conversion was reflected in sentencing practices as soon as the institution opened. Between 1800 and 1802, 70 per cent of property offenders sentenced to imprisonment were confined for hard labour, with the majority of these incarcerated in the house of correction.[128] As these patterns confirm, court sentencing practice was intimately related to and influenced by magistrates' administration of county prisons.

By the start of the nineteenth century, then, sentencing practice at the Surrey quarter sessions echoed that at the assizes: both were sentencing larger numbers of offenders to imprisonment; such sentences were usually accompanied by orders to put the offender to hard labour; and they were carried out primarily in the house of correction.

Middlesex and the City

In Middlesex and the City, the move by the highest court, the Old Bailey, to make more use of imprisonment was again the product of the disruption of transportation rather than an intensification of an established trend towards imprisonment at hard labour. The years preceding the war with America saw small numbers, on average five per year, sentenced to imprisonment, but until war broke out, the court depended almost entirely on transportation to punish

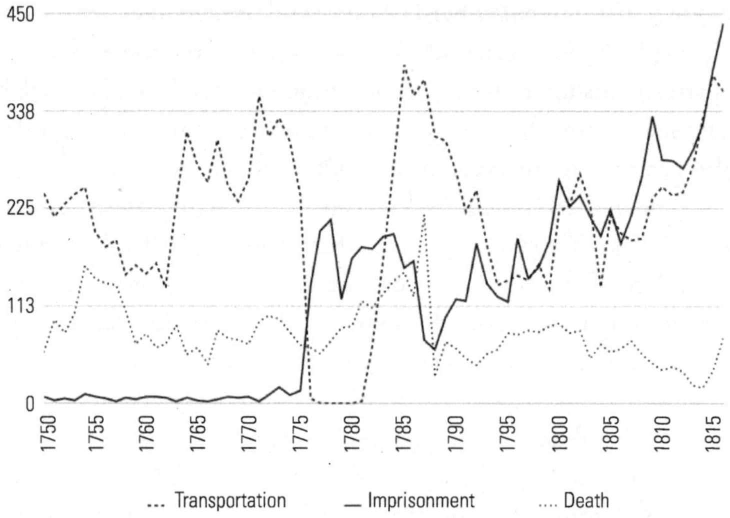

Figure 1.4 · Old Bailey: Death, transportation, and imprisonment sentences, 1750–1816. Tabulating year against punishment category, counting by punishments, between 1750 and 1816.

guilty offenders who were not sentenced to death, as shown in figure 1.4. Such was the Old Bailey judges' attachment to transportation that, from October 1781, they resumed sentencing offenders to transportation, despite an alternative destination not yet having been found.[129] Imprisonment did not replace transportation as the courts' primary substitute for execution. In the 1790s, as earlier, most of the condemned were pardoned on condition of transportation. The relatively few who were pardoned on condition they be imprisoned were generally older, over fifty-five years old, and sometimes sick or infirm.[130]

Simon Devereaux has suggested that the reliance on transportation in the lead-up to the war with America was linked to the amount of serious crime, especially burglary and highway robbery, which contemporaries believed had reached near-epidemic proportions in London after 1760.[131] Similarly, it seems that in the 1780s the quick return to transportation and the concurrent fall in sentences of imprisonment may have had less to do with judges' views of imprisonment and more to do with the social anxiety and chaos of the decade. The years following the Gordon Riots and the post-war crime wave saw judges become yet more willing to convict defendants and to order harsher punishments. There was a dramatic increase, for example, in the number and proportion of capital convicts actually executed in London in the 1780s – numbers unmatched at any other point in either the eighteenth or nineteenth centuries.[132] That a turn towards harsher sentencing in the 1780s would have led to an upswing in the numbers and proportions transported is unsurprising, as London judges continued to view transportation as "the minimally appropriate punishment" for certain offences, especially violent property crimes, which apparently were on the rise.[133]

When the Old Bailey judges finally resorted to imprisonment at hard labour in 1776, they did so in ways that minimized the effect on gaols and houses of correction. From July 1776 to July 1778, the judges sentenced 227 Middlesex offenders to imprisonment at hard labour. Only forty-five, less than 20 per cent, were imprisoned in the Clerkenwell house of correction while the remaining 182 were sent to hulks on the Thames.[134]

The justices at the Middlesex quarter sessions likewise relied on transportation to punish their most serious offenders, accused mainly of petty larceny or fraud, and turned to imprisonment at hard labour as a substitute only in 1776 when their preferred option was disrupted by war (figure 1.5). Like the Old Bailey judges, these justices returned quickly to their former sentencing practices after the war ended, though the numbers sentenced to transportation were dramatically reduced as compared with 1775 – perhaps in recognition of the fact that the justices could not in actuality transport offenders until Botany Bay was established.[135] They also preferred to send hard labour felons to the hulks rather than the house of correction. Those incarcerated in the latter were mainly women. Indeed, court practice and parliamentary legislation both suggest that in these years imprisonment at hard labour in a county prison was considered particularly suited to female convicts.[136]

The magistrates made greater use of imprisonment when dealing with less serious offenses. Most sessions from the 1720s onwards saw a handful of offenders sentenced to imprisonment. Imprisonment was used primarily as an attractive alternative, but more frequently as a complement, to corporal punishment and fines. Up to the 1790s, many if not most of those who were sentenced to imprisonment were also ordered to be whipped, to stand in the pillory, or to pay a fine.[137] By combining punishments in this way, the justices made them more dreadful. Such practices were common at the Old Bailey too, a court also seeking to intensify the pains of non-capital punishment. Over

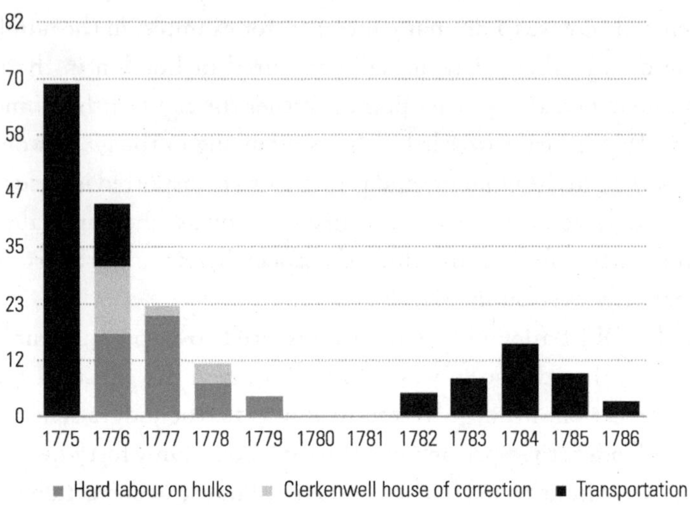

Figure 1.5 • Numbers sentenced to transportation and imprisonment at hard labour by Middlesex quarter sessions, 1775–86. Note: 1786 covers only sentences in January and February.

half of Newgate prisoners who received a prison sentence from the Old Bailey between 1789 and 1794 were also fined, while a quarter were ordered to be whipped.[138] Indeed, whipping saw a revival across London courts in the 1770s and 1780s. These trends should remind us that authorities in this period saw no need to choose between punishing the body and punishing the mind. In short, an endorsement of so-called 'enlightened' punishments need not entail a rejection of traditional, "brutal" practices.[139]

If we focus on one category of offence, assault, we can see how London magistrates, seeking a harsher penalty, increasingly opted for imprisonment over the previously favoured punishment, fines.[140] As Greg Smith has shown, in Middlesex, between 1780 and 1795, about 17 per cent of assault convictions were punished with a term of imprisonment, up from 9.6 per cent in the period 1760–75. In the City, this shift happened earlier: 21 per cent of assault convictions were punished with imprisonment in 1760–75 and 22.3 per cent in 1780–95.[141]

In choosing where to confine offenders sentenced to imprisonment, the Middlesex sessions had long made some distinctions. Specifically, those imprisoned with an order that they be put to labour or hard labour were directed uniformly to the house of correction, regardless of where they had been held prior to trial. Sentencing practice for those imprisoned without an order that they labour, however, was more irregular. Before the 1790s, such individuals were often confined in whichever institution they had been held in while awaiting trial. Afterwards, nearly all were directed by the sessions to the bridewell, regardless of where they had been held previously.[142] Lists created between September 1777 and January 1795 of "poor convicts" in the bridewell, a category which appears to have consisted of all those convicted at the quarter and assize sessions, attest to the regular usage of the bridewell as a site of punishment by these courts. In these years, the bridewell held between sixteen and 113 "convict" prisoners (sixty-four on average) each day.[143] Significantly, no such lists were compiled for New Prison.

In the City, by contrast, the justices continued to confine misdemeanants sentenced to imprisonment by the sessions in either Newgate or one of the compters.[144] There, the increasing use of imprisonment as a punishment did not lead to greater numbers of convicted offenders in the house of correction, Bridewell, for reasons which will be discussed below.

Historians have suggested that these sentencing patterns, particularly the reluctance of the higher courts to lessen their dependence on transportation and their unwillingness to imprison offenders sentenced to hard labour in a house of correction or gaol, indicate that neither the justices at the quarter sessions nor the judges at the Old Bailey were convinced of the benefits of imprisonment at hard labour in local prisons. Hitchcock and Shoemaker, for example, recently contended that "London's governors largely failed to implement, or even fully discuss, a substantial programme of prison reform in this period" and that "advocates of reformatory imprisonment had as yet had little impact."[145] They emphasize the 1790s as the crucial period of change.[146]

Certainly, the 1790s witnessed a clear break from earlier sentencing patterns. From that decade onwards, imprisonment became the most common sentence at the Old Bailey. To emphasize this decade only, however, is to miss the fundamental shifts taking place in the ideological outlook of London benches earlier in the period. In the 1760s and 1770s, magistrates across London moved decisively to repair and rebuild their prisons in order to accommodate a larger and more diverse population of offenders and to allow them to put into practice their belief in the reformatory potential of imprisonment at hard labour. In short, these years saw London authorities develop a coherent penal philosophy based increasingly on reformative imprisonment. The 1790s in Middlesex and Surrey, and the 1810s in the City, saw sentencing bodies acting in accordance with shifts in outlook which, due to practical and financial difficulties, were a long time in gestation, but which had germinated earlier.

Tracing a Shift in Outlook: Growing Interest in Reformatory Imprisonment

Middlesex

In September 1772, after a grand jury presented the county's gaol and bridewell as insufficient and requiring repair, the Middlesex bench commissioned an investigation into its prisons. Reporting their findings in October 1772, the committee urged the bench to substantially reconstruct both institutions.[147] With respect to New Prison, they justified their plans in traditional terms with reference to the building's "very feeble and insecure" structure which endangered the "health and safe keeping and well ordering" of the prisoners.[148] The work proposed for New Prison was confined to increasing the gaol's size, security, and salubriousness. Yet, their ambitions for the house of correction were far-reaching. The repair committee concluded,

> we are of opinion it wo[ul]d be highly beneficial to this county and the kingdom to have a more spacious house of correction fitted up and provided with a stock for every fitting kind of labour (whether profitable or not) to employ all persons comitted thither and we submit that such a comodious and well-furnish'd and well-ordered house of correction will be a means of amendment of the vicious poor and is a obligatory business of the justices.[149]

The committee, then, advocated for the refurbishment of the bridewell to make it a site of constant labour and endorsed the view that institutional labour promised moral reformation. This work promised benefits to the kingdom as a whole. Their comments testify to the fact that, in Middlesex, reformative imprisonment was associated explicitly with the house of correction.[150]

Between October 1772, when the rebuilding committee's plans were presented to the quarter sessions, and April 1773, when the sessions charged a new committee, composed of the same men as before, to oversee the prison work, the plan to reconstruct the house of correction under reformed principles was dropped. Why would this have happened if the magistrates were set on a reforming prison agenda?

When the magistrates reconvened in October 1772, questions were raised regarding whether the original committee was authorized to enquire into rebuilding the house of correction. The session order that had established the committee had directed them to consider the condition of the gaol and the sessions house; it did not explicitly name the bridewell.[151] The committee had justified their inclusion of the bridewell in deliberations by stating that its absence from the order must have been "some Mistake or Omission."[152] However, the May 1772 jury presentment, which had not only triggered the rate-funded rebuilding project but also authorized it, did not explicitly extend to the house of correction either. Though the jury surveyed both prisons, they presented only New Prison as "requisite to be rebuilt or at least to have a thorough repair made for the securing of the prisoners detained therein." However, in another confusing twist, one of the jurors, George Friend, had prepared a list of needed repairs as an addendum to the jury presentment, and this specified repairs to both prisons, though it focused mainly on New Prison.[153] Under the *Gaols Act* of 1699, the *County Rates Act* of 1738, and the *Justices Commitment Act* of 1743, justices could use county money to erect, repair, or rebuild a county building, including a house of correction or gaol, only if a grand jury presented it as insufficient, inconvenient, or in want of repair, and the justices, assembled at sessions, agreed to raise the money.[154] In short, if the May presentment extended solely to New Prison, then the committee's work could not legally extend beyond the gaol.

On top of this legal difficulty, the pressing need for repair at New Prison induced the magistrates to put building plans at Clerkenwell bridewell on hold. As the bench noted in April 1773, New Prison was "greatly the most out of repair," so they opted to "compleat such repair as they shall judge necessary to be done thereto before they proceed in the repair of Clerkenwell Bridewell."[155] The county spent £3,500 fixing and enlarging New Prison between 1773 and 1775, with only minor works conducted at the bridewell in this period.[156] The utter disrepair at New Prison took precedence over the magistrates' interest in preparing the bridewell to receive convicted felons.

It was probably the failure to proceed with reforming the bridewell that caused the Old Bailey judges and the magistrates at the quarter sessions to refrain from sending felons sentenced to hard labour to the bridewell in the 1770s and 1780s. Rather than totally rejecting imprisonment at hard labour, these committing bodies recognized that such sentences could not be realistically carried out without a significant reform of the bridewell. As the magistrates clearly stated in April 1773, the house of correction was "in so weak and insecure a state as not to be sufficient for the safe custody of the felons and others."[157] The various prison repair committees kept the Middlesex bench updated on the bridewell's state and communicated to them, regularly and forcefully, their views on the institution's limitations. In July 1777, for example, the committee informed the bench that the current bridewell was too small, and that, because it had been designed for the short-term confinement of vagrants and petty offenders, it was generally unsuitable for confining convicted felons. There was "no place within the said prison capable of holding or suited to the employment of the said convicts separate from the [other] prisoners pursuant to the directions contained in the act."[158] Hard-labour convicts who were sent to the bridewell were consequently kept in the garden behind the prison – a situation that was obviously unsuitable and untenable.[159] The magistrates' familiarity with the physical condition and layout of the house of correction probably made them particularly wary of sending large numbers of convicted felons there.

To further compound difficulties, Newgate was destroyed in the Gordon Riots of June 1780, forcing authorities to find alternative carceral arrangements. Prisoners who would normally have been sent to Newgate – the accused for trial at the Old Bailey, individuals sentenced and awaiting transportation, and City prisoners sentenced to imprisonment in Newgate – were all directed to the Middlesex prisons instead.[160] Only prisoners condemned to death remained in what was left of Newgate. The tense atmosphere following the riots, inmate overcrowding, and the influx of individuals accused of serious offences helped create, in Tim Hitchcock's view, a rebellious culture within the Middlesex prisons.[161] Nearly two years passed before Newgate, in February 1782, was able to accommodate its share of offenders convicted at the City sessions and the Old Bailey.[162]

Extraordinary measures taken by the Middlesex bench in the fall of 1780 highlight the severity of overcrowding and the justices' commitment to alleviating that pressure. First, the bench ordered constables and justices acting outside of sessions to send vagrants directly to the vagrant contractor, Henry

Adams, rather than to the house of correction.[163] Second, in October the bench requested that the sheriffs of London and Middlesex remove the debtors committed by them from the Clerkenwell bridewell, and in November, they informed the sheriffs that the county bridewell would not accept any more of their debtors.[164] Third, with the numbers of prisoners rising, the magistrates in November were forced to hire a space near the prisons to serve as a guardroom for the military guard who, since the riots, had patrolled the prisons. There was "no possibility of accommodating the Guard within the prisons," the justices reported, as the prisons were "so full" and numbers "daily increasing." The county, though, could not do away with the guards: due to the rising numbers there was "the greatest reason to fear should the Guards be withdrawn the prisoners would immediately affect their escape."[165] Finally, between 1777 and 1779, the magistrates spent £2,000 altering the bridewell to accommodate and set to hard labour "convict" inmates.[166]

The actions and words of the magistrates evince a clear and sustained concern over the number of inmates held in their prisons, especially the bridewell, and the dangers posed by confining together a heterogenous mix of offenders. As the magistrates on the prison committee, those with the greatest awareness of the problems faced by the institutions, declared to the bench in October 1780, "a far greater number of persons is now in general imprisoned there than what the building is capable of containing with safety and convenience[,] notwithstanding the alterations and improvements already made at a very considerable expence."[167] Given the frequency and urgency of such statements, it is not surprising that those justices were wary of committing additional offenders to either prison, especially when other options, namely the hulks, were available.[168]

The reopening of Newgate in 1782 allowed the magistrates to embark on the long process of redesigning and rebuilding their bridewell. This project, which began at the end of 1782, took over ten years to complete, with the new bridewell, Coldbath Fields, opening in 1794. Sentencing patterns at the Old Bailey changed immediately in response. Whereas in 1783–93, on average around 19 per cent of offenders were imprisoned and roughly 38 per cent transported, in 1794–1804, about 29 per cent were imprisoned and 25.5 per cent transported.[169] From 1794, the numbers annually imprisoned roughly matched, and generally exceeded slightly, the numbers sentenced to transportation (figure 1.4). Middlesex defendants, the "larger proportion" of individuals tried at the

Old Bailey, who were sentenced to imprisonment were committed uniformly to Coldbath Fields.[170] In this way, the practices of the Old Bailey came to match those of Middlesex justices acting summarily, who as we have seen had for some time used the bridewell (initially the old Clerkenwell bridewell) to confine individuals sentenced to imprisonment. That the numbers imprisoned grew consistently and significantly only after Coldbath Fields – the new, expensive, 'modern' bridewell – opened points to the pre-eminent role that the bridewell's construction played in enabling and encouraging justices to adopt incarceration on a wider scale.

At this point in London, there was little support for using imprisonment to punish habitual offenders, serious felonies, or reprieves, who were thought totally unsuited to punitive confinement. Instead, imprisonment became the punishment for those convicted of less serious, non-capital felonies, especially petty property offenses, which from 1718 had generally been punished by transportation. This set London somewhat apart from some other counties, which embraced imprisonment as a replacement for respites and for transportation somewhat more readily.[171] The Middlesex magistrates in 1791 actively campaigned against a parliamentary bill that would have allowed, as they saw it, "sending Criminals of the most abandoned and desperate sort after conviction and sentence" into the house of correction.[172] Admitting hardened convicts into the bridewell would be pointless, they argued. As William Mainwaring, the sessions' chairman, told the House of Commons in 1791, "it would be idle to imagine that any good purpose, either of reformation or contrition, could be effected on the minds of beings so abandoned to vice and infamy."[173] Worse, such practice would totally undermine the bridewell's purpose. It would "be extremely Prejudicial to the Morals of lesser offenders confined therein who are to be again set at large and prevent the salutary Effects to be expected from a well regulated House of Correction or Penitentiary house taking place."[174] For the habitual criminal, "banishment to the remote corner of the globe" was the only answer, as the chaplain of London's Bridewell noted in a 1798 pamphlet.[175] As such comments indicate, even those who generally embraced imprisonment and were committed to the expensive, time-consuming project of prison reform remained unconvinced about the suitability of imprisonment as a punishment for the most serious crimes, with those so convicted seen as troublesome and unamenable to reformation. Both imprisonment and transportation were required to fight against crime and disorder.

In 1772, the chairman of the Middlesex sessions, Sir John Hawkins, proclaimed the bench united in its ambition to "rebuild their prisons and ... to exert their utmost endeavours to substitute actual hard labour as a punishment, instead of transportation."[176] Hawkins surely overestimated the bench's support for imprisonment, but the evidence presented above certainly indicates that the slow adoption of punitive imprisonment at the higher courts stemmed primarily from structural rather than ideological considerations. Bringing these practical concerns and limitations into view helps us to understand the delays, not only on the part of the Middlesex magistrates in reconstructing and reforming their bridewell, but also on the part of the magistrates at quarter sessions and judges at Old Bailey in adopting imprisonment as a punishment. Even if these judicial bodies had come to believe that criminal offenders should be reformed at home rather than shipped abroad, and that this reformation could be actualized through imprisonment at hard labour, there was no way for them to put the experiment into practice until a reformed prison was built. Once the county built such a prison, defendants were sentenced to imprisonment in greater numbers and proportions.

Surrey

Such practicalities likewise shaped the adoption of reformative imprisonment in Surrey. There too the magistrates' intimate knowledge of the bridewell, especially its size, physical condition, and regime, informed their sentencing practice at the quarter sessions. As we have seen, the bench was reluctant, until the start of the nineteenth century, to imprison convicted offenders in the Southwark bridewell for punishment. This reluctance stemmed from the prison being judged unsuitable to hold such prisoners rather than from a principled rejection of imprisonment at hard labour.

A review of the county's prison-building efforts indicates that the justices sought to establish a system of reformatory imprisonment in their house of correction in the early 1770s. After a grand jury presented the Southwark house of correction and Surrey gaol, both built in 1720, as "too small unhealthy inconvenient and unsafe," the bench resolved to rebuild them. Work began at the gaol, where, in 1771, the justices built a new house for the gaoler and converted his old apartments into wards for debtors at a cost of nearly £700.[177] Their alteration of the bridewell proved considerably more expensive and extensive. In January 1772, the bench rejected a plan, costing £950, to repair and enlarge the bridewell, as had been done at the gaol, in favour of building an entirely new bridewell on a new site for the considerably larger sum of £2,500. The new bridewell divided men, women, and disorderly apprentices into separate wards and courtyards, whereas previously they had shared the prison space, and it included distinct workshops for each class. The provision of separate wards and the facilities for employment put this bridewell "in advance of nearly all bridewells of its date," as the architectural historian C.W. Chalkin has noted.[178] Furthermore, between 1767 and 1775, the justices built new bridewells elsewhere in the county, at Guildford and Kingston, costing the county another £2,340 and further attesting to the bench's interest in improving their stock of bridewells.[179]

Even after this work was carried out, sentencing practice at the quarter sessions did not greatly change. This was probably because the bridewell, even expanded, was too small to accommodate the growing numbers of felons and misdemeanants imprisoned by the quarter and assize sessions. In 1772, the year the new bridewell was built, only three property offenders were sentenced to imprisonment by the sessions; the following year, when the bridewell opened, the number jumped to twenty-six – a figure greater than the total number of property offenders (twenty-five) who had been sentenced to imprisonment over the previous decade.[180] Though the numbers imprisoned were not necessarily large, between eleven and eighteen property offenders a year between 1772 and 1775, the Southwark bridewell was very small: it could accommodate fewer than forty prisoners.[181] Moreover, since prison terms were usually for six months or longer, convicted offenders were relatively long-term inhabitants of the bridewell.[182] Consequently, any increases in the numbers sentenced to imprisonment would have had a considerable impact on the size of the daily prison population.

The pressures placed on prisons by changing sentencing practices do not seem to have overly concerned the assize judges; the Surrey magistrates, however, as supervisors of the county prisons, were more conscious of and receptive to those pressures.[183] Aware not only that the Southwark bridewell was small, but also that the assize judges sent a majority of their prisoners there, the magistrates may have chosen to divide their prisoners amongst the various

Surrey prisons to lessen the burden on any one institution. The burning down of the Southwark bridewell in June 1780 during the Gordon Riots further restricted the sessions' options. In these circumstances, it was unlikely, at least temporarily, that the magistrates would send more than a handful of convicted offenders to the bridewell.

Therefore, until 1801 when the bridewell in St. George's Fields was abandoned and incorporated into the new, reformed gaol at Newington, the only bridewell available for offenders in Southwark was small and frequently out of repair. Significantly, as soon as Newington bridewell opened – allowing for the full employment of a larger number of prisoners and the imposition of a stricter, more regimented discipline – magistrates' sentencing practices changed. Though the bench may have accepted the benefits of imprisonment at hard labour as early as the 1770s, they embraced the punishment in practice only when they knew their sentences could be effectively carried out.

City of London

Sentencing practice in the City of London diverged sharply from the practices developing in Middlesex and Surrey. In the City, as the use of imprisonment expanded, the judges at the Old Bailey sent their convicted offenders primarily to Newgate, while the justices at the quarter sessions divided theirs between Newgate and the compters. While such patterns may suggest a lack of concern with prison specialization, the Corporation in fact disapproved of this situation, though in the short term they deemed it inevitable.

Whereas the counties of Middlesex and Surrey each had at least one county-owned house of correction, the only house of correction in the City, Bridewell, was a charitable institution that was governed and funded by its own board of governors rather than the Corporation of London.[184] It is not entirely clear whether the Old Bailey judges or City justices in the late eighteenth century were empowered to sentence defendants to terms of imprisonment in Bridewell. On the one hand, there was clear precedent for this practice: some of the felons sentenced by the Old Bailey to imprisonment at hard labour between 1707 and 1718 were imprisoned therein.[185] Furthermore, several capital offenders were pardoned by the Old Bailey on condition of their being imprisoned in Bridewell, such as the eleven women sent there in 1705 to "Labour as idle and disorderly persons for the space of one whole year."[186] Such commitments became less frequent after the 1718 *Transportation Act*. On the other hand, a late-nineteenth-century historian of Bridewell, A.J. Copeland, suggested that City authorities had lost the authority to commit indicted offenders to the institution. He reported that in September 1713 the governors wrote to the Secretary of State informing him that in future felons from the Old Bailey would not be received at Bridewell.[187]

Regardless, by the early nineteenth century, City authorities evidently felt they could not use Bridewell in this manner. As the Newgate keeper told a parliamentary committee in 1811, there was no "house of correction or prison belonging to the City of London to which felons, sentenced to temporary imprisonment, can be sent from Newgate."[188] As a result, City authorities were actively engaged in securing funds, land, and authority to build a house of correction.[189] The Common Council had signalled their intentions in 1810 by resolving that "the evil effects arising from the crowded state of the gaols, would be greatly obviated by erecting a House of Correction for the reception of the minor classes of offenders, a measure which has been found highly beneficial to the administration of criminal justice in various parts of the kingdom, and to the moral reform of offenders."[190] Clearly, City officials not only understood the house of correction to be the proper place to confine those sentenced to imprisonment, but they believed they lacked such an institution. So, although the City opted to rely on Newgate (and, probably to a lesser extent, the hulks) to imprison convicted felons, they apparently viewed this reliance as temporary and highly inconvenient.[191]

In 1812, Parliament approved City requests to raise funds for prison-building. The Corporation was empowered to purchase ground to build a new prison, Whitecross Street, for debtors and others confined under civil process in the City and Middlesex, and to convert two old prisons, Giltspur Street Compter and Ludgate Prison, into a joint gaol and house of correction.[192] The reconfiguration of Giltspur was completed in 1816, after which those sentenced to hard labour for felonies and those convicted of assaults and misdemeanours at the Old Bailey or City sessions were directed primarily to the new house of correction.[193]

The City of London, more than either Middlesex or Surrey, had maintained a considerable degree of prison specialization throughout the eighteenth century, and yet, of the three jurisdictions, it was the last to build a house of correction to separate prisoners convicted and sentenced to imprisonment at the quarter and Old Bailey sessions from other kinds of prisoner. Compared with Surrey's Newington house of correction, finished a decade earlier, and Middlesex's Coldbath Fields, built over two decades earlier, this delay was considerable. It also placed incredible pressure on London's other prisons, especially Newgate, which had to accommodate not only pre-trial prisoners, debtors, and convicts awaiting transportation or execution, but now also convicts sentenced to imprisonment. The postponement, however, is largely explained by the City's pattern of prison-building in the second half of the eighteenth century.

From the 1750s to the mid-1780s, the various committees that dealt with the City's prisons were focused on the mammoth task of rebuilding Newgate. After years of disagreements over architectural plans, pricing, and sources of funding, reconstruction began in 1767, thanks to a £50,000 loan from Parliament secured on the City Orphans Fund.[194] Work was nearly finished (though late and over budget) when in June 1780 the prison was burned down by the Gordon rioters. Requiring three further grants from Parliament totalling £30,000 and a further five years, Newgate was finally completed at the end of June 1785. Taking over fifteen years to build and costing around £100,000 in total, it was "by far the largest prison undertaking yet built in England."[195] It was surpassed only in the nineteenth century when the government built the national penitentiaries of Millbank and Pentonville.

As building work at Newgate began winding down, City authorities turned their attention to the next immediate problem, the City compters. Wood Street and Poultry Compters had been declared "worn out and dangerous ... unfit to be replaced" by the Lands Committee in November 1770, a view repeated by the surveyor and sheriffs in the 1780s, while petitioners in Southwark asked the Lands Committee in 1776 to replace the Borough Compter with "a new Gaol upon a more extensive and better plan."[196] Borough was rebuilt between 1785 and 1788 at a cost of £2,357.6*s*.6*d*., after being severely damaged in the Gordon Riots.[197] Instead of repairing Poultry and Wood Street, the Common Council elected to build a new institution: Giltspur Street Compter. Having already exhausted the ordinary revenues for public building, the City sold £30,000 worth of three per cent consolidated bank annuities belonging to the Bridgehouse Estate to fund construction.[198] Work began in 1787 and finished in 1791, eventually costing the City about £30,141.

This record of significant building work in the late eighteenth century – which focused on rebuilding extant prisons that were crumbling under the enhanced pressure of prisoners, decades of insubstantial repairs, and recent, serious damage – goes some way to explaining the City's decision to delay building a new house of correction in the eighteenth century. On the one hand, the pattern of rebuilding suggests the Corporation acted only when necessity demanded. After all, over a decade passed between the Land Committee's declaration that Wood Street and Poultry Compters were unfit and the Corporation's sanctioning of comprehensive rebuilding work. Even then, the pace of change was glacial, with authorities spending five years wrangling over the site, the plans, and the estimated cost before work began. On the other hand, the City had many more prisons to care for than other jurisdictions, and in the late eighteenth century, it poured around £133,000 into the structure of the prisons alone. Such efforts indicate a considerable interest in and willingness to fund massive prison works.[199]

In the eighteenth century, London's governing elite was frustrated with the criminal law: its bloodiness as well as its leniency, its unpredictability, and its disproportionality. Some additionally came to believe that certain offenders, because of the nature of their offence or because of their age, gender, background, or demeanour, might be rehabilitated; or at the very least, they became convinced that rehabilitation, and in particular rehabilitation *at home* rather than abroad, was worth a try. In this context, authorities looked to the house of correction.

Changing views on the usefulness of imprisonment helped drive prison-building in London. Extensive reforms, or complete reconstruction, of bridewells were required to allow the courts to adopt imprisonment, or imprisonment at hard labour, on an expanded scale. The pattern of building was shaped by the interaction of evolving attitudes and changing opportunities, which played out at different speeds in different places. The demands on the time and resources of London's governing bodies differed by jurisdiction, allowing some to move more quickly, and spend greater sums, than others. Regardless, once the reformed bridewells opened, the number and proportion of offenders sentenced to imprisonment by quarter and assize sessions in the metropolis grew noticeably. The speed with which sentencing practice changed reflected the fact that by the time the counties opened the new institutions, the courts had already accepted the case for imprisonment at hard labour, hence their willingness to spend considerable sums and time on the projects.

CONCLUSION

As the uses of imprisonment expanded and the numbers incarcerated grew, London authorities responded by creating a more specialized prison system. Increasingly, they treated prisons as *either* custodial *or* punitive. Gaols and compters (where they existed) came to serve primarily as sites of custodial detention, where prisoners who were held for safe custody rather than for punishment (pre-trial prisoners, evidences, debtors, convicts awaiting transportation or execution) were sent, while houses of correction acted as places of punishment, receiving those who had been convicted – whether summarily or after jury trial – and sentenced to imprisonment. These practices were in some ways quite traditional, but in the late eighteenth century, authorities committed more firmly to adhering to them. So, while the trend in statute was to blur prison roles, the trend in practice, at least in London, was to assign the prisons, or in some cases reassign them, highly specialized roles.

Rethinking commitment practices may have been a central, unacknowledged tenet of the prison reform movement. The lack of research on the prison commitment practices of other counties makes this difficult to assess, but what has been done, and what can be gleaned from surviving prison rules, suggests that London's enthusiasm for classification, specialization, and separation was shared widely, and particularly by authorities known to be enthusiastic supporters of prison reform. In Gloucester, a centre of reforming activity, the bench at the end of the eighteenth century assigned specialized roles to the prisons under their control and instructed all magistrates to closely attend to the distinctions between prisons in their commitment practice. As in London, these moves further divorced custodial from punitive confinement.[200] The Staffordshire magistrates shared these ambitions, though they opted to assign specialized roles to distinct parts within one prison complex. As described in the 1792 rules, the Stafford county gaol and bridewell was really "three distinct prisons": a sheriff's prison (more commonly called a gaol) for debtors, those awaiting trial, and those held for want of sureties; a house of correction "for offenders chiefly committed for punishment by the magistrates"; and finally, a penitentiary house "for the punishment by hard labour of offenders convicted at any Assizes or Quarter sessions."[201] It is possible that the larger or more populous counties – that is, those with large numbers of prisons – or the wealthier counties – that is, those with more resources at their disposal – were able to make finer distinctions between prisons than smaller, less populous, or poorer jurisdictions. Counties may also have prioritized different divisions between inmates, above or aside from punitive and custodial status, and consequently, they may have opted to classify their prisons in other ways. Further studies will be necessary in order to properly understand and contextualize the craze for specialization in eighteenth-century England. Brief explorations of county archives suggest a certain amount of variation, but these also confirm that many counties followed each other in adopting some division between custodial and punitive confinement.[202]

In what follows we consider why London authorities made the choices they did: namely, why they selected the house of correction to serve as the site of punitive confinement, and why they picked the gaol and compter as sites of safe custody.

CHAPTER TWO

Specialization, Labour, and Punishment

"There are very few bridewells in which any work is done, or can be done. The prisoners have neither tools, nor materials of any kind; but spend their time in sloth, profaneness and debauchery."[1] The prison reformer John Howard, who toured England and Europe in the 1770s documenting the condition of prisons, had a low opinion of most English bridewells, especially their claims to keep inmates employed. Howard's views were broadly shared amongst those who undertook to visit prisons and to publish their observations in this period. William Smith, for example, a physician with an interest in medical provision in prisons, was similarly scornful of the employment at London's prisons when he published his account in 1776. Though he admitted to finding inmates in some bridewells at work, he characterized this as insignificant: "in this [the Southwark bridewell] and the other Bridewells they sometimes amuse themselves at beating of hemp: as to the quantity of work done, it seems to be a mere farce."[2]

Later reports by reformers suggest that little had changed in the nineteenth century. In the late 1810s, the Society for the Improvement of Prison Discipline and the Reformation of Juvenile Offenders (SIPD) claimed that the poor discipline in London prisons, especially the lack of employment for prisoners, was a primary cause of the recent, and much publicized, rise in juvenile crime. "The prisoner," their 1818 report evocatively claimed,

> enters a boy in years and a boy in vice; he departs with a knowledge of the ways of wickedness ... Idleness may have been the cause of his deserting the paths of virtue; the remedy of a London gaol is the impossibility of obtaining any employment, save what a pack of cards, or a game of chance, may haply afford him.[3]

In a footnote to this statement, the committee conceded that prisoners in Middlesex's Coldbath Fields bridewell were routinely put to work, but they swiftly discounted this evidence by arguing that the labour performed there – picking oakum – could "scarcely be designated labour."[4] Having established to their own satisfaction that prisoners did not work and that their idleness was a primary factor in their corruption, the SIPD proceeded to spend the next decade championing the treadwheel as a solution to the problem of prison work and urging authorities across the British Isles to adopt it as the main form of hard labour.

While the SIPD denied that prisoners laboured as a preface to promoting their preferred method of labour, other figures, including George Laval Chesterton, governor of the Middlesex bridewell between 1829 and 1854, deployed the image of the unreformed prison to magnify their reforming role. In his memoir, published in 1856, Chesterton painted a colourful picture of imprisonment prior to his keepership: "men and women, boys and girls were indiscriminately herded together ... without employment, or wholesome control; while smoking, gaming, singing and every species of brutalizing conversation and demeanour, tended to the unlimited advancement of crime and pollution."[5] Only through his unceasing service was the institution "transformed from one of the worst specimens of corruption and misrule into an establishment distinguished for industry, order and impressive discipline."[6]

These 'prison reformers' had clear motivations to depict prisons unfavourably, and yet their characterizations were widely accepted by early historians of the prison, many of whom saw the prison as yet another example of "the administrative indifference and incapacity" of the Hanoverian state.[7] It was agreed that magistrates, largely uninterested in carrying out the onerous aspects of their role, had abandoned their commitment to disciplinary employment so prison inmates did not work. However, since the mid-1980s, historians, delving into local county archives, have pushed back against the view that prisons were neglected and 'unreformed' before the final decades of the eighteenth century, one consequence of which has been the recovery of prison labour.[8]

Margaret DeLacy, in her study of Lancashire's prisons, found that, despite the disparaging remarks made by eighteenth-century commentators about the amount of work done, the county had a "relatively good record" of setting prisoners to work, and at the century's end, the justices came to regulate prison labour more strictly.[9] Beattie, too, in his exploration of punishment in Surrey, concluded that, throughout the eighteenth century, bridewells remained "in practice places of work and labour discipline."[10]

Despite presenting a completely different view of prison operation, such findings have not led to a broader reconceptualization of the pre-reform prison. Nor have they led to a greater investigation of forced labour in English prisons. This is surprising, not only because of the archival evidence, but also given the recent resurgence of interest in coerced labour and especially global convict labour. Historians of the British Empire have been pioneers of the field. Their research has not only uncovered the deep links between punishment and work, but it has also led to a re-evaluation of the significance of convict labour, including its role in developing the imperial state.[11] Yet, for England, we lack comprehensive studies, and so we know little about the nature, geography, and chronology of prison labour in the metropole.

The indifference to prison labour and the general acceptance of its unimportance to prison regimes has led historians to overlook the central ways in which labour shaped London's prison system. Specifically, the tradition of providing labour for inmates in some but not all prisons was the most significant factor driving commitment practice in London, including the patterns of specialization outlined in the previous chapter. Labour traditionally distinguished bridewells from gaols and compters, and throughout the period under study, it continued to do so – certainly in the metropolis and probably to a greater or lesser extent elsewhere. Indeed, insights that can be gleaned from existing scholarship on other counties and a brief look at some surviving archival sources suggest that London was not unusual in this regard.

At the end of the eighteenth century, local authorities, profoundly concerned over the state of the nation's morals and convinced of the potential malleability of individual character, grew increasingly interested in institutionalized labour. The judicial benches in Middlesex, Surrey, and the City came to believe that hard labour, when coupled with religious instruction and a certain degree of solitary confinement, could effect a transformation in the habits and moral character of offenders. In short, imprisonment at hard labour was endorsed as an antidote to the prevailing social disorder. These ideological shifts had far-reaching effects on London's prison system.

This chapter moves the study of labour in English prisons beyond the view imposed by nineteenth-century reformers and prison officers. In so doing, it recovers the actual pattern and significance of labour. Section one charts the place and practice of labour within houses of correction in the period before late-eighteenth-century reform, while section two considers labour in gaols and compters in the same era. Section three explains why labour assumed such a critical role in shaping committal decisions in the final third of the century. In particular, it traces the revived interest in work as a means of moral reformation and the impact such views had on bridewells and prison specialization.

I. LABOUR IN HOUSES OF CORRECTION

If you put him to hard labour, indeed Bridewell, London, is the fittest place.

Colonel Clarke, 16 December 1656[12]

Labour was central to the bridewell project from the start. It was the alleged unwillingness of large segments of the poor to work as elites expected that led Parliament in the sixteenth and seventeenth centuries to call for the establishment of houses of correction throughout England, and within these institutions, labour shaped daily life. Fifteenth- and sixteenth-century vagabond acts granted local authorities wide power to compel vagrant prisoners to work. Bridewells were to be equipped with "mills, turns, cards and such like necessary implements" of labour and governors empowered "to set rogues, vagabonds, idle and disorderly persons to work and labour (being able)."[13] Local ratepayers were not to bear the cost for supporting vagrants' incarceration. Rather, those confined had to work to support themselves: they "shall in no sort be chargeable to the county for any allowance either at their bringing in or going forth, or during the time of their abode there but shall have such as so much allowance as they shall deserve by their own labour and work."[14] The harder they worked, the better their material conditions within the bridewell.

While actual evidence of prisoner employment survives only sporadically from before the nineteenth century, what remains points towards, first, a widespread dedication to putting bridewell prisoners to work, and second, a fairly regular pattern of employment. At Bridewell, for example, all City men who accepted the governorship pledged to do their utmost to make it a site "for the oppression of Idleness the enemy of all Virtue, and the nourisher of good exercise which is the conquerour of all vice."[15] To fulfill such promises, governors in the sixteenth century set up occupations including cloth-making, nail-making, and working at the cornmill or bakehouse. Later employments included beating hemp, making tennis balls, silk-weaving, spinning candlewick, and making shoes. Individuals judged particularly troublesome were set to cleaning the city ditches or picking rags and waste-paper.[16] Reflecting on Bridewell's origins in 1819, a committee of governors stressed the reformative and penal purposes of labour: "a principal intent of the foundation was to teach poor (and perhaps chiefly vagrant) children useful trades, whereby they might thereafter maintain themselves honestly, without becoming a burthen to the commonwealth, and to punish idle Strumpets and Vagabonds by compelling them to labour."[17]

The Surrey justices likewise placed important emphasis on prison labour and expected inmates to work.[18] Before the county built its own bridewell in Southwark, they contracted with the City of London to allow Surrey magistrates, for a fee, to send "idle people" to Bridewell, where they would "scour the ditches about the city, cleanse the Thames and other works by which they may earn their meat and drink."[19] After the Southwark bridewell opened, the county reported in 1661 that it required a "more Convenient workehowse" as the current one was too "close for Ayre" and lacked sufficient light.[20] At that point, the bridewell had only one workroom, presumably shared by male and female prisoners, which contained eight blocks for beating hemp, though some justices aimed to have twenty.[21] Further elm blocks and mallets were purchased in the early 1700s.[22]

In Middlesex, the justices in January 1616, following the opening of the bridewell at Clerkenwell, ordered that "everie person committed thither shalbe sett to labour, and have no other nurture, then that he or she shall get with theire labour, except they be sick."[23] Echoing Parliamentary legislation, they linked county assistance, including food, to inmate productivity. Given this emphasis on labour, it is not surprising that the justices selected John or

Jacob Stoyte to serve as the first governor. Prisoner employment was central to Stoyte's petition to run the bridewell. He pledged to "keep and maintain ... in the mannuall trades of weaving, spinning of cotton wooles for drapery, and all other manufactures, fitt for the imployment and labour of such people as shall be committed unto him."[24] To put this ideological commitment into practice, the county supplied tools and paid for their repair. In February 1626, for example, the justices paid Jane Gott, the matron, seventeen shillings to reimburse her for repairing the women's spinning wheels, and in July 1632, they ordered that the hemp mills be repaired and a new mill made "so that a greater number of persons may bee imployed to labour."[25]

Although it appears that prisoners in London's bridewells generally laboured during the early years of each institution, because of the paucity of records, we know very little about how prison labour evolved in the ensuing centuries. When large numbers of records do survive, especially for the eighteenth century, these show that labour remained an essential part of bridewell punishment and hence a critical aspect of the institution's discipline. In October 1741, for example, a committee of Middlesex magistrates were concerned to find that "very little Labour had been for some time past demanded of the Prisoners or performed by them." While hemp may have been "very dear," as the keeper alleged, the magistrates were unequivocal:

> your Comittee were of Opinion & so they told ye sd. Keepr [that] it was expected he shou'd purchase Hemp & keep his Prisoners to Labour otherwise the Sentence of the Court wou'd be often by ye officer partly lessened & greatly eluded.

Bridewell inmates had to work because it was a central element of their court-ordered punishment. The governor was notified that "if he was not carefull in this Respect for the future he wou'd be complained of to the Court."[26] The court's threat of sanctions was probably a powerful motivator for the governor, but so too was the fact that inmate profits formed part of his income. At this point, the governor was not paid a salary, relying mostly in theory on prisoner fees. However, the governor claimed that, with many prisoners unable to pay, he had "no Income except what his Deputy pays him ... & w[ha]t arises from the Prisoners beating of Hemp."[27] Unsurprisingly, therefore, some governors petitioned the magistrates asking for more work tools, as Peter Creswell did in 1723, to ensure that prisoners could be kept to labour.[28]

Elsewhere in London, prison keepers were convinced magistrates placed great value on prison labour. In petitioning the tight-fisted Surrey justices for money and assistance to repair the bridewell's walls in 1701, the keeper emphasized the threat such disrepair posed to the prisoners' steady employment and the issues caused by inmates receiving unauthorized goods. With the walls "broken down and ruined," the prisoners were "neglect[ing] there worke" in favour of standing at the walls "begging of passengers."[29] Similarly, when another keeper sought permission from the justices to remove a troublesome prisoner from his custody in December 1725, he emphasized the negative impact that this prisoner's night-time ravings had on the others' work.[30]

Yet, by the eighteenth century, the range of work carried out at many bridewells seems to have contracted. Early attempts to train prisoners in skilled or semi-skilled labour, or in employments that they might pursue after their release from prison, had been largely abandoned, and instead, prisoners were engaged primarily in menial, arduous work.

At Bridewell, prisoners were set mainly to beating and spinning flax, bruising oyster shells, beating hemp, or netting and picking oakum.[31] In popular culture, Bridewell was especially associated with hemp, a plant with very tough fibres often used in this period to make rope and canvas for ships. The satirist Ned Ward in *The London Spy*, a travelogue on the city published between 1698 and 1703, observed that in Bridewell "Hemp and Labour fills each Room / Where Lords and Ladies sported," while John Strype in 1720 noted that the inmates were "forced to beat hemp in public view, with due correction of whipping, according to their offence."[32] The work was therefore unvaried, and the hours were long. When Howard visited in the 1770s, he found inmates working most of the day, from 8am to 4pm in winter, and from 6am to 6pm in summer.[33]

The scope of employments at Middlesex bridewell was also reduced. Until the end of the century, inmates, supervised by a salaried taskmaster, were mainly engaged in beating hemp.[34] In 1741 the governor estimated prisoners might earn about "three half pence a day or two pence" from beating hemp; three pence a day, he claimed, was "very great Earnings."[35] On work days in the 1750s, men were obliged to beat twelve "punnies," a twist of hemp containing two handfuls and weighing two to three pounds, and women eight.[36] By the 1770s, Clerkenwell boasted forty hemp blocks, so up to eighty prisoners could beat hemp simultaneously (table 2.1). From 1750s, the justices kept brief

Figure 2.1 · Beating hemp in London's Bridewell.

records of work done, evidencing steady employment.[37] Between the end of January and the start of April 1760, for example, prisoners worked up fifteen cwt (hundredweight) of hemp, and a further six cwt between April and May.[38]

Putting prisoners to work typically cost the county money, as table 2.1 illustrates. The wage paid to the taskmaster was one factor; the money expended on buying supplies was another. A more serious concern was the low price for beaten hemp, which, as a result of the invention of machines for dressing hemp, fell sharply in the 1770s from 2*s*.6*d*. per cwt to 8*d*.; prisons, whose inmates were seen as less capable or skillful than 'free' workers, could not expect to receive more than 6*d*. for each cwt (table 2.1). The difficulty of obtaining hemp and its low value led the county to prioritize picking oakum, an occupation that was well-established within London workhouses and which seemed to promise somewhat higher profits.[39] This task involved untwisting or picking apart old ropes, composed of hemp fibre and mixed with tar, to transform the rope back

Table 2.1 Profits and losses from prison labour at Clerkenwell Bridewell, 1772–74

	Profits received			Expended		Total loss to county
	Hemp beaten	Oakum picked	Wrought oakum sold	Wages to taskmaster	Oakum bought for work	
1772	[unreadable] for £2.12.6	4 cwt 1 qt for £4.1.0	7 cwt for £5.8.0	£7.13.0	£3.10.0	£2.0.6
1773	81 cwt for £2.0.6	—	—	£5.1.4	—	£3.0.10
1774	74 cwt for £1.17.0	—	£4.13.0	£4.13.0	—	£2.16.0

Source: Observations to explain articles contained in return from clerk of peace and treasurer, Apr. 1775, MSP, *LL*, LMSMPS506520136–143.

into loose hemp fibre. All wooden boats require oakum to caulk (seal and waterproof) their seams, and, given the size and importance of the British Navy in the eighteenth century, a supply of oakum was much in demand.[40] In a report to the bench in 1775, a committee of magistrates expressed their view that, if they could obtain a sufficient supply of old rope from different navy yards, "much Profit would accrue." By picking oakum for the Navy, prisoners might begin to redress the wrongs they had committed – in this way, "the labour of those persons might be applied to benefit that community whose ill conduct had tended before to injure and disturb it."[41] The county consequently contracted with multiple businesses which employed the prisoners to pick oakum.[42]

At Southwark bridewell, in contrast to the other institutions, the main activity throughout its history seems to have been beating hemp. In the 1730s, as in the 1660s, the bridewell possessed a supply of "blocks and beetles" for the prisoners to beat hemp upon, and the county contracted with local hemp dressers to ensure a steady supply of hemp. Reports confirm that prisoners were "kept to labour and work as they ought."[43] Between 1772 and 1774, the county earned an average of £30 annually from hemp-beating at their three bridewells.[44] Although the magistrates were apparently committed to beating hemp as late as 1781, by the following year, they recognized the impossibility of obtaining the product. Magistrates reporting on conditions at another Surrey house of correction at Kingston recommended that that "junk" and "oakham" be procured, "a more proper labour for the prisoners to be employed in and more useful to the publick."[45]

Even keeping prisoners to this work proved increasingly difficult in the late eighteenth century. Falling levels of industry were not a straightforward reflection of magisterial interest in or commitment to prison labour. Rather, getting prisoners to work was complicated by a variety of factors including supply systems, organizational structures, short prison terms, prison overcrowding, and the capabilities of inmates.

Most administrators faced difficulties acquiring a stock of materials for their prisoners. A committee of Middlesex magistrates in April 1775 lamented, "it is not at all times that Work can be procured even that little which is obtained is got with much difficulty, the Justices of the Peace for the County having been obliged more than once to solicit employment for these People by publick advertisement."[46] Bridewells may have struggled to attract contracts because they lacked individuals with expertise to oversee the prisoners at work. This was what a Southwark hemp-dresser suggested in 1738 when he sought (unsuccessfully) the keepership of Southwark bridewell. He provided the Surrey magistrates with a certificate signed by several hemp-dressers stating that they had taken their hemp beating away from the house of correction "for want of a skilfull keeper to see and take care of the said workmanship."[47] Another keeper noted the frustration of hemp-masters at the poor state of tools in the bridewell, which "damaged and spoiled" the hemp.[48]

The short length of time for which most prisoners were confined also presented difficulties for authorities trying to keep inmates to work. As a committee of governors appointed to consider work at Bridewell stressed in a 1797 report,

> three fourths [of prisoners] are committed only for seven days the first of which ... they can do but very little work[;] the morning they go out, they do nothing[;] Saturday being half a holiday on account of the prisoners washing and cleaning themselves for Sunday[,] and that intervening they are only employed three days and a half out of seven during their confinement.[49]

The short period left insufficient time for prisoners to learn and hone new skills. Unless the task set for prisoners was very simple, administrators had to rely on inmates bringing certain skills and knowledge into the prison with them. The spinning wheels at the Middlesex bridewell, for example, went unused until April 1797 when a prisoner, Mary Salmon, proved herself "well qualified to teach the female prisoners to spin."[50] Only her skill, and her willingness to teach fellow inmates, allowed the magistrates' ambitions to be realized. Generally, bridewell administrators had little choice but to try and find work for prisoners that required little or no training.

Crucially, changes in court practice at the end of the century meant that many – perhaps most – of those sent to metropolitan bridewells were totally incapable of any labour. City and Middlesex magistrates appear to have used their houses of correction as halfway houses or refuges for the poor and sick. The Bridewell prison committee in January 1795, for example, complained that "great numbers of sick people and infants utterly incapable of labour are sent to this prison by the magistrates with an order that they remain here until there be room for them at the hospital." Such commitments, they fumed, were "contrary to the intent and spirit of the charter" and "incompatible with the other objects of the institution which most particularly require that all persons committed to this House of Correction be capable of and be employed in hard labour."[51] The Middlesex magistrates likewise complained in 1775 that many prisoners were "incapable" of labour due to "Age, Sickness, or some personal disability."[52] In the short term, such protestations were in vain. City magistrates, confronted by large numbers of distressed people desperately needing temporary assistance, continued to send individuals who could not be employed in hard labour to Bridewell, practices that undoubtedly impacted productivity and profits at the institution, both of which remained low until the 1810s.[53]

Finally, serious overcrowding at London's prisons further frustrated the ambitions of bridewell administrators. The Middlesex bridewell was particularly impacted, first, by the disruption of transportation, and later, by the destruction of Newgate in the Gordon Riots. The latter event caused a variety of prisoners who would normally have been sent to Newgate to be incarcerated in Middlesex prisons instead. As an apothecary tellingly recalled in 1783, "at the time immediately following the Riots, the number of felons and debtors confined in Clerkenwell was so great as to render the place miserable beyond description. They almost lay upon each other when the season was sultry."[54] Under such circumstances, it became increasingly difficult to set prisoners to work. As the magistrates bemoaned in 1782, there was neither "room [nor] opportunity for employing the prisoners."[55]

In the face of these myriad challenges, bridewell administrators attempted to improve their existing labour systems and strove to keep inmates employed. At some point between 1760 and 1774, an additional room was built at Middlesex to separate male and female prisoners at work.[56] In September 1778, the county purchased new tables, benches, and other implements for picking oakum, and they erected a shed in which to dry oakum as well.[57] The Surrey magistrates and Bridewell governors also built new, separate workrooms for male and female inmates in the 1770s and 1780s respectively.[58] Despite the difficulties sketched above, some authorities still made some money off prison labour. One surviving account from the Middlesex bridewell shows gross profits from labour performed between 5 April 1783 and 2 March 1784 amounting to £37.6*s*.9*d*. For prisoners, earnings per head, at most 2*d*. a day, were exceptionally low. Even low-skilled, casual women workers, another group of low-wage earners, may have made on average 6.37*d*. daily in the 1780s.[59]

In their efforts to employ bridewell inmates, local authorities were supported by Parliament, who in 1782 passed legislation that, amongst other things, defined magisterial obligations regarding prison work and clarified its legality. As a whole, the act aimed to provide more "Order, Employment and Discipline" in bridewells. Inmates were divided into two categories, those ordered to hard labour and those not so ordered, and work separated into two types, work which was "not severe" and hard labour. The governor was empowered and instructed to employ all inmates "kept and maintained at the Expence of the County" in work that was "not severe," even if they had not been ordered by their commitment to be kept to labour. For such work, inmates would receive half their net earnings on discharge. Conversely, inmates ordered to hard labour were to be employed, unless sick, every day besides Sunday for at most twelve hours with breaks for breakfast, dinner, and supper. Remuneration was not mentioned.

Parliament broadly left local authorities, assembled at quarter sessions, to decide what constituted "hard labour," a term which was not defined further, and labour which was "not severe." They did, however, instruct bridewell governors to adapt the employments selected by the justices to "each person in such manner as shall be best suited to his or her strength and ability, regard being had to age and sex." The legislation placed other limits around the ability of justices to compel inmate labour. Although this was not made explicit, the act's phrasing suggests that only those sentenced to hard labour could be employed in hard labour. The King's Bench subsequently confirmed this line of interpretation. In an 1806 court case, the judges ruled in favour of a defendant who questioned the legality of his imprisonment at hard labour in Surrey's house of correction by pointing to the fact that the statute under which he was convicted did not specify that offenders be put to hard labour.[60] Second, the act's phrasing suggests that prisoners who had not been sentenced to labour and who were not dependent on prison authorities for their maintenance (food, bedding, and other necessities) could legitimately refuse to work.

A review of the practices and policies of London bridewells points to the enduring importance placed on labour within these institutions. Magistrates remained dedicated to the principle of putting inmates to work, at times going to great lengths to ensure this could be done. Consequently, when sending an offender for punishment in the house of correction, committing bodies could reasonably expect that they would be set to work, at least for part of their confinement. The same could not be presumed for gaols and compters, as authorities well knew. In these prisons, there was no general commitment to prisoner labour, so inmates typically were not set to work in the eighteenth century or before.

II. LABOUR IN GAOLS AND COMPTERS

Labour was not central to the foundation of gaols or compters, so the legality of work there was more ambiguous than it was in houses of correction. Under English contract law, free people could not form valid contracts under duress. Yet, as Sonia Tycko has recently argued with respect to seventeenth-century England, the state and its "collaborators" generally conceptualized prisoners as "captured commoners" who were "able to consent to serve without the option to refuse."[61] Imprisonment, she notes, made men dependent on charity; the social status and poverty of common prisoners left them no alternative but to agree to work. Another strain of thought explicitly viewed the offer of work in prison, sometimes even the requirement to work there, as charity. For instance, with respect to "unscrupulous" debtors, another category of non-convict prisoner, one author contended, "a Prison is the fittest place for them, and the best Charity to these is to provide so that they may be kept to work in Prison."[62] Such understandings of work and of the rights and obligations of commoners helped to justify the practice of permitting, persuading, and even coercing the work of prison inmates.

Until the nineteenth century, statute law said little about *compelling* the labour of gaol inmates who had not been so sentenced. However, from 1666, Parliament expressly authorized local authorities to provide voluntary work schemes in gaols and compters. Concerns about prison mortality principally prompted Parliament to pass the legislation which empowered justices to raise the county rate to provide their prisons with rooms, tools, and stocks for prisoners to work voluntarily; to hire persons to oversee prison work; and also to disburse profits to working prisoners. A stock of materials would prevent "poor and needy" prisoners, living "idly and unimployed," from "perish[ing] before their Trial" or becoming "debauched" and "instructed in the Practice of Thievery and Lewdness" in prison.[63] In short, parliamentarians, in sanctioning county-funded work schemes, hoped to provide prisoners with the means to support themselves. Additional legislation, allowing justices assembled at sessions to raise the rates to rebuild, finish, or repair public gaols, including to construct workrooms, further attests to Parliament's recurrent willingness to support local authorities who wished to use county money to set gaol inmates to work.[64]

Several English counties saw value in allowing prison inmates held for safe custody to work. When, at the end of the century, many drew up detailed, written regulations to formally govern their prisons, some specified that custodial inmates be encouraged to work and signalled the county's willingness to supply implements and materials. Some authorities claimed that the offer of employment was a kindness to inmates, a way to ease the horrors of incarceration, while also allowing them to recoup some lost earnings and ensuring habits of industry were not lost. Prison discipline reflected this: inmates were supposed to be allowed to choose the type of employment; there were no specified working hours; inmates were allowed some (but crucially not all) of the profits. Other prison keepers seem to have treated work more as a punishment, employing pre-trial inmates who had been in the prison repeatedly, particularly if they were "handy men and knew how to work," and sometimes forcing them to also wear a prison uniform.[65] Regardless, at many prisons, this encouragement was effectually compulsion, at least for poor inmates, as the county allowance was made conditional on accepting the county's offer of work. In Gloucestershire and many other counties, prisoners held for safe custody who accepted county relief were required to "execute any employment, of which he is capable (the same not being severe labour) to the best of his power or ability."[66]

At various points, some London authorities also seem to have shared such an outlook respecting the value of prison labour and the rights of inmates held for detention. Generally, however, London authorities opted against supplying gaol and compter prisoners with work. Furthermore, they never directly claimed the right to force inmates who had not been sentenced to hard labour to work.

Only at London's main gaol, Newgate, were efforts made to employ inmates. These infrequent attempts were resounding failures. In 1686, the London Aldermen considered building a "workhouse" in Newgate's Press Yard, but the plan was quickly dropped.[67] Over a century later, in September 1795, the Court of Aldermen approved a plan for employing pre-trial offenders in netting, making hammocks and sacks, and picking oakum. Under the proposal, separate workrooms would be fitted up for men and women; four overseers (two of each sex) and a clerk would be appointed, with salaries, to superintend the work.[68] Work was voluntary and was intended to "keep [the prisoners'] minds employed, bring Vicious habits to a sistem of Order & Industry ... & give them a rellish for Sobriety." The City would take on little financial responsibility for the programme: provisions for the work were to be purchased with the profits of prisoner labour, and salaries too would be paid from the earnings.[69] This plan was not carried out either. Finally, John Addison Newman, Newgate keeper from 1804 to 1817, claimed to have tried to introduce "a manufacture" into Newgate during his tenure, but, for reasons he did not specify, he too failed.[70]

There is no evidence that authorities sought to force prisoners in other London gaols or in the compters to work. Our firmest evidence comes again from the City, which not only left fuller records but also helpfully wrote down prison rules. In the seventeenth century, two sets of articles were drawn up and passed by authorities for regulating the compters. These touched on a range of issues of great concern to prison life, including prison fees, diet, charities, beds, and inspection by City aldermen. Neither made any mention of providing work for prisoners, forcing inmates to labour, or even allowing them to work at their trades.[71]

The absence of rules or guidance on work in the compters does not mean that prisoners were idle. Innes has shown that in the King's Bench, for instance, inmates played an important role in the prison economy, with prisoners providing goods or services to fellow inmates.[72] Some sold fruit, vegetables, or meat at the daily prison market while others turned their rooms into chandler's shops or restaurants.[73] Imprisoned professionals, such as doctors, lawyers, and writers, carried on their work, finding new customers inside the prison, while also retaining some of those without. At the Fleet, Ludgate, and Newgate, prisoners administered prison charity.[74] These examples generally come from debtors' prisons, and distinctively capacious ones at that, and are probably not wholly representative of the experience of criminals in gaols. Nonetheless, a variety of evidence suggests that criminal prisoners may have played similar, though perhaps not as diverse, roles. For example, there was a long-established practice of employing criminal prisoners, whether appointed by the keeper or elected by their fellow inmates, as wardsmen, keeping the "peace" within the gaol; as cleaners; as servants at the prison tap or coffeehouse; or as builders, carpenters, or plumbers.[75] Prison keepers also claimed that inmates "upon their own Request" or inclination could pursue their normal trades.[76] Some sold their services for a profit, whereas others aimed to gain the support of prison authorities and to lessen the pains of imprisonment. Finally, none of this accounts for illegal or disapproved-of activities, such as selling spirits from one's room or smuggling, but these widespread practices likely provided employment and income for countless prisoners in London.[77]

In sum, work in gaols and compters was voluntary, informal, and dependent not only on prisoners seeking out work, but also on their already possessing the skills and the means to perform it. These patterns suggest that, in London, magistrates did not view prison labour as essential to the good governance or ordering of their gaols and compters, an approach that contrasts markedly with their management of houses of correction.

Periodically, the lack of officially sponsored and officially directed systems of employment within London's gaols and compters seriously troubled local magistrates as well as some members of Parliament. In the eighteenth century, several committees were set up to investigate existing labour arrangements in the hopes of encouraging or even enforcing prisoner employment in these institutions, with little result. Why, if interest in prison labour was longstanding, at times widespread, and certainly apparent with respect to other penal institutions, did London authorities never move forward with labour plans at gaols and compters?

The question of legality arose only rarely, and the answers supplied were rather oblique, and yet, those that survive suggest that there was sufficient uncertainty amongst London's authorities regarding their powers over inmates who had not been sentenced to imprisonment to dissuade them from claiming their labour. In particular, the lack of a specific order by a court authorizing keepers to compel such prisoners' labour seems to have been crucial for Middlesex and City gaolers.

In December 1772, a committee of Middlesex magistrates explicitly asked William Pentlow, keeper of New Prison between 1751 and 1773, whether the officers "think themselves authorized to compel any prisoners to work at hard labour in any case, but when they are empower'd by the Committing Majestrate where hard labour is expressly mentioned." The keeper dodged the question of authority by responding that he "hath very seldom any committed to hard labour." Tellingly, though, he continued, "no prisonor is put to any labour, excepting the cleansing their own ward, by turns, in order for their preservation."[78] In other words, he did not employ his prisoners or set them to hard labour. In 1778, the keeper was again asked about prison labour, and his response provides a stronger indication that legal restraints, or his interpretation of how the law operated on prisoners, played a factor in his approach. He explained that the convicted inmates in his prison "had no Employment, as they were not sentenced to Hard Labour."[79]

John Addison Newman, the Newgate keeper, was more expansive and explicit when answering similar questions regarding prison labour before a parliamentary committee in 1810.

Asked whether it "would be possible to introduce any general system of work in Newgate," Newman replied no: "the persons in for trial are preparing for trial, and therefore could not have much opportunity for work; and the greater part of the others are transports or persons respited, who expect to be removed, and upon whom the law has had its operation, and they will not be forced beyond."[80] Newman did not elaborate on whether he believed he could force pre-trial prisoners to work; rather, he focused on practical restraints facing the employment of pre-trial prisoners, specifically their need to prepare for trial. With respect to transports and respites, however, Newman seemed to suggest that he lacked the legal authority to compel their labour.

In the 1820s, prison authorities' powers over inmates not sentenced to hard labour became a very public and heated subject for debate in England, locally and nationally. Controversy centred especially on claims that some authorities, notably North Riding magistrates, forced accused inmates held for trial to work on the treadmill.[81] The eventual result was the 1823 *Gaol Act*, which confirmed that only those sentenced to hard labour could be forced to do such work. Prisons were expected to provide "for the employment of other prisoners," but this employment was voluntary. Nonetheless, some types of work could be compelled: as the act clarified, "nothing herein contained shall be construed to extent to prevent the Justices from authorizing, at their Discretion, the Employment of any Prisoner in the Performance of any menial Office within the Prison, or for the Purpose of instructing others."[82] In adopting this position, English prisons diverged markedly from their Irish counterparts. There, the *Gaol Acts* of 1821 and 1822, which provided a model for the English act, authorized all prison keepers "full Power and Authority" to keep every "poor Prisoner" to labour, and further, they were explicitly required to keep such prisoners at work.[83]

It was more than the uncertain legal position of labour in gaols and compters that inclined London magistrates against setting up labour schemes there. Economic concerns undoubtedly played a role. In 1763, a Middlesex report noted that, under the 1666 *Poor Prisoners Act*, the magistrates could set up a labour system in their gaol; yet, the account's author(s) wrote, this act was "rarely if ever put in Execution" in Middlesex because "there were houses of correction already and the work there done but of little profit."[84] As this remark underscores, counties had limited financial resources from which to fund all county projects, among which prisons were only one. Though the magistrates continued to fund a costly work scheme in their bridewell despite the lack of profit, they were not willing to establish a similar system in the gaol. Perhaps, had bridewell work schemes been more profitable, they might have considered providing gaol prisoners with work too.

Perhaps the most significant factor shaping practice in London was fear – specifically, the fear that inmates would use work tools to escape, landing prison keepers in potentially serious trouble with the courts.[85] When asked about the lack of employment for prisoners held for examination and trial, prison keepers pointed repeatedly to the danger of supplying such inmates with tools and the likelihood of escape.[86] Even William Adkins, governor of Coldbath Fields, did not employ pre-trial prisoners, explaining, "we have no places for them to work in, and they would be getting out, if they had tools."[87]

Keepers and magistrates judged custodial prisoners, especially those awaiting trial and those post-conviction awaiting the execution of their sentences, particularly likely to escape.[88] Adkins, for instance, noted that whereas those who were convicted "very seldom" attempted to escape, "there are none that come to me [before trial], but what would be glad to get away; they frequently bring things with them to get out by, if they can."[89] Fear of punishment, especially transportation or execution, probably pushed some inmates to mount escape plans.[90]

These concerns had a significant impact on prison practice. Legally, prison keepers were personally responsible for any escapes, and they could be dismissed from their posts or even indicted if they failed to stop an escape. If a debtor escaped, the gaoler could be held liable to the creditor for the debt.[91] In July 1711, for instance, the Middlesex justices ordered that Francis Geary, the New Prison keeper, be imprisoned for trial at the Old Bailey for "negligently suffering" a prisoner to escape from his custody.[92] Another New Prison keeper pleaded guilty at the September 1733 quarter sessions to "wilfully suffering Ann Kersey to escape out of my Custody the said Kersey being committed by Warrant on suspicion of felony."[93] In some jurisdictions, Middlesex included, magistrates in the eighteenth century moved to make bridewell governors similarly liable for escapes. In October 1763, the justices resolved to "set down Fines and Penalties upon the said master and Governor" in the event that prisoners escaped from the bridewell.[94]

By placing a legal burden on keepers, magistrates sought to ensure that keepers remained attentive to their prisoners and actively sought to prevent escapes. This legal responsibility probably served to make keepers wary about allowing prisoners, whom they considered likely to escape, access to tools. Certainly, the City keepers seem to have taken their responsibility very seriously. Pointing to the large number of requests by keepers for security-related repairs in the seventeenth and early eighteenth centuries, Sheehan argued that keepers regularly inspected prison buildings and immediately notified the sheriffs or City Lands Committee if they found any physical defects posing a security risk.[95] Beattie likewise found the Surrey keepers alert to security threats and prepared to track down escapees, even at their own cost.[96] Fears that prisoners might attempt to escape were probably heightened in the London metropolis in the late eighteenth century as the number of escape attempts rose and prison populations became more violent.[97]

Since London authorities generally did not use county money to fund employment schemes in gaols or compters, by the late eighteenth century, these prisons lacked the provisions, staff, and workspaces needed to employ inmates, whether working voluntarily or at hard labour. As the New Prison keeper pointed out in 1772, "New Prison not being the Gaol appointed for Labour there is no Room particularly appropriated by the County for that purpose."[98] This historical pattern, whereby work was supplied for prisoners in bridewells but not in gaols, had a long-lasting effect on the metropolitan prison system. As the previous chapter showed, authorities in the late eighteenth century were moving to assign, or confirm, specialized roles to their prisons whereby custodial imprisonment was totally divorced from punitive imprisonment. In deciding where convicts sentenced to imprisonment as a punishment should be confined, authorities placed especial importance on the existence or non-existence of labour in the prison. In the City, Middlesex, and Surrey, local authorities settled on the house of correction as the site of punitive imprisonment as a result of its longstanding association with labour and the actual existence of labour systems in London's bridewells.

Further work is needed to assess how unique London's decision to concentrate labour systems exclusively in houses of correction was. Certainly, some counties took different approaches, especially in the early nineteenth century, and set up work systems in both gaols and bridewells, usually after rebuilding or extending them.[99] More striking, though, is the fact that, in the late eighteenth century, many, if not most, English bridewells set their inmates to work, at least sometimes. Extracts of returns submitted to Parliament on work in bridewells between 1772 and 1774 show almost all English authorities employing bridewell inmates, with common tasks including beating hemp, spinning flax and wool, picking oakum, and making items such as butchers' skewers and pegs for shoemakers.[100] The net annual profits reported, if reported at all, varied widely, from £32.10*s*.3*d*. reported by the Manchester house of correction for 1773, to £1.5*s*.6*d*. reported by Durham county bridewell for 1772.[101] For a later period, October 1783 to April 1789, the Norfolk magistrates reported that net earnings from prisoner labour at Wymondham house of correction amounted to £262.18*s*.5*d*. over this four-and-a-half-year period.[102] Across the country, there survive various orders for the purchase of work tools or installation of work machines, and there are also some cases of magistrates reprimanding or even dismissing bridewell governors who refused to keep the inmates at work or of them ordering the bridewell to be rebuilt to allow inmates to be properly employed.[103] As in London, these bridewells would have looked promising to committing bodies hoping to rely more extensively on reformative imprisonment.

III. USING LABOUR TO REFORM MANNERS

Concern over the state of contemporary morals provided a long-running theme in English thought, but anxieties were particularly acute in the later decades of the eighteenth century following the war with America and the outbreak of revolution in France.[104] In addition to these national concerns, Londoners in the 1780s were reckoning with the violence and destruction of the Gordon Riots and a crime wave (real and imagined) following the American war's conclusion. Such disasters, many believed, stemmed from the general immorality of British society. As the Middlesex magistrate Reverend Dr Samuel Glasse, who as a member of various prison committees soon became a leading force for reform in the county, contended, "there is an immediate connexion between the prosperity of a nation, and the virtuous conduct of its inhabitants"; he warned that "corruption and vice, when it becomes general, is more fatal to national happiness and national security, than all the designs of the most malevolent and most powerful enemy."[105]Another Middlesex magistrate, Patrick Colquhoun, who played an important role in police reform, similarly complained of the "profligacy and idleness which prevails in so great a degree to the unquestionable injury of society."[106] This widespread anxiety over the state of the nation sparked a new movement for the reformation of manners, modelled partly on an earlier campaign for moral reform that had flourished in the late seventeenth and early eighteenth centuries.[107] Men and women across the country were exhorted to work zealously to correct manners, improve morals, and punish vice. In this context, institutionalized labour, including prison labour, took on a renewed importance.

More than any other group, magistrates "set the agenda" for the campaign to reform manners, and those in London played a leading role.[108] In June 1787, George III, following the advice of William Wilberforce, issued a proclamation for the suppression of vice and immorality and for the promotion of religion and virtue in the kingdom. With royal backing, Wilberforce moved in earnest to recruit members for an elite society to sustain and guide enthusiasm.[109] Some of the earliest recruits to the Proclamation Society, as it came to be known, were Bridewell governors and London magistrates. Indeed, four – Brook Watson, Samuel Thornton, William Mainwaring, and Rev. Glasse – were named to the Society's ten-person executive committee, a position that underscores their deep involvement and leadership within the movement.[110] Less elite magistrates subscribed to the Vice Society, founded in 1802, which also sought to check immorality by enforcing laws against disorderly activity.[111] The men who joined these national campaigns had long sought to promote morality and suppress vice locally in their official capacity as magistrates, aldermen, or members of Parliament. Significantly, several had served on prison committees, while others had been involved in efforts to alleviate poverty and suppress vagrancy. Their membership in these campaigns reinforced their activism and prompted greater interventions.

Middlesex was a centre of reforming activity. In 1785, in an address to the grand jury, Mainwaring, the sessions chairman, castigated his fellows for their lax licensing of ale-houses and casual enforcement of the laws against disorderly behaviour, and he called on his peers to act more zealously in the performance of their duties: "we want activity and resolution to enforce [existing laws] … it is owing to our own supineness and cowardice, that the depravity of the times is got to the present alarming excess."[112] Many local notables rose to this challenge. A few months before the royal proclamation, in March 1787, the bench issued an order for the better observance of Good Friday, while in May, a grand jury, influenced by those amongst them who would go on to join the Proclamation Society, remonstrated against London's "general Spirit of Depravity." The latter called on magistrates to vigorously enforce the laws relating to vagrants, Sabbath-breaking, gaming, drunkenness, and other disorderly activity.[113] Welcoming the jury's intervention, the bench drew up a set of "Rules for the Better Ordering of Society," copies of which were distributed to every parish.[114]

Following the royal proclamation, the bench, again led by members of the Proclamation Society, took further steps to curb dissoluteness. They established a committee to inquire into the licensing of public houses and encouraged magistrates to join forces with the county's ministers, parish and peace officers, and principal inhabitants to ensure that the laws against, for example, profanation of the Lord's day and drunkenness were duly carried into

Table 2.2 Prominent magistrates who subscribed to the Proclamation and Vice Societies

	Proclamation society	Vice society
Bridewell governors	Brook Watson	Richard Clark
	Samuel Thornton	Richard Carr Glynn
	Sir James Sanderson	Thomas Bernard
	Thomas Bowdler	Henry Hoare
	Samuel Wegg	
	Thomas Bernard	
	Henry Hoare	
Middlesex magistrates	William Mainwaring	Patrick Colquhoun
	Nathaniel Conant	Frederik Matthew
	Edward Montagu	John Nares
	Rev Dr Samuel Glasse	Joseph Girdler
		William Bleamire
		Rice Davies
		John Groves
		Rev Dr Samuel Glasse

For evidence of governorship and magisterial activity: BMCG, 23 Sept. 1785, 28 June 1792, 30 Apr. 1795, *LL*, BBBRMG202090239, BBBRMG20209049, BBBRMG202100162; MGOC, 23 Oct. 1786, 25 May 1787, 21 Feb. 1793, May 1799, *LL*, LMSMGO556090270, LMSMGO556090339, LMSMGO556100286–91, LMSMGO556110341; "Minutes of Proceedings, Nov. 1785," MSP, LMSMPS507770247; "Minutes of Committee on Appointment of Licences to Publicans, 3 July 1787," MSP, *LL*, LMSMPS508240153; "Meeting of Justices Appointed to Act at Several Public Offices, 1792," MSP, *LL*, LMSMPS508760011.

For biographical information: Sue Brown, "Policing and Privilege: The Resistance to Penal Reform in Eighteenth-Century London," in *Institutional Culture in Early Modern Society*, ed. Anne Goldgar and Robert Frost (Leiden, Netherlands: Brill, 2004), 103–32; Innes, *Inferior Politics*, n83; History of Parliament Online, http://www.histparl.ac.uk; Oxford Dictionary of National Biography, https://www.oxforddnb.com/.

execution.[115] Mainwaring also used his position as a member of Parliament to push for new legislation to strengthen the powers of magistrates.[116] Similar efforts to better enforce the laws against disorderly and immoral behaviour were pursued in the City.[117]

Prisons were a key concern of the Proclamation Society.[118] Frustrated that reform had focused so squarely on prison health and therefore had "scarcely touch[ed]" on "the reformation of the morals of prisoners," the society commissioned a series of pamphlets, each of which targeted a different circuit, to guide magistrates embarking on reform.[119] The society also set up a subcommittee to correspond with those engaging in prison reform, to visit prisons, and to publish an updated account of the state of prisons. One especially active member, Thomas Bowdler, was a Bridewell governor who frequently served on the Hospital's prison committee between 1787 and 1793; in the 1780s he was also part of the commission tasked with finding a site for the construction of two penitentiaries as called for by the *Penitentiary Act* of 1779.[120]

The magistrates' involvement in the movement for moral reform points not only to their deep anxiety about rising immorality, but also to their belief in the redeemability of society and the human potential for reform. A sermon preached in 1777 by Samuel Glasse at the Magdalen Hospital, a refuge for penitent prostitutes, before numerous London magistrates and other elites epitomized such views. Addressing the "fallen" women before him, he proclaimed, "Great as thy Sin is, and offensive as thy Impurity must needs be in the Sight of Him … thou shalt experience to thy present Comfort, and, if it is not thine own Fault, to thy future Happiness and Salvation, that *the Son of Man Is not come to destroy Men's Lives but to save them: Go and Sin no more.*"[121] If they repented and made an effort to reform, even the greatest sinner might find salvation. For evangelicals, the possibility of salvation was God's gift to mankind; it was their duty to spread the word of God and to encourage others to live their lives in accordance with the gospel.

As part of this moral campaign, the magistrates joined a variety of existing voluntary organizations and founded new ones to advance religion, suppress vice, and improve manners. Significantly, many of these organizations promoted the provision of labour, often in combination with religious education and frequently in institutionalized settings, as the key to transforming a person's habits and character.

Much reforming energy focused on moulding or recasting the character of children. As part of a broader movement to educate the children of the labouring poor and to train them in new patterns of behaviour, numerous magistrates supported the establishment of schools that prioritized vocational training.[122] At schools of industry, students were daily instructed in industrial or "coarse" work with only a brief period set aside for learning to read.[123] According to their promoters, such instruction would "excite a spirit of virtuous industry among the children of the poor" and accustom them to their duties as future labourers.[124] Around six industrial schools were established in or near the metropolis in this period, at least one of which counted a Bridewell governor, John Clements, among its trustees.[125] The schools received considerable backing from the Society for Bettering the Condition and Improving the Comforts of the Poor (SBCP), which the Bridewell governor Thomas Bernard helped to found in 1796. The SBCP investigated and reported on the condition of the poor and on charitable schemes in England with the aim of supporting and publicizing good practices. Its donors included prominent Middlesex magistrates and numerous Bridewell governors, many of whom, such as Henry Hoare and Thomas Hibbert, served on the society's general committee.[126]

Other charities with notable support from the metropolitan magistracies provided vocational training and religious education to groups of children deemed particularly at risk of vice. The Philanthropic Society, founded in London in 1788, focused on educating the children of criminals, as well as vagrant or "criminal" children themselves. Occupational training was at the heart of the project. By institutionalizing "idle and criminal poor children" and educating them in "some useful trade or occupation," the society believed they could stem what they saw as the inevitable moral decline of "criminal" and poor children, provide them with needed skills, and make them "industrious and virtuous."[127]

Smaller numbers supported the Lambeth Asylum, founded in 1758 by the Middlesex magistrate John Fielding, as a refuge for orphaned or deserted girls. Some served as annual guardians, others as life guardians, and at least one left the Asylum money in his will.[128] The asylum used institutionalization, religious education, and vocational training to prevent these girls from falling into a life of vice – or, as a report explained, "anticipat[ing] the evil by implanting in tender minds the principles of religion and virtue; by cultivating in them habits of sobriety and industry."[129]

While many of these organizations used labour to remould the character of children, others applied this strategy to adults. The Magdalen Hospital for penitent prostitutes, also set up in London in 1758, relied on a combination of "labour and rest, prayer and reading" to care for and rehabilitate former prostitutes.[130] One of its founders, Robert Dingley, was a Bridewell governor. He was aided by two of Middlesex's leading magistrates, John Fielding and Saunders Welch, in designing and promoting the institution, while other London magistrates acted as governors.[131] Great importance was placed on the women's employment. As Jonas Hanway wrote, ostensibly in a letter to Dingley but more probably as promotional material for the Hospital, "we must find them employment, first for *their* benefit, that they may be the farther removed from temptation; and next for our own sake that by their labor they may repay the husbandman and manufacturer for their food and raiment, and ease the community by supporting themselves by their industry."[132] Such comments suggest the men saw employment as a necessary precondition for reformation and recognized its material benefits, including for the community that supported the women.

Those involved with the SBCP similarly believed it was possible to reshape the character of the poor, children and adults alike. They saw the encouragement of values such as thrift and industry as a key way to improve the poor's standard of living. The Clapham branch, for example, whose work was carried out primarily by influential, evangelical women, concluded that the "chief preservation of the poor from distress is their own steady industry" and consequently "principally directed" their attention to encouraging their industry by training children and adults in "useful occupations."[133] The SBCP was keenly interested in reforming prisons, and one suspects that such views on the industry of the poor coloured their proposals for prisons.

The men responsible for London's prisons, then, understood idleness, at least of the lower orders, to be immoral, productive of criminality, and a source of national misery. Their involvement in the various societies and projects discussed above points to a widespread and strongly held belief that society could be improved by setting the poor and the criminal to work, often in institutional settings, and instilling in them certain virtues, especially industry, thrift, and godliness. As Patrick Colquhoun expounded in a pamphlet on soup kitchens, "one of the greatest benefits that could perhaps be conferred on the labouring people, and upon Society in general, would be to establish institutions calculated to teach Frugality, and to instill principles of virtue and industry in the minds of the lower orders of the rising generation."[134] Such institutions, it was believed, could transform sinful and unproductive members of society into moral, productive ones. These endeavours, as Jonas Hanway argued, were well worth the time, energy, and money invested in them: "If those who have been a nuisance, become useful members to society, and the people grow more virtuous, the *ends of true policy* and *true charity*, are answered in the highest and most *proper* manner, and the *state* will be doubly repaid the *charge*."[135]

Some scholars, who link the growth of imprisonment to capitalism, have contended that British and European authorities embraced institutionalized labour, in prisons and workhouses, in the early modern period as a way to depress wages, keep the cost of labour down, and control the labour force.[136] The threat of confinement undoubtedly gave employers a strong hand, and some clearly used it to discipline their employees or coerce their labour.[137] Yet, institutionalized labour held a much broader appeal to contemporaries, whose interest in such projects was not necessarily linked to the supply or cost of labour. The language they used in advocating this measure suggests that they were as concerned with cultivating virtues as they were with instilling obedience. Or perhaps we might say that they sought to instill obedience through the cultivation of virtues.

Complementing their philanthropic work, the Bridewell governors and metropolitan magistrates, in their official capacity as prison supervisors, moved decisively in the late eighteenth century to reform the habits and morals of offenders through prison discipline. Their focus rested squarely on prisoners who had been convicted, whether summarily or after trial by indictment, and not on inmates generally. As in so many of their philanthropic ventures, labour played a central role in their plans to effect this moral transformation. These men believed that labour, when combined with religious education and a degree of solitary confinement, would lead to the reformation of convicted prisoners. Effecting this outcome was a primary goal of bridewell confinement, but not of confinement in gaols or compters. As this chapter has shown, bridewells had traditionally provided labour for their inmates, and they continued to do so in the late eighteenth century. For London magistrates, the enduring link between the bridewell and labour made the institution the natural vehicle for reforming offenders.

Setting forth the bridewell's objectives in 1794, the regulations for the newly opened Coldbath Fields in Middlesex proclaimed that "the primary objects of all prison regulations are safe custody, wholesome correction, useful employment and effectual reformation with a due regard to the health of the prisoners."[138] Prisoner employment played a central role in this reformation: "it [is] unquestionably true," the magistrates contended, "that the proper employment of prisoners is one leading step towards their amendment especially when united with due degrees of solitary confinement."[139] The prison committee instructed the bridewell governor to ensure that "every prisoner be employed as much as possible in a state of separation" and to consider this task a "main principle of this institution."[140] Shortly after the bridewell opened, the *Whitehall Evening Post* applauded the magistrates' efforts and predicted great benefits to society from the new discipline based on work and separation:

> the most sanguine hopes are entertained of [the bridewell] being productive of the most salutary effects, in reforming and restoring to Society and rendering useful, many individuals, who, under the old system, by living in idleness, and mixing with the most profligate of the human species, were ultimately returned upon the public infinitely more depraved than when the confinement commenced.[141]

While this depiction of the pre-reform bridewell was not quite accurate, it was nonetheless true that magistrates in this period committed themselves more actively to ensuring that the reformed bridewell was a site of labour discipline.

To the Surrey visiting magistrates, keeping the prisoners at labour was essential in order to inculcate amongst them a "spirit of industry," upon which, the magistrates believed, "the reform in the morals and conduct of prisoners" ultimately depended. "Bringing the prisoners into habits of industry" was the "grand object" of bridewell confinement, and a properly regulated house of correction would soon "diminish" the number of vagrants and petty offenders in the county.[142] "Our principle," the bridewell's chaplain explained, "is to make every man industrious." Reform, authorities stressed, depended on a combination of prison labour, separate confinement, and religious instruction. "Surely it will be universally admitted," the chaplain pronounced, that many criminals "are capable of being reformed by mitigated solitude and long continued habits of secluded industry, accompanied with reasonable admonition and religious instruction."[143] Soon after the new Southwark house of correction opened, the visiting magistrates, those appointed at each quarter session to visit and report on the county's prisons, expressed admiration for the new system, in which every prisoner (unless sick) was kept to labour. They optimistically concluded that the system of discipline "now promises fully to realise the hopes of the most sanguine, not only in the effect produced by the employment of the prisoners on their conduct and morals, but in the very essential saving of expence."[144] The new prison's "solitary cells, employment and regulations," the magistrates concluded, "will so strongly point out that prison as the fittest place of confinement for convicts in future."[145]

The Bridewell governors shared with their counterparts in Middlesex and Surrey the view that the house of correction was designed for "the encouragement of industry and the correction of idleness."[146] In a special report, a committee of governors stressed that "the only light in which a prison should be viewed" was "as a place where constant labour should take the place of destructive idleness, strict discipline, of habits of laxity, and moral reformation, of vice and profligacy."[147] They too expected their prison, if properly regulated, to "have a very great effect in the diminution of vice and misery and in the increase of industry and good habits of life within the metropolis."[148] In pursuit of these goals, the governors in the 1790s adopted a system of discipline which combined solitary confinement, "for a limited time to a certain degree," with "a moderate quantity" of labour, believing such a combination to be "by experience the best reformer of the vices punished by Houses of Correction."[149] Under this scheme, discussed in detail in chapter 4, only certain prisoners were subjected to separate confinement, but all were required to labour. A key function of this labour was to provide inmates with useful skills and profit to enable them to "obtain employment and livelihood" after their sentence expired.[150]

After the reformed houses of correction opened, a range of contemporaries testified to their success. In 1810, the governor of Southwark house of correction spoke of the numerous prisoners who had been rehabilitated by confinement: "I remember dustmen, carmen, men of the lower order of society, many men working in the brickfields, that had no trade, who are now going on well to my knowledge."[151] The Middlesex chaplain too affirmed that many former inmates "have made Resolutions of Amendment and now follow their lawful Occupations."[152] The governor of Coldbath Fields, William Adkins, credited the system of labour carried on in his prison with reforming the manners of his charges: "I have no doubt that hard labour would do more towards reformation of manners, and diminishing the number of prisoners, than any other mode that could be resorted to; and my opinion upon that is strengthened from almost every day's observation."[153] Such optimism likely encouraged magistrates to support efforts to extend imprisonment to more serious offenders, previously viewed as incorrigible, in the nineteenth century.

IV. CONCLUSION

At the end of the eighteenth century, some magistrates in England, including those in Middlesex, Surrey, and the City, moved to establish a system of reformatory imprisonment within their bridewells. As in so many of elite Englishmen's philanthropic ventures, labour played a key role in their plans to effect the moral transformation of criminal offenders. Faith in institutionalized labour was deep-rooted within English intellectual, religious, and legal thought, and at the end of the eighteenth century, it saw a strong revival as concerns with immorality, crime, and disorder intensified.[154] The resort to labour, then, was an established response, and it was closely connected to how elites understood the sources of crime and diagnosed the current chaos, in particular their conviction that the labouring classes were too idle and that idleness was a "never-failing inroad to criminality," as Patrick Colquhoun put it.[155] "Take away the cause," one contemporary remarked in the *Gazetteer and New Daily Advertiser* in May 1770, "and the effect will ease": "when, therefore, they found that the inevitable consequence of their crimes would be a scene of continued hard labour … I believe such punishments before their eyes would have a much better effect than hanging."[156]

Similar moves were also made outside London. Two leading reformers of the Salford bench in Lancashire, Thomas Butterworth Bayley and Samuel Clowes the Younger, proclaimed in 1783 that the "*leading* object of those who govern Houses of Correction" should be "to make prisoners better men." Moreover, they stressed, "it is well known that constant and laborious employment is the most friendly to the principles and habits of virtue." In 1785, the magistrates resolved to construct a new bridewell for 100 inmates with separate cells and facilities for labour.[157] Houses of correction were built or significantly altered along the same lines in Sussex in the 1770s, Norfolk in the 1780s, and Gloucester in the 1780s and 1790s, amongst others.[158] Like London magistrates, these authorities expressed great satisfaction with the new regimes: indeed, in 1811, the Reverend J.T. Becher, chaplain at Southwell house of correction in Nottingham, another widely recognized centre of prison reform, claimed, "in all instances that have come to my knowledge, the prisoners have been reformed," and he cited several specific cases of men who had worked diligently in prison, made considerable profit to support their families, and after discharge worked honestly at their newly learned trades. Becher continued, "we receive a man filthy, diseased, drunken, idle and profane; and that man in a short time becomes clean, sober, healthy, diligent, and to all appearance a good moral man."[159]

Scholars have not entirely ignored prison labour and its importance to confinement regimes in the eighteenth century. Some, for example, have placed labour at the heart of their accounts, but these scholars generally have understood prison labour in economic terms. Specifically, Rusche and Kirchheimer attributed the rise of imprisonment in Europe to fluctuations in the labour market and the increased value of criminal labour.[160] Certainly, magistrates had always hoped that prison labour would turn a profit, or at the very least, that profits might help offset the cost of running prisons. Concerns over the cost of employment schemes were frequently at the forefront of magistrates' minds and played a role in stymying efforts in some places. Still, profit was not the sole motivation leading elites to favour institutionalized labour as a punishment for crime. Consequently, such accounts have provided only a partial picture of labour's importance to confinement.

More commonly, historians have downplayed the significance of prison labour. Most have failed to recognize the importance that prison governing bodies attached to labour's ability to reform the morals and habits of criminal offenders at the end of the eighteenth century. Innes, for example, has noted that work had "a relatively less important place within reformed penal regimes," while Evans has stressed that, in the late eighteenth century, the idea that "industry should be the sole medium of moral improvement within prisons" was eclipsed.[161] Instead, historians have placed greater emphasis on newer methods of reformation, namely separate confinement and religious instruction. Certainly, these historians are right to draw our attention to the growing interest in means of reformation other than labour. As this chapter has highlighted, by the late eighteenth century, London magistrates no longer believed that labour alone was sufficient to turn convicted offenders into useful and reformed members of society. Rather, they advocated a combination of hard labour, religious education, and a degree of solitary confinement. As the following chapter will show, at the end of the century, magistrates across the metropolis redesigned and rebuilt their houses of correction to allow for the separate confinement of inmates, at least by night, and they introduced detailed codes to regulate prisoners' conduct, including their employment.

Nonetheless, in highlighting these other aspects, we should not downplay the role assigned to prison labour in reformed penal regimes. The tradition of labour in houses of correction, but not in gaols and compters, largely shaped patterns of prison specialization and led magistrates to identify the former as the appropriate site for corrective imprisonment. Labour was seen by magistrates as a crucial element of bridewell discipline, and it remained so into the middle of the nineteenth century, even as the magistrates' commitment to other aspects of reformatory discipline, such as separate confinement, waxed and waned. More than anything, it was the obligation to labour that defined the experience of bridewell inmates between the eighteenth and mid-nineteenth centuries and which set confinement there apart from that in gaols and compters.

In the mid-nineteenth century, certain prison reformers and administrators suggested that there was a choice to be made between prison systems based on putting prisoners to work and those based on solitude. Much of the historiography has naturally focused on the tensions between these two regimes – which came to be known as the separate and silent systems – and the fights between their respective promoters.[162] However, in the late eighteenth and early nineteenth centuries, prison reformers and local authorities tasked with implementing reform saw these elements as mutually reinforcing. In the words of the 1811 Holford Committee, established to consider the sort of penitentiary that the government should erect, penitentiary imprisonment was "a system of imprisonment, not confined to the safe custody of the person, but extending to the reformation and improvement of the mind, and operating by seclusion, employment and religious instruction."[163] These elements were equally essential to the project of turning convicted offenders into useful members of society.

CHAPTER THREE

Ideologies of Reform and Realities of Pre-Reform Prisons

In 1773, John Howard became high sheriff of Bedfordshire, a post that made him responsible, among other things, for the county gaol. His shock at seeing prisoners discharged at the sessions "dragged back to gaol" for failing to pay prison fees led him to search out a precedent for discontinuing them.[1] Initial visits to prisons in nearby counties spurred Howard to embark on a tour of all English and Welsh gaols and bridewells, and later some foreign prisons. He published a detailed account of his findings in 1777 in *The State of the Prisons in England and Wales*, which was extended and updated in later editions. In addition to providing statistical information on prisoners confined, descriptions of buildings, and details on prison administration, *The State of the Prisons* included an analysis of the prevailing bad practices in prison management and a scheme for reforming prisons. In the following two decades after its publication, England's prisons were substantially altered or rebuilt, frequently in ways that claimed inspiration from Howard.

John Howard was not the first person to take up the plight of prisoners or to consider the state of prison administration. Yet, historians who adopted a Whig or reform perspective, and even many who favoured a social-control perspective, often suggested that this was the case, and such a view continues to colour generalist, popular, and even some scholarly accounts of the prison.[2] Since the 1970s, however, historians have moved to recover an earlier history of penal experimentation, charting the various attempts by local and parliamentary authorities to amend the structure, organization, and operation of prisons before the end of the eighteenth century.[3] In common with that research, this work takes the pre-reform prison seriously, rather than caricaturing it, and highlights the long-running interest that justices had in their prisons. It also brings bridewells, rarely if ever considered in studies of prison reform, into the picture alongside gaols and compters. This approach reveals the early, deep, and widespread attachment to so-called "Howardian" reforms in England. Contrary to how they were portrayed by many reformers, London authorities were not ignorant of nor opposed to reform, or uninterested in their prisons. Instead, London justices in various ways anticipated and pioneered policies later taken up by reformers such as Howard. Underscoring these continuities in practice allows us not only to re-evaluate London's position within the reform movement, but also to see more clearly where Howard's proposals went further and to assess the extent to which local authorities adopted or adapted the newer reformist ideas in renovating their prisons.

Still, before Howard, there was no "prison reform" or "prison reformers" so conceived. There were ideas about good practice that informed prison administration, yet it was only in the 1780s that these projects of institutional amendment were sloganized as "reforms."[4] As well as the word "reform" doing new work from the 1780s, Howard, with the multi-edition publication of *The State of the Prisons*, gave the project of improving prisons a much higher profile and got the public interested.[5] Howard's work was the springboard from which an identifiable prison reform movement developed, and his ideas became a touchstone for those promoting prison reform and for local administrators seeking to implement reforms. As Gloucester's leading reformer, G.O. Paul, noted in his treatise, "it is impossible to enter on this Subject, without paying a Tribute of Respect to the incomparable Mr. Howard, the presiding Genius of Reform of these melancholy Mansions of Oppression and Distress."[6] For many local actors interested in reform but perhaps struggling to convince colleagues to assume a more active, costly role, referencing Howard and his specific critiques of a given locality's prisons probably helped to shame the bench and spur action.

Howard's complaints about contemporary prisons were numerous, multi-faceted, and wide-ranging, but broadly, he sought to prevent prisons from being destructive to the health and morals of prisoners. Howard asserted that, given the condition of prisons and the manner in which inmates were generally held, a period of confinement usually resulted in prisoners' loss of health or even life, and additionally, it "notoriously promote[d] and increase[d] the very vices it was designed to suppress."[7] Not only were most prisons "so decayed and ruinous," but there was also a want of food, water, and clean air. The indiscriminate association of prisoners and the prevalence of bad practices, such as gaming, drinking, general idleness, and demanding of garnish from new inmates, hardened morals. Certain conditions meant these problems remained unresolved: in particular, fee-taking by officers, the non-residency of gaolers, and the lack of regular magisterial oversight. As well as striving to improve the health and morals of prisoners, then, Howard hoped to change how prisons were run. While his account picked up some of the differences between gaols and bridewells, he was not interested in bringing these to the fore. Rather, he sought to identify common problems with all prisons, and to ensure that each prison, regardless of its function or status, was reformed. In what follows, we will explore these three areas of criticism in turn, considering, first, the applicability of Howard's critiques with regard to London prisons, and second, Howard's specific recommendations for reform.

I. RECONSIDERING HOWARD'S INTERVENTIONS

Prison Health

Despite Howard's claim that local authorities were generally "inattentive" to their prisons, interest in the health of prisoners was longstanding. Over the course of the early modern period, authorities increasingly took steps to improve prison salubriousness, especially by ensuring that the prisons were cleaned, at least occasionally and in some cases fairly regularly; by supplying the poorest prisoners with some provision of food; and by providing some medical care. The eighteenth century was especially significant in this respect, with efforts to keep prisons clean and healthy ratcheted up.[8]

While some local authorities paid for certain cleaning services such as emptying the privies, responsibility for prison cleanliness generally lay with the inmates.[9] At Clerkenwell bridewell, prisoners were tasked with keeping their wards "clean and free from vermin," while at Newgate prisoners made fires, washed tables and benches, and swept their wards every day.[10] Cleaning supplies were usually provided by the prisoners themselves, who used ward dues – payments traditionally claimed from inmates on admittance – to purchase mops, brooms, and other implements.[11] Some authorities also tried to ensure cleanliness through inspections. A system of annual inspections was established at Newgate in 1461, but these were rarely carried out. By the eighteenth century, however, inspections were more regular and widespread: the Middlesex justices visited their prisons to report on cleanliness from at least the 1750s, while the City Lands Committee made inspections from the 1760s.[12]

Prison health often became a concern following serious outbreaks of disease, especially when such outbreaks spread beyond the prison walls.[13] From the mid-eighteenth century, contemporaries focused on airflow as key to preventing epidemics. In 1752 or 1753, following a severe outbreak of gaol fever at Newgate which it was believed caused the death of several eminent men connected with the Old Bailey, the aldermen had ventilators installed throughout the gaol, as advised by the physician Stephen Hales.[14] Similarly in 1754, the Middlesex magistrates considered purchasing a ventilator to make the air in New Prison "more wholesome."[15] Still, it is notable that a concern with air quality had been well-established in the metropolis for many decades. The aldermen had installed an air-moving machine to combat the "corrupt air" of Newgate as early as 1535.[16]

To try to ensure that prisoners did not fall ill or starve, all London prisons provided at least some inmates with a small allowance of food by the mid-eighteenth century. Allowances were provided at bridewells earlier than at gaols, and because they were not guaranteed, they could be withdrawn. The 1557 Bridewell Ordinances specified that all inmates be given a "thin diet."[17] In practice, those who laboured received a somewhat more generous diet than those who did not. Moreover, committing governors reserved the right to withhold the allowance as added punishment.[18] In Middlesex, the bench elected to provide all bridewell prisoners with an allowance – 1*d.* daily to spend on necessary food – in October 1741 following a period of awful deprivation when several prisoners starved to death and others fell severely ill. Before this, inmates were largely at the mercy of individual keepers, who decided whom to support and how much to give.[19] In earlier years, the bench may have required that bridewell (and possibly even gaol) keepers provide provisions, out of their own pockets, to poor prisoners, but attention to this policy varied and by 1741 it had been forgotten.[20] Henry Wallbank, the governor at this point, reported that he gave those who laboured, of his own accord and at his own charge, "a Quartern Loaf among eight every Day" (a responsibility the magistrates subsequently assumed), but for the smaller numbers imprisoned for want of sureties, they had "nothing from him except wt he sometimes sent them to keep them from Starving."[21] Uniquely, in Surrey, the magistrates provided all gaol and bridewell prisoners with a pennyworth of bread a day from at least 1701.[22] At most gaols, however, only charity prisoners – those who resided in the free parts of prisons and who could not support themselves – were provided an allowance.[23] By the late eighteenth century, only the Borough Compter lacked a regular dietary allowance.[24]

Those who were forced to rely solely on the county allowance, or who lacked even this limited safeguard, unquestionably suffered great hardship. In 1712, Eliz [*sic*] Galaway, a prisoner in the Clerkenwell bridewell who, having served her sentence, was detained for an inability to pay fees, wrote of being "almost starved to Death for hunger," having almost lost the "use of all her Limbs," and not having "clothes to hide her nackedness."[25] In 1741, Wallbank described a fight between inmates over who would get to dip their bread first into a pot of water that had been used to boil beans. He observed, "they eat the Bread so dipt very greedily."[26]

Though London prisons generally did not employ salaried medical officers until the late eighteenth century, most formed informal arrangements with hospitals or individual medical men so that prisoners had some access to health care. From the mid-1660s, the aldermen arranged for City hospitals to send physicians to treat prisoners in Newgate and the compters when requested, and in Surrey, the magistrates found local surgeons or apothecaries who would attend and supply medicines to gaol and bridewell prisoners as needed.[27] Middlesex keepers who used their own money to aid sick prisoners were sometimes reimbursed.[28] More unusually, the governors of London's Bridewell paid a salary to an apothecary to tend to the prisoners from at least 1699.[29]

In the early 1770s, as Howard began investigating prisons, Parliament too turned its attention to the physical and spiritual health of prisoners. In 1774, they passed the *Health of Prisoners Act*, which ordered that separate infirmaries for men and women be built, baths be provided, cells be well-ventilated, prison walls be white-washed, and a salaried surgeon or apothecary be appointed.[30] Authorities across the metropolis responded with varying degrees of enthusiasm, often by ratcheting up their existing provisions a notch or two, specifically by appointing salaried physicians and ordering infirmaries be built.[31] Additionally, they applied voluntarily the provisions of the act to their houses of correction, to which it did not formally apply. The Bridewell governors, for example, in December 1774 ordered that bathing tubs be purchased, ventilators installed, and the prisons fumigated twice a week with tar or vinegar.[32] In 1776, they built two infirmaries, one for men and another for women, as well as an apothecary's shop.[33] Likewise in Surrey, the magistrates, as well as appropriating a room to hold sick prisoners, purchasing bathing tubs, installing pipes to supply fresh water to the inmates' yards, and purchasing clean clothes for inmates, also gave salaries to physicians already attending the prisons and ordered that the physicians regularly inspect the prisons and certify whether there had been any contagious diseases.[34]

Endorsing standards implicit in these customary practices and the new legislation, Howard pressed for infirmaries to be built, physicians to be appointed, baths (for washing) and ovens (for fumigating clothes and bedding) to be purchased, and hand-ventilators to be installed. Yet, Howard's proposals also went beyond current prison practice, even as recently enhanced. First, he sought to impose greater regularity and accountability by setting out clear guidelines and clarifying the respective responsibilities of prisoners and staff.[35] Second, while most authorities conceived of the dietary allowance as a safeguard for the indigent, Howard proposed that it be the main or primary source of food for inmates: prison authorities should provide a dietary allowance to each prisoner, regardless of their ability to supply their own provisions, and prisoners should subsist primarily, if not exclusively, on the county allowance.[36] Finally, Howard placed architecture at the centre of the discussion on prison health. Just as City authorities in the 1760s recognized that Newgate could not be made healthy unless it was totally rebuilt, so Howard advocated that most prisons be completely reconstructed. To assist local authorities in designing new prisons, Howard included a general plan for a wholesome prison. Prisons should be rebuilt on an "airy" and secluded spot, ideally near a body of water, and be composed of wards built on raised arcades, with large courtyards.[37]

Prisoner Morals

To Howard, prisons endangered the moral and spiritual well-being of inmates by allowing them to associate indiscriminately and to idle away their confinement, drinking, gaming, and quarrelling. Such claims undersold the degree of organization within eighteenth-century prisons. In London, as elsewhere in Britain and Europe, inmates generally slept communally in rooms with either a handful or, if in a common or charity ward, dozens of other prisoners. Such arrangements were not random, however. A prisoner's allocation to a particular area or room depended on their purchasing power, their status as a civil or criminal prisoner, their gender, and occasionally, their offence and character. The oldest divisions were those determined by wealth. The profit-driven nature of early modern prisons meant that prisoners were allowed to purchase accommodation to the quality of their choosing. Generally, prisoners with similar levels of wealth ended up congregating together. Those who paid the most lived in the most salubrious parts of the prison in superior chambers with relatively few ward-mates, while those without money, surviving on charity, were crowded into the most unpleasant and unhealthy spaces.[38]

Other ideas about how prisoners should be separated added extra complexity to prison organization. By the late seventeenth century, authorities often separated criminal and debtor prisoners, and in 1670, this separation was made mandatory by parliamentary legislation.[39] Howard, touring English prisons in the 1770s, found that nearly all authorities complied with this legislation, though a number of the noncompliant institutions, including the Borough Compter, were in London.[40] Nevertheless, even in compliant prisons, debtors and criminal prisoners were not kept entirely apart. Debtors may have had separate day and night wards, but many spaces were shared, including courtyards, some drinking and eating spaces, and the prison chapel.

London authorities had long attempted to keep male and female prisoners separate at night; the mid-eighteenth century saw attempts to ensure they were kept separate by day too.[41] The City Corporation committed to totally separating male and female prisoners at Newgate from at least 1755.[42] The Middlesex justices in July 1760 approved plans to erect brick walls down the centres of the gaol and bridewell to separate male and female prisoners into distinct sides of the prisons.[43] After their reconstruction in the 1770s, the Southwark gaol and the house of correction had separate courtyards, dayrooms, sleeping wards, and workshops for male and female inmates.[44] The London Bridewell's complete separation of male and female prisoners impressed visiting reformers in the 1770s.[45]

At some prisons, local authorities also attempted to classify and separate prisoners on the basis of their offences. The earliest and most frequent measures of this kind aimed to keep offenders accused or convicted of particularly serious offences away from other prisoners. In 1431, for example, the aldermen instructed that felons and those "suspected of great crimes" held in Newgate be "safeguarded in the basement cells and strongholds … and not allowed any intercourse with other prisoners."[46] Some prisons also kept condemned prisoners, those sentenced to death and awaiting execution, separate. At Newgate, from 1725, such inmates were held in solitary cells.[47] Middlesex's New Prison boasted a felons' room and a room for those confined for assaults from at least 1731; when damage to the former forced the keeper to imprison felons alongside the assaults, it led to a "great deal of mischeif & disturbance," which the keeper stressed when pushing for money to repair the gaol.[48] Other calls to keep certain categories of inmate separate were instigated by Parliament: consider the 1751 *Murder Act*, for example, which mandated that individuals accused of murder be kept in solitary cells.[49] In general, these kinds of measures were driven by concern over internal and external security and by a desire to intensify the dread of imprisonment.

Efforts to keep serious offenders away from the main prison body were complemented in the eighteenth century by schemes to isolate prisoners arrested but not yet charged with a crime. At the Poultry and Wood Street Compters, rooms were converted in 1737–38 into separate wards for night charges, while in 1772–73 the Middlesex magistrates added two rooms – one for males and another for females – for night charges at New Prison. At the latter, the rooms were placed at the entrance to the prison, over the gateway, perhaps a physical reflection of the peripheral place of night charges within the criminal justice system.[50] Grouping night charges into one or a couple of rooms allowed prison officers to limit the potential disruption caused by such prisoners. By the nineteenth century, the practice was also justified by health concerns. Only after they had been washed and examined by the surgeon were such prisoners allowed into other areas of the prison.[51]

Finally, at bridewells, authorities began to classify and separate inmates based on an evaluation of their character and criminal history. Throughout London, authorities created separate spaces for imprisoned apprentices, a group of prisoners considered to be young, relatively new to crime, and charged with minor offences. The Middlesex justices erected single cells to confine "disobedient and disorderly apprentices, separate from each other and from other prisoners" in 1771.[52] The Surrey justices followed suit in 1772.[53] Finally in

1799 the Bridewell governors ordered six "separate and distinct apartments" be furnished immediately for apprentices sent by the chamberlain.[54] The governors additionally considered isolating "the most incorrigible" prisoners, asking their surveyor to prepare plans for erecting "separate cells" for them in 1775, a measure probably driven by a desire to protect the morals of younger or more innocent prisoners. This work was not carried out; instead, the governors opted to place all criminal prisoners in cells.[55]

Howard based his system of classification on these established principles of separation. He called for debtors to be separated from felons, women from men, young offenders from old or hardened ones, petty offenders from serious offenders, and bridewell inmates from gaol inmates. While his proposed system of classification was not especially original, Howard went beyond common practice by insisting that the different classes be kept totally apart by both day and night. This more complete separation would be accomplished through architectural change. Respecting county gaols, he proposed all be divided into five main sections and that each class – male debtors, female debtors, female felons, young criminals, and male felons – be allocated a ward and adjoining court. He did not spell out his classification scheme for bridewells, but he seems to have envisioned at least three distinct groups: men, women, and apprentices.[56]

Howard broke most notably from existing practice by proposing that each prisoner have his or her own room. "I wish," he wrote, "to have so many small rooms or cabins in this ward, that each criminal may sleep alone."[57] Traditionally, prisoners slept in groups of varying size, and separate or cellular confinement was used either as a punishment, for those who acted disorderly in prison or who were sentenced to death, or as a security precaution, for those who posed a threat to other prisoners or who required special protection from others. Howard, by contrast, saw separate confinement as appropriate for all inmates, whether convicted or held for safe custody. He acknowledged that, in some prisons, it might prove impossible to prevent prisoners from associating during the day, yet he insisted that, at night, prisoners "should by all means be separated."[58] The "solitude and silence" would encourage reflection amongst inmates and "possibly lead them to repentance"; it would make escapes more difficult; lastly, it would keep prisoners safe from fellow inmates.[59] Howard was not the first to suggest that prisoners be held in separate 'rooms' or 'cells'; still, it was only from the 1780s, after Howard endorsed the practice, that it was more widely proposed.[60]

We turn now to the nature of prison life and find that prisons were neither as lawless nor as riotous as Howard claimed. Though early modern prisons are often caricatured as unregulated spaces, they were in fact governed by a range of local ordinances, parliamentary statutes, prisoner codes, and customary practices.[61] Generally, these rules, both formal and informal, did not focus on regulating the behaviour of prisoners, but some did attempt to impose a structure on inmates' days, while others placed restrictions on their conduct. For instance, there were fixed hours of locking and unlocking, when prisoners were shut in and released from their apartments, specified dining hours, and set arrangements for cleaning the prisons.[62] Divine service was held at specified times too, though generally prisoners were not required to attend.[63] Greater restrictions applied to prisoners at houses of correction, with most forced to labour for long portions of each day. At Clerkenwell, for example, prisoners started work by 10am and finished at 6pm, or earlier if they completed their tasks.[64]

Additional rules on prisoner behaviour were drafted and agreed to by prisoners themselves. In 1708–09, poor prisoners in the Poultry's charity wards adopted twenty-three regulations to govern their part of the compter. By one rule, prisoners who played games in the wards after locking up agreed to pay 6*d*. or lose their allowance for a week. More generally, inmates agreed to avoid talking or making noise in the common wards from 10pm until 6am.[65] These regulations were less about imposing morality and more about keeping the peace, and hence, they focused on regulating noise and establishing methods to deal with interpersonal conflicts between prisoners. How common such prisoner codes were outside of the City is difficult to assess given the nature of surviving records, but it would have made sense for inmates at other prisons to have formed similar agreements on acceptable and unacceptable behaviour to manage living in close proximity with strangers.

While there were some official restraints on prisoners' time and some restrictions on their behaviour, daily life was not closely regulated or supervised in early modern prisons. Once released from their wards, prisoners were free to spend most of the day as they chose within the confines of their designated wards and courtyards. Prisoners were allowed to drink without limitation, and though there were rules against gambling and gaming, such activities nevertheless continued.[66] Even bridewell prisoners were free to indulge in "vices" that Howard condemned once they finished their tasks. His interests may have been atypical of the average prisoner, but the printer Jacob Ilive found time to correct Smith's *Family Bible* for the press, walk about two miles in the yard each day, and learn Arabic after finishing work when imprisoned in Clerkenwell bridewell in the 1750s.[67] Other inmates, Ilive claimed, played games such as "Hunting the Slipper, Thread my Needle Nam, and Prisons and Bars," exchanged "Stories of their own Adventures," got drunk "as often as they c[ould]," and had sex.[68]

Howard called on prisons to introduce greater restrictions on prisoners' behaviour and time than were usually imposed. He urged administrators to issue rules against or clamp down on gaming, fighting, obscene language, and drunkenness.[69] In this way, he sought to make prisoner conduct more orderly and polite. He also proposed that prisoners work. The novelty of this proposition varied by institution. In the case of bridewells, Howard merely repeated established policy in London institutions by calling for workshops to be built and for prisoners to be kept at work, unless sick, for ten hours a day.[70] In the case of London's gaols and compters, his proposal constituted a departure from established practice. Howard thought all prisoners would benefit from working while incarcerated, and he claimed that many pre-trial prisoners had expressed to him a desire to work to "earn something for their more comfortable support." However, while he commended those gaols that allowed pre-trial prisoners to work, he did not insist that authorities provide them with labour or build them workshops. By contrast, he urged authorities to establish workshops for debtors who were willing to work. In this way, he argued, authorities could help debtors to preserve habits of industry and to contribute to their families' support.[71]

Howard also pushed for prisoners to be given a religious education. The 1773 *Gaols Act* had authorized justices to appoint clergymen to officiate in English and Welsh county gaols and to raise funds on the rates to pay them salaries. In 1815, this power was explicitly extended to houses of correction.[72] For some prisons, these acts changed little: the City Corporation had been paying salaries to prison chaplains for many years before parliamentary intervention, and the Bridewell governors had required inmates attend church on Sundays and holy days from at least 1599.[73] However, in Middlesex and Surrey the legislation was a spur to action. Justices quickly hired chaplains to attend not only their gaols but also their bridewells (table 3.1).

Table 3.1 Gaol chaplain salaries

Prison	Year remuneration granted	Type of remuneration	Annual amount	Notes
Newgate	1544	Salary	£10	
	1655	Salary Raise	£82	Total sum derived from salary, ancient stipend, and bequest for preaching to the condemned
	1685	Salary Cut	£30	
	1775	Salary Raise	£200	Total sum derived from salary, freedoms, residence, and ancient emoluments
City Compters: Wood Street and Poultry	1612	Salary	—	
	1655	Salary Raise	£75	
	1685	Salary Cut	£30	
Middlesex New Prison	1774	Salary	£50	Also appointed chaplain at Middlesex bridewell
Southwark Gaol	By 1775	Salary	£50	Also appointed chaplain at Southwark bridewell

Source: Sheehan, "System," 259–60; MGOC, 9 Sept. 1773, 9 Dec. 1773, *LL*, LMSMGO556050194–5, LMSMGO556060031; "Account of Salary Submitted by Clergyman," SHC, QS2/6/1776/Eph/23.

Howard reiterated the act's provisions by calling on authorities to build chapels and appoint salaried chaplains. He went further in calling for chaplains to be employed at bridewells too. Moreover, whereas the 1773 act had provided no instructions regarding the chaplain's duties, Howard clearly set out the officer's responsibilities: namely, preach a sermon and read prayers at least once on Sundays; read prayers on two additional days; and task a prisoner with reading a chapter of the New Testament each day before the prison allowance was distributed.[74] Additionally, the chaplain should not "content himself with officiating in public," but also "converse with the prisoners; admonish the profligate; exhort the thoughtless; comfort the sick; and make known to the condemned the Mercy which is revealed in the Gospel."[75] In short, Howard envisioned the chaplain playing a much larger role in prison life.

Administration

Finally, Howard believed that, to effect a thorough reform of prisons and ensure the physical and moral health of prisoners, the administrative structure of prisons needed amendment. "Without a due attention to the oeconomy and government of a prison," he wrote, "it is evident that no contrivance of structure can secure it from being the abode of wickedness, disease and misery."[76]

Traditionally, gaols and compters fell within the purview of the local sheriff, who typically appointed a deputy to run the prison in his stead. These prisons were largely self-financing. Keepers paid for the privilege of running the gaol; in return for their investment, they were authorized to take fees from prisoners, to benefit from customary perquisites, and to sell goods to prisoners. These men were answerable for most repairs and responsible for hiring assistants, who similarly relied on fees and the sale of goods to prisoners and their visitors for their income (notably at prison "taps").[77] Staffs were skeletal: often, a keeper and a handful of turnkeys or under-keepers, night watchmen, and runners. Until 1793, Newgate, for instance, was managed by the keeper, three turnkeys, and six runners or night watchmen.[78]

Between the sixteenth and eighteenth centuries a series of parliamentary statutes gave justices greater responsibility for maintaining and supervising gaols. These acts empowered justices to use the rates to maintain the fabric of gaols and to provide a variety of services and goods.[79] In many places, the acts simply caught up with what benches were already doing, but in others, including Surrey, the extension of magisterial authority prompted new investment in local prisons.[80] Across London, justices assumed much of the financial burden of running gaols and compters, including paying for prison repairs, funding county allowances, and providing keepers with larger salaries. Only the keepers of the Borough Compter and the Southwark gaol lacked salaries in the mid-1770s. Many authorities, including those of Middlesex by 1719, also banned keepers from employing deputies and required them to execute their office in person. The Middlesex gaol and bridewell keepers were also required to enter into a £500 bond with the county to secure their "well demeanor in, & executon of his Office."[81] By the time of Howard's tours, therefore, gaols and compters were already much less profit-driven and private than they had once been.

Table 3.2 Gaol keeper salaries

Prison	Year remuneration granted	Type of remuneration	Annual amount
Newgate	1735	Subsidy	No set price – Court decided keepers were entitled to a profit of £200 (excluding income from tap or other perquisites) so if annual profits fell below £200, Chamber would pay the difference.
	1744	Salary	£150
	1752	Salary raise	£200
City Compters: Wood Street and Poultry	1739	Subsidy	Same process to decide subsidy amount as at Newgate, but City estimated compter profits to be lower.
Middlesex New Prison	1753	Salary	£30
	1779	Salary raise	£70
Southwark Gaol	Between 1799–1802	Salary	£300

Source: Sheehan, "System," 230–1; "Petition of William Pentlow," LL, LMSMGO556030034–44; "Petition of Samuel Newport," LL, LMSMPS507320006; SSP, SHC, QS2/6/1799/Eph/7a–f; QS2/6/1806/MIC/23/5; Howard, *Prisons*, 24; James Neild, *An Account of the Society for the Discharge and Relief of Persons Imprisoned for Small Debts* (London, 1802), 274.

Increasingly justices required that other prison servants be paid salaries too, though they did not assume this burden themselves. The aldermen required that keepers pay weekly wages to their servants in 1732. In Surrey, it was the prison keepers who pushed for additional income from the bench to hire extra assistants.[82] While prison staffs generally expanded, institutions nonetheless continued to rely on inmates to fill several roles, as Howard alleged. Moreover, prison officers (except chaplains and physicians) still took fees, which, together with other benefits, accounted for the bulk of their income.[83]

At most houses of correction, justices were responsible for maintenance and supervision from the start. By a 1609 act, they were empowered to use the rates to pay salaries to their bridewell governors, and in London, as well as in other English cities, salaries were generally provided.[84] The Middlesex magistrates and Bridewell governors additionally paid salaries to a matron to supervise

Table 3.3 Bridewell governor salaries

Prison	Year remuneration granted	Notes
London Bridewell	1553	"Convenient stipends" were paid to all prison staff from the institution's establishment. The range of officers employed included taskmasters, taskmistresses, porters, cooks, and stewards.
Middlesex bridewell	1620s	At some point before 1689, the justices arranged for the governor's salary to be paid out of the rents received for New Prison gaol. After the new governor offered to do without his £80 salary, the bench (in 1719) discontinued it. The emolument was reinstated, at the lower value of £50, in 1752, only to be taken away in 1774. The salary was made permanent after 1779 in view of the "trouble and expense" faced by the governor in managing convict prisoners.
Southwark bridewell	1650s	Magistrates revoked the salary in the 1660s after keeper failed to carry out repairs and to pay for prisoners' bread. Salary restored by at least 1712. By 1724, the county provided lodgings in the prison for the keeper. Salary raised in 1729.

Source: R.H. Tawney and Eileen Power, *Tudor Economic Documents* (London: Longmans, Green and Co), 306–10; *LL*, LMSMPS500000043; BL, Ad MS 12496, document no. 236; "Order to Examine Money Spent on House of Correction," SHC, QS2/6/1724/Mic/6; "Petition of Daniel Parid, Keeper," SHC, QS2/6/1727/Ea/51–2.

the female prisoners.[85] By the 1720s, the Middlesex magistrates also provided lodgings to the governor and matron, who were expected to reside constantly in the prison and were forbidden from appointing a deputy to carry out their roles.[86] Since magistrates were not obliged to pay their governors' salaries, pay was sometimes suspended, usually to save costs. More broadly, neither the Middlesex nor the Surrey bench assumed full financial responsibility for operating or repairing bridewells. Instead, gaolers were expected to contribute to the prison's upkeep and operation. To do so, they chiefly relied on fees, providing prisoners with beds, and income from the tap.[87]

As for oversight, magistrates across London supervised their gaols, compters, and houses of correction in similar ways. They periodically sent committees to visit their prisons and report on their condition, but generally, justices were alerted to problems by prisoner petitions or by grand jury representations.[88] Any concerns were handled when reported to general court sittings. If an issue required greater attention, authorities in all three jurisdictions formed *ad hoc* committees to investigate and resolve the problem. The committees were promptly dissolved once solutions were found. Still, evidence suggests that magistrates exercised considerable oversight over their prisons, and that they became more involved from the end of the seventeenth or start of the eighteenth centuries. The Middlesex bench, for example, led repeated investigations into allegations of abuse by prison keepers between the 1690s and 1710s, resulting in numerous dismissals.[89] These and other accounts point towards magistracies that were fairly well-informed about the goings-on in their prisons and who were willing to intervene to correct irregularities.

The administrative structure that Howard envisioned for reformed prisons basically replicated existing London systems. He urged that each prison, in addition to a keeper, have a chaplain, a surgeon, and various turnkeys, and that the prison be supervised by the local magistrates. He also pushed for rules to be established and exhibited in prisons to govern operation. His proposals for prison operation, though, were distinctive. Namely, he aimed to eliminate its private and commercial aspects. He argued that county salaries should serve as officers' sole remuneration, and that the taking of fees from prisoners, the owning or benefiting in any way from the prison tap, and the selling of food or any other goods to inmates should be banned. Finally, Howard's plan envisioned local magistrates playing a greater supervisory role. Insisting that "the care of a prison is too important to be left wholly to a Gaoler," he suggested two systems of inspection be established to increase oversight. Under the first, justices would annually elect two from their number to serve as "visiting justices," visiting the county's prisons at least twice in every year. By the second, each prison would have an external inspector (a justice) who visited weekly.[90] These arrangements would have subjected prison keepers to a greater level of scrutiny than was customary, and they would have given magistrates a larger role in the day-to-day running of prisons.

II. REFORM MOVEMENT AFTER HOWARD

In the wake of Howard's publications, a reforming programme coalesced broadly along the lines that he had sketched. Yet, there was not total agreement. While many reformers may have aligned themselves formally with Howard, their proposals could take considerably different forms.

To start with, different reformers prioritized different aspects of reform. Some, especially those with medical backgrounds, focused on health in prisons; they principally promoted reforms that sought to improve cleanliness, air circulation, and nutrition in prisons.[91] Others were concerned chiefly with the improper association of prisoners. Some stressed the importance of prisoner labour above all else. Many were principally concerned with religious instruction and championed the role of the chaplain in reformed prisons.[92] A portion who focused on ill-treatment of inmates seem to have been concerned principally with safeguarding inmates' liberties and checking the state's coercive power.[93] Reformers' differing priorities might come into conflict. Many measures proposed to improve health in prisons threatened to undermine security, sometimes putting those who championed prison health at odds with those who aimed to better secure prisons.[94] The Proclamation Society thought Howard gave too much attention to health concerns and too little to the manner in which prisoners were confined.[95] In the nineteenth century, many reformers who stressed the importance of solitude came to see prison labour, which diverted the mind and was usually conducted in large groups, as an unwarranted alleviation of prison discipline.

Further differences emerged in the means proposed to give effect to shared objectives. Take the debate over indiscriminate association: while most were concerned to limit this, disagreements arose over the methods for classifying prisoners and the degree to which inmates should be separated. Some reformers, including Jonas Hanway and the Proclamation Society, pushed for a complete separation of all prisoners – a kind of confinement frequently referred to as 'solitary' or 'cellular.' For Hanway, solitude in imprisonment not only enabled those imprisoned for punishment to reflect, repent, and eventually be restored to society, but it also ensured that those committed for safe custody were guarded against their fellow inmates.[96] In his view, associated confinement was a punishment, and therefore, inappropriate for those confined for safe custody: "can any man of common sense say it is not a punishment to a man of the least sentiment, to be conducted to a prison, and there compelled to associate with the most atrocious offenders? … this is a cruel and unjust procedure."[97] The Proclamation Society likewise saw solitary confinement as beneficial to both the "guilty" and the "innocent." The former would confess their misdeeds, whereas the latter would be saved from the "blasphemous conversation of others of a different disposition."[98]

Others proposed a partial adoption of cellular confinement. Many suggested that it be limited to convicted offenders. In the 1780s, the London common councillor Josiah Dornford pressed for London's prisons to be rebuilt with a number of "separate apartments sufficient to promote solitude and labour" to hold convicts sentenced to imprisonment, but he did not suggest other prisoners be separated in this manner.[99] Likewise, Gloucester's G.O. Paul did not advocate total cellular confinement. Despite contending that "there is no possible degree of separation what will not bring with it additional perfection," Paul proposed that only convicted felons, held in either the gaol or the penitentiary, be confined in individual day and night cells.[100] For non-convict prisoners, he saw cellular confinement as a punishment, appropriate solely for the refractory.[101] Practical considerations may also have shaped their views. Building a prison with separate cells was not only more expensive, but it also required more space to build. For those responsible for executing plans, such as Dornford and Paul, these factors were probably at the forefront of their minds.

Howard made contradictory remarks about separate confinement. At one point he insisted that prisoners should "by all means be separate" by night, but elsewhere, he praised prisons, such as Suffolk county gaol, that slept prisoners in a "strong night-room" where each had a "crib-bedstead," which was "excellently contrived for cleanliness and health."[102] Similarly, in the section on proposed improvements for bridewells, he submitted, "in all prisons, it would be an excellent improvement to have little crib bedsteads for each person to lie upon separately."[103] Howard's remarks suggest he was less convinced of the necessity of separate or cellular confinement than people such as Hanway and the members of the Proclamation Society. Many who championed cellular confinement, however, did not read Howard in this way. John Brewster, for instance, saw complete solitude as an "opportunity" for prisoners to make "peace with God"; it allowed them to "purify" themselves from "all those evil Habits, and wicked actions, which rendered you dangerous to your fellow Citizens" so they might eventually "return into the world, and sustain your part in it with credit and reputation." Brewster repeatedly cited and credited Howard for proving the value of solitude.[104]

Reformers were also divided on prison labour. While all agreed that prisoners sentenced to imprisonment at hard labour must be forced to work, questions were raised over the labour of other inmates. Could such prisoners be forced to work? Should prisons make it possible for these inmates to work voluntarily? If they did, should this work be provided by the county? Should inmates receive any of the profits from their labour, and, if so, how much? Howard, we have seen, did not expressly call on prisons to allow accused offenders to work, or to provide work for them, but he did insist that debtors should be allowed to work if they wished. Other reformers thought magistrates should do more to ensure all prisoners, whether convicted or not, were employed. For instance, William Morton Pitt, active magistrate and member of Parliament for Dorset, insisted that "work rooms, means of employment, and some encouragement to industry, ought to be provided in *every prison*, and each person should be employed (whenever it may be practicable) in his own particular trade, or business."[105] In Gloucestershire, Paul designed a labour system whereby inmates detained for safe custody would be pressured into working by proposing the county allowance be withheld from prisoners who, though not legally obliged to labour, refused to work.[106] Other debates naturally centred on the spaces and organization of labour: whether inmates should work in groups or in solitude; for outside manufactories or merchants or directly for the keeper; and so on.

The traditional focus on John Howard has too often led scholars to miss the contested nature of prison reform in the late eighteenth century. Certainly, there was broad agreement over the direction that reform should take. The prison buildings themselves would be airier, cleaner, and stronger, assuring both the prisoners' health and their security; the prisoners would be classified and separated on the basis of these classifications; labour and religious education would play a greater role in prison operation; and finally, prisons would be governed by written rules, staffed by salaried public servants, and overseen by the local justices of the peace. Still, many of the details of prison architecture, administration, and regulation remained open to debate, with important implications for the path of prison reform in England. Just as reform ideas took diverse forms, so too did reformed prisons.

III. CONCLUSION

The decision to embark upon reform did not rest with most of those who put their reforming ideas into print, but instead with those who managed the prisons, the justices of the peace, or, in the case of Bridewell, its governing board. Of course, some who advocated reform in print also held these roles, but in order to move forward with their projects, they had to convince a majority of their fellow managers to pursue time-consuming and expensive reform projects. London magistrates needed little convincing. Indeed, as we shall see, these men eagerly welcomed the intervention of Howard and other high-profile reformers. They had long been attentive in managing their prisons, and in the eighteenth century especially, they assumed a more active role, introducing a raft of changes. Howard's work gave the magistrates greater license to embark on more thorough-going and expensive reforms. Although there was a blueprint for reform starting to take shape that London magistrates could draw on, there were many aspects still unresolved, leaving magistrates with a series of important choices to make. In what follows, we trace how London authorities translated theories of reform into practice.

CHAPTER FOUR

The Practice of Reform

The second half of the eighteenth century saw the blossoming of the penal reform movement. While interest in prisons was longstanding, the scale of building work, amount expended, and scope of ambition were unprecedented: nearly every county initiated and oversaw a rebuilding of its prisons, with around eighty-six either rebuilt or substantially renovated by 1800.[1] In London, every prison was either totally demolished and rebuilt or substantially reconstructed. This level of construction had not been seen since the Great Fire and represented a major rethink of the nature of prison buildings. The sums expended were vast. If we consider only major building work and exclude smaller repairs, then between 1767 and 1815, the City spent over £265,000 on its prisons (including nearly £4,300 by the Bridewell governors); Surrey about £50,000; and Middlesex about £78,000 (see tables 4.1–4.4). Prison building was part of a wider burst of public construction in this period, but even compared to other important civic projects, such as the rebuilding of key bridges or justices' sessions houses, the funds spent on prisons were remarkable.[2]

No authority in England spent more on their prisons than London justices. The City's Newgate was the most expensive prison built in England and Wales before 1800, followed by Middlesex's Coldbath Fields (constructed 1789–94) in second place, and Surrey's Horsemonger Lane Gaol (constructed 1791–99) in third.

Historians have offered a variety of explanations for local authorities' willingness to act on this scale and at this level of expenditure. Some have stressed the humanitarian origins of reform, associated with the spread of Enlightenment ideals or with evangelicalism: in rebuilding prisons, reformers sought to improve prison conditions and the lot of prisoners. Others have seen reform

Table 4.1 Prison-building in the City, 1767–1816

Prison	Years of work	Surveyor/architect	Estimated cost (£.s.d)	Money expended (£.s.d)	Type of work
Newgate	1767–84	George Dance the Elder and George Dance the Younger	£40,000	c. £100,000	Rebuilt
Borough Compter	1785–87	George Dance the Younger	£3,000	£2,593.8.2	Rebuilt
Giltspur Compter	1787–91	George Dance the Younger	£15,120	£30,141.3.1 (£9,772.13.4. spent on land)	New build
Whitecross Street Debtor's Prison	1812–15	William Montague	—	£125,810.0.0	New build
Giltspur Street Prison and House of Correction	1815–16	George Dance the Younger	—	£1,596.12.0	Alterations

Source: Chalklin, *Building*, 16; Chalklin, "Reconstruction," 24, 31; Sheehan, "System," 400; Stroud, "Giltspur," 129; PP, 1818, viii.275, 122.

Note: This account excludes work on prisons such as King's Bench and the Fleet, also remodelled in this period.

Table 4.2 Building at City Bridewell, 1775–97

Type of work	Years of work	Estimated cost (£.s.d)
Repairing and enlarging the men's prison and building 12 solitary cells for "most incorrigible"	1775–76	£192
Creating a men's infirmary	1776	£186.12.10
Creating a women's infirmary	1776	£126.4.10
Creating an apothecary shop	1776	£19.7.3
Building six cells for chamberlain's apprentices	1779	—
Solitary cells for female prisoners	1793–95	£856 in November 1793. Revised to more than £899 in July 1794
Solitary cells for male prisoners	1795–97	£1,362 in March 1795, revised to £2,850 in June 1796

Source: BPCM, 22 Mar. 1776, 29 Mar. 1776, 8 July 1779, 21 Nov. 1793, 11 Mar. 1795, 8 June 1796, LMA, CLC/275/MS33131/001; BCGM, 31 Jan. 1794, 10 July 1794, LMA, CLC/275/MS33011/025.

Note: This account may encompass only a fraction of Bridewell's repairs. A treasury committee report (1792) concluded the governors had spent £17,332.19s.7d. for repairs on Bridewell and Bethlem hospitals in 1775–92. The account does not specify how the money was allocated between the two institutions, and I cannot find evidence for the specific building work in prison committee minutes. Copeland, *Bridewell*, 150–1.

Table 4.3 Prison-building in Surrey, 1719–1801

Prison	Location	Years of work	Surveyor	Estimated cost (£.s.d)	Money expended (£.s.d)	Type of work
Southwark House of Correction	Borough High Street	1719	—	—	£550	Rebuilt
Surrey County Gaol	Borough High Street	1720–23	—	£2,551 + £142 for extras	£2,800	Rebuilt
Kingston House of Correction	Kingston	1760–62	—	£450 (includes £350 for the land)	—	New build
Guilford House of Correction	Guilford	1767	—	—	£853	Rebuilt
Surrey Gaol	Borough High Street	1771	George Gwilt	—	£689.13.0	Enlarged
Southwark HC	Hangman's Acre, St George's Fields	1772–73	George Gwilt	£2,682	£2,816	New build
Kingston HC	Kingston	1775	—	—	£1,037	Rebuilt
Southwark HC	Hangman's Acre, St George's Fields	1781	George Gwilt	—	£2,889.10.3	Rebuilt after Gordon Riots
Surrey Gaol	Horsemonger Lane, Newington	1791–99	George Gwilt	Under £40,000	£39,742.14.0 (includes £1100 for the land)	New build
Southwark HC	Horsemonger Lane, Newington	1800–01	George Gwilt	£950	£1,041	Addition to above

Source: C.W. Chalklin, ed., *Surrey Gaol and Session House, 1791–1824*, ix, xxi; Chalklin, *Building*, 157–8, 163–4; "Southwark Prisons," in *Survey of London*, 9–21.

Note: This table includes work done outside of Southwark to allow for a full understanding of the Surrey justices' prison-building and to serve as a comparison for the amount they spent on Southwark prisons. In addition to the amounts above listed, the justices paid for smaller repair work at the county gaol in 1784, 1787, and 1798, together amounting to over £600.

Table 4.4 Prison-building in Middlesex, 1773–94

Prison	Years of work	Surveyor/architect	Estimate cost (£. s. d.)	Money expended (£. s. d.)	Type of work
New Prison	1773–75	Thomas Rogers (county surveyor)	£3,500	£3,607	Enlarged
Clerkenwell House of Correction	1773–79	Thomas Rogers (s)		£4,204.7.1	Repairs
Coldbath Fields House of Correction	1788–94	Jacob Leroux (a); Aaron Henry Hurst (a); Sir Robert Taylor (advisor); James Paine (advisor); Thomas Rogers (s); S.P. Cockerell (clerk of works)	£27,361.4.11 in 1786. Revised in 1787 to £47,722.	£70,000 (includes c. £4,344 for the land)	New build

Source: Chalklin, *Building*, 163, 167; "Reconstruction," 25–7; "Account of Charges for Maintenance of Prisons, Sept. 1779," *LL*, lmsmps507200023.

as a "formidably severe disciplinary project" driven principally by a desire to exert greater control over prisoners, reduce their autonomy, and alter their personalities. Many have pointed to a fear of infectious diseases, especially gaol fever, prompting local authorities to care about the condition of prisons. Most have stressed the specific circumstances of the 1770s, especially the massive overcrowding in prisons occasioned by the war with America, as a primary motivation for reform. Architectural historians have also alerted us to statutory changes that made it easier for counties to borrow money to pay for new buildings in the 1780s – undoubtedly crucial for London, where authorities took on exceptionally large and expensive projects.[3]

All of these explanations suggest that within a county the same set of factors motivated change in every prison. In so doing they fail to consider and account for the fact that, within counties, reformed prisons were given diverse shapes. Though there were some common features introduced into a county's prisons, there were also notable differences. In particular, reform projects were tailored to fit each prison's role within the wider criminal justice system.

The pattern of reform in London suggests there was widespread concern over gaol fever, overcrowding, and, I would add, the run-down state of prisons, factors which drove and shaped reforming agendas universally. At all prisons, therefore, authorities took steps to make their prisons larger, healthier, and more secure. At gaols and compters, prisons that served mainly as sites of detention, this was as far as authorities generally went. However, at bridewells, prisons that acted mainly as sites of punishment, additional and more dramatic reforms were introduced. Circumstances alone – the threat of gaol fever, the disruption of transportation, prison overcrowding, and greater borrowing capacity – cannot explain the pattern of reform adopted at London bridewells. Not only did magistrates attempt to improve bridewells' administrative structures, but they also moved to create a moral environment within these prisons which was capable of transforming the character of those confined. At bridewells, philanthropic and disciplinary agendas fused.

I. HEALTH AND SECURITY

Although local authorities had repeatedly altered and repaired their prisons over the previous centuries, many were nevertheless run-down by the late eighteenth century, posing a serious threat to prisoners and to prison security. At Middlesex's New Prison, the women's ward required repair, as did the floors of the tap room and fines room; many locks and bolts had decayed; the walls were too low; the water pump, which provided prisoners with access to free water, was broken.[4] The Wood Street and Poultry Compters were probably in the worst condition. The City Lands Committee had declared the compters worn out, dangerous, and unfit to be repaired in November 1770, but no action had been taken. Subsequently, the Poultry's roof collapsed, twice, while at Wood Street the keeper was forced to move prisoners into his own residence to ensure their safety.[5] At other prisons, the extent of disrepair was less extreme and could perhaps have been resolved with repairs or alterations, but additional considerations prompted a complete redesign.

First, existing prisons were too small. Concerns about overcrowding were closely linked to a fear of gaol fever. In 1781, the Middlesex justices warned that, with their prisons "so crowded," "every thing is to be dreaded that may arise from infection and epidemick disorder."[6] An outbreak of gaol fever in Newgate in 1750, which spread to the Old Bailey courtroom and killed around fifty people, directly prompted the Corporation to consider rebuilding the gaol.[7]

Prisons, then, needed expanding. Setting out the legal case for a new house of correction in 1786, the Middlesex magistrates explained that the bridewell was not only "in a ruinous and decayed state unfit for the purposes of a House of correction," but it was also "not sufficient or convenient or wants to be enlarged."[8] Similarly, they resolved to rebuild their gaol on "a larger company of ground and with a greater number of useful appartments."[9]

Second, authorities increasingly attributed the poor health of prisoners and the recurrent bouts of gaol fever to the design of prisons, which were deemed too cramped, too dark, and not sufficiently airy. As the parliamentary act that authorized the City to raise funds to rebuild Newgate noted, the gaol was "so ill contrived, as not to admit of a sufficient Supply of fresh Air and Water, from which Circumstances the same is in general unhealthy, and often visited with a malignant Fever, called *The Gaol Distemper*, the fatal Effects of which have sometimes extended beyond the Prison Walls."[10] Descriptions of the prison from the 1760s confirm that it was intolerably stuffy, lacked open areas, and was so dark that prisoners were obliged to use "links and burners to go up and down" in the gaol.[11]

London authorities consequently moved to make their prisons "more secure[,] commodious[,] and healthy."[12] By introducing architectural and regulatory measures to improve health and security in each of their gaols, compters, and bridewells, local authorities across London brought these prisons into closer alignment with the model set out by reformers.

All London's prisons were enlarged, in some cases quite considerably. Justices determined the new capacities by collecting and reviewing past accounts of inmate populations. In Middlesex, the rebuilding committee decided to provide accommodation for 350 inmates in the new bridewell after the governor informed them that, at its fullest, the bridewell had once held 233 prisoners; other accounts show that on average it held 154 inmates between 1774 and 1784.[13] Not only did the committee's decision more than double the bridewell's capacity, but it reveals that the magistrates anticipated the daily population growing significantly after reconstruction.

The ambition of some projects ultimately proved unfeasible and had to be scaled back. When designing the new Giltspur Compter, the Common Council planned for 180 prisoners (100 debtors and 80 criminal prisoners), a little small for the greatest number held at Wood Street in the past thirty years (187) but which would comfortably fit the typical number held (fewer than 100).[14] The architect George Dance the Younger estimated that building the compter as directed would cost about £30,000; in addition, the City needed to raise at least £9,450 to pay Giltspur Street proprietors who, as a result of the building, were being forced to relocate.[15] Though the building committee approved the estimate, the City's governing bodies elected to raise only £30,000 to cover all related costs. Ultimately, half was allocated to compensating the street's proprietors, compelling the rebuilding committee to economize. In the final plan, 136 prisoners could be accommodated comfortably in Giltspur. Reports of prison stocks between 1800 and 1815 show the prison was not usually full.[16]

Authorities also moved to increase ventilation and light within prisons in line with contemporary medical thinking. Many inmates were moved to less populous sites. The Surrey magistrates relocated their bridewell in 1772 from its place on the busy Borough High Street to a new site in Hangman's Acre that was larger, more open, and detached from other buildings. In 1790, they moved their gaol to a three-and-a-half-acre plot in Newington, a suburb of Southwark.[17] In addition, the justices ordered that no buildings except a fence (maximum height of six feet) be erected and no pigs be kept within forty yards of the gaol's boundary wall in order to ensure "a circulation of pure and wholesome air," so "preventing the gaol fever and other malignant diseases."[18]

Likewise, the Middlesex magistrates in 1785 opted to purchase for £4,000 an eight-acre plot of land, recommended by John Howard, on which to rebuild their bridewell; this was larger and healthier (abutting a tributary of the Fleet) than the site originally chosen (and purchased for £1,600 in 1783). According to one magistrate who supported the switch, the justices rejected the initial site on the grounds that it guaranteed "neither Air, nor Space, nor Privacy."[19] The anonymous magistrate further remarked, "in general, Space to breathe in, Space to work in, Space for Health, Exercise, and Labour, is to be considered as a *sine quo non*, an absolute Essential, in constructions of this sort."[20] The justices' decision considerably increased the prison's projected cost. Their surveyor had estimated that, if they used the land already owned, the prison would cost £14,939, whereas with the new site, the estimate grew to £27,000 in 1786, revised in 1787 to over £47,000.[21] City authorities also recognized that prisons should be erected in "open and unconnected" spaces, yet in the built-up City, this was not possible.[22] In 1815, the aldermen claimed that if Newgate were built to accommodate the number of inmates usually held within the gaol, with "all the space, not only for air and exercise but for day-rooms and sleeping cells," then the gaol would occupy at least thirty acres.[23]

Magistrates improved ventilation by creating expansive, open courtyards at the centres of prisons.[24] The courtyards not only allowed a "free currency of air" to pass through the entirety of prisons, but they also provided prisoners with space to exercise. More broadly, there was an emphasis on all rooms, even the dungeons, being exposed to "thorough air and light." At Coldbath Fields, for example, the solitary cells were equipped with two windows on either end of the cell for air and light to flow through, while larger rooms such as the chapel had ventiducts, airholes, and ventilators to ensure circulation.[25]

Administrators also added several new or improved facilities to improve inmate health. Fresh pools or cisterns with pumps were installed in courtyards to give inmates access to fresh water. New privies were built. Fireplaces were erected and stoves placed in the prisoners' dayrooms to ward off the cold. Infirmaries were added to the few prisons, such as Southwark gaol, that still lacked them.[26]

Architectural measures were complemented by new regulations aiming to ensure prison cleanliness and inmate health. Some policies, such as the establishment of a schedule for wall-scraping and white-washing, were ordered by Parliament, but many others were devised locally. At New Prison, the magistrates appointed certain prisoners "sheds-men" and "sheds-women," tasked with washing the courtyards and wards each morning. Indeed, much of the responsibility for cleaning continued to lie with the prisoners.[27] Other rules focused on the bodies, clothes, and habits of prisoners. At Bridewell and Coldbath Fields, prisoners entering the prison were to be stripped, bathed, and sometimes shaved; their clothes were washed, fumigated (or destroyed), and replaced with a county uniform.[28] Prisoners at Southwark and Coldbath Fields had to wash their faces and hands each morning and keep their hair short.[29]

Not everything changed. Despite authorities recognizing that prison health depended on good nutrition, inmates at gaols and compters still had to provide most of their own provisions, aside from the daily loaf of bread provided by London magistrates to all prisoners.[30] There remained, then, an unwillingness on the part of county and city officials to assume full financial responsibility for prisoners. What authorities did do was assume greater responsibility for charity prisoners. The City, for example, decided to provide bedding to poor inmates, and by January 1785, the first month of the policy, it had delivered seventy-five rugs each to Wood Street and Poultry, 349 to Newgate, and twenty to Borough Compter.[31] Yet, as Sarah Howell, imprisoned in Newgate, wrote

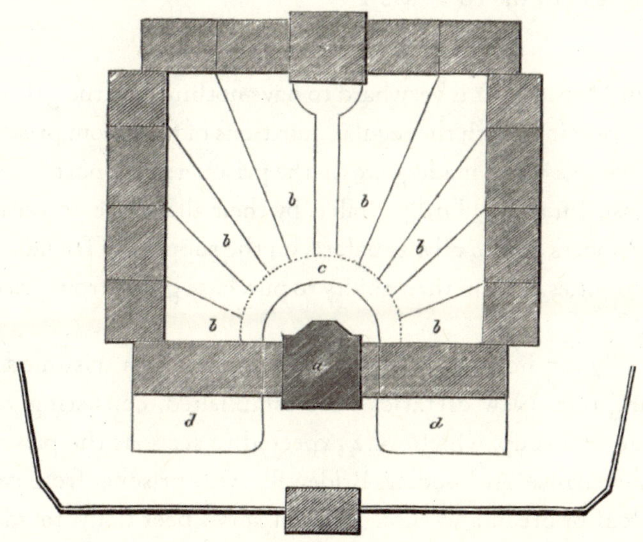

Figure 4.1 • Plan of Surrey Gaol, Horsemonger Lane, Newington. Key: (a) Keeper's house; (b) Courtyards for criminal prisoners; (c) Officers' station area; (d) Courtyards for debtors.

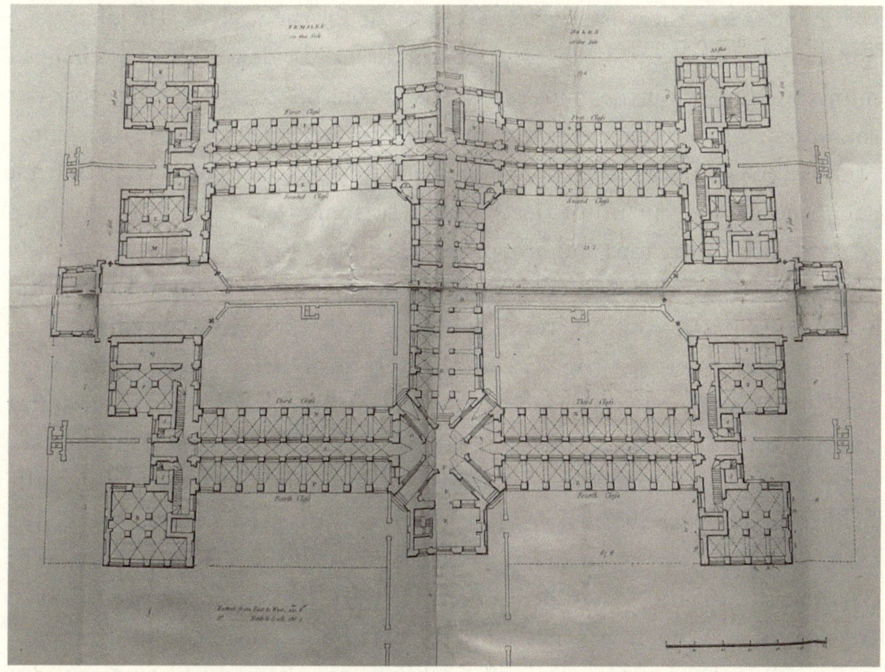

Figure 4.2 • Plan of Coldbath Fields, ground floor, 1788.

in a letter in May 1817, "it is very hard to have nothing but the gale alouance."[32] Even when combined with the regular donations of food from prison charities, the allowance was "quite inadequate to [the prisoners'] support," as even a City keeper stressed in 1814. "Hardly ... able, by their allowance, to exist," gaol and compter prisoners had to rely, as before, on the support of friends and family, on prison charities, and on their ability to purchase goods from prison vendors to survive.[33]

Conversely, at houses of correction, authorities assumed a greater provisioning role. New dietaries were established, consisting generally of bread, meat, and soup, which were expected to serve as the prisoners' main source of sustenance. At London's Bridewell, every prisoner from 1792 received a quarter loaf of bread and three pints of small beer daily, in addition to a pint of broth, made with 10 oz of meat and thickened with oatmeal or onions, four days a week, and on the other three days, a pint of milk pottage and a quarter-pound of cheese.[34] Crucially, the food allowances were provided *only* to inmates who had been sentenced to imprisonment. Others – whether held for trial, re-examination, debt, or to give evidence – received only bread and water and were otherwise expected to provide for themselves. The diets were not accepted without controversy. At Middlesex's bridewell the diet changed numerous times over the 1790s as the prison committee struggled to work out the amount of food they deemed appropriate for "criminals."[35] The provisioning of other goods followed a similar pattern. At houses of correction, but not gaols and compters, authorities supplied prisoners with bedding, clothing, coals for fires, and mops and brooms for cleaning.[36]

The pattern of provisioning in London prisons certainly reflects local authorities' desire to keep costs down, but it also tells us something about how authorities viewed the state and its responsibilities and how they were starting to mark out imprisonment for punishment. Perhaps magistrates did not provide for gaol and compter prisoners because they did not see such inmates as the state's responsibility. These prisoners were principally held for safe custody on the initiation of private prosecutors. The state's task, therefore, was to ensure that they were held securely, without undue harshness, until they could be brought to court. Moreover, while the loss of freedom of movement was incidental to custodial detention, other freedoms, it was believed, should be retained. Such inmates, therefore, should continue eating, drinking, sleeping, dressing, and perhaps even working as before. This meant paying for or bringing their own food, bedding, and so on. Some clearly fought for these "rights": "what right has the Keeper to hinder any Prisoner from bringing in his or her Bed and Bedding ... and use them during his or her imprisonment," asked an anonymous pamphleteer, unimpressed with Middlesex's management of its prisons.[37] It was only when an inmate was in danger of, say, starving or going naked that the state, or rather the prison keeper, would step in – just as was the case outside the prison.

Conversely, prisoners who had been sentenced to imprisonment by the magistrates or by the quarter and assize sessions were undoubtedly the state's responsibility. In recognition of this, magistrates had long accepted, at least in theory, that such inmates should be provided with food and other necessaries, although in practice they were wary of assuming total financial responsibility. Increasingly, however, magistrates linked the provision of prison allowances – especially of food but also in some places of bedding and clothing – to the restriction of the traditional ability of inmates to maintain themselves; moreover, they started seeing this restriction as a vital part of the punishment of imprisonment. As magistrates on Middlesex's prison committee informed bridewell inmates in January 1810, they had "no right" to "indulgences" such as receiving food and articles from friends and family: "they were in the prison to receive punishment for the crimes of which they had been convicted and by their sentence entitled to bread and water only." Such policies clearly set, and were intended to set, punitive imprisonment apart from custodial imprisonment. This was reflected in bridewell policies in the early nineteenth century, where the few inmates who were held for safe custody were expressly "at liberty to receive any food their friends send in."[38]

The development of this policy, however, was slow and halting, with the definitive change occurring only in the 1810s and 1820s. In Middlesex, for example, rules passed in 1795 forbade convicted prisoners from receiving or purchasing extra provisions, but almost immediately, concerns were raised about the cost of the policy and the "heavy demands of the county rate." In December 1798 the magistrates voted by a close margin to repeal the regulation. Afterwards, all prisoners could receive "common plain food (not liquor) from their friends."[39] This privilege came at a cost. Those who opted to receive provisions from friends were required to forsake the prison allowance, a condition that suggests the change in regulation was driven by the county's desire to economize. Those who voted for the change argued that it was "reasonable"

Figure 4.3 · Exterior view of Coldbath Fields, 1798.

and "just" that those who "violated the laws and disturbed the peace and security of the public" should be a charge on their friends rather than the county.[40] In practice, however, it allowed convicted prisoners with funds or friends to improve their standard of living, while those without could not. As this example underscores, it took time for magistrates to work out the conditions that punitive imprisonment would entail. Disagreements over which food policy was more punitive and a desire to keep the rates at an acceptable level led the magistrates to tinker continually with the rules. What remained constant, however, was the view that those held for safe custody should be free to supply themselves.

Finally, prisons were rebuilt to be more secure. To prevent escapes and to limit communication with the outside world, prison walls were raised or rebuilt thicker. Some authorities additionally built new boundary walls, as at Coldbath Fields (figure 4.3), whereas other authorities simply eliminated external windows, as at Newgate.[41]

Within prisons, authorities sought to achieve greater security by increasing the staff's effective power to supervise and inspect inmates. At Newgate, a watchhouse and sentry box was installed on the roof, where at least two guards, with dogs and firearms, kept watch all night.[42] In Surrey, the gaol keeper's house was placed in the centre of the prison and new windows gave him "an opportunity of inspecting the prisoners."[43] Howard had hoped that strengthening prison walls and increasing facilities for inspection might allow authorities to do away with the common practice of keeping prisoners in fetters, irons, and handcuffs, but many prisoners continued to be restrained nonetheless.[44] Perhaps this reflected the fact that, despite the thick, tall walls, prisons remained porous, with visitors and goods admitted fairly readily. In practice, however, irons added to the physical discomfort and pain of imprisonment, a punishment which remained concerned with subduing bodies as much as minds.

Throughout London, then, authorities introduced into all their prisons, regardless of type, many of the measures that prison reformers had deemed necessary for the safe custody of prisoners. They expanded institutions to cope with larger inmate populations; they made them airier, lighter, and somewhat more secure. Yet they differed from reformers such as Howard in refusing to see a county allowance of food and bedding as necessary for a prisoner's safe custody. Instead, London magistrates linked provisioning to punishment, taking responsibility only for those sentenced by courts while leaving custodial inmates to fend for themselves, unless they were totally destitute. As the next section explores, authorities diverged more thoroughly from Howardian reform in other aspects.

II. A PLAN FOR MORAL REFORM

Howard and other leading reformers had sought to make prisons orderly places capable of shaping the conduct of inmates and of reforming – or at the very least safeguarding – their morals. London magistrates shared these ambitions only up to a point. While they sought to transform prisons that functioned mainly as sites of punishment into "school[s] for moral discipline," they were less interested in reshaping the environment and the administrative structure of prisons that served primarily as sites of custodial confinement. Indeed, they ultimately interpreted many of the measures urged by reformers to curb indiscriminate association and to restructure prison life as punitive measures, fit only for inmates sentenced to imprisonment, rather than as policies that should necessarily attend incarceration.

Gaols and Compters

At custodial prisons, London's local authorities adopted some measures to curb prisoner association, as urged by reformers, but generally, the policies introduced drew on established prison practice, rather than on the reformers' more novel proposals. Similarly, they did not move to restructure prison life. Instead, they continued to allow prisoners to organize their own lives within prison, so long as this was compatible with keeping them in safe confinement.

Classification

For decades or even centuries, local authorities had attempted to limit the indiscriminate association of prisoners by adopting classification systems, allocating prisoners to particular niches within these, and endeavouring to keep the classes somewhat separate. During the reform period, interest in classification and separation intensified, with local authorities turning to architectural solutions to ensure different classes were kept separate. However, although distinctions between prisoners were more clearly marked in the new buildings, space continued to be allocated according to established conventions. Arrangements varied, but most institutions separated inmates by a combination of civil or criminal status, gender, and purchasing power, while some additionally separated prisoners on the basis of offence, commitment type, or age. This represented a continuation of, rather than a novel departure from, pre-reform practice.

In London, reform on the new model began at Newgate, redesigned and rebuilt between 1769 and 1784. Following plans drawn up by his father in the 1750s, George Dance the Younger removed prisoners from their traditional place in the gate of Newgate and placed them into three quadrangles: one for debtors, one for male "felons" (that is, criminal prisoners), and one for female "felons."[45] Each quadrangle was self-contained and included its own courtyard, day rooms, and sleeping wards. Additionally, the Press Yard was retained, so condemned prisoners were kept totally separate.

This system of classification did not take account of newer ideas about organizing prisoners: it did not consider the legal basis on which a prisoner was committed, the nature of the offence, the age of the prisoner, or the inmate's character. The felon quadrangles consequently held a mixed bunch: felons alongside misdemeanants, the young with the old, hardened or experienced

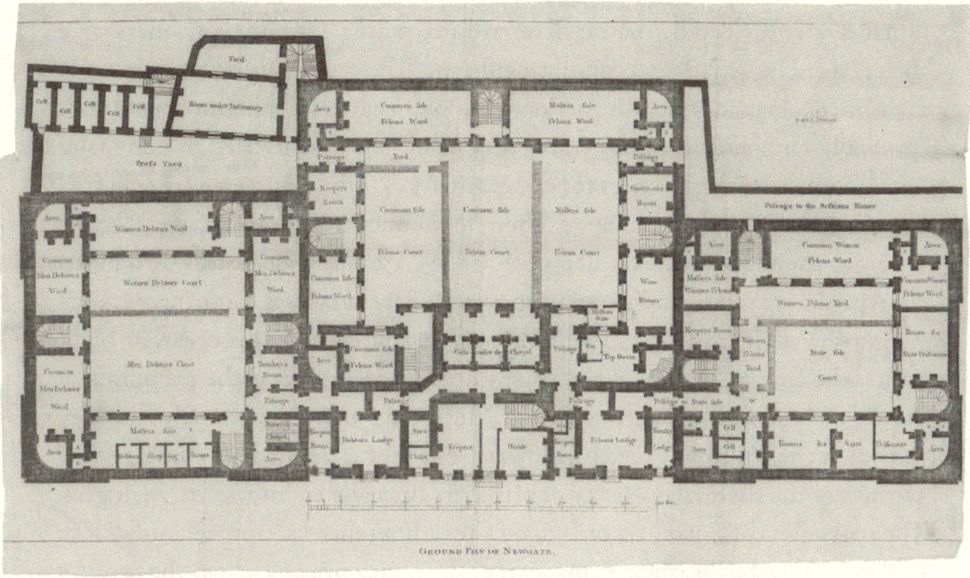

Figure 4.4 • Ground plan of Newgate, 1808.

offenders with new ones, and custodial with convicted prisoners. This conglomeration was obviously anathema to reform ideology.

Within the quadrangles, the overriding principle of division remained inmate wealth. So long as they could pay the entrance fee, any inmate, unless condemned to death, could remove themselves from a common side to the master and state yards.[46] These divisions were not in any of the building plans; rather, they were added during construction in the 1780s at the behest of councillors on the gaol committee.[47] Such divisions were popular with wealthier inmates, and they also brought needed income, which probably explains the committee's decision. Ultimately, though, the additions reversed novel attempts to put prisoners in the same class on equal footing, and they placed added pressure on prison space. While the master and state sides were rarely full, the common sides were regularly overcrowded.[48] Taking space away from poorer prisoners to create additional room for wealthier ones not only increased the hardships faced by poorer or less connected inmates, but it also made disease far more likely and potentially built up resentment within the prison.

The Surrey justices introduced a scheme of classification and separation similar to but somewhat more extensive than that pursued at Newgate. First, inmates were divided by their civil or criminal status. Criminal prisoners were then divided by gender and commitment type. The generally greater number of male prisoners made finer distinctions possible. They were split into four classes (probably: prisoners for trial, transports, fines [those sentenced to periods of imprisonment], and prisoners for re-examination), while women were collected into one class.[49] In total, there was room for about 112 male and fifty-six female criminal offenders, and sixty debtors.[50] Each class was allocated its own paved courtyard, day room, and sleeping spaces. Different classes came into contact only at the chapel, and even there, they sat separately.[51] As this overview highlights, the Surrey justices were generally more receptive to the proposals of prison reformers than were City and Middlesex justices. Not only did they introduce the divisions urged by Howard, but they expanded his model to take account of the particular variety of prisoners typically committed to their gaol. The sparseness of Surrey records makes this difference in approach difficult to explain. Nonetheless, their management of county prisons across the century suggests, first, that they saw the gaol as being as much their responsibility as was the bridewell, and second, an eagerness to adopt the latest reform policies.

This degree of separation was not replicated at other prisons, which generally held fewer people than Newgate or Surrey gaol. At Middlesex's gaol, inmates were already divided by sex and to some extent by wealth, as those with funds could pay to stay in nicer rooms. In the late 1790s or early 1800s, the bench, under pressure from magistrates on the prison committee, ordered three night rooms built – one for male felons held for trial, one for male fines ("persons imprisoned for a certain, limited time"), and one for female fines.[52] During the day, however, inmates were not divided by commitment type or offence. At Borough Compter, classification was based primarily on whether a prisoner was a debtor or criminal. These two groups were separated by a brick wall splitting the compter into two sides. Despite the growing expectation that male and female prisoners would be kept totally apart, in the compter, they continued to associate by day, sharing both a courtyard and day rooms.[53]

The organization of these prisons suggests that, where populations were large and diverse, authorities were more willing to introduce extensive systems of classification and to try harder to keep such classes separate; where populations were smaller or more homogenous, elaborate attempts to classify and separate prisoners were not deemed worthwhile. Financial cost was an important factor here, as the abandonment of some plans to extend classification and reduce inmate association highlights. The committee tasked with rebuilding Giltspur in the 1780s originally proposed a scheme that took account of prisoners' commitment type, in addition to their civil or criminal status, gender, and wealth. They intended to keep the proposed ten classes entirely separate. When forced to retrench, however, the City abandoned the most novel aspects of the proposal. They dropped the separation of "criminal" prisoners into those for trial and those for punishment. They allowed the different classes to associate during the day. Finally, purchasing power remained significant, with male "felons" (convicted and pre-trial) divided into common and master sides according to their means.[54] Their attachment to new theories of classification seemed relatively shallow, in short.

Methods of Confinement

The forms of accommodation adopted by London authorities generally remained traditional, despite reformist enthusiasm for separate or cellular confinement. In the City and Middlesex, nearly all prisoners spent both day and night in associated confinement.[55] Cellular confinement was associated primarily with punishment. Before the reform period, cells were sometimes used to punish refractory inmates and to isolate convicts sentenced to death, and such uses continued after prisons were rebuilt. Additionally, from the 1780s, magistrates began building cells to hold at night inmates sentenced to imprisonment as a punishment; by day, these prisoners associated in wards with members of their classes.[56] Cellular confinement, therefore, was time-limited; moreover, it did not entail solitary confinement. At Giltspur, between two and four criminal prisoners slept in each so-called single cell.[57] Even Newgate's condemned cells, though designed to hold one prisoner, likewise held two or three at the keeper's discretion.[58] Often, prison cells were used for purposes for which they had not originally been intended. At Borough Compter, a prison which rarely received inmates for punishment, cells were given over to night charges and vagrants.[59] At Giltspur, though the cells were designed to hold only the convicted, they came to hold prisoners for trial and for re-examination too after the financially strapped City authorities combined the pre-trial and convicted classes into one general criminal prisoner class.[60] The fact that prisoners were not confined alone in cells probably assuaged City concerns about holding pre-trial prisoners in them.

The failure of some authorities to adopt cellular confinement along the lines that the reformers had envisaged at the end of the eighteenth century has usually been explained in terms of the economic cost of constructing individual cells.[61] Economic feasibility, however, was only one factor, and it was probably less important than magistrates' growing conviction that cells should primarily be for punishment.[62] Not all local authorities viewed cells in this way, however. The Surrey magistrates seem to have accepted the view that cellular confinement was appropriate for all criminal prisoners, whether held for safe custody or punishment. Even there, though, the cells were intended only for sleeping. By day, criminal prisoners congregated by class in day rooms and courtyards. Moreover, in practice, cellular confinement was even more limited, as only male prisoners accused or convicted of a criminal offence were held in cells, with female inmates and debtors remaining in wards.[63] Across London, then, single cells were only used irregularly to hold non-convict prisoners.

Regulating and Reorganizing Prison Life

London authorities showed little interest in controlling the conduct or reshaping the habits of gaol and compter prisoners. By and large, they continued to delegate to prisoners the right to organize their own lives. In other words, London magistrates did not treat these inmates as guilty individuals requiring reform; instead, authorities saw their responsibility over these inmates as limited to keeping them physically confined and safe.

Work and religion consequently played a minor role in reformed gaols and compters. Prisoners were still required to clean their wards, but beyond this, they were not forced to labour. They might work voluntarily, as in pre-reform prisons, but administrators neither set aside designated spaces for labour nor provided tools – hardly an encouragement to labour. Authorities claimed that prisoners rarely chose to work.[64] Unless condemned to death, prisoners were not required to attend divine service.[65] Indeed, some prisons did not hold religious services at all. The Borough Compter, for example, lacked a chapel and a chaplain until the late 1810s.[66] Typically, gaol chaplains played limited roles. Newgate's Ordinary, for instance, never visited privately with inmates, leading a parliamentary committee in 1813–14 to conclude that he "knows nothing of the state of the morals in the Prison." This was appropriate, the Ordinary explained, because Newgate mainly served as a detention centre. "If," he noted, Newgate "was a house calculated for reformation and so on, it might be different."[67]

The conviviality and intemperateness of prison life survived the reform period. Despite the passage of legislation aimed at cracking down on the "disorderly" environment, prisoners generally were allowed to spend their days gaming, gambling, socializing, and drinking, with only minor changes.[68] In 1784 an act was passed which banned gaolers and other officers from selling or having an interest in the sale of alcohol. Although keepers lost their incentive to encourage drinking, inmates continued to acquire alcohol and the prison taps remained open. Indeed, in the City, the taps served as important centres for the City's nightlife.[69] At Newgate, the prisoners formed a drinking society, the "Free and Easy Club," which organized regular parties that included live music, dancing, singing, and a free-flowing supply of beer and spirits to which visitors flocked. City authorities banned visitors from such gatherings in 1808, but the inmates continued without them.[70] Further regulations were introduced in the 1810s to somewhat curb alcohol consumption. The Newgate keeper in 1813 ordered that prisoners could have only one quart of beer or one bottle of wine in their possession at once; that alcohol not be admitted into the prison after 8pm; and that habitual drinking (tippling) be banned.[71] Yet, the amount of alcohol that a prisoner could receive each day was not limited. So long as inmates followed the above restrictions, they were free to send out for or receive from visitors unlimited quantities of beer, porter, and wine. Finally, although prisoners were not supposed to get drunk, prison officers generally did not punish inmates who did.[72]

Reformed gaols and compters may have had higher walls and fewer windows, but they remained accessible to the local community. At Newgate, visitors were "indiscriminately admitted" from 9am until 9pm, while the Southwark gaol was open to visitors from 9am until 6pm. Visitors to male, but not female, prisoners could enter the gaol's main wards, and their visits were not closely supervised.[73] To some extent, relaxed visiting hours were necessary. Prisoners preparing for trial might need to meet with lawyers, friends, and character witnesses, while debtors needed to liaise with creditors and others to sort out their affairs.[74] Additionally, since inmates remained responsible for supplying most of their provisions, they relied on the openness of prisons to receive goods from visiting friends and family and to purchase provisions from outside vendors. The comparatively loose security meant prisoners continued to acquire spirits and other illicit goods fairly easily despite parliamentary and local restrictions. Prisoners at the Borough Compter, for example, formed an alliance with various local pubs, and in one ruse, serving girls smuggled in gin for prisoners under the cover of collecting their beer pots.[75]

The lax regulations at gaols and compters might also benefit wealthy inmates confined for punishment. When William Cobbett, the radical writer and publisher, was imprisoned in Newgate in 1810 following his conviction for seditious libel, he paid twelve guineas weekly to rent rooms at the top of the governor's residence, where he entertained visitors with food and refreshment from midday to 10pm; his family was allowed to stay overnight.[76]

At the start of the nineteenth century, gaols and compters in London were generally cleaner, healthier, larger, and more secure, but they were not more orderly. Nor were they less costly for inmates, who paid considerable amounts in fees, rent, and for provisions. Prison life in London's gaols and compters, therefore, changed only to a limited extent in this period. Such efforts as were made to shape prisoners' conduct and habits came mainly from philanthropic reformers, who started visiting the prisons regularly in the mid-1810s (see chapter 6).

Houses of Correction

As houses of correction became the primary receptacle for convicted prisoners sentenced to imprisonment, magistrates in Surrey and Middlesex and the Bridewell governors moved to transform this category of prison into proper places of punishment and sites for moral reformation. In pursuit of this goal, they devised systems of classification that drew on reformist principles of separation; they adopted separate confinement on a major scale; and they designed and introduced detailed regulations to shape the conduct of bridewell prisoners.

Classification

By the early 1780s, prisoners at London bridewells were already separated by sex, commitment type, and age; during the reform period, authorities adopted additional principles which tried to take account of an inmate's offence and personal character.

The Middlesex system, devised in the 1780s, was the most extensive. Male and female prisoners were divided into four classes each. The first class was composed of convicted felons and atrocious offenders; the second of "petty convicts," those convicted of "lesser" offences in and out of the sessions; the third of prisoners committed to await trial and to give evidence; and the fourth of all other petty offenders, described in one source as "persons committed for Assaults, for acts of Vagrancy Etc."[77] In addition, the prison committee requested the governor endeavour to separate "apprentices from criminals, and boys from old offenders" and to keep "those committed for a first offence, or a crime of lighter description, from those who are become inveterate in evil habits."[78] In other words, they endeavoured to separate prisoners by age and criminal experience as well as by offence and commitment type. Over the years the magistrates added more divisions. By 1802, the miscellaneous fourth class had been divided into two classes, one exclusively for vagrants and another for disorderly apprentices and evidences.[79] After 1808, children imprisoned alongside their parents were kept apart from them in special apartments.[80]

The Surrey justices, devising a new code of classification in 1801, likewise looked to separate prisoners by sex, offence, criminal experience, and age. However, they applied such divisions only to male prisoners.[81] Female prisoners were treated as an afterthought with all placed together – a particularly surprising decision given that most urban bridewells in the eighteenth century were either dominated by women or more equally split between the sexes.[82]

Classification was less elaborate at Bridewell, probably due to its less diverse population. Male and female inmates were classified as either "prisoners" or "vagrants." "Prisoners" were summary convicts imprisoned for punishment, whereas "vagrants" were imprisoned to be passed back to their place of settlement. These groups were kept totally separate from one another. Within these classifications, certain kinds of prisoner – notably, apprentices and *Lottery Act* vagrants – were isolated from the others.[83]

In principle at least, classification on the basis of purchasing power was rejected. None of the London bridewells were divided into master and common sides, and some institutions explicitly articulated this principle in new regulations. Middlesex's 1802 rules, for example, prescribed that the governor "shall allow no distinction to be made, either in lodging or diet, between the wealthy and indigent prisoners."[84] In practice, however, prison committees and prison keepers made fairly regular exceptions, allowing certain prisoners to purchase superior accommodation and privileges. At Coldbath Fields, for example, a rule had developed by 1800 which permitted inmates convicted of misdemeanours to pay to stay in nicer rooms. So, when a royal commission visited that year, they found one misdemeanant occupying a "commodious sitting room, and a neat Bed Room with in it"; he had a fellow prisoner to wait on him; and he was allowed to procure as much liquor as he desired.[85]

Cellular Confinement

All London bridewells adopted cellular confinement. The Bridewell governors had investigated the possibility of confining prisoners in single cells as early as October 1775, and over the years, they had continued, periodically, to debate the benefit of cells. Concerns about cost had repeatedly stymied change – until 1792, when the governors ordered the prison rebuilt.[86] "All prisoners who are sent to this Hospital for punishment," they declared, "ought to be kept in solitary confinement and a reasonable portion of work assigned them to perform every day." Female prisoners moved into their new accommodation in 1795,

Figure 4.5 · Bridewell's pass room for vagrants.

Table 4.5 Plan for cells and wards, Coldbath Fields

	Single cells		Communal wards	
	Male	Female	Male	Female
1st Class: "Convict" Felons	26	32	—	—
2nd Class: "Petty Convicts"	56	52	—	—
3rd Class: Prisoners for Trial or Evidence	12 or 18	18	—	—
4th Class: Miscellaneous Petty Offenders	32	15	76	43

Source: "Repair committee," LMA, MA/G/GEN/0032; "Plans, elevations and sections of house of correction," LMA, MJ/SP/1786/02; "Report from committee appointed to inspect plans," *LL*, LMSMPS508070086–LMSMPS5080700867.

and the men moved at the end of 1797.[87] Not all inmates were held in cells. Vagrants, those imprisoned in order to be passed, were still accommodated by day and night in large, communal wards (figure 4.5). When, in the 1740s, Parliament legislated that vagrants must be passed via bridewells, they surely had intended to make this process more penal, but over time, the confinement of these vagrants in bridewells morphed self-consciously into a matter of simply holding people, as the case of Bridewell highlights.

In Surrey, all inmates slept in separate cells, but during the day, they associated in classes – though in practice class divisions were only irregularly maintained.[88] In Middlesex, the degree to which inmates were kept separate varied by classification. At night, the first three classes slept separately in cells, but the fourth class slept in communal wards (table 4.5). Separation during the day was linked to conviction status and offence type. The magistrates hoped to keep those sentenced to imprisonment separate as much as possible, so they directed that these prisoners work in their cells and be released for only a handful of hours each day: to wash, eat, exercise, and attend divine service. These activities were carried out in the company of their classmates.[89]

The rules on separation were more relaxed for other inmates. Those held for trial were released from their cells during the day and mixed with members of their class in designated wards and courtyards.[90] Debtors and pass vagrants lived and slept in communal wards.[91] Yet, some unconvicted prisoners suffered the same conditions as the convicted because the bench had not planned for their confinement. Prisoners for re-examination were restricted to their sleeping cells because the bench had not allocated a yard or dayroom to them, and judged it inappropriate for such inmates to associate freely with others.[92]

There were several important exceptions to this general system of separate confinement. First, some forms of labour could not be done alone or in a cell, so certain prisoners worked outside them. For example, some women were employed in the washhouse and the laundry, while some men, mainly convicted offenders, were employed in manufacturing shops as carpenters, tailors, turners, shoemakers, and sawyers.[93] In December 1798, the Middlesex governor reported that, on average, forty male prisoners were released daily from close confinement to work, and that they were constantly supervised by three prison servants.[94] Second, prisoners worked by task, and once they finished their tasks, they were released from their cells, "at liberty to be in Society with each other."[95] Consequently those who were physically and mentally able to work quickly spent more time outside their cells. Finally, the rules on separate confinement were significantly relaxed during the winter months. As no provision had been made for warming the cells, all inmates were, by turns, given access to rooms with fires during the day to keep warm.[96] There were only ten or twelve rooms in the prison equipped with fireplaces, so male prisoners gathered in groups of about fifteen while all women shared one room. With more prisoner classes than fires, some prisoners were removed "from their own to another class, to receive the benefit of the fire."[97]

In spite, then, of the enthusiasm expressed by some reformers, including certain London magistrates, for solitary imprisonment, most inmates in London bridewells were held in some degree of association. Night-time solitary confinement was popular, especially for inmates convicted of criminal offences, but day-time confinement to cells was often deemed impracticable.

Regulating and Organizing Prison Life

At the bridewells, new rules aimed to transform the habits and moral character of prisoners by attempting to control, to varying degrees, their every action and interaction. Prisoners in Coldbath Fields were the most intensely surveilled. Every hour of every day was scheduled: "the first Bell shall be rung at six

Table 4.6 Daily routine at Coldbath Fields, c. 1820–23

Time	Activity
6:30 to 7:00	Prisoners unlocked, washing, etc.
7:00 to 8:30	Prisoners commence oakum picking and various other works
8:30 to 9:15	Breakfast
9:15 to 10:15	Divine Service
10:15 to 14:00	Picking oakum and various other works
14:00 to 15:00	Dinner
15:00 to 17:00	Work and exercise
17:00 to 17:30	Giving in work
17:30 to 18:00	Supper
18:00	Locking up for the night
Note	Each boy attends school for at least an hour each day

Source: LMA, MA/G/GEN/0589. Dated to 1820–23. Clearly drawn up before the treadwheel was introduced.

o'clock from Lady Day to Michaelmas Day, at seven o'clock during Winter half year: in half an hour the second Bell shall be rung, and the Prisoners of the first and second class shall singly be conducted to the cisterns to wash …"[98] And on it went. By comparison, the regulations for Southwark and City bridewells provided more of a general outline for prisoners' days rather than a regimented timetable.

Everywhere, prisoners' days revolved around work and religion, regardless of whether the inmate was committed to labour or not.[99] Authorities adopted different methods for managing labour. The Surrey magistrates appointed a superintendent and contractor to oversee work.[100] At Bridewell, prison labour was presided over by a taskmaster and hemp-dresser between the 1770s and 1792, and afterwards by a superintendent and his wife.[101] In Middlesex, justices initially appointed a taskmaster to direct and supervise labour, but in 1796, after deciding that an insufficient amount had been done under his supervision, the justices dismissed the taskmaster and instructed the governor to assume his responsibilities.[102] Many inmates worked by task: at Southwark, for instance, men were expected to pick 22lbs of oakum a day and women 18lbs.[103] Prisoners were entitled to keep varying portions of their earnings. Generally, those committed to hard labour could receive, at most, one-third of their earnings, given to them on their leaving prison, while prisoners not committed to hard labour were given half. Governors were also allowed to keep a portion, usually one-third of net earnings, as "stimulus to his activity and reward for his attention."[104] In addition, prison committees typically ordered that prisoners on their discharge be given at least a few shillings, and some who were deemed particularly needy or deserving were given items such as shoes and shirts.[105]

Religion was central to efforts to reclaim criminal offenders, so other hours were occupied by prayer and religious instruction. As the Middlesex magistrates emphasized, "much of our Hopes of the Prisoners Reformation will depend on the Chaplain's zealous and conscientious, as well as prudent Discharge of his Duty."[106] At each bridewell, the chaplain preached at least one sermon on Sundays and holidays, and prisoners were excused from work to attend. Twice weekly, chaplains additionally read prayers to the prisoners; they occasionally delivered "short but affectionate" exhortations to prisoners to "consider their Situation and to form Resolutions of Amendment"; and they instructed (or appointed someone else to instruct) prisoners in the catechism.[107] Magistrates supplied prisoners with books of moral and religious instruction for private study.

Some bridewells also provided a more secular education. The chaplain at Coldbath Fields reported in 1796 that he sometimes taught young prisoners reading and writing "as he sees necessary."[108] Indeed, authorities' primary concern in this regard lay with the young. A school was set up at Coldbath Fields from at least January 1808, when a report noted that children were making "great" progress in their learning.[109] In 1816, the visiting magistrates noted that a "great alteration in [boys'] behaviour has taken place for the better" and recommended that boys be required to pick less oakum so they could dedicate more time to school.[110]

Magistrates placed considerable emphasis on the conduct of inmates. In a preface to the Middlesex rules, written in 1794, the magistrates warned that "the good effects of solitary confinement will be prevented if the prisoners are not restrained from talking aloud, singing indecent songs, uttering oaths, blasphemes and improvocations – which divert or disturb other prisoners from the reformation that is wished for."[111] At all London bridewells, conversation between prisoners was discouraged, profane swearing was forbidden, and games and pastimes were banned.[112] Additional servants were hired to enforce the new codes of conduct, and inmates who broke the rules were punished.[113] At the City Bridewell, those who behaved in "a riotous or disorderly manner" or were adjudged "guilty of any indecent or filthy behaviour" could be put in the stocks and given a reduced allowance, and, if the misbehaviour continued, whipped.[114] At Middlesex, inmates were ominously warned that any "refractory and obstinate conduct" would be "opposed by adequate punishments, until subdued."[115]

Many magistrates also targeted inmates' drinking habits. Parliament had banned spiritous liquors from all prisons in the 1780s, but at bridewells, local administrators imposed additional restrictions. By the end of the century, Surrey and Middlesex justices had prohibited most of their prisoners from receiving or purchasing beer, porter, or wine.[116] Conversely, the City Bridewell allowed all prisoners three pints of small beer as part of their daily allowance.[117] Yet, even in Middlesex and Surrey, there were several exemptions to the general ban. Debtors and state prisoners were still allowed to order beer and wine from local taverns, and the surgeon could order beer or wine for sick or aged prisoners. Additionally, in Middlesex, the keeper gave a strong pint of beer a day to convicted prisoners who worked at either particularly onerous trades, such as in the laundry, or skilled trades, such as in the prison's manufacturing shops.[118] Alcohol, then, was generally disallowed for prisoners incarcerated for punishment, but exceptions were made, especially to reward good conduct.

Finally, administrators placed restrictions on the ability of prisoners to see their friends. From December 1782, Bridewell prisoners could receive visitors only at 8–9am and 12–1pm; they were allowed one visitor a day; the visit was restricted to half an hour; and it was supervised by a prison officer.[119] At Southwark, visitors were required to speak to prisoners through a railing and in the presence of a turnkey.[120] Boundaries were even more tightly policed in Middlesex. The bridewell's rules specified that inmates could not receive any visitors, unless the committing or visiting magistrates provided written approval. Visitors with such an order could visit inmates daily, but only between 12pm and 2pm, and they were newly banned from the bridewell's interior wards.[121] In spite of this apparent strictness, however, visitors came in great numbers, suggesting that either the requirement for an order was ignored or orders were easily obtained. Finally, in an attempt to crack down on contraband, officers were supposed to search all parcels brought for prisoners, though they were usually too busy.[122]

Magistrates in Middlesex also seem to have contemplated further restrictions on visiting rights in an attempt to intensify the "pains" of imprisonment: banning inmates from obtaining any food and provision beyond the county allowance. In the short term, this policy was dropped to reduce prison expenditure, but in the longer term its impact was considerable.[123] Namely, from this point onwards, magistrates insisted that the ability of inmates to receive extra provisions was a privilege, not a right.[124]

While Middlesex authorities periodically contemplated a more serious attack on traditional inmate privileges in their quest to punish and reform criminal offenders, City authorities were less interested in fighting such a battle. At Giltspur house of correction, for example, opened in 1815, City governors allowed inmates to freely receive visitors and food brought in by friends, practices a parliamentary committee deemed "perhaps ... too much indulgence" for a correctional establishment.[125]

III. IMPROVING THE QUALITY AND ACCOUNTABILITY OF ADMINISTRATION

Finally, the degree to which authorities moved to adopt reformist ideas on prison administration differed by jurisdiction and prison type. In the City and Middlesex, magistrates did not embrace administrative reform at their gaols and compters, but they did at houses of correction. Such moves reflect the greater interest these authorities generally took in bridewells and their larger sense of responsibility for convicted, as opposed to unconvicted, inmates. Yet in Surrey, where reform ideas so often made greater headway, the magistrates introduced new methods of administration into the gaol and house of correction equally.

In the City and Middlesex, gaols and compters remained semi-private institutions where the nature of office-holding did not greatly change. The salaries paid to certain prison officers increased, but the raises were not intended to replace income from prisoner fees and other emoluments, which continued to account for the majority of officers' incomes. In the 1810s, for example, when the Newgate keeper received £450 annually in salary from City authorities, he took in between £600 and £1,000 from prisoner fees and rents yearly.[126] Primarily, keepers' salaries were raised to compensate them for the substantial losses they sustained in being deprived of the profit from prison taps.[127] Only in Surrey did magistrates tie the provision of a county salary to the discontinuance of taking fees from criminal prisoners.[128]

Magistrates could have shouldered more financial responsibility for gaols by using the county rate to fund salaries for all prison officers, but they opted against this.[129] With the keeper still primarily responsible for hiring and paying salaries to his staff, the logic of prisoner fees remained. As the Poultry keeper pointed out in 1814, if he were barred from taking fees from prisoners, his salary would be inadequate to support the running of the prison.[130] Servants likewise depended mainly on fees and emoluments for their income. In 1815, when each Newgate turnkey received an annual salary of £27.6*s*.9*d*., each also received £100 from fees and for admitting strangers into visiting rooms; other emoluments added an extra £93.14*s*. yearly.[131] While these gaols and compters continued to be run for the profit of their officers, at bridewells, officers were banned from taking fees or accepting gratuities from inmates. In lieu of such proceeds, they either were given salaries or saw their salaries raised.[132]

We have seen how London authorities uniformly drew up detailed, written regulations for the government of their bridewells. These rules touched not only on the behaviour of inmates, but also on prison staff. The effect was to limit the autonomy previously enjoyed by prison officers by clarifying their obligations and making them accountable to justices if they failed to fulfil their specified duties. These rules, the Middlesex justices stressed, should be considered "as peremptory and as superseding all discretionary power in the Governor."[133] In Surrey, the magistrates followed the advice of prison reformers and the provisions of recent gaol legislation by establishing rules to manage their gaol, as well as their bridewell, both of which stated the duties of each officer precisely.[134] Surrey authorities apparently saw some benefit to providing clear guidance to all prison officers, regardless of the prison in which they worked. City and Middlesex authorities, by contrast, did not bother to draw up new rules for their custodial prisons. In this, they again showed themselves to be less concerned with and responsible for the operation of gaols and compters.

Within very broad guidelines, keepers and their inferior officers were left to determine how to run the institutions. This lack of guidance increasingly frustrated keepers and sheriffs, especially as the duties of prison management became more onerous with swelling inmate populations and greater public scrutiny. In 1797, for example, the London sheriff lamented the "want of rules and orders, system and method … with regard to the economy and management of

Newgate," while in 1813, John Addison Newman, who had served variously as the keeper of Ludgate, Giltspur, and Newgate, alerted City authorities to the "real need for specific, detailed regulations" to govern the prisons.[135] Nonetheless, such calls were ignored until Parliament intervened in the mid-1810s (see chapter 6). As a general rule, officers took the least confrontational and least onerous path: specifically, they left prisoners to organize their affairs themselves. Inmates continued to manage and distribute charity money; to collect garnish or ward dues to pay for communal services; and to hold positions of authority, including acting as surgeons' assistants, as chaplains' clerks, or as wardsmen, tasked with supervising and reporting on the activities of other inmates.[136]

The establishment or expansion of written prison rules was an important step in the transformation of prisons from semi-private to public institutions. Another important step was the development of inspection systems. Parliament, following Howard, favoured the appointment of visiting justices who would supervise prison operation. This principle was embedded in the 1779 *Penitentiary Act,* and such a system was explicitly called for in houses of correction and latterly in gaols by legislation passed in 1782 and 1784 respectively.[137] London justices typically adapted these models to suit their own needs, but as a whole, these authorities, to varying degrees, became more attentive in supervising their prisons, especially their bridewells.

The Middlesex magistrates and the Bridewell governors developed the most extensive arrangements. The former experimented with appointing visiting justices to supervise their prisons first in 1781 and again in 1794, but primarily they relied on committees of magistrates.[138] In 1796, the bench established a permanent prison committee, which met at least sixteen times a year. In the 1790s, the justices founded a subcommittee to supervise prison operation more closely, and in 1809, they additionally appointed two visiting justices.[139] These various committees dealt primarily with bridewell issues, held their meetings at the bridewell, and only occasionally visited the gaol.[140] The Bridewell governors established a permanent prison committee even earlier, in 1775. It was composed of twelve men who met monthly to "inspect and regulate all matters appertaining to the prisons and prisoners."[141] In 1792, they founded a prison subcommittee who met weekly at the prison.[142] Elsewhere in the City magistrates took on a looser supervisory role with inspections less frequent. The City neither appointed visiting magistrates nor established a permanent prison committee, but rather continued to set up temporary committees to investigate and resolve issues relating to their gaols and compters as they arose.[143] Only the Surrey justices made an effort to treat their prisons similarly: from 1799, they resolved to appoint at each quarter sessions two visiting magistrates to visit, inspect, and report on both their gaol and their house of correction.[144]

The adoption of administrative reforms at London's houses of correction and at Surrey's gaol brought these prisons into close alignment with the model sketched out by reformers such as Howard. By the end of the eighteenth century, these prisons were run by salaried officers, whose duties were clearly set out for them; the prisons were financed completely by the county bench; and their operation was closely supervised by magistrates. As a whole, these reforms targeted the discretionary power of prison officers and of inmates. To a certain extent, they substituted a rules-based system of management for the customary one based on discretion. Yet, in another sense, they simply replaced one system of discretionary management for another. Specifically, the new policies set up magistrates as the managers and ultimate arbitrators of prison practice. Visiting magistrates and magistrates on prison committees decided how inmates should be classified, set to work, dieted, accommodated, taught, and so on, often tweaking, bending, or outright contravening the written rules, and even parliamentary statute, in the process. Conversely, gaols and compters in the City and Middlesex continued to be run for the profit of the officers; they were funded only in part by local authorities; and they were supervised by magistrates in a haphazard fashion, as before.

IV. CODA: PRESUMING INNOCENCE

Together, the last four chapters have traced how, over the course of the eighteenth century, London magistrates came increasingly to believe that tried and untried prisoners should be kept apart and treated differently. In recognition of this, magistrates began to create – or perhaps we should more accurately say re-create – a more specialized prison system, where prisons were treated as either custodial or punitive. At the end of the century, when they moved to reform their prisons, the magistrates tailored the programmes to take account of the distinctions between pre-trial and post-conviction incarceration. Before we consider how this prison system evolved in the nineteenth century, we must first reflect on why London magistrates pursued these policies.

The decision to totally separate prisoners sentenced to imprisonment as a punishment from prisoners held temporarily in confinement presupposes an acknowledgment that these categories of prisoner are materially different. It further suggests a recognition of the presumption of innocence for those not convicted by a court and an unwillingness to act beyond what the law has ordered. The assumption that the accused are innocent until proven otherwise has ancient roots, yet until the very end of the eighteenth century, such a standard of proof was not in operation at London's trial courts.[145] Instead, as Beattie has stressed, it was the accused who had to prove an accusation false. The burden of proof slowly began to shift from defendant to prosecution at the end of the century with the transformation of judicial practice, especially the rise of the adversarial criminal trial. Early-eighteenth-century prosecutorial developments, such as the reward and crown witness systems, quite obviously disadvantaged the accused and heightened concerns over false accusations, perjury, and mistaken conviction. In response, Langbein has argued, judges initiated a series of changes, including the general allowing of defence counsel and the development of laws of evidence, which as a whole provided greater safeguards to criminal defendants.[146]

Greater sensitivity to and concern over treatment of criminal defendants impacted how contemporaries thought about the rights of the accused and the purposes and conditions of pre-trial detention. From the 1780s, various local officials in England voiced with greater regularity and clarity the view that pre-trial detention should be separate and different from punitive confinement in recognition of the accused's legal status. A Gloucester grand jury in 1783 proclaimed it "inconsistent with the humanity and wise discrimination of the spirit of the laws, that the unfortunate should share a common fate with the infamous, or that the barely accused should without distinction, be classed with the convicted prisoners."[147] Meanwhile, in Edinburgh, the Lord Provost and the Deputy Sheriff authored a pamphlet in 1782 which defined a jail for unconvicted prisoners as "nothing more than a temporary habitation, where the prisoner is to be confined, in the first instance, till his guilt or innocence shall be legally investigated; and, during that confinement, he ought to be denied no comfort that can be afforded him, consistent with good morals, decency, and the detention of his person."[148] These ideas, as the grand jury address quoted above makes especially clear, were part and parcel of a wider movement to reform the criminal law along 'enlightened' principles. As is well known, this period saw a concerted push to diversify the range of punishments available to the courts so that punishments could be proportioned to the specific offences charged. Such proposals were driven by fears regarding the pernicious effects of punishing various categories of offence, from petty theft to murder, the same. Such a penal system was not only unjust and irrational, but it "levels all distinctions of guilty, enervates the arm of justice, and in its consequences tends to multiply capital offences among the mass of mankind."[149] Similar concerns motivated attempts to distinguish pre-trial and post-conviction incarceration.

But what conditions should distinguish these two forms of confinement? We traced in chapters 2 and 3 how various elites, within and without the government, became convinced at the end of the century that imprisonment for punishment should entail coerced labour. As chapter 4 stressed, the men responsible for prisons in a given locality, usually magistrates, went to great lengths to adapt their prisons so that every inmate confined for punishment could be put to work. Other widely accepted features of punitive confinement included cellular confinement, at least for part of the day, and mandatory religious instruction.

Less attention was paid to those held in prison for safe custody, but generally, most agreed that such inmates should be treated more leniently than those sentenced to imprisonment as a punishment. G.O. Paul, for instance, contended that "DEBTORS, and the UNCONVICTED, should doubtless, be allowed to employ the Gratuity of Friends, or the Wages of their own Industry, to make Life more comfortable; but under such Restrictions, as the good Government of the Prison renders indispensable."[150] The nineteenth-century prison reformer Thomas Buxton emphasized that because those accused of crimes were "innocent in the eye of the law till their guilt is proved," their confinement was "not imposed as a penalty, it is merely permitted as the only method of insuring the appearance of the person suspected, on the day of the trial"; consequently, "no principle of justice can defend the infliction of any severities on the unconvicted."[151] In short, the presumed innocence of the accused justified, and indeed necessitated, that prisoners held for custodial purposes be kept apart from prisoners held after conviction and that their treatment be less severe or coercive. Official government policy on prisons in the 1830s took the same line. Describing "confinement of an innocent person (for in such a light must a prisoner awaiting trial be regarded)" as a "legal anomaly," the Prison

Inspectors for the Home District insisted it was irrational and unjust to subject such inmates to the "discomfort and privations to which the law sentences" those imprisoned for punishment.[152] Some commentators went further and claimed such punitive treatment of the detained was illegal: "previous to trial, the same degree of rigorous treatment which might afterwards be both lawful and salutary, would before the prisoner is proved to be guilty, be both unlawful and unjust ... the prison to this class of its inhabitants is a place of detention only and not of coercion or punishment."[153]

What constituted a "coercive" or punitive measure was up for debate. Jonas Hanway, writing in 1775, argued that, because the accused were innocent until proven guilty, they should be held in separate confinement while incarcerated: "Can any man of common sense say, it is not a punishment to a man of the least sentiment, to be conducted to a prison, and there compelled to associate with the most atrocious offenders? I will be bold to say, this is a cruel and unjust procedure."[154] The Bridewell governor Thomas Bowdler came to a similar conclusion after touring English gaols in the 1790s: "let the society reflect, that several of these men may be, and some probably are, innocent; and that if any of this description, or any penitent malefactor, is disposed to think seriously, he is obliged constantly to hear the blasphemous conversation of others of a different disposition."[155] Holding such low opinions of the character of convicted prisoners and so concerned with the "contamination" of guilty offenders, these men came to see associated confinement as a punishment. On similar grounds, some reformers argued that custodial inmates should be allowed and indeed encouraged to work: "you have no right to debar him from the craft on which his family depends ... no right to ruin his habits, by compelling him to be idle."[156] Similarly, when the Prison Inspectorate called for untried inmates to be held in separate confinement and for them to be subjected to greater supervision, instruction, occupation, and restraint in their pastimes, the men argued that authorities had a duty to protect the morals, feelings, and character of untried inmates; such were the real "rights to which every untried prisoner has an inalienable claim."[157] As these comments underline, the debate over the appropriate and legal treatment of prisoners in the early nineteenth century was explicitly fought in terms of prisoner rights.

When explaining their new specialized policies, most London authorities initially did not make such broad ideological or legal arguments. Instead, they highlighted the practical difficulties they faced in using one institution for both custodial and punitive purposes. In April 1796, for example, the Middlesex prison committee recommended that the bench issue an order advising magistrates not to send untried prisoners to the house of correction on account of "such persons being seldom employed and generally conducting themselves (chiefly because they are idle) in a disorderly manner."[158] The different expectations for and rules governing custodial and punitive prisoners made it highly inconvenient for prison managers to hold the tried and untried together, but there was nothing inherently wrong or illegal in using the bridewell for custodial purposes. As a magisterial committee found in 1799, Coldbath Fields was "well adapted for the purposes of its institution as a house of correction, as well as for those of close and separate confinement and safe custody."[159]

Opinion in London began to shift in the face of prisoner protest. The claims and actions of "state prisoners," individuals charged by the government with crimes against the state who were confined in London prisons in sizable numbers during the French and Napoleonic Revolutionary Wars, were especially influential in shaping magisterial policy. State prisoners vociferously protested their confinement and the severity of conditions that they were forced to endure. These inmates made a nuisance of themselves within prisons: at Coldbath Fields, they disrupted divine service, regularly called on the magistrates to complain, hatched escape plans, and tried to incite a "riot" among the prisoners, amongst other things.[160]

The prisoners' actions prompted magistrates on the prison committee to step up their opposition to using the bridewell as a site of safe custody and to harden their commitment to specialization. In May 1798, a committee stressed that "the Practice of sending State Prisoners, previously to their Trial, to the House of Correction, was found to be very detrimental, and to break in upon the System established for the Management of that Prison." Detaining pretrial prisoners, they later complained, "greatly disturbs the Tranquillity of the Prison, and opens the Door to Irregularities unknown in the ordinary Management of it."[161] At this point, tranquillity, system, and management remained at the forefront of magistrates' minds, but this began to change after state prisoners went public with their complaints. Some inmates had powerful allies in the press and in Parliament, one of whom, Sir Francis Burdett, made a crusade against Coldbath Fields, "the English Bastille," and its magisterial administrators central to his campaign for election to Parliament. Widely circulated rumors of "inhumane cruelty" and illegal restraint forced the government to appoint a royal commission to investigate the prison's operation, a relatively unusual and intrusive step.[162]

It was in this context that London authorities, hypersensitive to attacks on their character and conduct, started to make broad statements about the injustice of conflating pre-trial and post-conviction incarceration. In December 1799 the bench issued an order emphasizing that regulations at houses of correction, which had "the punishment of prisoners solely in view," subjected non-convicts to "a coercive discipline contrary to the ancient usage of prisoners."[163] Their commitment to this idea was closely related to their desire to get state prisoners removed from their house of correction, as the magistrates blamed them for ruining their reputations and making them a target of "public odium."[164] Still, the royal commission investigating alleged abuse at Coldbath Fields came to a similar conclusion regarding pre-trial detention in bridewells. They found that custodial prisoners were "pressed by the severity of the established discipline and accommodation," constituting an "Excess of Punishment which ought to be alleviated."[165] Such views were expressed more widely in London in the nineteenth century. The Giltspur keeper, for example, when asked by the City aldermen to prepare a list of possible rules for his prison in 1815, reminded them that different rules were needed to govern pre-trial as opposed to convict prisoners. Compter prisoners, "consisting principally of persons before trial," he stressed, "ought not to be subject to the strict regulations which persons [are] liable to who have been convicted."[166]

The conclusions that London magistrates came to regarding the appropriate conditions of confinement for non-convict prisoners differed starkly from that of the more zealous reformers within and outside government. While the latter viewed associated confinement, lack of discipline, absence of labour, and want of religious instruction as harmful and intolerably punitive measures for non-convict prisoners, the London magistrates instead saw separate confinement, forced labour, mandatory religious instruction, and bans on visitors and additional provisions as the punishments. Such measures, they contended, were appropriate only for convicted offenders or those who broke prison rules. The developing views on a prisoner's guilt and on the distinctions between custodial and punitive confinement impacted not only prison commitment practice, but also local authorities' approach to prison reform.

In 1811, the parliamentary committee on penitentiary houses painted a very unflattering picture of Newgate, with its porous boundaries, loose regulations, and profit-driven structure. "It is obvious," they proclaimed, "that the reformation of offenders is not to be looked for in a place of confinement conducted upon the plan here described."[167] City authorities would probably have agreed. They never set out to turn Newgate, in their view primarily a site of detention, into a prison for the "reformation of offenders." Its regulations, architecture, and administration reflected this. The same was true at other sites of detention, namely gaols and compters, in London. As a consequence of the reform movement, these prisons became ever more distinct from houses of correction, with authorities increasingly deeming it inappropriate for committing bodies to treat the prisons interchangeably.

CHAPTER FIVE

The Rise of Imprisonment, 1815–50

If courts and magistrates were not totally convinced by imprisonment in the eighteenth century, by the nineteenth, there seem to have been few doubts concerning its usefulness. In London, growth in prison commitments was slow or stagnant in the first decade of the century, when England was at war with France and its allies, but the numbers ballooned after the conclusion of the Napoleonic Wars in 1815. While it was normal for criminal prosecutions to rise after wars ended, prison commitments in London continued growing even after the post-war boom, reaching unprecedented numbers.[1]

Commitments to Middlesex's two prisons reached their peak in 1832, with 20,325 people committed in total, and declined thereafter, especially after 1834. Strikingly, the decline occurred as the county's population grew. In the City, commitments continued to rise through the 1830s, and in the case of Southwark, the 1840s. These jurisdictions also saw population growth.[2] The City's population actually fell between 1801 and 1811, and again between 1821 and 1831, but it rose between the 1830s and 1850s. Meanwhile in Southwark, the population grew steadily from the start of the nineteenth century and expanded considerably between 1841 and 1851 (table 5.1).

Neither changes in population size nor the alternation of peace and war can entirely explain the shifts that took place in prison commitment practice. It was not simply that many more people were being imprisoned; prisons were also being used in different ways. In particular, forms of imprisonment that were employed commonly in the eighteenth century were used with less frequency in the nineteenth, and conversely, forms employed irregularly in the

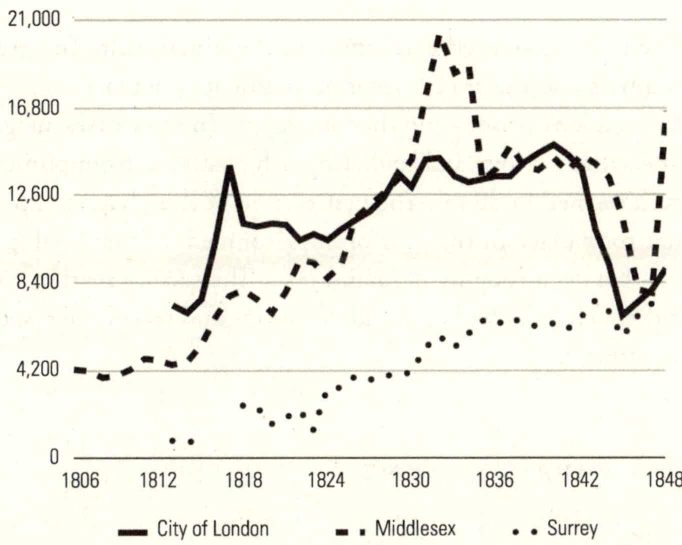

Figure 5.1 · London prison commitments, 1806–48. Note: City of London includes Borough Compter, Poultry, Giltspur, Whitecross, Bridewell, and Newgate. Surrey includes Surrey gaol, Southwark bridewell, and Brixton; Middlesex includes New Prison and Coldbath Fields. Middlesex's New Prison closed for reconstruction in 1846–47 which is partly why commitments in those years were so low.

Table 5.1 London populations, 1801–51

	Middlesex	Westminster	City within walls	City without walls	Southwark
1801	535,329	153,272	75,377	54,151	67,448
1811	670,282	162,085	55,484	65,425	72,119
1821	837,012	182,085	56,174	69,260	85,905
1831	1,032,605	201,842	55,778	67,905	91,501
1841	1,227,355	222,053	54,626	70,382	98,098
1851	1,521,282	237,425	54,752	73,117	172,863

Source: "Abstract of Answers and Returns under Act for Taking Account of Population of Great Britain (Enumeration abstract), 1801–02," *PP*, vi.1 (9); *PP*, 1812, xi.1 (316); *PP*, 1822, xv.1 (502); *PP*, 1833, xxxvi.1 (149); *PP*, 1843, xxii.1 (496).

eighteenth century were used extensively in the nineteenth. The growth in prisoner numbers and the transformation of inmate populations posed new problems for London's prisons and their managers. In some cases, magistrates' efforts to specialize prisons and to distinguish custodial from punitive confinement even seemed in doubt. The first section of this chapter explores the changes that took place in the uses of imprisonment – custodial, punitive, and debtor – between roughly 1800 and 1850. The second section considers the impact these changes had on London prisons and traces the responses of London magistrates.

I. USES OF IMPRISONMENT

Custodial Imprisonment

In the nineteenth century, prisons continued to serve as detention centres for the safe custody of individuals arrested at night, suspects awaiting examination or trial, witnesses held to give evidence in trials, and convicts awaiting the execution of their sentences. Indeed, in London, the numbers annually imprisoned for custody grew significantly – an increase that was related to patterns of policing, population growth, and an increased willingness on the part of victims to take their disputes before the courts.

London had long maintained a fairly sophisticated system of policing, and in the seventeenth and eighteenth centuries, the intensity of policing expanded. The local authorities who managed London's wards and parishes not only increased the size of their forces, but also reorganized and professionalized them. In addition, new forces were set up in the latter half of the eighteenth century, including the Bow Street Runners and the officers attached to London's stipendiary magistrate offices, with support from the Home Office.[3] The pressure for reform intensified after the Napoleonic Wars ended, in the context of the usual post-war crime wave and changing governmental agendas. While the City Corporation moved to gain greater authority over the ward structures of policing, the government took steps to gain control over policing across the metropolis.[4] In 1829, these reforming efforts culminated in the passage of the *Metropolitan Police Act*, which established a centralized police force of 3,000 men under the control of the Home Secretary for the metropolitan area, excluding the City.[5] In 1839, a separate police force, under the control of the City Corporation, was established along the lines of the Metropolitan Police.[6]

Historians still debate the impact of the new, centralized forces. Some claim that the new police prompted a greater crackdown on crime and that the emphasis on crime prevention led to greater policing of suspicious persons. In short, London became more intensely policed and greater numbers were arrested. Others, however, have stressed continuity in practice and theory between the 'new' and 'old' police. The new officers did not usher in such a radical improvement in policing, while the old officers were neither as ineffective nor as corrupt as some contemporaries alleged.[7] Regardless, it is clear that the forces arrested considerable numbers of Londoners each year. Returns provided by the Metropolitan Police, for example, show that in the 1830s they detained on average 67,981 individuals each year, and in the 1840s, an average of 64,792 individuals. The City of London police forces, meanwhile, took an average 11,618 individuals into custody annually in the 1840s.[8] It seems likely that most arrests took place at night, so many of those taken into custody by these various forces were incarcerated, at least for a few hours.[9]

The impact of these changes in policing on London's prison systems was mixed. To start with, the expansion and formalization of police forces led to fewer night charges being committed to prisons. Increasingly, policing bodies took full responsibility for night charges. Suspects were brought to watchhouses, magistrates' offices, or police stations when arrested at night, as was common in the eighteenth century, but no longer were they regularly transferred to a county, borough, or city prison prior to being taken before a justice. This transition happened earliest in Middlesex, in the 1810s, but even in the City and Surrey, where night charges were still sometimes sent to prisons, this practice was becoming more unusual.[10] From the late 1830s and early 1840s, officers were explicitly instructed to confine charges only in their stationhouses or watchhouses. Consequently, the few prisons that had continued to receive some night charges, namely the Borough Compter and Giltspur Prison, received no more after September 1839 and July 1842 respectively.[11]

Despite this shift in responsibility for charges, arrest patterns nonetheless impacted prison commitments. This period saw a dramatic rise in the volume of business at summary courts and public offices, due partly to population growth but also to more proactive policing, especially in the daytime. Drew Gray found that over the course of ten months in the 1780s the justices at

Guildhall and Mansion House together dealt with around 1,294 full hearings; in 1837, at Guildhall alone, the magistrates handled cases against 4,339 individuals.[12] Caseloads grew at the public or police courts too: whereas, in 1831, the magistrates staffing these offices together dealt with 49,037 cases, by the mid-1850s, they heard around 100,000 a year.[13] As the number of cases grew, so too did the number imprisoned to await examination and trial, who generally were incarcerated in prisons.

Victims shaped incarceration patterns too. Some scholars have argued that the professionalization of policing, and of the criminal justice system more broadly, caused the erosion of England's participatory legal culture and, eventually, the disappearance of the victim as an "active participant in the prosecution process."[14] While the police did assume a growing prosecutorial role in the nineteenth century, victims remained responsible for initiating most judicial proceedings at least until 1880.[15] As a comparison between the number of cases heard by magistrates and the number taken into custody by the new police forces underscores, many of the cases tried summarily were initiated by private individuals without assistance from the police. The magistrates' growing caseloads therefore also reflect the fact that Londoners remained willing throughout the period to take their disputes before the courts.[16]

London magistrates sent large numbers of accused offenders to prison to await examination. Estimating the numbers imprisoned on this basis is complicated by the fact that surviving commitment accounts either did not distinguish types of commitment, grouped examination prisoners together with night charges, or completely excluded such prisoners. Still, it seems that thousands were imprisoned for examination each year. In Middlesex, they were sent mainly to New Prison, where in the 1830s and 1840s, on average 2,903 were annually committed.[17] In the City, they were confined in Giltspur prison. Accounts for the City are patchier than for Middlesex, but they suggest that, on average, Giltspur received about 5,458 examination and charge prisoners each year.[18] Finally, in Surrey, examination prisoners were sent exclusively to the county gaol, which on average received 950 such prisoners annually.[19]

Up to the middle of the century, it remained uncommon for those examined at London's summary courts to be sent for jury trial. In 1831, for example, when 49,037 offenders were brought to the public magistrates' courts, only 2,955 (6 per cent) were committed for trial. In 1842, the figure was 6.7 per cent (4,431 defendants).[20] Yet, as London's citizens brought more and more disputes

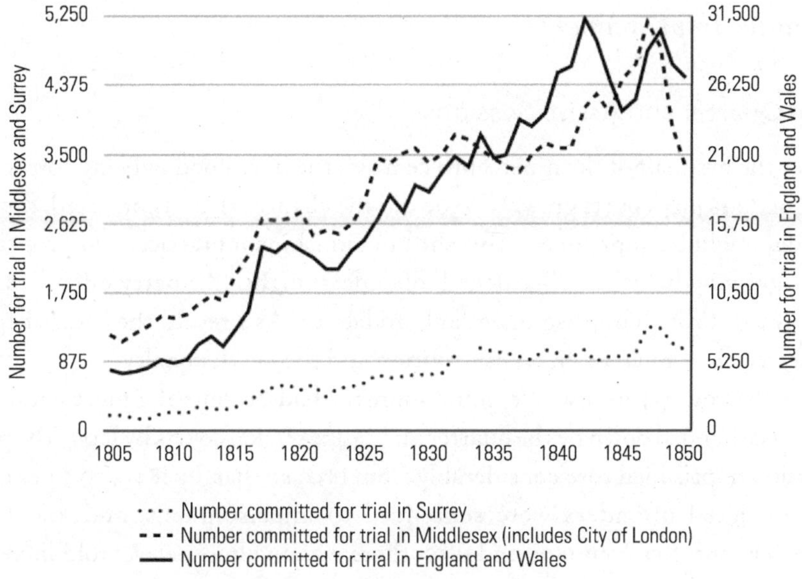

Figure 5.2 · Persons committed for trial in Surrey; Middlesex and the City; and England and Wales.

before the courts, total numbers committed for trial at the quarter and assize sessions grew dramatically. Across England and Wales, the number increased more than sixfold between 1805 and 1846, from 4,605 individuals to 30,349. This rate of growth was mirrored in Surrey, where, in 1805, 199 persons were committed for trial compared to 1,296 in 1848. Growth was slower in Middlesex and London, but there too, the number committed for trial in 1848 (4,856) was four times greater than in 1805 (1,217). The increase in prosecuted crime in London surpassed the increase in population growth. Given that most of the cases tried at the jury courts were prosecuted by victims, the rise in cases suggests that London's residents were more willing to prosecute crime than previously.[21]

Mostly, those committed for trial were imprisoned. Bail was granted only rarely in the nineteenth century, reflecting restrictions on magistrates' authority to allow bail, a traditional presumption against the process, and the need for the accused to find sureties.[22] Consequently, an increase in the numbers sent for trial also meant an increase in the numbers confined to prison.

Punitive Imprisonment

The Quarter and Assize Sessions

Over the first half of the nineteenth century, the likelihood of being convicted at London's jury courts grew.[23] So too did the chances that, if convicted, the offender might be imprisoned. This shift in punishment practices was propelled by a growing belief that 'hardened' offenders might, like petty offenders, be reformed through imprisonment at hard labour. As a result, the courts began to lessen their reliance on transportation and the death penalty.

In the country as a whole, imprisonment had become the most common sentence handed down by the quarter and assize session courts by 1805. The proportion imprisoned rose considerably from 1832, so that, by 1840, 79.5 per cent of convicted offenders were sentenced to imprisonment, and, by 1860, 85.7 per cent. Between 1805 and 1850, there was an almost elevenfold increase in the number imprisoned from 1,680 to 17,602 (figure 5.2). Practice in Surrey closely mirrored the national pattern, but in Middlesex and the City, the ascendancy of imprisonment was slower. Only from 1832 did imprisonment account for at least half of sentences handed down by the quarter and assize courts. From then, however, the proportion imprisoned rose considerably and consistently (figure 5.3).

In Middlesex and the City, doubts over the prison's efficacy as a punishment persisted into the 1830s, with the courts continuing to prefer transportation when punishing certain categories of serious offenders. The capital's attachment to transportation ensured the punishment's continued existence, despite the serious reservations that had been raised since the 1760s concerning its operation. It also set London's penal practice apart from the rest of the country.[24] The outsized reliance on transportation reflected the seriousness of crime in London and Londoners' perception of the metropolis as particularly crime-ridden.[25] Some metropolitan officials considered their offenders to be more dangerous and irredeemable than those elsewhere. "I am aware that a criminal of the metropolis is, in many respect[s], of a different character from one of any other place in the kingdom," the Middlesex magistrate G.B. Mainwaring wrote in 1819; "that he is possibly the offspring of crime, trained and disciplined in its pursuit, and that plunder is his process; and it may be said, that his reformation is impracticable."[26] Metropolitan authorities valued

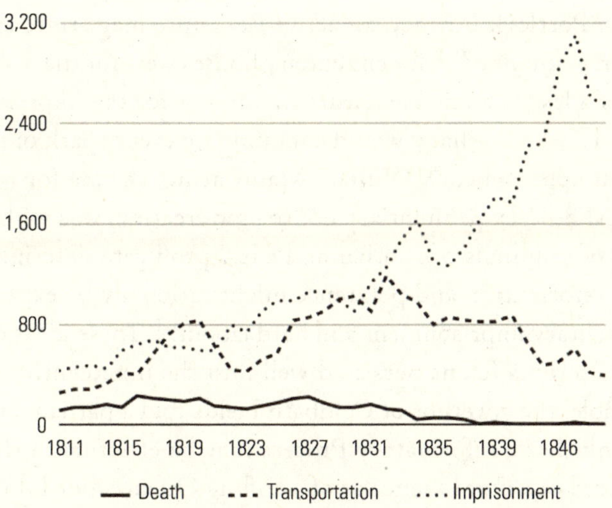

Figure 5.3 · Punishments in the City and Middlesex, 1811–50.

transportation for its perceived severity and considered it to be a greater deterrent to their supposedly inveterate criminals. The Newgate keeper, giving evidence in 1847 before a Lords committee, insisted that defendants viewed transportation as "the most severe Punishment that can be Possibly inflicted upon them, next to the full Sentence [death]."[27] "Hardened offenders," some alleged, "do not dread [prison] at all"; instead "the comfort of the Prisons, which is very great, detracts materially from the deterring Influence."[28] Terror and violence, then, remained crucial to the functioning of the criminal justice system, especially in London, which slowed the adoption of imprisonment there. As the 1847 Lords Committee on the criminal laws recognized, transportation could not be abandoned, for "no hope exists of Imprisonment being so far rendered more formidable as to supply in all respects the place of Transportation."[29]

Metropolitan authorities also questioned whether imprisonment could reform serious offenders. Many seem to have shared the view of G.O. Paul, the architect of prison reform in Gloucestershire, who opposed the general imprisonment of convicts reprieved from death and any convict who misbehaved in prison.[30] Indeed, some in the 1790s insisted that using penitentiary houses to punish serious felons was a "perversion" of the institution's purpose. One such man, Peniston Portlock Powney, an active Berkshire magistrate and MP for New Windsor, maintained that penitentiary houses were for the "confinement of offenders of a less incorrigible nature ... and not for the imprisonment of hardened felons, whose villany would contaminate every spark of remaining virtue which it approached."[31] William Mainwaring, the MP for Middlesex, agreed: "The Middlesex penitentiary house now erecting, was with a view to the reception of criminals of another and a less profligate description, upon whose minds reformation and penitence might rationally be expected to be produced by solitary imprisonment and hard labour."[32] These ideas on the imprisonment of serious felons persisted well into the nineteenth century. In 1847, for example, the governor of Coldbath Fields told a parliamentary committee, "I think that a reformatory Process may be effectual in the Case of Parties convicted of a first Offence or of a trifling Offence, but I do not think that any reformatory system will succeed with those who have adopted theft as trade."[33]

Lacking confidence in the prison's ability to deter, punish, or reform serious and hardened offenders, the metropolitan courts that handled the most serious crimes – the county assizes in Surrey and the Old Bailey (later Central Criminal Court) in London and Middlesex – continued to rely heavily on transportation, especially in periods of social, political, or economic unrest. Courts that handled less serious crimes, by contrast, embraced imprisonment earlier. In Middlesex, for example, on average 76 per cent of convicts tried at the quarter and general sessions in 1815–17 were sentenced to imprisonment, compared to 5.9 per cent transported, while in 1828, 87.5 per cent were imprisoned. Similarly, at the Southwark quarter sessions, on average 71.7 per cent of convicts were imprisoned and 16.5 per cent were transported in 1815–17.[34] Such patterns confirm that, generally, the courts did not view transportation and imprisonment as competing or opposing, but rather as complementary, punishments. Together, they ensured that the aims of deterrence, punishment, and rehabilitation were properly balanced, and that punishments were made proportionate to the offences committed.

Attitudes towards transportation began to shift from the 1830s. The punishment came under sustained attack in this period, first from critics in Britain, who condemned the punishment as ineffective, oppressive, and arbitrary, and who were supported by the Whig government after their success in the 1830 election, and later (perhaps more significantly) from an anti-transportation movement in colonial Australia, whose extensive, sustained, and organized opposition to transportation "*forced* a dramatic change in penal policy on a deeply reluctant metropole."[35] In 1833, the number transported from Britain to New South Wales and Van Diemen's Land peaked and thereafter went into permanent decline.[36] Transportation continued until 1868, but by the mid-1840s, imprisonment had replaced transportation as the primary punishment for even serious felonies. One important effect of the winding-down of transportation was the unprecedentedly large numbers of convicted felons who were funnelled into London's punitive prisons; alongside them were growing numbers of misdemeanants sent by the sessions (figure 5.3).

Studies of English imprisonment often focus on this moment between the 1820s and 1840s when imprisonment became a primary method for punishing felonious crime. Most, however, concentrate on the national penitentiaries of Millbank (opened gradually in 1816–22) and Pentonville (opened in 1842). These were significant moments in Britain's penal history, but they tell only a small part of the story of felony imprisonment. Crucially, neither Millbank nor Pentonville received prisoners sentenced to imprisonment by the quarter or assize courts. Initially Millbank only admitted prisoners who, originally sentenced to transportation, were pardoned by the Home Office on condition that they be imprisoned.[37] A series of controversies and general dissatisfaction with its regime led the government in 1843 to designate Millbank a convict "depot," where those sentenced to transportation were held temporarily before being sent either abroad, to the hulks, or to a prison. Pentonville, the government's "model prison," was also designed for offenders sentenced to transportation. Select male convicts, chosen by the Home Office, spent eighteen months in the prison in almost total solitude and separation in preparation for their transportation to Australia.[38] The numbers who experienced incarceration in the national penitentiaries were small, especially by comparison with those imprisoned in county or city prisons.[39] If, therefore, we seek to understand how the courts' growing use of imprisonment impacted prisons and their administration, or if we are interested in felons' experience of incarceration, we must look to prisons run by local authorities, especially houses of correction, where such prisoners were held.

Summary Imprisonment

The imprisonment of convicted offenders by the quarter and assize sessions was not the only or even the primary reason why prison numbers grew. Chiefly, prison commitments grew because of the numbers convicted and imprisoned under summary process (table 5.2). The rise in such prisoners stemmed from several related factors: the nature of crime (or at least arrests), the nature of prosecutions, and practice at the summary level.

Most people arrested in nineteenth-century London, and indeed in other English cities and towns, were charged with petty offences.[40] As a result, most people accused of crimes were tried summarily rather than by indictment. Summary trial became more dominant in the nineteenth century as the number of regularly constituted petty sessions grew and as Parliament passed a raft of new and amended legislation which broadened summary jurisdiction to include numerous crimes formerly triable on indictment only. The *Wilful and Malicious Trespass Act* of 1820, the *Larceny Act* of 1827, and the *Criminal Justice Act* of 1855 formalized magistrates' jurisdiction over certain property offences; the 1828 *Lansdowne Act* sanctioned the summary prosecution of simple assault.[41] In London, these acts recognized and made legal practices that were already common at summary sessions. Such legal legitimation likely encouraged and hastened the transfer of property and violent crimes to the summary sessions.[42]

The likelihood of being convicted before summary courts rose in nineteenth-century London as magistrates gradually moved away from practices involving diversion – informal sanctions not including indictment, fines, or imprisonment – towards policies that prioritized the maintenance of order. At the stipendiary offices, between 1831 and 1852, for example, defendants were almost as likely to be convicted as they were to be discharged. On average 50 per cent of defendants saw their cases dismissed while 43 per cent were summarily convicted and 7 per cent sent for trial. Other parts of England saw even lower discharge rates in the mid-to-late nineteenth century.[43]

The harsher approach to managing disputes may reflect the erosion of magistrates' traditional discretion. The openness of summary hearings, particularly in London where lawyers and pressmen were increasingly in attendance, together with growing criticism over the extent of summary jurisdiction, may have prompted justices to apply the law more punctiliously, diminishing their

Table 5.2 Commitments to English and Welsh prisons by class, 1837–50

	Prisoners for trial at sessions	Summary convictions	Deserters awaiting a route	Re-examined and discharged	Debtors	Total
1837	27,469	59,364	—	—	—	86,833
1838	25,600	56,736	—	10,024	—	92,360
1839	24,956	57,455	1,083	10,569	9,636	103,699
1840	27,093	63,979	1,691	14,951	11,808	119,522
1841	27,085	63,296	1,508	14,347	13,001	119,237
1842	31,160	70,507	1,521	11,260	13,951	128,399
1843	29,871	73,196	1,119	9,685	13,586	127,457
1844	26,682	71,298	1,074	9,263	11,792	120,109
1845	25,083	66,042	943	7,916	2,490	102,474
1846	25,033	64,899	1,093	9,052	3,847	103,924
1847	28,139	67,481	1,312	9,421	4,527	110,880
1848	30,086	84,271	1,388	9,985	8,782	134,512
1849	28,752	90,963	1,111	9,982	8,519	139,327
1850	26,463	80,608	883	9,534	7,806	125,294

Source: "Inspectors of Prisons of Great Britain I. Home District, Tenth Report," *PP* (1845), xxiii.1 (674), vi; ibid., "Twelfth Report," *PP* (1847–48), xxxiv.373 (925), v; ibid., "Twentieth Report," *PP* (1857, session 1), vii.1 (2169), xii.

capacity to act as informal mediators. Changes in the character of the magistracy and in the administration of the summary courts may also have led to a decline in arbitration. First, under the direction of the Home Office, London's stipendiary magistracy was increasingly professionalized. From 1822, all such magistrates were trained barristers, and in 1825 their salaries were raised to attract more qualified candidates. Second, in the 1840s, a standard set of procedures for magistrates operating summarily was established.[44] By formalizing and standardizing summary proceedings, these developments may have curtailed justices' room for manoeuvre. Strikingly, at older summary courts, which in this period were still staffed by amateurs, the "mediation-based ethos" of traditional summary proceedings seems to have predominated longer.[45]

Usually, the summarily convicted were either fined or imprisoned in a house of correction. Fines ranged from 4 shillings to £30; prison terms ranged from seven days (very unusual by the nineteenth century) to three months. The decision to fine or imprison was shaped by statute law, the nature of the offence, the given offender, the wishes of the victim, and the individual magistrate.[46] Together, these changes in summary practice brought growing numbers of summary convicts into London prisons for punishment.

Debtor Imprisonment

Imprisonment for debt, as a civil process, lies at the margins of this study, which is concerned chiefly with the evolution of criminal imprisonment. Nevertheless, debtor imprisonment cannot be ignored totally, as a portion of debtors incarcerated in this period were held in London's criminal prisons.

In London, the number of debtors annually incarcerated grew considerably from at least the 1790s.[47] The rise stemmed especially from the number of small debtors coming before courts of requests. These courts offered a faster, cheaper, and easier route to recovering debt by allowing residents to sue to recover debts of 40 shillings or less without recourse to trial by jury.[48] More than 100 courts of requests were established in England between 1690 and 1830, the majority at the end of the eighteenth century.[49] London boasted at least five such courts: Westminster, Southwark, City, Tower Hamlets, and Middlesex.[50] The jurisdiction of some of these courts expanded in the early nineteenth century as new legislation authorized them to consider debts of up to £5 and later £10.[51] Consequently, the number of cases before these courts grew spectacularly: in the 1820s, they heard around 200,000 cases annually; in the 1830s, over 300,000; and in the 1840s, about 400,000.[52]

Initially, more cases meant more imprisoned debtors. In 1798, at least 1,943 debtors were imprisoned in London; in 1812, at least 3,492 debtors; and in 1828, at least 6,678. The pattern after 1818 is difficult to trace given the surviving records, but evidence from Surrey gaol and Whitecross Street suggests commitments for debt may have levelled off or even declined slightly in the 1830s before falling dramatically in 1845.[53] Decline was the result of legal change: the 1844 *Insolvency Act* exempted individuals with debts under £20 from incarceration.[54] Not all debtors were held in 'criminal' prisons, but sizeable numbers were, as later discussions will show, with considerable impact on prison operation.

II. LONDON'S SPECIALIZED PRISON SYSTEMS

The growing number of prisoners posed a variety of challenges for London magistrates. In some jurisdictions, shifts in court practice propelled authorities to make radical changes in their manner of allocating prisoners between prisons, whereas in others, practice remained largely the same. Nonetheless, there were some common themes. First, all sought to make their prisons even more specialized, and in this pursuit, they continued to differentiate between gaols and compters, on the one hand, and houses of correction, on the other, though they did so in somewhat distinct ways. Second, bridewells remained reserved for convicted offenders. Finally, all jurisdictions moved to expand and improve their ageing prisons, leading to another burst of reforming activity.

Middlesex

Middlesex's prisons were already highly specialized by the end of the eighteenth century. The gaol, New Prison, served mainly as a receiving prison, holding inmates for safe custody, while the house of correction, Coldbath Fields, was largely dedicated to "the correction of culprits" and "the punishment of prisoners."[55] Nineteenth-century changes in the flows of prisoners, sketched above, did not alter this fundamental distinction. Indeed, the division hardened as committing bodies fell into line, voluntarily or after some persuasion, with the bench's commitment policies.

Support from external bodies helped the bench to discourage the few justices and courts who persisted in using the gaol and house of correction in unsanctioned ways. The bench's opposition to holding pre-trial inmates in the house of correction, for example, received powerful support in 1800 and 1809, respectively, from two royal commissions who called on the county to remove all custodial prisoners from Coldbath Fields. Indeed, the authors of the 1809 report strongly suggested that such commitments were unlawful, and they urged magistrates to issue a "positive order" against them.[56] Such interventions point not only to the wider, and perhaps more strident, support for specialized prisons systems beyond the London magistracy, but also to broader support for looser prison conditions for pre-trial detainees. Support from the Court of King's Bench, meanwhile, allowed the magistrates to remove debtors from their prisons. Although the bench had long opposed such commitments to

New Prison and Coldbath Fields, they continued because certain courts, namely courts of request, were authorized by statute to imprison debtors in county gaols and bridewells.[57] After years of frustration, the bench in July 1832 instructed their keepers to "refuse to receive into their custody all debtors committed, or to be committed by the Court of Requests for the Tower Hamlets," the primary culprit. Although the court protested, the policy was upheld by the King's Bench.[58]

Changes in legislation also played a role in compelling committing bodies to adhere to the bench's policies. In some cases, the magistrates may have played a role in drafting such legislation. In 1821, for example, the prison committee wrote to the parliamentary committee responsible for drafting what became the 1823 *Gaol Act* to impress upon them the "necessity of committing only prisoners convicted" to houses of correction. When the Tower Hamlets court sought to force the magistrates to accept their debtors, the magistrates pointed successfully to the *Gaol Act* for support.[59] The magistrates also managed to exclude capital and other serious felons from New Prison after years of wrangling, following the formation of the Central Criminal Court in 1834.[60] The parliamentary legislation establishing the court set clear boundaries between crimes that could be tried at local or general sessions and those that had to be tried at the CCC – a division that previously had been obscure. Under the act, the sessions were restrained from trying persons charged with capital offences and other serious crimes including housebreaking, bigamy, forgery, assault with intent to commit felony, conspiracy, larceny by clerks and servants, and manslaughter.[61] The act did not require that individuals imprisoned to await trial at the CCC be imprisoned in Newgate, but this was how the Middlesex magistrates interpreted it. When, on occasion, a suspect charged with a serious crime was committed to New Prison to await trial, the prison committee promptly challenged the commitment. In November 1837, when the Thames Police Office committed a man charged with murdering seven people to New Prison for re-examination, the prison committee warned that such commitments were against the gaol's "charter." After securing the Attorney General's support, the magistrates directed the gaol keeper to refuse entry to persons "charged with capital felonies, either when committed for re-examination or for trial." To ensure the order was complied with, the justices sent copies of the resolution to all the county's petty sessions and magistrate offices.[62]

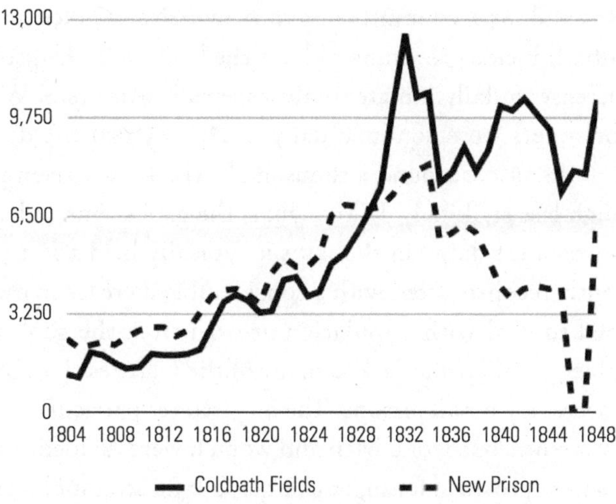

Figure 5.4 · Commitments to Middlesex prisons, 1804–48.

As this later example highlights, greater administrative capacity and increased surveillance over prisons also aided the magistrates' efforts. In 1837, a separate prison committee was formed to oversee New Prison, and the committee magistrates actively policed the gaol's boundaries. When in December 1837 a magistrate sent a summary convict to New Prison for punishment, the committee wrote to him to inform him "that this is not the proper place of confinement for such a prisoner."[63] They took similar steps to remove the occasional witness who was imprisoned in New Prison.[64]

As a result of shifting sentencing practice and the bench's commitment to specialization, New Prison was increasingly restricted to prisoners confined to await examination or trial, who accounted on average for 97 per cent of commitments between 1830 and 1848, while Coldbath Fields was limited chiefly to receiving convicted prisoners sent by the summary, quarter, and assize session courts for punishment, who made up 99.8 per cent of commitments between 1836 and 1848.[65] While the essential role of Middlesex's prisons remained unchanged, the prisons were nonetheless affected by changes in the volume and character of prisoner flows. Specifically, these shifts helped prompt a large-scale reconstruction of the county's prisons, and they also considerably altered the makeup of the bridewell population.

Between 1805 and 1848, commitments to New Prison tripled and commitments to Coldbath Fields grew ninefold. At the bridewell, the growth led to a sustained increase in daily inmate totals, especially after 1812. Whereas, on average, 214 prisoners were confined daily in 1812, by 1821 the daily average was 400, and in the 1830s, around a thousand.[66] The New Prison population grew too, though less strikingly. In the 1780s, the gaol seems to have held an average of 123 prisoners daily; in the 1810s it typically held 200 to 230.[67] The bridewell, recently reconstructed with a considerable increase in capacity, was better equipped to deal with population growth than the gaol, which was two decades older, smaller, and lacked many of the features that, by the 1810s, were deemed necessary for all prisons. The magistrates particularly viewed the classification system as outdated. Men and women were divided, and separate sleeping rooms were provided for night charges, but no attempt had been made to divide inmates according to kind of offence, form of commitment, age, or record of past offending.[68]

Between 1816 and 1818, the magistrates rebuilt the gaol. It cost the county £39,429.16*s*.6*d*., and made room for 240 prisoners – though, as the keeper told a parliamentary committee in 1818, up to 340 could be conveniently accommodated.[69] Male inmates were separated into five classes: adults committed for felonies; three classes of adults imprisoned for misdemeanours, breaches of peace, and want of sureties; and lastly, prisoners younger than fourteen. Female prisoners were split into three classes: felons; misdemeanants and those held for want of sureties; and women of "outrageous or disorderly character."[70] These changes brought New Prison into line with what might be termed Howardian notions of classification.

New Prison was again demolished and rebuilt in 1845–47. This time expanding numbers played no role in driving reconstruction. In fact, the gaol's population had shrunk from the 1830s, as, with the Middlesex sessions meeting more regularly, pre-trial prisoners spent less time in detention.[71] Instead, magistrates decided to build anew after endorsing the separate system of confinement, a system that, up to this point, the justices had repeatedly refused to apply to their gaol. Instead, inmates were held in association. Male inmates generally slept in groups of fifteen, and females in groups of seventeen, though between twenty-five to thirty might sleep together in one room when the gaol was especially busy.[72] The gaol boasted only four cells (two for each sex) where prisoners who desired to be alone could be placed.[73] The new gaol, renamed

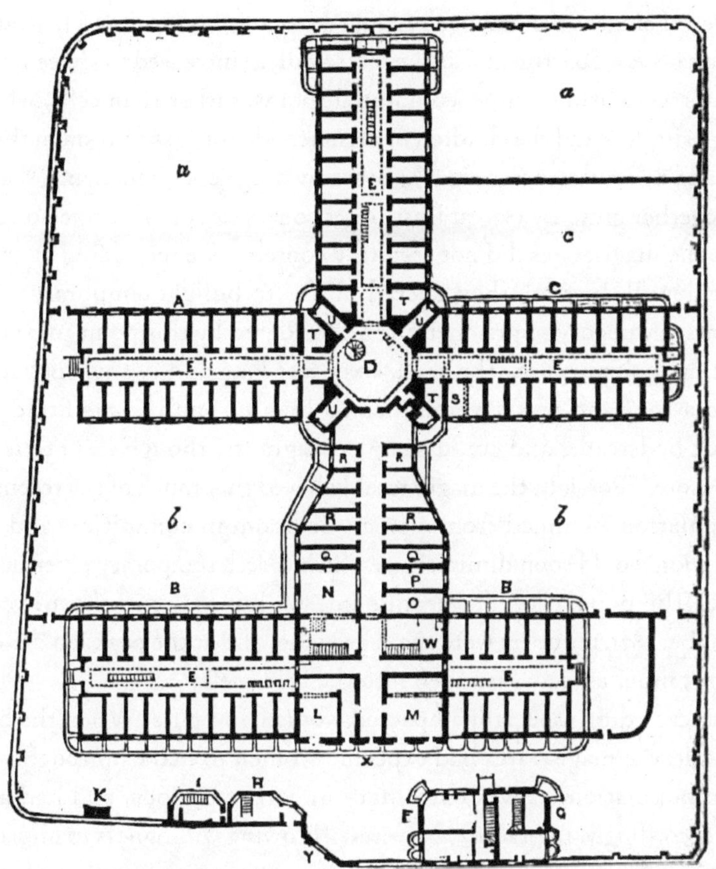

Figure 5.5 · Ground plan of Clerkenwell House of Detention.

Middlesex House of Detention, was modelled on Pentonville and completed at a cost of £28,000. Composed of five wings of single cells, it could accommodate 300 prisoners in separate confinement.[74]

Almost as soon as it opened, Coldbath Fields struggled with overcrowding. As early as 1797, the magistrates had to accept that the pressure of numbers made it impossible to keep all prisoners in solitary confinement. By 1800, the number of single cells had been reduced from 230 to 202, and the number of double cells (or "apartments" as they were called) increased to sixteen.[75] By 1808, vagrants were held in large, communal rooms, rather than cells, while some young prisoners and the children of prisoners slept in association in the schoolroom and nursery respectively.[76] As overcrowding kept intensifying, the number held together grew. By 1821, at least 117 prisoners slept in three-person cells.[77]

Yet the magistrates did not seriously contemplate rebuilding or expanding the bridewell. Instead, they elected in 1821 to build a temporary "shed" for vagrants, a category of prisoner often considered by this point to be marginal to the prison's purpose. The shed, sixty feet long and twenty-four feet wide, lacked a roof and was covered instead by a tarpaulin, was fitted up with barrack bedsteads, and could sleep 80 vagrants, though in practice it held many more.[78] Possibly, the magistrates believed that much of the recent growth in population stemmed from a post-war boom in committals and that the population would soon diminish, in which case, a temporary extension would suffice. The population *did* decline in 1821, but this was short-lived. From November 1821, numbers were again growing, and at the peak, on 7 November 1822, 775 inmates were crammed into the bridewell.[79]

Overcrowding especially impacted women and girls. When the bridewell was built, the magistrates had expected women to make up roughly half the prison population, as was customary in earlier periods, and had allocated space accordingly. In practice, however, a growing willingness to imprison men and to use imprisonment for more serious offences meant that men quickly came to outnumber women. To accommodate the greater numbers of men and boys, officials appropriated rooms and cells originally allotted to women. By 1822, only forty-three of the bridewell's 266 cells were set aside for women. This shrinking of female space was especially problematic since the number of women held roughly doubled between the 1790s and early 1820s.[80]

By the early 1820s, magistrates knew that the growth in the daily population was not temporary, but opinion on the bench was divided regarding how best to manage overcrowding. Some, especially those on the prison committee, advocated the costly solution of constructing additional buildings, but more favoured makeshift, inexpensive measures. In 1822, in response to prison committee agitation, the bench appointed a committee to inquire into the necessity and practicality of expanding the bridewell.[81] Though the committee found that 800 sleeping spaces were needed to accommodate the prisoners,

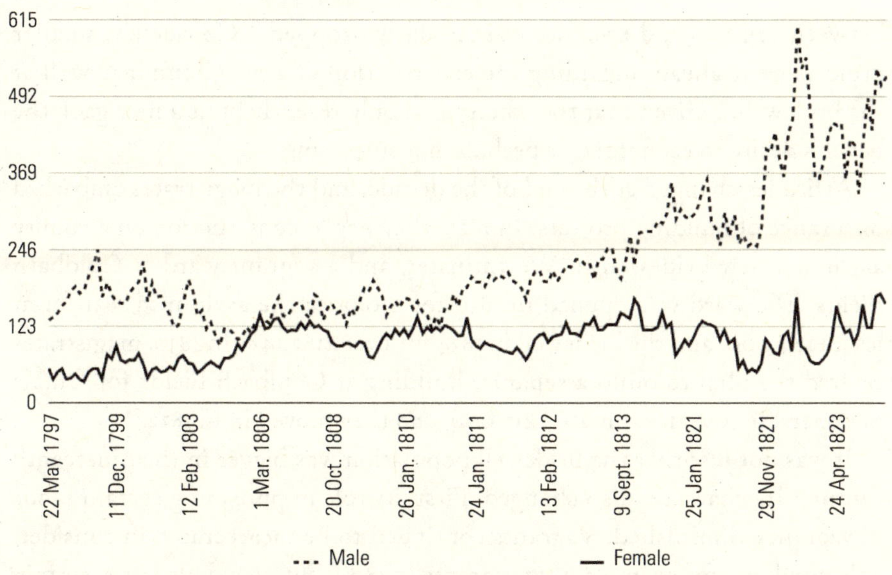

Figure 5.6 · Daily inmate population at Coldbath Fields, 1797–1826.

double the bridewell's present capacity, they argued that this could be accomplished without new buildings. "By adding two bedding places to the single cells now containing only one and by increasing them in the other cells where it is practicable," the committee proposed, "the number of sleeping places may so be increased without affecting the security of the prison, that it will not be necessary to alter or increase the present building at any material expence."[82] For those justices who sought to cut back on prison expenditure, this was a convenient finding. In the following years, the magistrates converted numerous small rooms and cells into communal night wards equipped with barrack bedsteads, relatively low-cost alterations.[83] Such efforts formally ended, at least temporarily, the practice of separate confinement at Coldbath Fields.

There was a general reluctance among the bench's members to spend any considerable sums rebuilding or enlarging their prisons, with several projects rejected or delayed indefinitely. In 1824, for example, the magistrates began planning a new female wing for Coldbath Fields, estimated to cost roughly £20,600.[84] Although the magistrates advertised for architectural plans, they deferred work on this project in 1825.[85] An 1826–27 plan to rebuild New Prison, which would have provided accommodation for 500 prisoners at a cost of between £29,600 and £35,000, was similarly dropped.[86] Conversely, smaller projects went ahead, including the construction of a new boundary wall at the bridewell.[87] Given that the county had only recently built a new gaol, the bench's desire to economize is perhaps not surprising.

Attitudes changed at the end of the decade, and the magistrates embarked on a range of building projects. In 1829, they began construction on a county asylum, a new bridewell in Westminster, and a vagrant ward at Coldbath Fields. The ward was opened in 1830 for £10,000; the asylum in 1831 for at least £124,000; and the bridewell in 1834 for over £182,144. In 1830, magistrates revived the plan to build a separate building at Coldbath Fields for female prisoners. It cost an estimated £12,000, and they moved in in 1832.[88]

It was not just that the bridewell population was bigger in the nineteenth century. Its character also changed. First, its role in punishing certain kinds of vagrancy diminished. Vagrants continued to be incarcerated in considerable numbers (for example, 1,117 vagrants in 1816), but on a daily basis, certain vagrants, namely those confined to be passed, were increasingly uncommon.[89] Unique accounts collected by the prison committee in 1823 show that, on an average day, the bridewell held sixty-nine "vagrants," probably pass vagrants, who accounted for 13 per cent of the population.[90] On 11 August 1834, there were sixty-three "vagrants," again probably pass vagrants, making up 6 per cent of inmates. Other types of vagrant populated the bridewell in larger numbers, including those labelled "rogues and vagabonds" (186 individuals or 19 per cent of inmates in August 1834) and prostitutes (102 or 10 per cent). All these prisoners were convicted under the *Vagrancy Acts*, but prison authorities conceived of them – and indeed treated them – differently. While rogues, prostitutes, and other disorderly people were classified as "convicts" in prison records, those confined to be passed were labelled "vagrants."[91] The former were understood by magistrates as appropriate targets of bridewell discipline, but the latter, increasingly, were not. Consequently, from 1823, pass vagrants were committed in smaller numbers. This represented a considerable shift in how the bridewell was conceptualized and in the reality of its daily population.

Second, and relatedly, the bridewell increasingly became a site for the punishment of serious, criminal offences. Most commitments to Coldbath Fields in the first half of the nineteenth century were for relatively minor offences. Indeed, the vast majority were summary convictions, which on average made up roughly half of annual commitments in the late 1810s, 69 per cent of

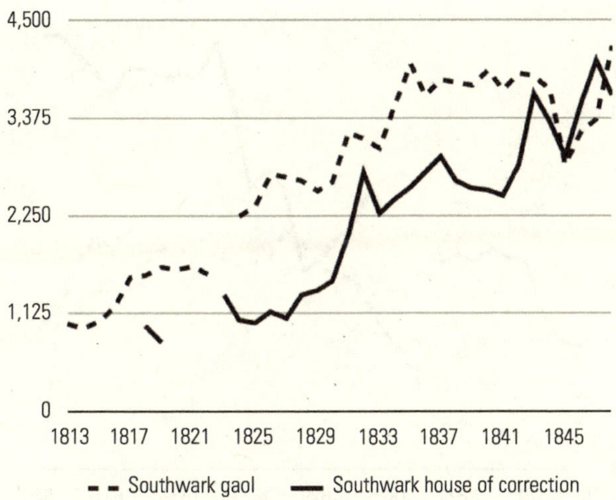

Figure 5.7 · Commitments to Surrey Prisons, 1813–48.

commitments in the 1820s, and 85 per cent between 1836 and 1844.[92] On a daily basis, however, the bridewell was populated, especially from the late 1830s, by more serious offenders. This is evidenced, first, by the growing presence of inmates who had been convicted after trial by indictment, a category of offender typically charged with a more serious offence than those convicted summarily. For example, half of those confined on Michaelmas 1839 and 63 per cent on Michaelmas 1847 had been convicted after trial by indictment.[93] Second, the proportion of felons grew. On Michaelmas 1831, felons accounted for 21.1 per cent of the inmate population; on Michaelmas 1839, they made up 38 per cent; and on Michaelmas 1845, 55.6 per cent.[94] These shifts in the nature of the inmate population, as the next chapter explores, prompted a series of reforms to the bridewell's daily regime.

Surrey

In Surrey, as in Middlesex, magistrates responded to the growing number of prisoners by attempting to cement the division between the gaol and the house of correction. In Middlesex this division marked the boundary between punitive and custodial confinement. In Surrey, however, this division came to separate those confined with an order that they be put to labour from those

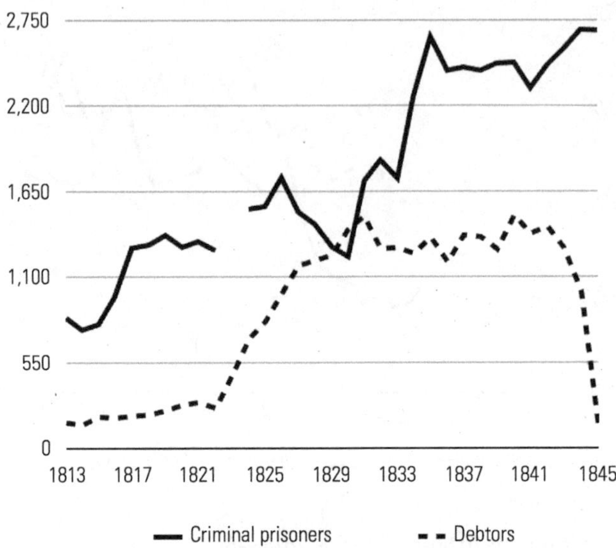

Figure 5.8 · Criminal and debtor commitments to Surrey Gaol, 1813–45.

imprisoned without labour. Prisoners confined for punishment with labour were sent to the house of correction; all others were incarcerated in the gaol. So while the house of correction served an exclusively punitive function, the gaol's role was more mixed, with it acting as a site of safe custody, a place of punishment, and a setting for debtor imprisonment.

Nineteenth-century changes in flows of prisoners did not impact the division between gaol and bridewell, but they did alter the gaol's role and function. Two developments were particularly transformational: the rise in the number of small debtors sent to prison annually and the growing use of imprisonment without hard labour to punish misdemeanants and petty offenders. Other counties faced these challenges, but Surrey's approach to dividing its prisoners meant that its gaol was uniquely impacted.

Between the 1790s and 1820s, Surrey county gaol was primarily a criminal prison. Most commitments were for examination or trial or for lack of sureties. In addition, a certain number of debtors, around 150 or so, were committed yearly. However, in 1823, the Southwark court of requests began sending debtors to the gaol in vast numbers. As a result, debtors came to account for a larger proportion of annual commitments (figure 5.8).

Table 5.3 Commitments to Surrey Gaol, 1836–45

	For trial	For re-examination	Summary convictions	Debtors	Sentenced to prison without hard labour	Unknown	Total
1836	1,168	723	544	1,195	—	0	3,630
1837	1,059	950	378	1,300	—	0	3,687
1838	1,039	971	410	1,358	5	0	3,783
1839	1,101	952	418	1,276	3	0	3,750
1840	1,059	957	451	1,449	9	0	3,925
1841	798	884	393	1,379	5	0	3,694
1842	790	946	432	1,427	5	291	3,891
1843	662	1,085	529	1,287	5	285	3,853
1844	961	1,079	592	1,008	25	0	3,665
1845	445	1,170	932	192	468	10	3,217

Source: "Inspectors of Prisons, Home District, Second to Eleventh Report, 1837–46," *PP*.

Even after 1830, when the gaol again received many more criminal than debtor commitments, debtors remained prominent within the daily population given their generally longer terms of confinement. On an average day between 1825 and 1844, half of inmates were confined for debt.[95] Only a change in the debt laws in 1845, which exempted from incarceration individuals with debts under £20, brought about a decline in debtor commitments, ultimately causing the number held in the gaol to drop.[96]

A range of criminal prisoners were sent to the gaol for confinement. Most were for trial or examination, but a considerable portion had been convicted. Capital convicts, transports, and convicts whose judgments had been respited were held in the gaol until their sentence could be executed. Additionally, the gaol received offenders sentenced to imprisonment without hard labour by summary, quarter, and assize session courts. Mostly, these individuals were charged with minor assaults, and they were imprisoned for non-payment of penalties; smaller numbers were convicted of other misdemeanours.[97] Over the period, the number of convicted offenders sent to the gaol generally grew (table 5.3).

In the late eighteenth and early nineteenth centuries, most criminal inmates held in the gaol had been confined to await examination or trial, but by the 1840s, the gaol was increasingly populated with convicted prisoners confined for punishment. In part, this stemmed from the practices charted above: namely the Surrey sessions' growing use of imprisonment without hard labour and their decision to commit such offenders to gaols. Additionally, the foundation of the Central Criminal Court in 1834, extending the jurisdiction of the court to parts of Essex, Kent, and Surrey, played an important role.[98] Surrey offenders who were formally committed for trial at the CCC were either removed from the county gaol into Newgate or were committed directly to Newgate.

Uniquely amongst London prisons, Southwark gaol was neither rebuilt nor expanded at any point in the first half of the nineteenth century. This stemmed from the prison's relative newness, its design, and its inmate population size. Unlike many other prisons, Surrey apparently did not struggle with overcrowding.[99] Although the population swelled in the 1810s, the magistrates' decision to build a new bridewell at Brixton, discussed below, relieved pressure on gaol space.[100] From 1820, the gaol could accommodate 336 prisoners, 230 in separate cells. The capacity was extended to 364 in 1832 by increasing the number of prisoners in each room or cell. As this suggests, the magistrates were not fully attached to the policy of holding gaol prisoners in single cells at night. Still, the magistrates' decision in the 1790s to adopt cellular confinement at the gaol, alone of all London magistrates, proved especially felicitous. At the conclusion of the Napoleonic Wars, the movement for prison reform revived, and notable proponents, influenced by experiments in America, stressed the necessity of confining all prisoners in single cells for either part or all of the day. Although Surrey did not actually do this, prison reformers, including the prison inspectors William Crawford and Whitworth Russell, who had a notably acrimonious relationship with many local authorities including the City of London, were occasionally complimentary about the gaol's cells.[101]

The gaol's cells not only impressed prison reformers; they also made the magistrates more willing to send minor convicted offenders imprisoned without labour to the gaol. Unlike many other English gaols, the Surrey gaol had the facilities to keep convicted offenders totally separate from custodial prisoners and debtors and to accommodate them in cells at night. Separation was made easier after 1820, when bridewell prisoners were removed from the gaol and their wards were reallocated to gaol prisoners. By 1835, the number of classes had expanded to thirteen, with inmates divided by gender, conviction status, offence type, and age.[102]

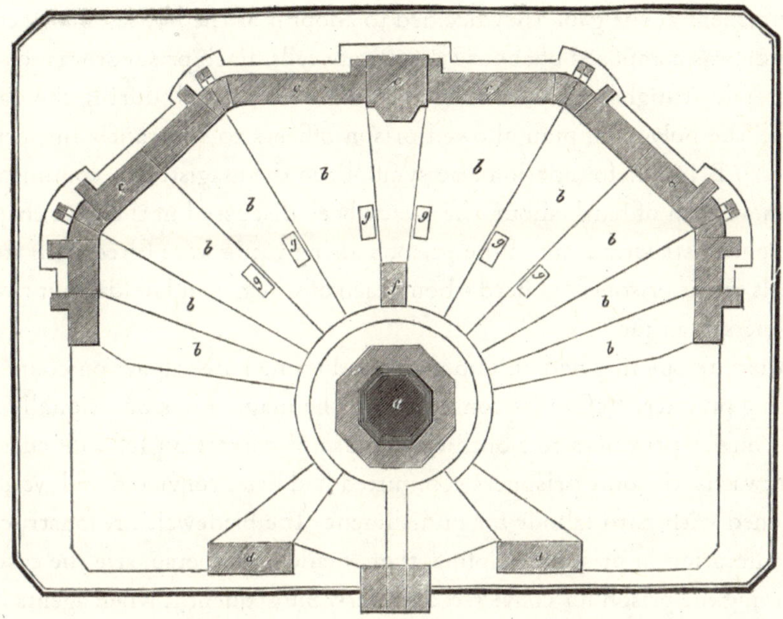

Figure 5.9 • Plan of Brixton House of Correction, 1826. Key: (a) governor's house; (b) airing courts; (c) buildings containing day rooms on lower floors and single cells on upper stories; (d) infirmaries; (e) chapel; (f) mill house; (g) treadwheels.

At the start of the nineteenth century, the Southwark house of correction was located within the walls of the county gaol at Horsemonger Lane. The bridewell's capacity was relatively small, accommodating only fifty prisoners; this was in line with the bridewell's small population, which, in the 1790s, was roughly thirty-eight inmates.[103] However, as various courts sentenced more offenders to imprisonment with hard labour, so the bridewell's population expanded. On its fullest day in 1818, the prison held 121 inmates, more than double its intended capacity. The greater use of imprisonment by the summary, quarter, and assize sessions prompted the magistrates to build a new, larger house of correction, entirely separate from the gaol, to accommodate the anticipated numbers.[104] The new bridewell, built on three acres at Brixton Hill, opened in 1820.

The decision to build reflected more than a growing inmate population; it also signalled the Surrey bench's evolving views on bridewell confinement. At the same time that magistrates were loosening their commitment to cellular confinement at the gaol, they decided to adopt it at the house of correction. Brixton was composed of about 130 separate cells. Each prisoner was to sleep separately at night and then to be released from the cell during the day to work. The polygonal plan allowed prison officers to constantly inspect inmates.[105] Brixton's foundation also symbolized the magistrates' commitment to a new form of hard labour, the treadwheel, discussed in the next chapter. During construction, six of the prison's airing yards were fitted with treadwheels to put prisoners to hard labour, each of which could hold about twenty prisoners at a time.[106]

Brixton's opening had an important and immediate impact on court sentencing practice. Before its construction, the magistrates occasionally sent non-convict prisoners to Southwark house of correction for safe custody. Afterwards, the only prisoners committed had been convicted and were imprisoned with hard labour for punishment. The bridewell's reconstruction and alteration in prison discipline, then, made more persuasive the case for reserving the prison for convicted offenders. Subsequently, when agents from the Prison Discipline Society visited in 1822, they found much to admire: as the report detailed, the bridewell was

> appropriated to the reception of prisoners sentenced to hard labour; a sentence which the magistrates are at length enabled to carry into effect, according to the strict tenour and design of the statute, as with the exception of the very few confined by the casualties of sickness or debility, all the prisoners are steadily employed in working the treadmill.[107]

Such practices confirm that the magistrates designed Brixton as a labour prison, and they help to explain why convicted offenders sentenced to imprisonment without an order to labour were directed by the magistrates, in summary and quarter sessions, to gaols rather than to the bridewell, where they would break and disrupt labour discipline.

The growth in annual commitments to Brixton from 1820 led to a sustained increase in daily inmate totals, prompting a partial abandonment of night-time solitary confinement. By 1835, about twenty of the men's cells held three prisoners in each, and fifteen of the women's cells held two or three in each.[108] The growing population, combined with pressure from the Prison Inspectorate to adopt the Pentonville model of imprisonment, pushed the justices in 1847 to agree to build a new house of correction for 700 prisoners at Wandsworth, which opened in 1851.[109] They subsequently sold Brixton for £13,000 to the government, who, after some alterations, used it as a female convict prison.[110]

Mostly, prisoners were committed to Brixton after summary conviction: on average, 2,479 prisoners accounting for 87 per cent of annual commitments between 1836 and 1845. Large numbers were summarily convicted under the *Vagrant Acts*; others were convicted for offences against the games laws, revenue laws, or bastardy laws; under the metropolitan or local police acts; from courts-martial; or as deserters. Unfortunately, in considerable numbers of cases, the specific summary offence was not specified, which frustrates attempts to trace commitment patterns. Additionally, an average of 370 convicted offenders were sent annually from the assize and quarter sessions.[111]

Over time, Brixton seems to have become populated more and more by serious offenders, mirroring the shift that took place at Coldbath Fields. A paucity of records makes this difficult to assess, but until the 1840s the bridewell appears to have held mainly petty offenders convicted summarily; afterwards, the proportion of felons held grew, as did the proportion of inmates convicted at the quarter or assize sessions. For example, between 1825 and 1840, felons on average accounted for 26 per cent of the bridewell population, whereas between 1841 and 1847, they made up 44 per cent. Similarly, when the prison inspectors visited Brixton at Michaelmas 1837, 74 per cent of inmates had been summarily convicted, whereas at Michaelmas 1844 this figure was 50 per cent.[112]

In Surrey, magistrates focused their energies on specializing the bridewell. They were very successful with Brixton, admitting only convicts sentenced to imprisonment at hard labour. The gaol, by contrast, served increasingly as a catch-all institution. While it served primarily as a site for custodial detention, it also acted as a punitive prison and a prison for debtors.

City of London

By the end of the eighteenth century, there were six prisons in the City over which the Corporation had jurisdiction: Newgate, Bridewell, Ludgate, and Giltspur, Poultry, and Borough Compters.[113] The large number made it possible for the City's prison system to be in some ways more specialized than those in other parts of the metropolis. It possessed a prison, Ludgate, exclusively for debtors, and its supply of compters made it uniquely capable of differentiating between the various kinds of merely custodial prisoner. Additionally, with Bridewell, the City could isolate petty offenders convicted summarily from all other types of punitive and custodial prisoner. In other respects, however, the City lagged behind. Unlike Surrey and Middlesex, the City neither founded nor specially designated a prison to hold the growing numbers annually sentenced to imprisonment after trial by indictment. Without an alternative, such prisoners ended up in Newgate or, less commonly, the compters, a situation much despised. Additionally, Ludgate was too small and its jurisdiction too limited to contain all those imprisoned for debt, so criminal prisons were regularly called upon to house debtors. In prisons such as Newgate, therefore, debtors mixed with criminal prisoners, pre-trial prisoners consorted with convicts, and felons associated with misdemeanants.

The 1810s saw the City embark on a new wave of prison-building. Partly this project was driven by overcrowding and fears of gaol fever, but it was also prompted by the Corporation's desire to rationalize its prison system. By constructing new prisons and adapting existing ones, City authorities were able to alter the allocation of prisoners between prisons. By doing so, they established possibly the most specialized prison system in England.

First, the City moved to totally disassociate debtor and criminal imprisonment. The presence of debtors in many City prisons became more problematic as both the number annually committed and the number daily confined grew. At Newgate, nearly 40 per cent of prisoners committed between 1808 and 1815 were debtors, and on an average day in 1810–16, the gaol held 185 debtors.[114] By comparison, in 1747–64, Newgate typically held eighty-two debtors who accounted for less than 14 per cent of commitments.[115] Debtors were even more dominant at the Giltspur Compter, built in the 1790s to hold night charges, those awaiting examination, and debtors. Between 1805 and 1815, they made up 69 per cent of the daily population.[116] Such increases stemmed from a country-wide rise in debtor commitments and from the declining condition of the Poultry Compter, which previously had received many City debtors.

The debtors in Newgate and Giltspur were not just a "great inconvenience"; their presence put the prisons, and the city more broadly, in "danger of contagious Disorders."[117] To alleviate these difficulties, and especially to relieve Newgate, the City ordered the construction of a new prison, Whitecross Street, exclusively for debtors.[118] After Whitecross opened in 1815, the City's civil prisoners were uniformly transferred there, and from this point, criminal prisons were no longer expected to receive prisoners for debt. Only the Borough Compter continued to hold criminal prisoners together with debtors, a unique case discussed below.

After removing debtors from (most of) the City's criminal prisons, the Corporation stepped up efforts to divorce pre-trial from punitive confinement. Resistance to incarcerating convicted offenders alongside non-convicts, on both ideological and practical grounds, grew in the 1800s and 1810. The decision to act was probably also influenced by the growing numbers sentenced to imprisonment with hard labour by the quarter and Old Bailey sessions who needed to be accommodated. The 1812 act that had allowed the City to raise funds to build Whitecross Street also authorized them to convert two adjoining prisons, Ludgate Prison and Giltspur Compter, into a new institution, the Giltspur Prison and House of Correction, completed in 1815.[119] Though run by the same keeper, the prison and house of correction were totally distinct institutions with different systems of classification and rules. The prison side held a miscellaneous mix: convicts sentenced to imprisonment without hard labour; night charges and inmates for examination; prisoners for trial; and vagrants to be passed. They were united by the fact that none could be set to hard labour – very similar, in this sense, to how the Surrey gaol functioned. Conversely, the house of correction was specifically and exclusively created for those sentenced by jury courts to imprisonment with hard labour.

Giltspur's foundation transformed sentencing practice and the nature of confinement in the City. After it opened, nearly all offenders sentenced to imprisonment for felony or misdemeanour were sent to the house of correction side of that institution.[120] The exceptions were incarcerated in Newgate or the prison side of Giltspur. Their different treatment stemmed from the fact that they had been sentenced to imprisonment *without* hard labour. Generally, those sent to Newgate had been convicted at the Old Bailey, or later the CCC, of "royal offences," such as uttering (that is, passing) counterfeit money, or of political or religious crimes, including libel and blasphemy, which had long been punished, if the offender was imprisoned, by a stint in Newgate.[121] Mostly, such individuals were already confined in Newgate when sentenced; it was exceedingly rare for individuals to be sentenced to confinement in Newgate if they had not been committed there to await their trial.[122] Giltspur Prison, meanwhile, received misdemeanants sentenced to imprisonment without hard labour from the City quarter or general sessions.[123] Giltspur House of

Correction remained the City's main punitive prison for indicted offenders until 1852, when, as a result of growing commitments and the City's conversion to separate confinement, a new house of correction, Holloway, opened.

Like their counterparts in Surrey, then, the City magistrates were trying to differentiate the experiences of confinement for different kinds of convicts. In pursuit of proportional sentencing, City judicial authorities sentenced offenders convicted of crimes they deemed less serious to imprisonment without hard labour, and they specified that such convicts be incarcerated in prisons known to have a less severe disciplinary regime. Their sentencing practices also ensured that Giltspur House of Correction held only prisoners sentenced to hard labour, and therefore that the same discipline applied to all inmates. Uniquely, City convicts sentenced to imprisonment by the quarter and assize sessions were generally not imprisoned alongside summary convicts. While the former went to Giltspur, the latter were sent to Bridewell. At Bridewell, all inmates were confined after summary conviction.[124]

The prison side of Giltspur, meanwhile, served as an important site of custodial detention. The vast majority of commitments were confined as night charges or for examination. In 1836, 4,669 individuals, out of a total 5,295 commitments, were confined on this basis to Giltspur Prison and House of Correction. Likewise, in 1841, out of the 6,870 commitments to Giltspur, 5,990 were night charges or remand prisoners.[125] Smaller numbers were committed to await trial: perhaps between 110 and 260 individuals annually in the 1830s and 1840s. All such prisoners had been accused of misdemeanours and were committed for trial at the City quarter sessions.[126] To sum up, then, by converting Giltspur Compter into a prison and house of correction, the Corporation made it possible not only to distinguish and separate into distinct institutions three different kinds of convict, but also to distinguish and separate different kinds of custodial prisoner.

The City's efforts to separate custodial and punitive imprisonment and to disentangle criminal and debt imprisonment did not extend to the Borough Compter. In that part of the City, the lack of alternative prisons to which to commit offenders and the Corporation's unwillingness to build more meant that all City prisoners in the Borough were sent to the compter.

Between the 1780s and 1814, the compter primarily received and held debtors, but after 1814, when the City re-established a regular magistracy in the Borough, the number of criminal commitments rose considerably, as indeed did debtor commitments (again, an effect of the rise of small debt courts). In 1814, 202 debtors and forty-nine criminal offenders were committed compared to 760 debtors and 1,074 criminal offenders in 1821.[127] The inmate population also grew, prompting concerns about overcrowding and contagion. Fears about disease, anxieties over debtors and criminal prisoners mixing freely, and intensified scrutiny by Parliament and prison reformers combined to propel the compter's enlargement in the late 1810s.[128] Once completed, the alterations made it possible for the keeper to classify and separate his prisoners according to sex, offence, and committal type. Whereas previously prisoners were simply divided into "criminals" and "debtors," in the extended compter, prisoners were split into five classes: male debtors, male prisoners charged with felony, male misdemeanants (tried and untried), night charges (male and female), and female prisoners (criminals and debtors).[129] The compter continued to serve a mixture of roles into the 1830s, receiving night charges, prisoners for re-examination, individuals for trial, summary convicts, and debtors. Despite its renovation in 1818 and the easing of overcrowding after 1823, however, the prison continued to be something of an embarrassment for the City.

III. CONCLUSION

In the nineteenth century, the use of imprisonment expanded markedly, bringing unprecedented numbers into London's prisons. Changes in commitment practice imposed new demands on institutions to which their managers had to respond. Though the individual benches took distinct approaches, a common theme was to step up efforts to specialize prisons. Consequently, by the middle of the century, it was exceedingly rare for an untried prisoner to be incarcerated in a house of correction, or conversely, for an offender sentenced to imprisonment with hard labour to be confined in a gaol or compter. A key area of divergence was what courts did with individuals imprisoned without an order that they labour. In Middlesex, officials prioritized conviction status, and so they chose to confine such individuals in the bridewell with other individuals sentenced to imprisonment. In Surrey and the City, by contrast, authorities focused on labour status, so they sent such offenders to gaols. Different attitudes towards prison labour, and the discretion afforded to local authorities in employing inmates sentenced to simple imprisonment, played an important role in shaping these commitment practices. Namely, while City and Surrey officials opted against setting convicted offenders not sentenced to hard labour on lighter employments, the Middlesex magistrates put these inmates to work.[130] In Middlesex, then, bridewell discipline was not impacted by the presence of inmates not sentenced to hard labour because these prisoners were not suffered to remain idle. More broadly, nineteenth-century commitment practices suggest a desire by local officials to rationalize prison operation, making it easier for prison officers to impose a more uniform discipline in each prison, and by the conviction that custodial and punitive confinement should be kept as separate as possible.

The new uses of imprisonment significantly impacted the character of prison populations. In particular, the courts' growing attachment to imprisonment as a punishment for both serious and petty crime markedly altered the makeup of houses of correction. These prisons, which were originally designed to punish and correct vagrants, were increasingly dominated by convicts who had been convicted of relatively serious offences, a shift with momentous but heretofore unrecognized consequences for prison operation.

CHAPTER SIX

An Age of Prison Improvements

Reform and Discipline

The period following the conclusion of the Napoleonic Wars in 1815 was one of intense anxiety across Britain. Economic depression followed the onset of peace. Falling prices and a post-war slump in trade and manufacturing led the labour market to contract. The rapid demobilization of troops, over 300,000 of whom returned to Britain in 1815–17, further glutted the labour market and pushed down wages.[1] As economic conditions worsened, the cost of poor relief rose. London was seen to have particularly high rates of pauperism, and in real terms, costs of relief more than doubled between 1813 and 1832. Escalating rates placed added strain on social relations, and attitudes towards the poor shifted and hardened.[2] The resurgence of popular radicalism, related to growing economic hardship, a general disillusionment with the government's handling of the war, and renewed resentment against "Old Corruption," further intensified class strife.[3] Moreover, as the last chapter highlighted, criminal indictments were soaring, generating widespread fears about growing levels of crime. In this climate, interest in improving domestic government and reforming manners was reignited. Deep interest in penal reform from across the ideological spectrum, by the public and from government authorities, spurred a burst of new building (including the decision by Parliament to build the first national penitentiary), the foundation of several new pressure groups focused on prison reform, heated debate regarding the path of reform, and a spurt of new legislation. It was, as one contemporary remarked, an "age of prison improvements."[4]

Reformative philosophies, many historians have argued, dominated penal policy and practice in the first half of the nineteenth century. Contemporaries insisted that the task of punishment was to "reform the guilty, and to restore them as useful members of community."[5] The means advocated for achieving this end differed. Prominent Evangelical and Quaker groups such as the Society for the Improvement of Prison Discipline and for the Reformation of Young Offenders (SIPD), established in 1815, looked to establish a transformation based on sympathy.[6] Prisoners would be reformed through the personal influence and moral persuasion of reformers who used kindness to "soften" the hearts of offenders and awaken their sympathetic feelings. Such views were based on Christian notions of spiritual revival.[7] Other voices stressed, for example, the cultivation of industriousness as the best way to achieve prisoner reformation, but it was those associated with the Prison Discipline Society who played key roles in shaping penal policy in the period.[8] By mid-century, however, widespread disillusionment with reformatory philosophy, combined with growing belief that crime was committed by members of a "definable social class in need of discipline," prompted a reappraisal of prison policy. Increasingly, the punitive aspects of imprisonment were emphasized, and authorities came to adopt a regime of "hard labour, hard board, and hard fare."[9]

Some historians have put the date for this transformation earlier. As Michael Ignatieff noted, it was fashionable in the 1820s to deride the "spurious benevolence" of Elizabeth Fry and the Prison Discipline Society, whose work, though well-meaning, was compromised by the "fallacious idea" of "reformation through the medium of moral persuasion."[10] Other reformers, though they claimed individuals like Fry as inspirations, advocated "more terrifying" practices.[11] Crucially, theirs was a modern dread. As Sydney Smith, the Anglican parson and cofounder of the *Edinburgh Review*, remarked, "a return to prison should be contemplated with horror – horror, not excited by the ancient filth, disease, and extortion of jails; but by calm, well-regulated, well-watched austerity – by the gloom and sadness wisely and intentionally thrown over such an abode."[12] As magistrates across England came to believe that "nothing but the terror of human suffering can avail to prevent crime," as one Staffordshire justice wrote, they concluded that a prison should be a "place of terror to those without, of punishment to those within."[13] R.A. Cooper has shown how the

Prison Discipline Society responded to the critiques that it focused too much on the physical well-being and moral welfare of prisoners by reorienting its objectives. By 1822, its adherents were emphasizing hard labour and regular employment in combination with "spare diet, occasional solitary confinement and habits of order and silence," whereas previously, they had stressed cleanliness, nutrition, religious instruction, and prisoner classification.[14]

Such views, scholars argue, promoted a "tightening up of social controls" within prisons, bringing a "newly authoritarian tenor" into prison administration and refashioning prisons as sites of "orderly disciplinary confinement."[15] As evidence of this transformation, they cite the introduction of the treadwheel and the general shift towards unproductive labour, the development of the silent and separate systems, the withdrawal of traditional privileges such as receiving visitors and extra provisions, the imposition of leaner diets, and the demise of prisoner self-government. Certainly, the advent of these measures in English prisons from the late 1810s supports the notion that attitudes and practices were changing prior to mid-century.

This chapter reconsiders prison reform and prison experience in this contested period. It considers, first, the rationale behind schemes to harshen prison discipline; second, the scope or universality of these schemes; and finally, the practical impact of tougher measures on prisoner experience.

I. TIGHTENING DISCIPLINE

In explaining why prison reformers and authorities may have pushed to transform prisons into bleaker, harsher places from the 1820s and 1830s, historians typically point to hardening attitudes towards both criminal offenders and the poor. Gradually, many came to believe that the existing systems of poor relief and criminal punishment only aggravated the respective problems of pauperism and crime and that stronger deterrents were needed to stop, on the one hand, the poor from seeking relief, and on the other, individuals from committing crimes.[16] Crucially, attitudes were hardening at a moment when material conditions within prisons were apparently improving. Prisons now provided all inmates with food, bedding and clothing, and access to medical care; in short, they offered a respite from the exposure of the streets. These improvements demanded a change in discipline. "Each additional comfort for the body," Robin Evans argued, "required a compensating subtraction of mental sustenance."[17] In explaining the need for tougher measures, as Ursula Henriques and Margaret DeLacy have emphasized, many commentators pointed to the principle of "less eligibility," which required "the life of the criminal under punishment ... be harder than that of the lowest paid honest labourer."[18] As conditions outside the prison worsened, concerns grew that prisons had become too cushy, anxieties reinforced by various reports claiming that individuals deliberately committed crimes in order to be admitted to prison.[19] A report from a committee of London aldermen, published in 1815, encapsulates the shifting views:

> A Prison ought to be furnished with every reasonable means to secure the Health of the Prisoners; but on no consideration ought indulgence to be carried so far, as that it shall cease to punish as a Prison. It ought to be of sufficient Terror to be avoided by the guilty, and not to possess so much of accommodation as to be sought as an Asylum by the Indolent and Profligate.[20]

Broadly, then, hardening attitudes towards the poor and the criminal combined with fears that prisons had become a boon to such groups propelled local authorities to introduce tighter measures.[21]

These interpretations posit ideology as the driver of change while only cursorily, if at all, considering the impact of court practice on prison discipline. Some scholars have referred in brief to the part played by the rapid growth of prison commitments, which helped encourage harsher attitudes towards prisoners.[22] Margot Finn has additionally pointed to changing prison populations, arguing that as criminal prisoners came to outnumber debtors, English gaols shed the "lax and disorderly practices and conditions associated with the debtor's prison."[23] Court practice, however, played a more central role in driving authorities to restructure prison discipline, and its relationship to ideological change requires greater attention. In London, the introduction of harsher measures related specifically to the growing use of imprisonment *as a punishment* and to the presence of convicts *sentenced to hard labour* in prisons. If we posit a change in attitudes, we need also to register that it operated selectively.

In introducing tougher measures, local authorities were responding consciously and specifically to new sentencing practices that saw imprisonment become the most common punishment handed down by all London courts,

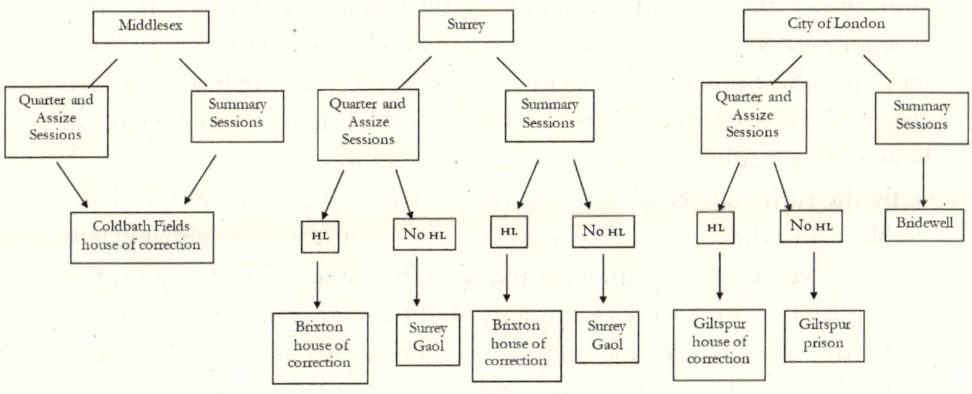

Figure 6.1 • Sentencing offenders to imprisonment in London. HL stands for hard labour.

including the Old Bailey, in the nineteenth century. London authorities aimed to make imprisonment for punishment, especially imprisonment for the punishment of serious offences, more dreaded. This desire was closely bound up with the move to restrict the death penalty and to end convict transportation. Organized opposition to these punishments grew from the 1810s and swelled from the late 1830s.[24] Those who sought to repeal the capital code or to abolish transportation needed not only to delegitimize existing penal solutions but also to present compelling alternatives.[25] The tightening of discipline at punitive prisons was part of this broader effort.

It was bridewells – and generally not gaols or compters – that saw the introduction of tougher measures in London in the 1820s. As we saw in the last chapter, offenders sentenced to imprisonment by London's summary, quarter, and assize courts were sent mainly to bridewells – though exact arrangements differed somewhat by jurisdiction (see figure 6.1).

As a result, by the 1810s if not earlier, London's bridewells served almost exclusively as prisons for convicted offenders. Previously, those sentenced to imprisonment were charged mainly with vagrancy or another petty offence, and some but not all were confined with an order of hard labour. From the 1820s, however, the makeup of bridewell populations began to change. The majority, if not all inmates, were confined for labour, and a growing proportion were charged with serious misdemeanours and felonies. These were the exact sorts of prisoners at whom harsher practices were aimed. Conversely, local authorities expressed some discomfort in subjecting certain petty offenders, especially vagrants incarcerated to be passed, to a harsher penal regime. It was only after these prisoners were either removed entirely or reduced considerably in number that authorities adopted more challenging forms of labour at houses of correction.

By the early nineteenth century, the poor were increasingly viewed as a problem, and their immorality was cited as a main reason for growing poverty. Such views were encapsulated and promoted by successive parliamentary investigations into mendicity, vagrancy, and policing in London.[26] The 1815 committee on mendicity, for example, proclaimed that "an immense proportion of [London beggars] are idle, profligate and lazy, and living in a great dissipation."[27] The 1838 committee on metropolitan police offices similarly concluded that "of the number of beggars to be met with in the streets of London, it is computed that nine out of ten are gross imposters."[28] These committees argued for greater severity in prison discipline to deter the disorderly poor. The committee investigating the laws on vagrancy, for example, claimed, "the threat of commitment has lost its terror"; prisons operated "rather as a bounty upon delinquency than as actual chastisement" to the extent that the vagrant "steps forward as a volunteer for prison."[29]

Many in positions of authority in London, however, did not share this highly negative view of the poor – as a select committee observed with some dismay, "all the Magistrates are not governed by the same views of the pernicious tendency and inexcusable character of the vice of mendicancy."[30] Those responsible for punishing or providing relief to the poor continued to cite distress as a primary cause of vagrancy, and many still emphasized a distinction between the deserving and the underserving poor.[31] The Middlesex magistrate G.B. Mainwaring, for example, told the committee on vagrancy that magistrates generally made "a moral distinction" between "a vagrancy which arises from destitution" and that "proceeding from imposture and intentional delinquency"; while he would punish the latter with the full force of the law, the former he would treat as an "object of charity."[32] Metropolitan authorities believed that many, if not most, of those who were imprisoned as vagrants were destitute rather than delinquent. As Mainwaring posited, "the destitute are the more willing and easier objects of apprehension, and greatly exceed those whom the law has designated rogues and vagabonds, and intended to punish. It is therefore the poor, rather than the guilty, who are principally subjected to the law."[33] Francis Hobler, clerk to the Lord Mayor of London, similarly submitted that those whom the select committee designated as vagrants were in fact "poor persons called vagrants ... who give very lamentable accounts of their distresses." Yet the ability of magistrates to order relief for such poor persons was constrained by the requirement that they hold a legal settlement. In such circumstances, Hobler reported that City magistrates deliberately convicted these "poor creatures" as vagrants and imprisoned them in Bridewell for seven days. Such action allowed the magistrates to relieve the poor by offering them shelter, food, access to medical care, and assistance travelling back to their settlements.[34] Their confinement was expressly understood as an act of charity.

Their treatment within bridewells reflected this. Pass vagrants, or "seven day vagrants" as the authorities often called them, constituted a separate class at Coldbath Fields, distinct even from other vagrants, with their own ward and courtyard. Over time, pass vagrants came to share their yard with debtors and inmates too old or infirm to work. This grouping made a certain sense as all had an anomalous status within the prison: namely, they did not work. Consequently, they were not labelled as convicts nor were they subjected to separate confinement. At City Bridewell too, pass vagrants were classed separately and held apart from other summary convicts, and they were accommodated in large wards rather than in separate cells.[35]

From the late eighteenth century, magistrates pushed forcefully to remove pass vagrants and other petty offenders imprisoned without hard labour from bridewells. G.B. Mainwaring told an 1821 parliamentary committee that "an exclusive receptacle [for vagrants] would be desirable on the grounds that it would exclude vagrants from houses of correction, which should be appropriated to the heavier sentences in execution."[36] Such a position had some wider support: in 1850, Joshua Jebb, Surveyor-General of Prisons and later Director of Convict Prisons, similarly advocated for vagrants to be held in separate buildings "so that they might not come inside the prison at all."[37] At Bridewell, governors on the prison committee called on City magistrates to stop sending prisoners who were "not within the intention of the institution which required that all persons admitted ... be kept to hard labour"; for similar reasons, they also deprecated the commitment of "sick and diseased persons" to Bridewell, many of whom were confined to await admittance to hospital.[38] In a special report, published in November 1819, a committee of governors expressed hope that a contemplated revision to the Vagrancy Laws might allow them to exclude pass vagrants and thereby dedicate the institution to hard-labour prisoners. While they described the former as confined "under the fiction of their being offenders against the law," the latter they proclaimed "those objects, who appear to fall more particularly within the original design of the hospital, as a house both of correction and occupation."[39] Indeed, in 1822, Parliament passed an act which did away with the requirement for magistrates to commit to prison for at least seven days all those convicted of vagrancy.[40] This legislation had an immediate impact on court practice and prison operation. After 1822, no pass vagrants were committed to Bridewell. Subsequently, the governors moved forward with their plans to transform Bridewell into a place of "constant labour ... strict discipline ... and moral reformation."[41] In 1823, the prison committee recommended installing treadwheels in the prison, and by the end of the year, both male and female prisoners were employed on them.[42] In bridewells across London, including Giltspur and Southwark, the treadwheel was generally adopted only after the institution was restricted to hard-labour convicts.[43] Where vagrants and others not sentenced to hard labour were still admitted, as at Coldbath Fields, treadwheel labour was reserved explicitly for the more serious offenders sentenced to hard labour.[44]

Alongside the treadwheel, London magistrates introduced a range of new measures that aimed to tighten bridewell discipline and make confinement more unpleasant. The changes introduced into Coldbath Fields are characteristic of London policies. In 1821, magistrates on the prison committee suggested that prisoner visiting hours be restricted and that the admittance of food from outside the prison be discontinued.[45] Such changes were not accepted immediately, perhaps indicating disagreement amongst the bench regarding the appropriate treatment of prisoners and also reflecting prisoner opposition to the changes. Nonetheless, by 1829, the visiting justices had banned inmates confined after conviction from receiving food, clothing, or other necessaries beyond the gaol allowance, except under exceptional circumstances.[46] In 1835, they ordered that convicted prisoners be prohibited from receiving visits or letters from friends during the first six months of their imprisonment; prisoners committed for examination, meanwhile, had to have their visits supervised by the governor or a turnkey.[47] Moreover, in December 1834, silence was imposed on the prison. All convicted prisoners were required to remain silent by day and night; singing and whistling were "strictly prohibited," as were any attempts to communicate, including by "signs, writing, or stratagem"; "any unnecessary looking round or about" was also forbidden. Breaches (of which there were many) were punished by stoppage of food, solitary confinement, or corporal punishment. So, Daniel Harnett in May 1843 was struck a dozen times with a birch rod for persisting in singing in chapel and for singing and whistling in cells, while Johanna Welch, accused of dancing and singing obscene songs, was kept in solitary confinement on bread and water for fourteen days in June 1843.[48]

In adopting more punitive measures, authorities hoped to make prison a viable alternative to transportation and execution, punishments traditionally seen as more despised by offenders. Especially hard measures were introduced, therefore, only after authorities accepted the prison as the replacement for the other punishments and once bridewells came to be populated by more serious offenders sentenced to hard labour. The close connection between hard-labour prisoners and stricter regimes is confirmed by the path of reform at London's gaols and compters. At these prisons, none of the "hallmarks" of the punitive prison were adopted – at least until the late 1830s when Home Office influence over prison policy expanded. Instead, the reforms introduced to custodial prisons in the 1810s and 1820s focused mainly on improving the conditions of confinement, eliminating the private aspects of prison operation, and professionalizing the administration of prisons. Generally magistrates resisted attempts to make detention more punitive.

II. LOCAL RESISTANCE

In the 1810s, the Howardian programme of reform remained unfinished at most of London's custodial prisons. As we saw in chapter 4, City and Middlesex magistrates had opted against introducing into these prisons many of the measures suggested by Howard and his fellow reformers, deeming such reforms either unnecessary or inappropriate. So, although the new gaols and compters were generally larger, healthier, and more secure than their previous incarnations, they were still managed and organized in traditional ways. Prison officers continued to rely on prison fees as the main source of their income; inmates were still expected to supply most goods and provisions themselves; prisoners were not classed by offence, age, or character; they associated in large groups by day and night; detailed rules were not drawn up; inmates were not required to attend divine service, nor were they provided with work or education.

The situation in Southwark was different. There, magistrates had introduced into the gaol and bridewell alike measures aimed at improving health, security, and prison administration, *and* at creating a moral environment. They banned fees and gave salaries to all officers; introduced classification systems based on sex and commitment type; adopted a degree of separate confinement; established rules to manage the prisons; and set up a system of visiting magistrates to inspect and report on the prisons. They did not go beyond this, though. As in Middlesex and Surrey, gaol prisoners were not put to work nor were their conduct or daily routine closely supervised by prison authorities.

As enthusiasm for reform grew after 1815, the continued failure of London's authorities to adopt the full Howardian programme attracted renewed criticism. Local authorities were put under increasing pressure to adopt reforms by new pressure groups, on the one hand, who stepped up efforts to publicize abuses in the current system and who intensively lobbied central authorities for change, and on the other hand, by national governmental authorities, some of whom began to take a more activist approach to reform. Between 1813 and 1818, for example, Parliament appointed five select committees and a royal commission to look into London's prisons.[49] The use of select committees was a fairly unusual (though soon to be common) move: before this, the last such committee appointed by Parliament to inquire into prisons without a preceding request from the authority concerned was Oglethorpe's famous 1729–30 gaols committee.[50] Meanwhile, the Home Office assumed a leading role in the drafting of penal policy. Home Secretaries, notably Henry Addington, Lord Sidmouth, and Robert Peel, along with some MPs, increasingly sought to compel local authorities to act by passing a series of new acts relating to the management of prisons.[51] Some were explicitly aimed at changing practice in London. Ultimately, the greater appetite by ministers and MPs for setting the agenda in penal policy brought to a close the "era of permissive penal legislation" and diminished the capacity of local authorities to act independently in this area.[52]

It was in this context that City and Middlesex authorities finally accepted the need to adopt a degree of reform at their gaols and compters. The City Corporation, for example, was spurred to reform following extensive parliamentary criticism of its prisons. By taking action, it hoped to defend local self-government and demonstrate that external interference was unnecessary. This is not to say that reform was entirely forced upon the City or that its interest in reform was superficial or solely tactical. Indeed, the City had already been in the process of reviewing its administration and regulation of prisons, but greater public, especially parliamentary, attention certainly sped reform up.[53] The decisions leading to reform in Middlesex are harder to recover given the shortage of records covering the 1810s, but one suspects that parliamentary and government pressure and the influence of the SIPD, especially from those members who were also county magistrates, similarly played a role.

The reforms introduced into City and Middlesex gaols had several aims. First, they looked to improve conditions, especially by providing all prisoners with a dietary, bedding, and fuel allowance. Second, they aimed to clarify prison administration, particularly by establishing written rules, which laid out the duties of each prison officer and set out a clear daily routine, and by banning officers from taking fees or profiting from the sale of goods sold in the prison. Unsurprisingly, therefore, most new regulations dealt with the duties of prison officers. Some authorities also sought to expand their classification systems and to harden divisions between classes. Finally, they increased magisterial oversight over prisons by setting up permanent committees to visit and supervise prison operation.[54] Crucially, magistrates rejected proposals, made by reformers within and outside Parliament and even by some of their own members, which if implemented would have made confinement far more severe for inmates detained for safe custody.

The new written regulations placed several restrictions on prisoners' time, behaviour, and privileges, which together made daily life at gaols somewhat more structured. Yet, none of this amounted to the close monitoring of inmate conduct or the minute control of the daily regime that was common in London houses of correction and which reformers and central government figures sought. As before, there were set hours for unlocking and locking, and prisoners were required to perform a variety of cleaning tasks, but additionally, inmates were required to attend daily divine service.[55] Before New Prison was rebuilt in 1816–18, there was no religious attendance and no chapel. The new gaol, however, included a chapel where the chaplain read prayers daily to the prisoners and additionally instructed them in the Holy Scriptures. On Sundays, the chaplain also held morning and evening services, preaching two separate sermons.[56] Apparently, magistrates supported reformers' calls for religion to play a larger role in gaol life. Yet in practice, the effects of religious policies varied by institution. In Newgate, for example, the prison chapel was too small for all inmates to attend service until alterations were made in 1828.[57]

The new rules also fixed more clearly hours and policies for the admission of visitors and provisions. Such policies had existed already, but they were somewhat fluid and not necessarily written down. The new rules were lax by comparison with those at houses of correction. At Giltspur Prison, visitors were allowed from 10am till 2pm, and at Borough Compter, they were admitted from 8am until 7pm, with shorter hours on Sunday. At Newgate, New Prison, and Surrey gaol, visitors were newly prohibited from entering the prison's interior wards; instead visits took place in designated rooms or at the prison gates. Conversely, at Giltspur, visitors were still admitted into the wards.[58] As this suggests, the boundaries of custodial prisons remained porous, even as punitive prisons became increasingly inaccessible. Custodial prisoners could still see their friends and relatives on a daily basis; they could send and receive letters; and they were allowed to receive provisions, including food, drink, bedding, and clothing, from outside the prison.

With respect to their behaviour, prisoners generally were expected to stay clean, keep relatively quiet, and not fight. At New Prison, inmates who did not wash each morning were prohibited from seeing visitors, while at Newgate inmates were instructed not to curse, swear, or fight.[59] Such expectations were not new, but it appears magistrates hoped to better police them, as highlighted by the considerable expansion in the number of detailed instructions issued to prison officers and, later, by attempts to introduce a graduated system of fines for officers who failed to adhere to instructions.[60] Other traditional privileges were maintained with some tweaks that suggest a slightly stronger focus on internal prison order. For instance, while magistrates did not ban criminal prisoners from buying beer, as some reformers had urged, they did introduce measures to clamp down on excessive drinking. At Newgate, prisoners were barred from sending out for beer, so they could purchase it only from the "beer man," a publican contracted to supply the prison. By the 1830s, the beer man visited once a day between 12pm and 1pm, and prisoners were limited to one pint a day, though, as the prison inspectors complained in 1835, "no steps are taken to limit the supply to the regulated quantity; no account is taken of the quantity brought into the prison, nor of the number of pints served to the different wards."[61] At New Prison, inmates could send out for beer only after noon and for no more than one pot (specifically limited to a pint) a day. Rules were more lax, as always, at Borough Compter, where a debtor, known as the "captain," was allowed to keep a tap and supply prisoners, whether debtors or criminals, with "whatever quantity may be called for"; the tapster received a halfpenny on every quart he sold, an encouragement to keep the beer flowing.[62]

To a certain extent, inmates' freedom of movement within prisons was limited in this period by the extension of classification to encompass prisoners' ages, offences, and commitment types. Inmates were newly restricted from associating with those outside their class. Yet, such systems operated imperfectly, and new divisions were sometimes dropped – such as the requirement to separate young female prisoners from adults.[63] At some institutions, including Giltspur Prison, classification remained rudimentary into the late 1830s, so prisoners mixed freely. Crucially, within their classes, inmates socialized, played games, read books and newspapers, exercised, smoked tobacco, and drank, at least into the late 1830s, irrespective of parliamentary injunctions on such behaviour.[64]

Reformers had pushed repeatedly for pre-trial prisoners to be employed in light, voluntary employments. The 1823 *Gaol Act* had looked to aid such objectives by explicitly empowering magistrates to provide light employment to unconvicted prisoners; the legislation even permitted their compulsion to work. London authorities, however, seemed unmoved by their authority to force non-convicts to work, and aside from some cleaning tasks, they generally opted against employing gaol and compter inmates. Consequently, prison inspectors complained repeatedly into the 1850s that most gaol prisoners spent their days in idleness – complaints which were probably overblown.[65] This approach set London authorities apart from those elsewhere in England who forced non-convict prisoners to work, even at hard labour.[66]

Generally, magistrates did not concern themselves overmuch with the behaviour of custodial inmates, but there were some key exceptions. First, authorities took notably greater interest in juvenile prisoners, mainly boys, who were also subjected to greater restrictions within prisons. Children had long been seen as more malleable and susceptible to influence than adults, and within London, elites had repeatedly set up private organizations and institutions targeted at shaping the habits and morals of youth. Moreover, this period saw growing concern about juvenile crime and its apparent rise. The SIPD, who took a leading role in debates, saw juvenile crime as a problem closely related to poverty, to a lack of education, and to bad parenting. Their solutions focused on a change of environment and education.[67] Across London, prison authorities began insisting that boys held before trial should be given lessons, especially in reading and sometimes in writing, just as boys held after conviction were. The boys' school at Newgate was founded by the Ordinary, Rev. Dr Horace Salisbury Cotton, soon after his appointment in 1814. Boys were required to attend lessons for four hours each day. Cotton instructed them in the catechism while a prisoner-appointed schoolmaster taught them to read. A separate school for the children of convicted female prisoners was set up in Newgate in 1817 by Elizabeth Fry.[68]

Second, at City gaols, greater attention was paid to and restrictions placed on female inmates. Voluntary reformers, rather than local officials, drove these efforts. At Newgate, Borough Compter, and Giltspur Prison, Elizabeth Fry sought and received permission to hire a matron to supervise some female prisoners and to set up and enforce rules. Magistrates required Fry to gain "the consent of the female prisoners," who she claims "unanimously expressed to support the plan, and to abide by whatever rules might be established," which suggests the women were not, at least in theory, forced to comply.[69] The Newgate women were divided into new classes; given "suitable employment" such as needle-work and knitting; and banned from a wide variety of "inappropriate" activities including begging, gaming, card-playing, immoral conversation, and reading improper books.[70] Initially, Fry's jurisdiction extended only over women who had been tried and convicted, most of whom were awaiting transportation.[71] However, she gradually assumed responsibility over all women. In 1820 or 1821, she set up a school for adult, untried women, who were taught to read.[72] Fry and her female followers later extended their efforts more widely. They applied to form a "Ladies' Committee of Visitants" at Southwark gaol, to promote "industry, cleanliness, religious instruction and good order among female prisoners," but their offer, though gratefully received by some magistrates, was rejected by the bench.[73] Other counties, including Middlesex, were more receptive, so across England, ladies' committees were set up to visit female prisoners.

As these examples indicate, City magistrates delegated responsibility for the moral care and secular instruction of juveniles and convicted women in gaols to philanthropists such as Fry and to prison chaplains, who were given wide license to develop policies for those under their care. As these projects depended on the energy of individual philanthropists, prison officers, and convicted prisoners who (in the boys' case) taught the prisoners, educational and work schemes occasionally fell into abeyance. It also meant that provision was patchy across prisons. At Giltspur, for example, a school for boys was set up under the chaplain's superintendence only in 1838.[74]

Middlesex and Surrey magistrates set up schools for boys in their gaols slightly later than the City's Newgate, from at least 1821 and 1825 respectively.[75] One must also wonder about the content and quality of the education provided, with some chaplains expressing highly negative views on prison education and, more broadly, on the boys' potential for reformation.[76]

The pattern and content of reform in the 1810s to 1830s shows London authorities continuing to distinguish the conditions of confinement in custodial prisons, namely gaols and compters, from those in punitive prisons, namely houses of correction. Their unwillingness to introduce measures which might turn their gaols into "schools of morals" increasingly put the magistrates out of step with the wider prison reform movement.[77] Their stance was regularly criticized, even by fellow London officials. The New Prison chaplain, for example, was especially scathing about the discipline, or lack thereof, in the gaol. "He feels it his duty again to call attention to the moral discipline of this Prison," he reported to the visiting justices in 1833, "as not only calculated to defeat all his efforts for the spiritual improvement of the prisoners but as also tending greatly to the increase of corruption and wickedness." He identified as key impediments features which the magistrates had consistently represented as distinctions of pre-trial custody. Namely, a "general reform" was stymied by "the fact of [inmates] spending the greater part of their time in idleness and profligate conversation, in yards of from 20 to 70, without any other moral control, *in the yards*, than that of a fellow prisoner as wardsman; and the fact that great number leave the prison without employment."[78] In the following years, these aspects came under sustained assault, not only from some prison officers, but also from the SIPD, and more significantly, the Prison Inspectorate.

III. PRISON LABOUR

While calls to introduce harsher policies may not have seemed particularly attractive to London magistrates when administering their custodial prisons, such appeals made greater headway at punitive prisons. But, in introducing these measures, were local authorities turning away from the goal of prisoner reformation and towards a primarily punitive, terrifying, and deterrent discipline, as some scholars have alleged? How did the new, stricter measures operate in practice? To answer these questions, the remainder of this chapter considers the adoption and impact of one of the key tougher measures: prison labour. Such an exploration suggests we cannot view labour in the nineteenth century as either purely penal or primarily deterrent. On the contrary, labour systems were designed to benefit the running of prisons, and they were intended to play a critical role in the reformation and rehabilitation of convict prisoners. Consequently, even as London magistrates adopted more punishing forms of work, they continued to stress the importance of useful and productive labour. We will start by revisiting the hallmark of the new labour regimes, the treadwheel, so often presented as symbolic of the general shift towards punitive discipline, before examining other forms of labour.[79]

Treadwheels

Designed by William Cubitt, an engineer and millwright from Norfolk, in 1818, the treadwheel was a great, elongated wheel, equipped with wooden steps and sufficient for ten to twenty people to stand in a row on one side; as those on the wheel stepped together, the wheel turned. It was arduous work: as one inmate explained, it was like "ascending an endless flight of steps."[80] Importantly, the work required neither training nor particular skills. It was, though, potentially dangerous, as several accidents and various investigations underscored.[81] The power generated by the inmates' treading could be (and was originally intended to be) used to grind corn or pump water, but in popular imagination and many historical works, the treadwheel is generally associated with pointless, monotonous, and back-breaking labour.[82] Yet, the wheel was not solely adopted at houses of correction for its perceived onerousness. Rather, magistrates believed the wheel would be taxing, useful, and potentially reformative.

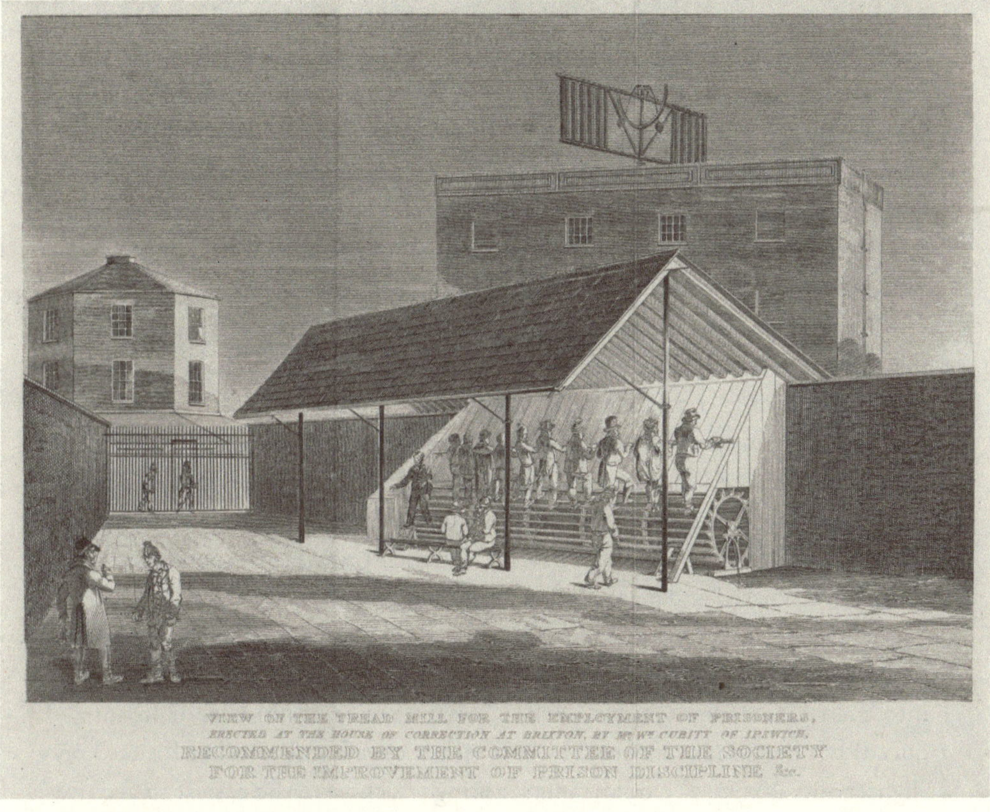

Figure 6.2 • View of the treadmill, 1823.

In 1819, the Middlesex bench appointed a committee to inquire into labour at Coldbath Fields. The impetus for such an investigation was a letter from G.B. Mainwaring, a magistrate at Worship Street police court, the county treasurer, and a former MP, who subsequently exercised considerable influence over the committee.[83] Mainwaring hoped to convince the county to adopt the recently invented penal treadwheel, the first of which had just been installed in Bury St Edmunds Gaol. Its severity particularly appealed to him, and he endorsed the wheel as "labour, which shall really work the body and subdue (properly discipline) the mind." He liked that treadwheel labour could be minutely regulated by officials. He believed that, on the wheel, a prisoner could not shirk his task. Nonetheless, Mainwaring did not view treadwheel labour as pointless, nor did he value it solely for its deterrent potential. Rather, he asserted that the treadwheel, by giving prisoners a "mechanical habit of industry," would be the "the surest means" of reforming them: "if, therefore, habits be given him, from which he acquires health, strength, peace of mind, and the honest means of support, surely it is not beyond probability, that many, even the worst of men, may profit by the acquisition of such habits."[84] As we have discussed already, belief in the redeemability of incorrigible offenders, so low in the eighteenth century, grew in the early nineteenth; the treadwheel, and the promise it held out to magistrates such as Mainwaring, was part of the reason for this momentous shift.

Mainwaring's view of hard labour as both punitive and reformative was widely shared by influential reformers. The Prison Discipline Society likewise stressed that labour should deter crime and improve criminals. In an 1821 report, they proclaimed themselves "the decided and unequivocal advocates for hard labour such as is calculated to alarm the criminal, and necessarily produce weariness and exhaustion"; but they stressed, "in this as in every other branch the reformation of the criminal must be kept in view."[85] In their private correspondence, SIPD members discussed and commended Mainwaring's efforts.[86]

Mainwaring's committee drew up a questionnaire on prison labour which they sent to bridewell governors across England and which provides a glimpse into their aims. One question asked "what species of hard labor (if introduced) has been most effectual … as a means of reform"; another focused on "lighter and auxiliary" employments, asking which were the easiest to acquire and in which "prisoners have shewn the greatest disposition to industry, and from which the best habits have been produced."[87] The magistrates also sought greater information on the sorts of hard labour that were "most effectual as a punishment" and which acted as a deterrent causing recidivism rates to fall. The magistrates' questionnaire reveals these men searching for a tool that would not only reform the habits of prisoners, but also punish them and deter them from crime. Some responses gave the magistrates great encouragement. John Orridge, keeper of the gaol at Bury, claimed, "I have no doubt that [the treadwheel is] the most efficient mode of employment for reforming the prisoner that has yet been adopted in prisons."[88]

These letters also provide a unique glimpse into how local policy was worked out. In particular, magistrates throughout England looked to other counties for inspiration, corresponding with one another or visiting other prisons, in pursuit of successful policies. Formal avenues for such discussions had been established in the late eighteenth century by groups such as the Proclamation

Society. They organized national conventions for magistrates to discuss social policy issues and established a sub-committee to correspond with those engaging in prison reform, to visit prisons, and to publish an updated account of the state of English prisons (see chapter 2). These efforts were continued in the nineteenth century by the SIPD and, on a more informal basis, by individual magistrates and county benches. In these years, the Middlesex magistrates reached out to officials in Gloucester, North Leech, Oxford, Dorchester, Lancashire, Ilchester, Wiltshire, and Warwick, while the City magistrates sent agents on a tour of all English prisons in 1815.[89] The reforming efforts of London magistrates, though not a primary model for other benches in this period, were similarly watched and debated.[90]

The committee ultimately recommended that treadwheel labour be adopted in the Middlesex bridewell: "upon full consideration of the present employment of the prisoners in this prison it appears to your committee not to be productive of any beneficial result and that it is therefore absolutely necessary to change the present system."[91] The bench subsequently commissioned William Cubitt to build eight treadwheels.[92] Their decision suggests that by 1820 most magistrates believed the treadwheel offered the best chance at punishing, deterring, and reforming bridewell prisoners.

In some respects, the treadwheel was a logical choice of employment for many London bridewells. It offered magistrates a way to employ large numbers in regular employment that did not require extensive training. As we have seen, bridewell populations were generally quite large in London; the period individuals were confined was very short; and in the 1810s magistrates faced serious difficulties obtaining work for their inmates, especially the men. City Bridewell committee records, for example, show the inmates frequently unemployed in this period.[93] The governors struggled to obtain supplies of hemp and oakum, and while the female prisoners were sometimes employed on flax machines and spinning wheels, these often broke, and the labour required training. The prison committee eventually hired a woman to superintend flax spinning, but the committee soon found it "almost impossible" to procure material to supply the machines and "extremely difficult" to dispose of the spun yarn.[94] A special committee appointed in 1819 to consider this predicament bemoaned the fact that "various expedients have been suggested, and have all failed in their turn."[95] In these circumstances, the treadwheel proved an especially attractive option.

In London, treadwheel labour also helped to cover some of the cost of operating prisons. Magistrates set prisoners to grinding corn and grain and to pumping water for prison use. They had bakehouses built (often using prisoner labour) so that other inmates could bake bread from the grains and corns milled. Prison labour, then, supported inmates' diets. Some jurisdictions also sold the bread outside the prisons or used it to supply other county institutions, including gaols and hospitals. Surrey, for example, made around £239 annually between 1824 and 1831 from selling prison bread.[96] Margaret DeLacy noted in her study of Lancaster prisons that magistrates, "sensitive to increases in the rates," were "never enthusiastic about demands that they convert profitable prison manufactories into places of worthless and unpleasant activity."[97] In London, as in Lancashire, a desire to offset the costs of prison operation and to limit tax rises remained at the forefront of magistrates' concerns, regardless – or perhaps in spite – of wider ideological shifts in penal philosophy.

The treadwheel's adoption did not herald the end of productive or reformative labour. Certainly, magistrates were attracted to the wheel because it seemed more exacting than other forms of hard labour, but additionally, magistrates valued its industrial potential. They also hoped that, by introducing an employment that offered a constant supply of labour, they might accustom inmates to regular industry. Such interests drove similar uses of the treadwheel outside of London, where wheels were used to grind grain into flour, to run power looms, and to pump water for the prison.[98]

Beyond the Wheel

Though scholarly and popular accounts of the nineteenth-century prison focus extensively on the treadwheel, this was not the only – and in some prisons not even the main – method used to employ prisoners. Instead, magistrates continued to prioritize useful and profitable employment, with inmates filling vital roles within the institutions as well as engaging in a wide range of productive employments, at least some of which were explicitly intended to supply prisoners with income and useful skills.

Prisoner labour was essential to the maintenance, operation, and government of London prisons, especially bridewells. Though the number of staff expanded in this period, bridewells still counted on inmates to fill a variety of posts, a situation that enabled magistrates to limit expenditure on staff salaries. Health care, for example, depended on prison labour. Inmates served as nurses and cleaners in the infirmaries, and they were all responsible for ensuring their own bodily cleanliness, not just by washing themselves, but also by acting as barbers and launderers. Education, spiritual and otherwise, was likewise sustained by prisoner labour. Inmates acted as teachers or teaching assistants in prison schools, and they served as assistants or clerks to chaplains. We have seen how inmate labour was central to keeping themselves fed. As well as treading the wheels and baking bread, some also worked in the kitchens, and others tended prison gardens, whose produce was used to enrich the standard dietary allowance. Additionally, inmates were responsible for keeping themselves clothed, making and repairing the prison uniforms and shoes. A few acted as servants for prison officers, cleaning their rooms or houses and washing their linen and clothes. Finally, prisoners played a crucial role in maintaining discipline, primarily by serving as yardsmen or wardsmen, superintending the actions of their fellow inmates.

Bridewells could not have operated without this labour. The number of posts held by prisoners was extensive, and considerable numbers of inmates were engaged in these tasks. A list of prisoners employed in so-called "menial" employments in Coldbath Fields on 13 September 1823, for example, counted sixty-one prisoners, about 11 per cent of the population.[99] By May 1836, 272 prisoners (31 per cent of inmates) were so employed.[100] In the 1830s, as in the 1820s, many worked as cleaners; others as warders or monitors, upholding the silent system; yet more as craftsmen, such as carpenters, gardeners, and painters.[101] The range of employments also expanded. In keeping with the increased emphasis on prisoner cleanliness, new positions, including an "inspector of blankets" and "scourers of bedding and blankets," were created. Additional crafts were introduced, including smithing, knife-making, and book-binding.[102] To offset some of the cost of prison education, magistrates set up a printing office where prison lesson books were set in type and worked off by the inmates.[103]

Prisoners could secure significant benefits from filling these roles. All were excused from hard labour, even if they had been so sentenced, and many positions came with additional perquisites, such as extra food or a beer allowance.[104] Uniquely at Giltspur wardsmen were allowed to sell, for their own benefit, various articles, including coffee, butter, sugar, tea, eggs, and sometimes beer, to fellow inmates.[105] Inmates could also receive more direct pecuniary incentives. In September 1810, the Middlesex prison committee ordered Mary Alice Edge be given two guineas on her discharge for her "good conduct" and service as a nurse in the women's infirmary. Similarly, in September 1825, James Bowler, a "felon," was allowed £2 on his discharge since he had "done a good deal of work" as a bricklayer and whitewasher in the past year.[106] Prison committees gave other inmates goods in return for their service. In October 1818, Bridewell authorities ordered a shift be purchased for Sarah Adam, who remained in prison after her release to nurse a fellow inmate.[107] Coldbath Fields's 1823 rules specified that inmates who worked "diligently and faithfully" for the prison would receive "rewards upon their discharge."[108] These gifts were part of a wider system of rewards employed by London bridewells, discussed in greater detail below, which enabled authorities to incentivize good behaviour.

Although the benefits attached to these positions likely made them attractive to inmates, only a limited number could be so employed. Some prison governors consequently tried to link the positions to good behaviour, such as Coldbath Fields' governor who in 1818 noted that his selections for yardsmen were based on prisoners' "good conduct" within prison.[109] The Brixton governor instead prized skill and experience, choosing "the intelligent and the clever" to serve as yardsmen.[110] Often, those chosen had been sentenced to long periods of hard labour. Local administrators believed the "long prospect of confinement" made such prisoners "anxious to retain their situations," and they would therefore conduct themselves appropriately.[111] These practices worked against attempts to treat similar types of prisoner equally and to tailor treatment to offence type, offending history, and behaviour, but they also made it easier for officers to run the prisons.

Mostly, prisoners were engaged in some form of "hard labour," a nebulous term with no clear definition. As the Lords committee on prison discipline in England's gaols and bridewells remarked in 1863, "there is the widest possible difference in the opinions held as to what constitutes hard labour."[112] This is hardly surprising, as eighteenth-century prison legislation had left decisions about the kinds of labour at which inmates might be employed to county magistrates, while nineteenth-century legislation was largely silent on the sorts of employment that qualified as hard labour.[113] Many prison reformers and some London magistrates aimed to place all prisoners sentenced to hard labour on the treadwheels, but the wheel never replaced other forms of hard labour. This was partly a question of practicality. Coldbath Fields had an immense (and unusual) capacity to put prisoners on the wheels ("upwards" of 300 could fit on them each day), but even there, the bridewell population was too big.[114] The same was true at Brixton and Giltspur.[115] At prisons with smaller populations outside of London, the difficulty and expense of operating treadmills, which required regular maintenance by a specialist, was apparently a more serious barrier to extending mill labour.[116] London authorities differed as to how they decided which prisoners should work the wheels. While at Giltspur men were chosen based on their strength, at Coldbath Fields those employed on the wheels had been convicted of the most serious offences.[117] Though magistrates could have purchased additional wheels, they did not, opting instead to employ inmates in a range of other, mainly useful tasks.

By and large, hard labour systems were designed to support the running and maintenance of bridewells. Throughout London, magistrates interpreted "hard labour" as including various kinds of building trades, which allowed them to use inmates to construct and maintain their prisons. Thus, male prisoners in Southwark bridewell were employed in building the new house of correction at Brixton in 1820.[118] At Coldbath Fields, male inmates were set to levelling the ground and digging the foundations for the new female ward in the early 1830s.[119]At Giltspur, male prisoners worked as carpenters, stone masons, and sawyers.[120] While male prisoners were engaged in construction work, female prisoners worked in prison laundries.[121] The magistrates built a new washhouse in Coldbath Fields's female prison in the 1830s, which provided employment for around sixteen prisoners, who were chosen on the basis of their "conduct" and "fitness for the occupation." In recognition of the severity of the labour, the magistrates gave the laundry women a pint of beer a day for their health.[122] The Bridewell governors did the same.[123] Additionally, prisoners made many of the goods required in prisons. At Giltspur, male prisoners who were not strong enough to work on the corn mill were set to breaking flax, which was then spun into yarn by female prisoners, later woven on the loom by male prisoners, and finally made into bedding by female prisoners.[124] Women were also engaged in producing and maintaining the prison uniforms that all London bridewells had adopted by the early nineteenth century.[125]

The Middlesex magistrate and philanthropist Jonas Hanway commented in 1776 that if prisoners, during their incarceration, would "learn the religion of their country; and how to get their bread when they are restored to liberty, by any particular labour or mechanic art, the end of imprisonment will be answered."[126] The expansion of productive work at houses of correction in the

Figure 6.3 · Tailoring in Coldbath Fields, 1874.

1830s and 1840s suggests such interests continued to shape the approach of London magistrates. In Middlesex, male prisoners had long been engaged in making shoes and clothes, but while at the start of the nineteenth century only a handful were engaged in this work, by 1849 around seventy-six worked as tailors and shoemakers each day, and in 1855, around 160.[127] This arrangement had clear benefits for the county: many of the items produced were sent to clothe inmates at New Prison and the county asylum at Hanwell.[128] This and other work, such as making "utensils" for the Westminster bridewell, allowed the county to save on costs, while allowing some prisoners to learn a trade that might help them secure employment on their discharge.[129] The administrators specifically instructed that young boys, sentenced to at least a year in prison, be employed in such work, alongside older prisoners with greater experience.[130] They were interested, in short, in training up those they saw as inexperienced in both work and crime.

In addition to producing goods for the county, inmates made items for the magistrates to sell. At Brixton in 1844, female prisoners were completely occupied with making clothing for slop shops, stores which originally supplied cheap clothing to the navy and army, but whose trade in ready-made clothing had expanded rapidly from the 1830s.[131] Female prisoners were generally engaged in various forms of clothes production. Most knit or did needlework, while some produced the clothes fastenings known as hooks and eyes.[132] At Coldbath Fields, female prisoners were formally instructed in coarse work: as the matron explained to prison inspectors in 1849, this vocational training ensured that prisoners who came in, "as the great majority do, knowing nothing" left prison "with a knowledge of how to knit a stocking or hem a strap."[133]

The Middlesex magistrates were especially eager to form relationships with manufacturers to employ prisoners. Several businesses contracted with them to employ inmates in picking oakum.[134] From the 1830s, the numbers so employed and the profits made expanded. In 1833, for example, the prison made £280.18*s*. from picking oakum. To manage this labour, the visiting magistrates in 1834 standardized the amount of oakum picked: 5lb each day for male prisoners, 3lb for female prisoners, and 1lb for children.[135] By 19 May 1849, 315 prisoners were picking oakum and another eleven were preparing it.[136] The magistrates also introduced mat- and rug-making into the bridewell. Under the scheme, prisoners made mats and rugs for an outside manufacturer who paid for two superintendents to instruct the prisoners in this work as well as in carding and spinning flax and other materials.[137] The contract was initially for two years, but the magistrates were so pleased with the results that they decided to continue on a more permanent basis and to increase the number trained.[138]

The Middlesex magistrates increasingly stressed the benefits of manufacturing work over other forms of hard labour, such as the treadwheel and picking oakum. In an 1842 report, they concluded that the conduct of prisoners engaged in manufacturing was "in every respect better" than the conduct of other prisoners.[139] In 1847, they judged that the prisoners employed in trades had been "impressed with the utility of such labours," and as a result, they attended to the work with "a vigilance and promptitude which had never been shown at the labour of the tread-mill, which they appear invariably to consider with disgust, as an unavailing and unproductive devotion of labour and time."[140] Such comments suggest that the magistrates viewed manufacturing work as more reformative and therefore preferable to other forms of labour. Inmates also seem to have preferred this work, another determining factor. The profits probably pleased the magistrates too: in 1849, they made £1,234.2*s*.11*d*.

net profit from manufacturing and other work done by the prisoners, excluding the work done "for the benefit of the county," such as construction work. Unsurprisingly, in 1848, they updated and renewed their contract with one Charles Dagnall, a rope and sacking manufacturer, who continued to pay the county for the prisoners' labour.[141] Into the 1860s, Middlesex officials stressed that unproductive labour had "a bad effect" upon inmates' minds and that "the more profitable the labour for the prisoners is the better."[142]

The "support" or training offered to inmates was heavily gendered. In the eighteenth century, most men and women worked at the same trades in prison, but by the nineteenth, women were siloed into either prison laundries or clothes production. Such shifts may have reflected the growing focus on domesticity and women's position within the home in the nineteenth century.[143] Regardless, they concentrated women in especially low-paying industries often viewed derogatorily as low-skilled. Young male prisoners, by contrast, were singled out for training in skilled manufacturing work. Some forms of prison labour may have been designed to offer a route to occupational or financial betterment, but these schemes usually excluded female inmates.

Across London, then, there was continued, and even increased, interest in employing some prisoners in useful and profitable trades. Support for productive labour eventually put some local authorities at odds with Parliament and the Home Office. From the 1860s, prominent figures within these spheres increasingly argued, controversially, that industrial occupations constituted "light labour," "so much less penal, irksome, and fatiguing" than treadwheel, crank, and shot-drill labour. The latter employments properly merited the designation of "hard labour" and should be prioritized, even if the labour was unproductive or could not be made profitable.[144] Although this view acquired the force of law in 1865, justices throughout England frequently ignored it, continuing to designate industrial employments as a type of first-class, or severe, labour.[145]

Scholars have sometimes suggested that, as attitudes towards criminals hardened in the 1820s, authorities stopped paying wages to prisoners for their labour. Certainly, reformers increasingly opposed remunerating prisoners, as they believed profit "necessarily weakens the character and abates the severity of punishment."[146] In London, however, magistrates continued to pay prisoners a small portion of the profits of their labour either as direct payments for work done or through an informal system of rewards. Some authorities paid inmates set amounts, such as at Giltspur where prisoners working on the mill were allowed two pence for every bushel of wheat ground. The profits were divided equally among the prisoners, who, on average, received six pence each weekly.[147] Other prisons, such as Brixton, set designated proportions.[148] Additionally, the Surrey visiting magistrates were also empowered to "furnish such of the prisoners as may have behaved themselves with propriety" with "decent" clothing and some money on their discharge so to "provide the means of present sustenance until they can obtain employment."[149] Some prisoners received relatively large sums on their discharge, such as Mary Keaton, given twenty shillings by the Middlesex prison committee for her "great diligence" in teaching female inmates.[150] Others received funds on discharge in recognition of their indigency. Since records for these disbursements do not survive, it is not possible to estimate how many were helped in this way or how much they were given.[151]

At the City's Bridewell, the value of rewards as incentives to industry was so prized that a special committee of governors in 1819 argued that "if the entire profit of the work were applied to this object, we are convinced it would not be bestowed in vain."[152] The prison committee and sub-committee minute books are littered with orders that certain prisoners be gifted particular sums of money or items of clothing, frequently for being "very industrious" and often because they were "in very great distress."[153] A few were explicitly paid for work performed: the vagrant prisoner James Campbell, for example, was paid £2.19s. on his discharge for dressing the hemp.[154] Many more were given items without explanation.

The emphasis on useful trades and the continued provision of profits point to magistrates' ongoing concern about prisoners' fates on release. Officials continued to stress that recidivism was not solely due to the moral failings of inmates. Many pointed to the difficulty that prisoners faced in finding employment after their discharge, and others emphasized the lack of support given to those struggling to re-enter 'polite' society. In his 1826 report to Parliament, for example, the chaplain at Brixton noted, "if distress occasioned by loss of character, and consequent inability to obtain employment, did not counteract them, by urging the offenders, when liberated, to seek subsistence in a return to dishonest practices, the instances of re-commitment would probably be much less frequent."[155] Rather than tougher punishments, he pushed for the county to allocate greater funds to the Surrey Refuge of the Destitute.

The Refuge, which furnished employment to discharged prisoners, helped, the chaplain claimed, "render permanent" the "good impressions which the temperance, regularity and habits of industry, enforced in the prison, leave, for a time at least, on the minds of the prisoners."[156] In short, prison discipline worked; the problems were the short period in which inmates were exposed to it and society's response to ex-prisoners.

Magistrates throughout London testified to the pressing need for more support for ex-prisoners. "The insufficiency of such existing institutions as are open to the repentant prisoner," the Middlesex justices reported in 1842, was "a serious impediment in the way of reformation." They stressed that the relief "most needed" by prisoners was "actual employment, and that on the moment of their discharge, before the good impressions produced in the prison have become effaced by a return to their former haunts and companions."[157] If gainful employment could be located for prisoners on their discharge, these magistrates believed that ex-convicts, cured of their former habits as a result of bridewell discipline, would not turn again to crime. In recognition of the difficulties faced by ex-offenders returning to society, magistrates sought to equip their inmates with skills that might aid them in securing employment after their release and to supply them with small sums of money or with clothing to help them find their feet. In England as a whole, concern over recidivism additionally led magistrates to expand prison education and to form close relationships with refuges and asylums dedicated to assisting and improving recently discharged prisoners.[158]

Authorities who embraced the silent, rather than the separate, system, as in all the bridewells under study here, are often portrayed as unconvinced by the efficacy of reformation by imprisonment.[159] However, the efforts to employ prisoners and to educate and support them after their release suggest we cannot view prison discipline as primarily deterrent or punitive. Local authorities across the period continued to prioritize reforming inmates (and making money off them) even while turning prisons into more austere, authoritarian sites. More generally, for English elites, there was nothing incongruous about wanting punishment to hurt more and adhering to a reformative philosophy of imprisonment.[160]

In London, these efforts centred on houses of correction, prisons that held individuals sentenced to relatively short terms of imprisonment, from a few weeks to a few years, with hard labour. Prisons that functioned mainly as sites of safe custody, namely gaols and compters, continued to operate differently in the early nineteenth century. There, the hallmarks of the punitive prison – the treadwheel, separation or total silence, the elimination of visiting rights, and so on – were not introduced, in recognition of the more lenient treatment that magistrates believed untried prisoners deserved, and magistrates paid little attention to the inmates' moral condition, in acknowledgment of their presumed innocence.

CONCLUSION

Specialization or Uniformity

I. CENTRALIZATION, BUREAUCRATIZATION, AND CREEPING UNIFORMITY

The practice of regulating prisons that primarily held prisoners for safe custody differently from prisons that primarily held offenders sentenced to short terms of imprisonment came under increasing pressure, especially from the 1830s, as the Westminster government's control over prisons expanded. The Home Office, with the support of Parliament, pushed more and more for prisons across the country to be organized and administered in a uniform fashion. All, they argued, should have characteristics typically associated with punitive prisons.

The passage of the 1823 *Gaol Act*, promoted by Home Secretary Robert Peel, marked an early success for these wider objectives. It introduced for the first time a general set of standards for prisons. The act declared "due Classification, Inspection, regular Labour and Employment, and Religious and Moral Instruction" to be "essential to the Discipline of a Prison." Magistrates were instructed to introduce into all their prisons a designated classification system, religious and educational instruction, and labour. To encourage compliance, the act required that magistrates submit annual reports to the Home Secretary on the state of their prisons. The jurisdiction of the act was limited, applying only to large county gaols in England and Wales and to seventeen smaller English towns, but the City, Middlesex, and Surrey were all included.[1]

Home Office control and the push for uniformity increased further in subsequent years. In 1835, two select committees on prison discipline, one in the Commons and the other in the Lords, recommended greater severity, uniformity, and central inspection in the administration of prisons.[2] Following the publication of the Lords' report, the chairman of the committee, the Duke of Richmond, approached the prime minister, Lord Melbourne, to prepare a prison bill.[3] The 1835 *Prisons Act* empowered the Home Secretary to establish a prison inspectorate, composed of at most five men, to visit prisons across the country and report on their conditions to the Home Secretary.[4] The act further required magistrates to submit prison rules to the Home Secretary for approval. In practice, this authority devolved to Whitworth Russell and William Crawford, the inspectors for the home district, which included London. These men had long been involved in prison reform in London: Russell as Millbank chaplain and Crawford as a founding member and secretary of the SIPD. Although they could not compel local authorities to act, they used their platform to embarrass local authorities, especially by publicizing their administrative failings, and to promote their favoured system of imprisonment, the separate system.[5] In 1839, they convinced Parliament to pass an act that formally authorized the adoption of the separate system, and moreover, gave the Home Secretary the authority to approve – or reject – all new prison building schemes.[6] In 1840, the Home Office proposed the building of a "model" prison to demonstrate the separate system's benefits and to encourage its adoption by local authorities. Pentonville, which opened in 1842, had a clear impact on British prison design.[7] By 1850, at least fifty-five prisons had been erected or improved on the basis of the Pentonville model and six more were in progress; it also inspired the design of prisons abroad.[8]

Initially, London magistrates fiercely resisted the push for centralization and uniformity in prison administration. They argued against many of the measures ordered by the Home Office and by Parliament, and they dragged their feet in implementing them. Those in the City, ever alert to threats to their self-government, were particularly combative.[9] Yet, from the late 1830s, the magistrates also began adopting some of the measures promoted by central authorities and reform groups which they had previously deemed too punitive for custodial inmates. For example, in the wake of the 1835 *Prisons Act*, magistrates clamped down on gambling, gaming, and smoking in gaols.[10] At Giltspur Prison and Surrey gaol, but not at Newgate, New Prison, or Borough Compter, untried prisoners were also prohibited from purchasing beer.[11] At the bigger gaols, including Newgate and New Prison, magistrates started to enforce silence among the prisoners.[12]

Some jurisdictions were generally more receptive to the new tenets of reform. In Middlesex, but not in Surrey or the City, magistrates on the prison committee took on board reformist ideas about labour in custodial prisons in the late 1830s and set up voluntary labour systems in their gaol. Female prisoners were encouraged to take up needlework, knitting, cleaning, and cooking, while male prisoners were urged to act as carpenters and bricklayers. Despite this enthusiasm, however, only a handful of untried prisoners worked. The number who could be employed in building work was necessarily limited, and although there was more scope for female employment, the matron often found inmates unwilling to be employed, "notwithstanding the latitude [menial offices] afforded them, and the extra allowances they receive in consequence," she noted with dismay in 1844.[13]

The advocates of the separate system also made greater headway in Middlesex. In the fall of 1837, the magistrates ordered that wooden partitions be constructed to divide prisoner wards into smaller rooms; they began to provide some prisoners with separate sleeping berths; and they built a few dozen separate cells "upon the plan recommended by the prison inspectors."[14] In January 1838, the quarter sessions voted to keep untried prisoners in separate confinement on all occasions. They resolved to tear down and rebuild the gaol, and the prison committee invited the prison inspectors and government engineer to visit the prison and advise the magistrates on a particular plan.[15] Yet soon thereafter, interest in rebuilding the gaol cooled. It took another eight years before the magistrates demolished the gaol and pressed ahead with constructing a new prison. In Surrey, the bench adopted the separate system only in 1857, and instead of building a new prison, they opted to adapt the existing gaol, against the wishes of the inspectorate.[16]

Debates amongst the Middlesex magistrates and the prison officers, preserved in committee papers and prison reports, suggest that there were probably constant voices on the London benches who pushed to make custodial confinement more punitive in the nineteenth century. However, it was only at certain moments that such proposals received a warm hearing, and it was even rarer that action was taken. In Middlesex, for example, the chaplain constantly pressured the magistrates to introduce a stricter discipline into the gaol. He seems to have viewed gaol prisoners, despite their not having been convicted of an offence, as morally dubious and potentially if not actually criminal. Gaol discipline, therefore, needed to impress upon them "the misery as well as guilt of a criminal course ... urging them to forsake their evil ways as the only means of present and future happiness."[17]

Measures introduced into London's gaols and compters from the late 1830s indicate a shifting attitude towards untried prisoners and custodial detention. In particular, there seems to have been a growing willingness to restrict traditional inmate privileges, to police behaviour, and to enforce moralizing codes of conduct. In practice, however, other concerns – including the time and expense of implementing certain changes, and rivalries between various officials – served to slow the introduction of these changes. The impact of these changes on prison life at London's custodial prisons awaits further investigation. What the pattern of reform suggests, however, is that as uniformity and centralization made greater headway, the distinction between custodial and punitive confinement, between innocence and guilt, which had coalesced over the course of the eighteenth century at the instigation and activity of local magistrates, may have begun to fade away.

II. REWRITING THE HISTORY OF IMPRISONMENT, 1700–1850

Since the 1980s, social historians writing about the history of punishment have often been charged with uncovering lots of new evidence, but not using this to suggest "larger overviews, theoretical models, or methods of approach."[18] This book has certainly presented much new evidence on the use, administration, and experience of criminal confinement in London from the eighteenth to mid-nineteenth centuries; nonetheless, it has also attempted to do something more. Namely, it has sought to change how scholars study punishment, how we explain the expansion of imprisonment, and how we understand the nature of prison discipline.

This work has made a plea for studying punishment in a particular way. Specifically, I have tried to show why we need to consider the processes through which individuals came to be incarcerated alongside the management and experience of confinement. This is not done often enough in prison history. Yet, court commitment and sentencing practice indelibly shaped and was shaped by the nature of punishment. Moreover, charting court practices and recovering the actual practice of prison operation are as key to explaining changes in the history of punishment as tracing shifts in attitudes, ideas, and circumstances. This methodological point has wider implications for studies of punishment generally, not just at this time and place.

This study of court practice in London has unquestionably shown that the use of imprisonment expanded considerably between 1700 and 1850. Scholars have long been aware of this trend in general terms, but heretofore no work has attempted to trace the patterns of prison use so closely, at so many different courts, and in multiple jurisdictions. Such an exploration confirms that, from the eighteenth century, London courts increasingly used prisons not just to punish felons, but also to punish petty offenders and misdemeanants and to detain individuals temporarily in safe custody. These different uses of imprisonment were driven by distinct impulses and had distinct timelines.

Prisons had long been used to hold individuals temporarily until they could be examined by a justice, be tried by or give evidence before a court, have their sentence executed, or provide sureties to guarantee their appearance at sessions, their good behaviour, or their indemnifying of another party. The numbers imprisoned on a custodial basis grew as London expanded and as more Londoners took their disputes before the courts. Meanwhile, authorities turned to imprisonment to punish criminal offences of all sorts out of frustration with the available punishments, in particular the over-reliance on the gallows and the various problems this created for the administration of justice. Humanitarians and disciplinarians alike sought a penal system that promised predictability and proportionality: that is, they wanted certainty that guilty offenders would be punished and that the punishments would fit the crimes alleged. Increasingly, many also wanted punishments that would reform offenders, reducing crime by 'curing' malefactors. For this purpose, elites turned to hard labour.

The appeal of imprisonment, especially at hard labour, as a punishment for petty crime was recognized quite early by magistrates acting outside of formal sessions, who over the course of the eighteenth and nineteenth centuries took on more and more responsibility for adjudicating criminal disputes. Sentencing an offender to a term of imprisonment was seen as an effective way to add pain to a sentence of corporal punishment or a fine. It was also hoped that, by being removed from their usual environment and subjected to hard labour, the prisoner might become accustomed to discipline and industry. Such an intervention was especially crucial for petty offenders, who, if they were not corrected sharply, would become further debauched and prone to greater criminality, or so it was generally believed. London magistrates also made great use of prison sentences when assembled at their quarter and general sessions, often in combination with other sanctions, to punish misdemeanours. Such penalties became increasingly common from the second half of the eighteenth century. In London, magistrates were able to make extensive use of imprisonment at hard labour because they had built, stocked, and maintained houses of correction. This possibly set London authorities apart from other jurisdictions, who had perhaps let their bridewells, or more accurately their systems of labour, fall into decay.

The judges at the Old Bailey and the Surrey assizes embraced hard labour as a punishment for felony at the end of the seventeenth century in the context of a growing aversion to executing all convicted felons, a belief that other available options short of death were insufficiently punitive, and a desire to make convicted offenders useful to the state. Between the late 1710s and early 1770s, London courts favoured putting convicts to work overseas, via transportation, rather than keeping them incarcerated at home. Transportation had several advantages: it allowed authorities to push the problem of troublesome individuals elsewhere; it was thought a tougher punishment; and it was generally accepted that some convicts, seen as especially hardened or charged with particularly heinous crimes, were irreclaimable and so were unsuited to penitentiary confinement.

By the late eighteenth century, the English magistracy, Parliament, and the reading public broadly had become more confident in the ability of hard labour to suitably punish and thoroughly reform criminals. This confidence combined with growing opposition to transportation, especially from the colonies but also at home, to convince many that efforts to reform convicts through labour at home were worth trying on a broader scale. Consequently, in London, the numbers and proportions of felons sentenced to imprisonment at hard labour grew from the 1770s. The real expansion in prison sentences came slightly later – crucially, after magistrates had rebuilt, expanded, and redesigned their houses of correction along reformed lines. In this sense, the state and capacity of prisons closely conditioned changes in court practice.

Some scholars, highlighting the failure of the *Penitentiary Act*, have suggested that the development of "large-scale organised imprisonment" failed at this juncture because it was "anathema to the British" who "repeatedly rejected" imprisonment at hard labour because it "infringed upon the liberties of 'free-born subjects.'"[19] Yet, there was little to no opposition raised to imprisonment on these grounds. Instead, principled opposition to hard labour in the 1770s focused on convicted offenders working *outside* prisons on public works. This was likened by some parliamentarians to slavery, which, it was claimed, apparently unironically, was "no less abhorrent to the spirit of the constitution than to the feelings of an Englishman."[20] Increasingly, those who supported extending hard labour at home argued that it should be carried out within the walls of a prison and be accompanied by solitude and religious instruction. As one anonymous commentator explained,

> Hard Labour in public … can never be considered by a wise Statesman, but as a temporary expedient in the want of proper prison room, to confine him, till brought to a right mind. Let him be habituated to Labour at Arts, by which he may earn his Bread in the World: this alone can answer the purpose you have in view.[21]

National penitentiaries were not built in the late eighteenth century, but the penitentiary idea nonetheless found wide purchase. Several counties including Middlesex, Surrey, Gloucestershire, Lancashire, and Oxfordshire constructed large prisons self-consciously on the penitentiary model. In this sense, large-scale imprisonment *was* embraced by the end of the eighteenth century, especially for petty offenders and certain felons, and its adoption stemmed from a renewed belief in the reformatory qualities of imprisonment. Such views were not confined to a small group of reformers but were shared widely by county justices throughout England. What was rejected at this stage was not the penitentiary, but central government control and oversight over prisons. Indeed, into the middle of the nineteenth century, administration of punishment remained firmly in local hands.[22] In London, this meant the development of a varied penal system that relied extensively on prisons, transportation, and execution to punish, deter, and reform criminals.

Prison historians have gone to great efforts to explain how the "squalid conditions of local prisons and the spectacle of the scaffold were replaced with the sanitary and disciplinary regimen of the modern penitentiary."[23] Yet such an endeavour is misguided as it misunderstands the changes that took place during the long eighteenth century. We have seen already that the greater use of imprisonment as a punishment did not lead straightforwardly or immediately to the abolition of the death penalty. The widespread adoption of imprisonment at hard labour as a punishment for felony came about a century after the punishment was first mooted following extensive experimentation both with other punishments and with using imprisonment for lighter offences. Similarly, there was no overnight transformation in prison conditions. London magistrates had long been interested in their prisons, which were neither as squalid nor as lawless as late-eighteenth-century prison reformers, and twentieth-century prison historians, claimed. Nevertheless, changes in court practice unquestionably altered how magistrates approached their prisons. Greater use of imprisonment prompted magistrates to assume greater responsibility for and control over their prisons and to embark on more expensive and ambitious plans for their reform. Again, many of the central aims – to improve health, to strengthen security, to impose greater order – were not new, but they were pursued with greater vigour and more financial support from the late eighteenth century.

Court practice had another impact: it forced local authorities to grapple with the difficulties presented by managing larger and more diverse prison populations and to think seriously about how they defined and wanted to distinguish the different kinds of confinement. Although prisons had been founded to serve particular functions, the original differences between them had eroded somewhat over time as legislation and court practice extended the uses to which imprisonment could be put and endowed committing bodies with broad flexibility when deciding where and how to incarcerate those who came before them. Most London magistrates in the eighteenth century made some use of these powers, especially when pressed for prison space, and consequently, bridewells sometimes held sizeable numbers of pre-trial prisoners while gaols and compters occasionally received convicted prisoners for punishment. Frustration with the multi-purpose nature of individual prisons and with the heterogeneity of inmate populations grew as the use of imprisonment expanded. In this context, London authorities opted to use the flexibility granted to them by custom and statute to tailor their commitment practices in pursuit of creating a more specialized prison system.

Throughout the metropolis, local authorities came to treat prisons as either custodial or punitive. More and more, prisoners for punishment, especially those sentenced to hard labour, were sent to houses of correction while prisoners for custody were directed to gaols and compters. These policies, which drew on traditional commitment practices, solidified in the late eighteenth century and hardened even further in the early nineteenth. By this later point, it was almost universally accepted in London that it would be unjust to send an individual detained solely for safe custody to a house of correction, and conversely, that it would be inappropriate to direct an individual sentenced to imprisonment with hard labour to a gaol or compter. A response to swelling prison populations, prison specialization made headway as a policy because it allowed magistrates to rationalize and streamline prison commitment practices and prison operation; it promised to ensure that the guilty were properly punished and hopefully reformed; and it helped to safeguard the rights of the accused.

One key aim of specialization was to punish the guilty more effectively. For the vast majority of individuals sentenced to imprisonment as a punishment, labour was a fundamental aspect of their sentence. This was why most such offenders throughout the eighteenth century had been directed to houses of correction, as, at these prisons, magistrates could reasonably expect that inmates would work. Heightened fears over societal decay and a renewed emphasis on institutionalized labour as key to moral reform prompted London magistrates at the end of the century to insist on these commitment practices. Not only would this allow magistrates to concentrate those imprisoned with hard labour in specific institutions, a useful practice for prison management, but it also would ensure that those so sentenced did in fact labour. Yet, by this point, London magistrates no longer believed that labour alone could turn criminals into useful members of society. Instead, they advocated a combination of hard labour, religious education, close surveillance, and a degree of solitary confinement. Magistrates subsequently embarked on bold and expensive reform programmes to put these convictions into practice. Though London is not typically seen as a centre of prison reform activity in the eighteenth century, its magistrates poured considerable energy and funds into rebuilding their prisons.

Major reforms were also introduced into gaols and compters, those prisons that mainly served as sites of custodial detention. Reforms aimed to make custodial prisons healthier, larger, more secure, and better managed. They did not seek to create a moral environment capable of transforming the character of those reformed. In this, they differed materially from the reforms introduced into houses of correction. Again, this reminds us how closely court practice shaped the forms that prisons took. In gaols and compters, magistrates did not introduce labour systems; they did not adopt separate confinement; only Surrey adopted (partial) cellular confinement; they did not make divine service mandatory; they did not attempt to closely surveil or regulate inmate behaviour; they did not clamp down on traditional, "disorderly" pastimes such as drinking, smoking, and gaming. Ultimately, the effect of these policies was to create two distinct forms of confinement in London: custodial and punitive.

The discipline at reformed gaols and compters reflected the magistrates' growing belief that confinement for custody should entail less severe restrictions than confinement for punishment. Indeed, London authorities came to argue that bridewell confinement – with its strict diet, forced labour, separate confinement, and restrictions on visits – subjected pre-trial inmates to unlawful severities. In this sense, prison specialization was driven by a desire to better protect the innocent as well as by a wish to punish the guilty. The new sensitivity to the rights of the accused in detention was closely linked to broader shifts in the nature of criminal trials and to concerns over the treatment of criminal defendants. It also stemmed from the actions of prison inmates themselves, who put considerable pressure on magistrates at the end of the eighteenth and start of the nineteenth centuries to treat them in particular ways.

The conclusions that London magistrates came to regarding the appropriate conditions of confinement for non-convict prisoners differed starkly from those of the more zealous reformers within and outside government. These differences in opinion became more prominent, and more problematic for London magistrates, from the 1810s, with the revival of the prison reform movement. London prison policy was particularly scrutinized and debated in newspapers, pamphlets, and Parliament, with magistrates regularly required to justify their policies and defend their reputations. Meanwhile, their scope for independent action was increasingly reduced by the growing power of the Home Office. Under these conditions, London magistrates accepted that they would need to assume greater responsibility for and oversight of their gaols and compters. In addition to improving conditions and clarifying prison administration, they expended some effort in making custodial prisons more orderly and less lively. Yet, into the middle of the nineteenth century, magistrates resisted, to varying degrees, many of the proposals put forth by reformers within and outside government to make custodial prisons more punitive. Resistance was especially fierce in the City, where traditional prison practices and rights consequently survived the longest.

The nineteenth century saw broader attempts to transform English prisons of all types into bleaker, harsher places. Historians typically explain such efforts by pointing to the growing disenchantment with reformative philosophy and the harsher attitudes towards the poor and criminal offenders. Changes in penal practice are not typically referenced, but in London, these played an important role in leading magistrates to introduce tougher measures into their houses of correction. Alongside commentators in the press and officials in government, London magistrates looked to make confinement more unpleasant for the serious offenders who were increasingly populating their bridewells. In so doing, many hoped to transform imprisonment into a plausible replacement for transportation and execution.

Even as London magistrates embraced more severe measures from the 1820s, they remained committed to moral reform. They continued to believe that prisons should rehabilitate, as well as punish, criminal offenders. Consequently, they extended secular education, expanded productive labour and industrial training, set up systems to provide inmates with small sums of money on their discharge, and established relationships with prisoner aid societies. At least until 1850, then, harsher attitudes towards convicted criminal offenders did not result in a general loss of faith by magistrates in the potential of reformation. Nor did it cause magistrates to lose all compassion for prisoners. Instead, many magistrates and prison officers, though in ways that were deeply paternalistic and patronizing, showed a broad recognition of the challenges that people faced in earning an honest living and a willingness to do more to support those they deemed obedient and repentant.

How common or distinctive London's prison system was in eighteenth- and nineteenth-century Britain awaits further investigation. As this study has shown, penal and prison policy in this period was intensely local. Magistrates had vast flexibility and wide discretion not only in their court sentencing practices, but also in designing and regulating their prisons. This was a period of great penal experimentation across Britain. The decisions that were made reflected local conditions and circumstances as well as individual personalities and beliefs. What the few existing studies of prisons suggest is that London magistrates were not alone in trying to refine their prison systems in the late eighteenth century to make them more rational, efficient, and orderly. Their growing belief in reformative imprisonment was not unusual, nor was their enthusiasm for specialization. Possibly, their moves to divorce custodial and punitive confinement found traction elsewhere, as they stemmed from broadly held views on innocence and guilt. Moreover, justices communicated fairly regularly across county lines when designing their prison systems, and the practice of some counties had a considerable impact on practice elsewhere. Finally, London's experience suggests that it is worth paying more attention to jurisdictions that are not typically seen as pioneers of reform. A close examination of London's court practice and its prison regulation between roughly 1750 and 1840 suggests not an uninterested magistracy nor a resistance to change, but rather, an intense interest in reorganizing and remaking its prison system.

Notes

INTRODUCTION

1 Daniel Defoe, *A Tour thro' the Whole Island of Great Britain*, 3 vols, 1724–26 (London, 1725), 2: 137.

2 Sidney and Beatrice Webb, *English Prisons under Local Government* (London: Longmans, Green, 1922); Leon Radzinowicz, *A History of England Criminal Law*, vol. 1 (London: Stevens, 1948).

3 For a full account of this literature see Joanna Innes and John Styles, "The Crime Wave: Recent Writing on Crime and Criminal Justice in Eighteenth-Century England," *Journal of British Studies* 25, no. 4 (1986): 383, 410–11.

4 Michel Foucault, *Discipline and Punish*, trans. Alan Sheridan (London: Allen Lane, 1977).

5 Ibid., 82.

6 David Rothman, *The Discovery of the Asylum: Social Order and Disorder in the New Republic* (Boston: Little, Brown and Company, 1971); Michael Ignatieff, *A Just Measure of Pain: The Penitentiary in the Industrial Revolution, 1750–1850* (London: Pantheon Books, 1978); Robin Evans, *A Fabrication of Virtue. English Prison Architecture, 1750–1840* (Cambridge: Cambridge University Press, 1982).

7 Foucault, "The Subject and Power," in *Michel Foucault: Beyond Structuralism and Hermeneutics*, ed. Hubert Dreyfus and Paul Rabinow (Chicago: University of Chicago Press, 1983), 208–9.

8 My thanks to an anonymous reader for Oxford Historical Monographs for this point. Foucault is a divisive figure amongst historians. See Randall McGowan, "Power and Humanity, or Foucault among the Historians," in *Reassessing Foucault: Medicine, Power and the Body*, ed. Roy Porter and Colin Jones (London: Routledge, 1994), 91–112.

9 Georg Rusche and Otto Kirchheimer, *Punishment and Social Structure* (New York: Columbia University Press, 1939); Dario Melossi and Massimo Pavarini, *The Prison and the Factory: Origins of the Penitentiary System* (London: Palgrave, 2018).

10 Ignatieff, *Just Measure*. See also his later comments: Michael Ignatieff, "State, Civil Society, and Total Institutions: A Critique of Recent Social Histories of Punishment," *Crime and Justice* 3 (1981): 153–92.

11 John Beattie, *Crime and the Courts in England, 1650–1800* (Oxford, UK: Oxford University Press, 1986), 308–9, 421, 555–9.

12 McGowen, "The Body and Punishment in Eighteenth-Century England," *Journal of Modern History* 59, no. 4 (1987): 651–79; "Civilizing Punishment: The End of the Public Execution in England," *Journal of British Studies* 33, no. 3 (1994): 257–82. See also Peter King, *Punishing the Criminal Corpse, 1700–1840* (London: Palgrave, 2017).

13 Pieter Spierenburg, "Punishment, Power and History: Foucault and Elias," *Social Science History* 28, no. 4 (2004): 607–36; Peter Spierenburg, *The Prison Experience: Disciplinary Institutions and Their Inmates in Early Modern Europe* (New Brunswick, NJ: Rutgers, 1991).

14 Excellent work on court sentencing cited regularly in this work includes Peter King, *Crime, Justice and Discretion in England* (Oxford, UK: Oxford University Press, 2000); Robert Shoemaker, *Prosecution and Punishment: Petty Crime and the Law in London and Rural Middlesex* (Cambridge: Cambridge University Press, 1991); Drew Gray, *Crime, Prosecution and Social Relations: The Summary Courts of the City of London in the Late Eighteenth Century* (London: Palgrave MacMillan, 2009).

15 This approach was used in Beattie, *Crime and Courts*. Vic Bailey also stresses the importance of considering punishment "in all its manifestations": "judicial sentencing, law making, and the administration of legal penalties." Victor Bailey, *The Rise and Fall of the Rehabilitative Ideal, 1895–1970* (London: Routledge, 2019).

16 Joanna Innes's work is a notable exception. Innes, "Prisons for the Poor: English Bridewells, 1555–1800," in *Labour, Law, and Crime: An Historical Perspective*, ed. Francis Snyder and Douglas Hay (London: Tavistock, 1987), 42–122. Innes's article looked at England over several centuries, and as a result, remained quite broad.

17 Richard Bell, "Dens of Tyranny and Oppression: The Politics of Imprisonment for Debt in Seventeenth-Century London" (PhD diss., Stanford University, 2017); P.H. Haagen, "Imprisonment for Debt in England" (PhD diss., Princeton University, 1986); Margot Finn, *Character of Credit: Personal Debt in English Culture, 1740–1914* (Cambridge: Cambridge University Press, 2003); Tawny Paul, *The Poverty of Disaster: Debt and Insecurity in Eighteenth-Century Britain* (Cambridge: Cambridge University Press, 2019); Alexander Wakelam, *Credit and Debt in Eighteenth-Century England: An Economic History of Debtors' Prisons* (London: Routledge, 2020).

18 Terms such as 'local government' and 'central government' were not often used in the period, but they are nonetheless useful here as they help us to distinguish between local bodies, especially justices of the peace, who operated largely independently of the centre at least until the nineteenth century, and Parliament and the agencies and offices under its direct remit. On this see Innes, "Central Government 'Interference': Changing Conceptions, Practices, and Concerns, c. 1700–1850," in *Civil Society in British History*, ed. Jose Harris (Oxford, UK: Oxford University Press, 2003), 39–60.

19 Rosalind Crone, with Lesley Hoskins and Rebecca Preston, *Guide to the Criminal Prisons of Nineteenth-Century England*, vol. 1 (London: London Publishing Partnership, 2018), 4. For studies, see Helen Johnston, Barry Godfrey, and David J. Cox, *Penal Servitude: Convicts and Long-Term Imprisonment, 1853–1948* (Montreal and Kingston: McGill-Queen's University Press, 2022); Elaine Farrell, *Women, Crime, and Punishment in Ireland: Life in the Nineteenth-Century Convict Prison* (Cambridge: Cambridge University Press, 2020); Ignatieff, *Just Measure*; Ben Bethell, *"Star Men" in English Convict Prisons, 1879–1948* (Abingdon, UK: Routledge, 2023); Catherine Cox and Hilary Marland, "'He Must Die or Go Mad in This Place': Prisoners, Insanity, and the Pentonville Model Prison Experiment, 1842–52," *Bulletin of the History of Medicine* 92, no. 1 (2018): 78–109.

20 Clifford Dobb, "London's Prisons," in *Shakespeare in His Own Age*, ed. Allardyce Nicoll (Cambridge: Cambridge University Press, 1964), 87–100; W.J. Sheehan, "The London Prison System 1666–1795" (PhD diss.; College Park, MD: University of Maryland, 1975); J.R.S. Whiting, *Prison Reform in Gloucestershire, 1776–1820* (London: Phillimore, 1975); R.A. Cooper, "English Prison Reform 1773–1835: A Study in Administrative Change" (PhD diss.; Chapel Hill, NC: University of North Carolina, 1975); Eric Stockdale, *A Study of Bedford Prison, 1660–1877* (London: Phillimore, 1977); Beattie, *Crime and Courts*; Margaret DeLacy, *Prison Reform in Lancashire, 1750–1850* (Manchester, UK: Manchester

University Press, 1986); W.J. Forsythe, *A System of Discipline – Exeter Borough Prison 1819–1863* (Exeter, UK: Exeter University Press, 1983).

21 The patchy survival of pre-1780 records is partly responsible for these chronological and geographical limitations. For pre-1780 histories see Bell, "Tyranny"; Esther Brot, "By Their Own Hand: Prisons in the City of London, 1700–1755" (PhD diss., King's College, 2022); Wakelam, *Credit*. Additionally, Rachel Weil is working on a project on imprisonment in gaols in seventeenth-century England. Early modern literary scholars have also helped to shed light on carceral experiences. See "Prison Writings in Early Modern England: Special Issue," *Huntington Library Quarterly* 72, no. 2 (2009); Ruth Ahnert, *The Rise of Prison Literature in the Sixteenth Century* (Cambridge: Cambridge University Press, 2013).

22 Webbs, *Prisons*, 13–15, 160–7. The Webbs' findings are problematic. See Kiran Mehta, "Courts and Prisons" (DPhil diss., University of Oxford, 2021), 13.

23 Seán McConville, *History of Prison Administration, 1750–1877* (London: Routledge, 1981), 67; Evans, *Fabrication*, 19, 52–3; DeLacy, *Lancashire*, 23, 56.

24 Innes, "English Bridewells," 94; Beattie, *Crime and Courts*, 492–3.

25 The records that survive are: "Prisoners Awaiting Trial, Books," LMA, WJ/CC/B; "Prisoners Awaiting Trial, Rolls," LMA, WJ/CC/R; "Lists of Prisoners Tried," LMA, WJ/CP. The rolls cover the house of correction for 1716–65. The books for the gatehouse cover 1720–65. The books for the house of correction cover 1701–1832, but the later period is notably thin, with only ten books for 1775–1832. WJ/CP/A covers the bridewell for 1838–47 while WJ/CP/P covers the gatehouse for 1693–1765.

26 Kenneth Goodacre and E. Doris Mercer, eds, *Guide to the Middlesex Sessions Records, 1549–1889* (London: Greater London Record Office, 1965), 14–15; Sidney and Beatrice Webb, *English Local Government from the Revolution to the Municipal Corporations Act* (London: Longmans, Green, 1908), 223–5.

27 Ralph Pugh, *Imprisonment in Medieval England* (Cambridge: Cambridge University Press, 1968), 1–3.

28 William Alfred Morris, *The Medieval English Sheriff* (Manchester, UK: The University Press, 1927), 150; Pugh, "The King's Prisons before 1250," *Transactions of the Royal Historical Society* 5 (1955): 2.

29 Custodial imprisonment was made obligatory for certain offences. Edward Peters, "The Prison before the Prison," in *Oxford History of the Prison*, ed. Norval Morris and David Rothman (Oxford, UK: Oxford University Press, 1995), 31; Pugh, *Imprisonment*, 5.

30 5 Hen IV c. 10.

31 Margery Bassett, "Newgate Prison in the Middle Ages," *Speculum* 18, no. 2 (1943): 234; Pugh, "Prisons," 1, 12.

32 The shrievalties of London and Middlesex were joined sometime between the 1040s and mid-1100s, which is why Newgate served both counties. Sheehan, "London Prison," 21; Susan Reynolds, "The Rulers of London in the Twelfth Century," *History* 57, no. 191 (1972): 337–57.

33 Mary Alexander, "Aspects of the Early History of Guildford and Its Castle" (PhD diss., University of Reading, 2004), 59, 118, 135.

34 Surrey lacked a gaol for a period of years. "Southwark Prisons," in *Survey of London*, vol. 25, *St George's Fields*, ed. Ida Darlington (London: London County Council, 1955), 9–21, *British History Online*, http://www.british-history.ac.uk/survey-london/vol25/pp9–21.

35 Penny Tucker, *Law Courts and Lawyers in the City of London, 1300–1550* (Cambridge: Cambridge University Press, 2007), 97–8, 131–2, 138–40.

36 Pugh, *Imprisonment*, 110.

37 Caroline Barron, *London in the Later Middle Ages: Government and People* (Oxford, UK: Oxford University Press, 2004), 167–8, fn110.

38 Bruce Watson, "Compter Prisons of London," *London Archaeologist* 7, no. 5 (1993): 116; Johnson, *Southwark and the City* (Oxford, UK: Oxford University Press, 1969), 223.

39 Bridewell's early history has been well studied. A.J. Copeland, *Bridewell Royal Hospital Past and Present* (London: Wells Gardner Darton, 1888); E.G. O'Donoghue, *Bridewell Hospital, Palace, Prison, Schools*, vol. 1 (London: Bodley Head, 1923); Paul Griffiths, *Lost Londons: Crime, Control, and Change in the Capital City, 1550–1660* (Cambridge: Cambridge University Press, 2008); Jennifer Cryar, "The London Bridewell: Defining Deviance in Early Modern London" (PhD diss., Queen Mary University of London, 2022).

40 Spierenburg, *Prison Experience*, 23–6. See also Michel Foucault, *Madness and Civilisation*, trans. Richard Howard (New York: Pantheon, 1973).

41 18 Eliz I c. 3; 39 Eliz I c. 4.

42 7 Jac I c. 4.

43 Innes, "Bridewells," 73.

44 Bassett, "Newgate," esp. 233n3; K.J. Kesselring, *Mercy and Authority in the Tudor State* (Cambridge: Cambridge University Press, 2003), 27–32; Helen Carrel, "The Ideology of Punishment in Late Medieval English Towns," *Social History* 34, no. 2 (2009): 312–14; Christine Winter, "Prisons and Punishments in Late Medieval London" (PhD diss., University of London, 2012), esp. 17–23, 26–31.

45 Pugh, *Imprisonment*, 40–1.

46 Peter King, "Summary Courts and Social Relations in Eighteenth-Century England," *Past and Present* 183, no. 1 (2004), 124–7. See also Douglas Hay, "England 1562–1875: The Law and Its Uses," in *Masters, Servants, and Magistrates in Britain and the Empire*, ed. Douglas Hay and Paul Craven (Chapel Hill, NC: University of North Carolina Press, 2004): 59–116.

47 King, *Discretion*, 83; Thomas Sweeney, "Extension and Practice of Summary Jurisdiction in England c. 1790–1860" (PhD diss., University of Cambridge, 1985).

48 Michael Dalton, *The County Justice* (London, 1697); Giles Jacob, *The Modern Justice* (London, 1716); Samuel Blackerby, *The Justice of Peace his Companion* (London, 1711); Richard Burn, *Justice of the Peace, and Parish Officer*, 6th ed. (London, 1758). See "laborious" in Thomas Dyche and William Pardon, *A New General English Dictionary*, 11th ed. (London, 1760).

49 27 Geo III c. 37; 13 Car II c. 11. See also 4 Geo I c. 7; 6 Geo I st. 1 c. 13; 1 Geo I st. 2 c. 46.

50 27 Geo III c. 11. The act specified: "it shall be lawful for any justice … to commit either to the common Gaol, or to any House of Correction, within his or their respective Jurisdictions … such Vagrants, and other Criminals, Offenders, and Persons charged with or convicted of small Offences, as by any Law now in force, or hereafter to be made."

51 Robert Shoemaker and Timothy Hitchcock, *London Lives: Poverty, Crime and the Making of a Modern City* (Cambridge: Cambridge University Press, 2015), 70, 71–5.

52 Shoemaker, *Prosecution and Punishment*, 166–7; Beattie, *Crime*, 293.

53 See also Spencer Weinreich, "Unaccountable Subjects: Contracting Legal and Medical Authority in the Newgate Smallpox Experiment," *History Workshop Journal* 89 (2020): 22–44; Beattie, *Crime*, 292–3.

54 6 Geo I c. 19.
55 22 Geo III c. 64; 101 "English Reports" 1329.
56 Innes, "Bridewells," 74–5.
57 18 Eliz I c. 7; 3 W&M c. 9; 10 Will 3 c. 12; 6 Ann c. 9. On benefit of clergy: Beattie, *Crime and Courts*, 141–7; Beattie, *Policing*, 19; John Langbein, "Shaping the Eighteenth-Century Criminal Trial," *University of Chicago Law Review* 50, no. 1 (1983): 37–41.
58 City men were not alone in promoting hard labour. See Beattie's discussion of John Brewer and his failed 1693 bill in Beattie, *Policing*, 302, 316–21, 326–34.
59 18 Eliz I c. 7; 21 Jac I c. 6; Innes, "Bridewells," 75; Langbein, "Shaping," 38.
60 6 Ann c. 9.
61 See "Petitions to Queen Anne, George I, etc, of and rel. to detained criminals," British Library, Add MS 61618, and "Correspondence between Secretary and City Justices," LMA, MJ/SP/1706/02/018–19. On sentencing: Shoemaker and Hitchcock, *London Lives*, 67; Innes, "Bridewells," 89–90.
62 Beattie, *Policing*, 473.
63 16 Geo III c. 43; 19 Geo III c. 74. On these acts see Simon Devereaux, "The Making of the Penitentiary Act, 1775–1779," *The Historical Journal* 42, no. 2 (1999): 405–33.

CHAPTER ONE

1 Textiles were prominent objects of crime in this period. John Styles, "Spinners and the Law: Regulating Yarn Standards in the English Worsted Industries, 1550–1800," *Textile History* 44, no. 2 (2013): 145–70.
2 "Police intelligence," *Morning Chronicle* (London), 17 July 1834, 4. All newspaper articles cited in this work were accessed on British Newspaper Archive, https://www.britishnewspaperarchive.co.uk/, or British Library Newspapers, https://www.gale.com/intl/primary-sources/british-library-newspapers.
3 Gray, *Summary Courts*, 78–82; John Beattie, "Sir John Fielding and Public Justice," *Law and History Review* 25, no. 1 (2007): 61–110.
4 "Police," *The Morning Chronicle* (London), 18 Nov. 1822, 4, col. a.
5 Ibid.
6 *The Standard* (London), 25 Jan. 1828, 4, col. b.
7 John Paul, *The Compleat Constable* (London, 1785), 92.
8 "Police officer" includes the night watchmen, constables, marshalmen, beadles, and Bow Street Runners. For policing in London: Elaine Reynolds, *Before the Bobbies: The Night Watch and Police Reform in Metropolitan London, 1720–1830* (Basingstoke, UK: Macmillan, 1998); John Beattie, *First English Detectives: Bow Street Runners and Policing of London, 1750–1840* (Oxford, UK: Oxford University Press, 2012).
9 Robert Burn, *The Justice of the Peace, and Parish Officer*, 3rd ed. (London, 1756), 50.
10 Gray, *Summary Courts*, 2.
11 Most recent work on this is Rosalind Crone's Local Lock-Up Project, https://www.prisonhistory.org/local-lock-up/. See also Tim Hitchcock, "'You bitches … die and be damned': Gender, Authority and the Mob in St Martin's Roundhouse Disaster of 1742," in *Streets of London*, ed. Tim Hitchcock and Heather Shore (London: Rivers Oram, 2003), 69–81.

12 "Trial of Mary Powell, Mary Smith, Mary Brown" (t18090215-75), 15 Feb. 1809, *Old Bailey Proceedings Online* [hereafter OBO], http://www.oldbaileyonline.org, version 8.0, accessed 20 Jan. 2019.

13 Tony Henderson, *Disorderly Women in Eighteenth-Century London* (London: Longman, 1999), 129. See also Andrew Harris, *Policing the City: Crime and Legal Authority in London, 1780–1840* (Columbus, OH: Ohio State University Press, 2004), 13.

14 "Statement of Persons taken by Metropolitan Police, 1831–32, 1833," *U.K. Parliamentary Papers* [hereafter PP], https://parlipapers.proquest.com/, version 1.51, 225, xxxii.387.

15 Henderson, *Disorderly*, 130.

16 "Inspectors of Prisons of Great Britain I, Home District, Fourth Report, 1839," PP, xxi.1 (210), 276.

17 On the longevity of the use of compters see "Folio cclxvi b" in *Calendar of Letter-Books of the City of London, H: 1375–1399*, ed. Reginald Sharpe (London: His Majesty's Stationery Office, 1907), 366–79, BHO, http://www.british-history.ac.uk/london-letter-books/volh.

18 "Report on Gaols in City of London, 1813–14," PP, iv.249 (152), 41.

19 Copeland, *Bridewell*, 63; BCGM, 4 Mar. 1802, LMA, CLC/275/MS33011/025. Originally consulted on microfilm at LMA, but some records are also available online: "Minute Book," BCB-25, Bethlem Museum of the Mind, https://archives.museumofthemind.org.uk/BCB.htm.

20 These calculations include offenders against the criminal and poor laws. Debtors have not been included. "Poultry Compter Charge Book (9 Nov. 1802–22 Sept. 1804)" and "Giltspur Compter Charge Book (26 Aug. 1807–6 June 1809)," LMA, CLA/030/01/014; "Southwark Compter Charge Book, 8 July 1814–30 Dec. 1820," LMA, CLA/031/01/003.

21 Ibid. In both cases, these are the earliest charge books surviving that list criminal prisoners.

22 "Memorial of John Teague, Keeper of Giltspur, and of Edward Kirby, Keeper of Poultry, 14 June 1814, Court of Aldermen Gaol Committee Papers," LMA, COL/CA/GAC/03/001. By comparison, historians have found that unskilled men could expect to earn on average about 13*d.* daily in the 1780s and 23*d.* in the 1810s while women could earn about 6*s.*4*d.* in the 1780s and 9*s.*7*d.* in the 1810s. Jane Humphries and Jacob Weisdorf, "The Wages of Women in England, 1260–1850," *Journal of Economic History* 75, no. 2 (2015): 432.

23 Keepers sometimes recognized there was no point in chasing some prisoners who they knew were unable to pay the fees. Sheehan, "System," 224–6.

24 "Cash Book of Samuel Newport, Keeper of New Prison, 1790–98," LMA, MA/G/CLE/0032–033.

25 Howard, *The State of the Prisons in England and Wales* (1780), 170, 174, 208; Howard, *Account of Lazarettos in Europe*, vol. 2 (London, 1789), 245; James Neild, *State of Prisons in England, Scotland and Wales* (London, 1812), 57, 60, 229, 292, 485.

26 "Prisoner returns, 1808–19," LMA, CLA/032/01/037; "Report of Committee on Prisons in City of London and Southwark, 1818," PP, viii.297 (275), 123–4.

27 LMA, CLA/030/01/019.

28 Ibid. When an offender was discharged by proclamation, it normally indicated that the prosecutor, usually the victim, had not appeared to prosecute. If the offence was vagrancy-related, offenders might be committed for the sessions even though there was no intention to put that offender on trial, and once the sessions came round, they were discharged by proclamation.

29 LMA, CLA/031/01/003.

30 For example, "Petition of Ann Saunders, 9 Oct. 1754," *London Lives, 1690–1800* [hereafter *LL*], (http://www.londonlives.org, version 2.0), LMSMPS504350028; "Rolls on Death of William Pimlott, 14 Nov. 1768," *LL*, LMSMPS505890002.

31 "List of Prisoners Tried (Papers), 1724–53," LMA, MJ/SP/1724/01/033–4, MJ/SP/1724/10/142–4, MJ/SP/1736/01/065-6, MJ/CP/P/046–7, 075–8, 196–8, 226–7; "Prisoner Rolls, Dec. 1744," LMA, MJ/CC/R/004.

32 "Petition of Samuel Price, 9 Sept. 1732," *LL*, LMSMPS502850017.

33 "London, Jan. 25," *Stamford Mercury* (Stamford, Lincolnshire), 30 Jan. 1772, 2 col. 4; LMA, MJ/SP/1724/01/033–4.

34 MPCM, 19 Mar. 1796, LMA, MA/G/GEN/0302, 0308; MGOC, June 1793, *LL*, LMSMPS508850188.

35 MPCM, 13 Aug. 1796, LMA, MA/G/GEN/0308.

36 "Appendix 7," in "Commissioners Report on Cold Bath Fields, Dec. 1800," *PP*, 132, 77; MPCM, 25 Feb. 1796, LMA, MJ/SP/1796/02/03; MPCM, 11 Dec. 1802, LMA, MA/G/GEN/0002.

37 "Third Report from Select Committee on Police of the Metropolis, 1818," *PP*, viii.1 (423), 13, 291.

38 Ibid., 51, 82.

39 "Police intelligence," *The Morning Post* (London), 11 Jan. 1836.

40 Ibid. The Mendicity Society was formally established in London in 1818 to tackle the "alarming prevalence" of begging, though it had roots in earlier efforts started by Matthew Martin in 1796. For the society see M.J.D. Roberts, "Reshaping the Gift Relationship: The London Mendicity Society and the Suppression of Begging in England 1818–1869," *International Review of Social History* 36, no. 2 (1991): 201–31, here 208; Lynn MacKay, "The Mendicity Society and Its Clients: A Cautionary Tale," *Left History* 5, no. 1 (1997): 39–64.

41 In addition to studies cited below see King, "Summary Courts," 125–72; Norma Landau, *The Justices of the Peace, 1679–1760* (Berkeley, CA: University of California Press, 1984); Landau, "Summary Conviction and the Development of the Penal Law," *Law and History Review* 23 (2005): 173–89; Bruce Smith, "Circumventing the Jury: Petty and Summary Jurisdiction in London and New York City, 1790–1855" (PhD diss., Yale, 1996); Greg Smith, *Summary Justice in the City: A Selection of Cases Heard at the Guildhall Justice Room, 1752–1781* (Suffolk, UK: London Record Society, 2013); Douglas Hay, "Master and Servant in England: Using the Law in the Eighteenth and Nineteenth Centuries," in *Private Law and Social Inequality in the Industrial Age*, ed. Willibald Steinmetz (Oxford, UK: Oxford University Press, 2000), 227–64.

42 King, *Discretion*, 86.

43 "Select Committee on Police of Metropolis, 1834," *PP*, xvi.1 (600), 189.

44 Beattie, *Policing*, 91–4, 108–10, 144. Each alderman was expected to serve for one day at a time – a system quickly adapted as aldermen filled in for one another or chose to sit for days in a row.

45 These calculations exclude the mass of administrative business that came before the courts and include only examinations in which a full hearing, beyond the issuing of a warrant, took place. For more on Kettilby: Kiran Mehta, "Summary Justice in Eighteenth- and Nineteenth-Century Southwark," *Crime, History and Societies* 24, no. 1 (2020): 59–90.

46 For urban/rural comparisons see Innes, "Bridewells," 69, 100–1.

47 Figures drawn from a sample of thirty-eight days between 25 Mar. 1811 and 2 Dec. 1817. CAGCP, 1812–17, LMA, COL/CA/GA/03/001–002.

48 "Home Office Criminal Registers, Middlesex," HO 26/1–7. Accessed on Digital Panopticon, "England and Wales Criminal Registers (Middlesex), 1791–1802" [dataset], version 1.0 (Jan. 2018), https://doi.org/10.15131/shef.data.5688700.v1.

49 LMA, CLA/030/01/019.

50 The Giltspur committal books do not generally indicate whether prisoners committed for trial were moved or not, so I compared Giltspur charge books with Newgate calendars, which list all prisoners committed to Newgate for trial. I am assuming those prisoners committed for trial who could not be found in the Newgate calendars stayed in Giltspur. "Home Office: Newgate Prison Calendars, 1782–1853," The National Archives [hereafter TNA], HO77, accessed on http://www.findmypast.co.uk.

51 The justice's power to commit prisoners to both Newgate and Surrey gaol was probably dependent on where the crime was committed, but the limited amount of detail provided in Kettilby's notebook and in the registers does not allow us to confirm this.

52 "Southwark Charge Book," LMA, CLA/031/01/003. Some of those moved to Surrey gaol were removed under *habeas corpus*.

53 "Money received by John Kinsey [?] from John Law, 5 July 1824," in "Bills, 1824," CAGCP, LMA, COL/CA/GAC/03/005. "Money paid by John Law, 10 July 1824," in ibid.

54 LMA, CLA/031/01/003.

55 24 Nov. 1778, 3 Aug. 1780, 7 Aug. 1780, LMA, CLA/031/03/001.

56 Gray, "Proceedings," 217, 228. This percentage is drawn from 158 outcomes – fifty-four were discharged (or reprimanded and discharged), fifty-three imprisoned, twenty-one passed, and five sent to hospital, with twenty-five unknowns. Gray's "vagrancy" includes those prosecuted as beggars, vagabonds, vagrants, and prostitutes.

57 I have written in greater detail about the Bridewell Court of Governors and about commitments to houses of correction in a forthcoming publication entitled "Revisiting English Bridewells: 'Prisons for the Poor'?." About 8 per cent of those convicted were charged as vagrants (i.e. wandering/lodging in open air, begging, refusing to give account of settlement, common vagrant, etc.), but in total, around 66 per cent were charged under the *Vagrancy Acts*, which covered a broader array of actions and conditions. BCGM, 22 Jan. 1778–25 Apr. 1788, *LL*, BBBRMG202080642–BBBRMG202090324.

58 Gray, "Proceedings," 140.

59 1809 is the earliest year for which full commitment records survive. "Bridewell Commitment Books, 1809–23," LMA, CLC/275/MS33138/001–002.

60 BPCM, 1775–1802, LMA, CLC/275/MS33131/001–002; BPSCM, 1792–1805, LMA, CLC/275/MS33132/001–002.

61 LMA, CLA/031/03/001. In another instance, a man was sentenced to be imprisoned in a bridewell as a disorderly person, but for some reason ended up in Surrey gaol.

62 For a full discussion, see Mehta, "Courts and Prisons," 47.

63 "Surrey Sessions Papers," Surrey History Centre [hereafter SHC], QS2/6/1778–82, 1792–96, 1800–02, 1812–16, 1820.

64 Variations of "gaol delivery" lists can be found in three different record series at the LMA. MJ/CP/P (June 1690–June 1794) are handwritten lists of prisoners and their sentences after trial, copies of which were sent to prison keepers. Some of these lists are stored in the justices' sessions papers (MJ/SP) rather than catalogued separately. Finally, lists of prisoners – which take a slightly different format, but similarly say what happened to prisoners at the sessions – were included in the sessions book minutes (MJ/SB/B). As the following notes show, I have consulted and used all these record types.

65 "Lists of Prisoners, 1739–95," LMA, MJ/CC/B; 1730–1821, MJ/CC/R; 1747–1859, MJ/CC/V.
66 LMA, MJ/SP/1724/01/033–34, MJ/SP/1724/10/142–4, MJ/SP/1736/01/065–6, MJ/CP/P/046–8.
67 LMA, MJ/CC/B/075–6, MJ/CC/R/003–4, 019, 034, 041, 051, 061, 066, 070–3.
68 Innes, "Bridewells," 95; Shoemaker, *Prosecution and Punishment*, 169, 175–6.
69 Unfortunately, calendars from the 1770s onwards mostly do not state the legal basis of commitment. However, they almost always state the offence. In these years, between one-third and three-quarters were confined for a violent, property, or felony offence – that is, crimes for which offenders could not, strictly speaking, be summarily convicted. Some were probably confined summarily anyways, but we know that at least a portion were explicitly held for trial. So, if anything, these percentages overestimate custodial commitals. "Prisoners committed to House of Correction, Oct. 1769–Sept. 1772," *LL*, LMSMPS506240151; LMA, MJ/CC/R/076/07, 14, 19, 21, 23, 25; LMA, MJ/CC/B/068, 078–81.
70 MJ/CC/B/001, 007, 009, 010.
71 "Prisoners committed to New Prison, Sept. 1769–Sept. 1772," *LL*, LMSMPS506240152; LMA, MJ/CC/B/016–032.
72 "Prisoners Committed," *LL*, LMSMPS506240151–2.
73 4 Geo IV c. 64.
74 MPCR, LMA, MJ/SP/1803/10/019.
75 MSP, Apr. 1787, LMA, MJ/SP/1787/04. In 1815, 88 prisoners were committed for trial, but of those only 16 were tried. The 1786 account only specified those committed for trial who were tried, which is why I have compared the actual trial numbers rather than the (larger) number committed for trial. If the total number committed for trial in 1786 was five times greater than the number eventually tried, as was true in 1815, then perhaps around 440 persons were committed for trial in 1786, which would have accounted for 27 per cent of committals.
76 For this development, see ch. 5.
77 On this authority see "Committee on Petition from London on Newgate, 1765," *LL*, LMSMPS505470045.
78 Ibid.
79 Ruth Paley, "The Middlesex Justices Act of 1792: Its Origins and Effects" (PhD diss.; Reading: University of Reading, 1983), 34; David Bentley, *English Criminal Justice in the Nineteenth Century* (London: Hambledon Press, 1998), 8. As he notes, the quarter sessions, in theory, had jurisdiction to try all crimes except treason.
80 "Report of Committee on Removing Prisoners to Newgate, May 1727," *LL*, LMSMPS502430085– LMSMPS502430092
81 Ibid., LMSMPS502340088.
82 Ibid.
83 "Case of Middlesex Respecting Newgate, Apr. 1765," *LL*, LMSMPS505470039. For evidence of transfers see LMA, MJ/CC/B.
84 "Prison committee, Oct. 1772," *LL*, LMSMPS506240141–LMSMPS506240143, LMSMPS506240145.
85 "Mayor's Orders to Prison Keepers, Oct. 1772," LMA, MJ/SP/1772/10/088.
86 In this respect the policy was imperfect: felons for trial were still sent in the first instance to New Prison, and they remained there until a few days before trial, so within the gaol, serious and petty offenders continued to mix.
87 "Case of Newgate," *LL*, LMSMPS505470039.
88 "Draft Orders, Sept. 1775," *LL*, LMSMPS506560156, LMSMPS506560163.

89 PP, Dec. 1800, 132, 81.

90 "County Day Draft Minutes," LMA, MJ/SP/1803/10/019. The committee urged the bench to send a recommendatory order to the police offices and acting magistrates to remind them of the policy.

91 "Gaol and Bridewell Calendars," SHC, QS2/6/1778–82, 1792–96, 1800–02, 1812–16, 1820. For more detail see Mehta, "Courts and Prisons," 56.

92 "Westminster Sessions, Dec 13," *Jackson's Oxford Journal* (Oxford), 18 Jan. 1823.

93 The willingness of authorities to execute the capitally convicted varied across England. Areas furthest from London tended to see significantly fewer executions. Peter King and Richard Ward, "Rethinking the Bloody Code in Eighteenth-Century Britain: Capital Punishment at the Centre and on the Periphery," *Past and Present* 228 (2014): 159–205. On capital punishment generally see Simon Devereaux, *Execution, State and Society in England, 1660–1900* (Cambridge: Cambridge University Press, 2023). For the fate of Old Bailey convicts sentenced to death see Robert Shoemaker, "Sparing the Noose: Death Sentences and the Pardoning of Old Bailey Convicts, 1763–1868," in *Cultural Histories of Law, Media, and Emotion*, ed. Katie Barclay and Amy Milka (New York: Routledge, 2022), 237–58.

94 Beattie, *Crime*, 438, 444, 457.

95 Gwenda Morgan and Peter Rushton, *Rogues, Thieves and the Rule of Law* (London: UCL Press, 1998), 71–5, 154–6.

96 A. Roger Ekrich, *Bound for America: The Transportation of British Convicts to the Colonies, 1718–1775* (Oxford, UK: Clarendon Press: 1987), 23–7.

97 They might have sentenced prisoners to hard labour on the roads, or canal-building, or perhaps to work in mines. John Langbein, "Historical Origins of the Sanction of Imprisonment for Serious Crime," *Journal of Legal Studies* 5, no. 1 (1976): 39–44. For the approaches of other countries, see Clare Anderson, ed., *A Global History of Convicts and Penal Colonies* (London: Bloomsbury, 2018).

98 Beattie argues that whipping was not thought "to provide an adequate substitute for transportation," so it was mainly used in cases of petty larceny or grand larceny (in Surrey, but not in the City and Middlesex) when the sums were not too considerable. Beattie, *Crime*, 544–6. See also Hitchcock and Shoemaker, *London Lives*, Figures 7.8 and 7.10.

99 5 Anne c. 6.

100 See introduction, part iii.

101 MGOC, 9 Apr., 14 May 1719, *LL*, LMSMGO400000142–5, LMSMGO400000150.

102 Significantly, hard labour, in this bill, was intended to serve as "visible and lasting Examples of Justice to others." Beattie, *Crime*, 521–2; Morgan and Rushton, *Rogues*, 173.

103 16 Geo III c. 43; 19 Geo III c. 74.

104 Simon Devereaux, "Convicts and the State: The Administration of Criminal Justice in Great Britain during the Reign of George III" (PhD diss., University of Toronto, 1997), 144, 190, 217, 223.

105 King, *Discretion*, 263, 266; Beattie, *Crime*, 540–1, 547; Devereaux, "Convicts," 126–9, 137–9; Hitchcock and Shoemaker, *Lives*, 332–5.

106 The Westminster government may have signalled its willingness to allow transportation to wind down in 1772 when they stopped paying the costs for transporting London and Home Circuit convicts and paying the bounty to merchants who transported them. More likely, however, this reflected the growing profitability of the trade. Beattie, *Crime*, 546–7; Farley Grubb, "The Transatlantic Market for British Convict Labour," *Journal of Economic History* 60, no. 1 (2000): 94–122.

107 Ignatieff, *Just Measure*, 74–5.
108 Hitchcock and Shoemaker, *Lives*, 322–3, 325. For further support of this position, see also work on pardon refusers: Lynn Mackay, "Refusing the Royal Pardon," *London Journal* 28, no. 2 (2003): 21–40; Simon Devereaux, "Imposing the Royal Pardon," *Law and History Review* 25, no. 1 (2007): 101–38.
109 Pamela Cox, Robert Shoemaker, and Heather Shore, *Victims and Criminal Justice: A History* (New York: Oxford University Press, 2023), 190–8.
110 King, *Discretion*, 267.
111 Ibid., 270.
112 Ignatieff, *Just Measure*, 79. For the Enlightenment see Anthony Draper, "Cesare Beccaria's Influence on English Discussions of Punishment, 1764–1789," *History of European Ideas* 26, no. 3 (2000): 177–99.
113 John Beattie, "London Crime and the Making of the 'Bloody Code,' 1689–1718," in *Stilling the Grumbling Hive: The Response to Social and Economic Problems in England, 1689–1750*, ed. Lee Davison et al. (Stroud, UK: Alan Sutton, 1992), 58.
114 King, *Discretion*, 263–5.
115 Beattie, *Crime and Courts*, 546.
116 Ibid., 563, 577.
117 Ibid., 532–3.
118 Ibid., 561.
119 Ibid., 578, 594, 597.
120 Ibid., 563.
121 On the longevity of corporal punishments globally, but especially in eighteenth- and nineteenth-century Europe, see Guy Geltner, *Flogging Others: Corporal Punishment and Cultural Identity from Antiquity to the Present* (Amsterdam: Amsterdam University Press, 2014), 68–77.
122 Beatie, *Crime and Courts*, 578.
123 Ibid., 578, 580, 593. In 1776–82, 42.8 per cent of imprisonment sentences for property offenders were carried out on hulks compared to 53.3 per cent in houses of correction. In 1783–87, only 8.3 per cent of sentences were carried out on hulks. No offenders were so sentenced in 1788–1802. On the hulks' mortality rates see Howard, *The State of the Prisons*, 428; Hitchcock and Shoemaker, *Lives*, 335–7. Around one in three of all convicts sent on board the hulks died in the late eighteenth and early nineteenth centuries. High rates of mortality continued into the nineteenth century: Anna McKay, "'Allowed to die?' Prison Hulks, Convict Corpses and the Inquiry of 1847," *Cultural and Social History* 18, no. 2 (2021): 163–81.
124 Beattie, *Crime and Courts*, 580.
125 Ibid., 563, 580, 602.
126 Morgan and Rushton, *Rogues*, 187–8.
127 Beattie, *Crime and Courts*, 605.
128 Ibid., 608.
129 For the experiments in transporting convicts to the African coast, America, and Honduras, see Hitchcock and Shoemaker, *Lives*, 372–3; Emma Christopher, *A Merciless Place: The Lost Story of Britain's Convict Disaster in Africa* (Oxford, UK: Oxford University Press, 2011), ch. 10–15; Hamish Maxwell-Stewart, "Transportation from Britain and Ireland, 1615–1788," in *Convicts and Penal Colonies*, 183–210.

130 Richard Ward and Lucy Williams, "Initial Views from the 'Digital Panopticon': Reconstructing Penal Outcomes in the 1790s," *Law and History Review* 34, no. 4 (2016): 893–928, here 900, 909–11.
131 Devereaux, "Convicts," 142. Devereaux quotes one foreign visitor, writing to a friend in Jan. 1775, as noting, "it is said that voluptuousness, evil and debauchery have never been so rampant in London as they are at present."
132 Devereaux, "Execution and Pardon at the Old Bailey, 1730–1837," *American Journal of Legal History* 57, no. 3 (2017): 447–94. See also Hitchcock and Shoemaker, *Lives*, 362–7.
133 Devereaux, "Convicts," 142.
134 "Account of Middlesex Prisoners Delivered for Hard Labour from Newgate," LMA, MA/G/GEN/1132.
135 For the founding of Botany Bay, see Emma Christopher and Hamish Maxwell-Stewart, "Convict Transportation in Global Context, c. 1700–1788," in *Cambridge History of Australia*, vol. 1, ed. Alison Bashford and Stuart McIntyre (Cambridge: Cambridge University Press, 2013), 68–90.
136 16 Geo III c. 43. After this period, hulks were mainly used as a place to hold convicts sentenced to transportation until they could depart. This pattern parallels earlier experimentation with hard labour: Beattie, *Policing*, 342–3.
137 "Middlesex Sessions Minute Books," LMA, MJ/SB/B/0114–127, 0155, 0283–8, 0329, 334; MSP, MJ/SP/1724/01/33–4, MJ/SP/1724/08/43–6; MJ/CP/P/044–8, 076–8, 196–200; MJ/SP/1787/04.
138 TNA, HO 26/1–7.
139 Hitchcock and Shoemaker, *Lives*, 362–5; J.S. Cockburn, "Punishment and Brutalisation in the English Enlightenment," *Law and History Review* 12, no. 1 (1994): 155–79. See also how the bodies of the condemned were treated: Richard Ward, "The Criminal Corpse, Anatomists, and the Criminal Law," *Journal of British Studies* 54 (2015): 63–87; Peter King, *Punishing the Criminal Corpse, 1700–1840* (London: Palgrave, 2017).
140 Smith, "Violence," 325.
141 Ibid., 310, 436. These calculations exclude unknown punishments.
142 Ibid., 323.
143 "Convict bills," MSP, LMA, MJ/SP/1777–95.
144 Smith, "Violence," 322.
145 Hitchcock and Shoemaker, *Lives*, 330.
146 Ibid., 403.
147 "Grand Jury Presentment, 2 May 1772," MSP, *LL*, LMSMPS506190007–LMSMPS506190008; MPCR, Oct. 1772, *LL*, LMSMPS506240141–LMSMPS506240145. The county had undertaken substantial repairs at these prisons only a decade before, also in response to a grand jury presentment: "Presentment, 7 July 1760," MSP, *LL*, LMSMPS504850056–LMSMPS504850061; MPCP, 19 Jan. 1762, *LL*, LMSMPS505060104.
148 *LL*, LMSMPS506240141–LMSMPS506240145.
149 *LL*, LMSMPS506240143.
150 The justices saw some reason to try to reform the morals of gaol, as well as bridewell, prisoners, but this was to be accomplished solely through religion rather than physical labour or employment. The magistrates initially planned to build one chapel to serve both prisons for "the better recovering of the prisoners from the present profligate & abandoned state." Ibid.
151 *LL*, LMSMPS506240156.

152 *LL*, LMSMPS506240141–LMSMPS5062401415, LMSMPS506240156, LMSMPS506240158.
153 *LL*, LMSMPS506190007–LMSMPS506190008.
154 11 Will 3 c. 19; 12 Geo II c. 29; 17 Geo II c. 5. Conditions replicated in 24 Geo III c. 54.
155 "County Day, 21 Apr. 1773," *LL*, LMSMPS506290110–LMSMPS506290111. This view of the prisons was confirmed by the grand jury, the first repair committee, and a quarter sessions order. *LL*, LMSMPS506240141–LMSMPS506240145.
156 C.W. Chalklin, "The Reconstruction of London's Prisons, 1770–1799," *London Journal* 9, no. 1 (1983): 25.
157 *LL*, LMSMPS506290110.
158 MPCM, 17 July 1777, LMA, MA/G/GEN/0001.
159 Ibid.
160 MPCR, LMA, MJ/SP/1781/PC/0031.
161 Tim Hitchcock, "Re-negotiating the Bloody Code: The Gordon Riots and the Transformation of Popular Attitudes to the Criminal Justice System," in *The Gordon Riots*, ed. I. Haywood and J. Seed (Cambridge: Cambridge University Press, 2012), 185–202.
162 *LL*, LMSMPS507510134.
163 By 9 Jan. 1781, Adams had received 89 vagrants who otherwise would have been confined to the bridewell.
164 MPCM, 10 Nov. 1780, 27 Oct. 1780, LMA, MA/G/GEN/0001.
165 "Expenses of Prisoners Normally at Newgate, 1780," LMA, MA/G/GEN/0234; MPCM, 10 Nov. 1780, MA/G/GEN/0001.
166 "Draft Orders, Oct. 1777," MSP, *LL*, LMSMPS506750051; "Index, Oct. 1778," MSP, *LL*, LMSMPS506840104, LMSMPS506840108; "Account of Edward Hall for Money Paid by Him for Subsistence of Poor Convicts, 12 Feb. 1779," MSP, *LL*, LMSMPS507110064.
167 MPCM, 27 Oct. 1780, MA/G/GEN/0001.
168 For example: MPCM, 2 Mar. 1781, LMA, MA/G/GEN/0001.
169 *OBO* (http://www.oldbaileyonline.org, version 8.0, Mar. 2018), tabulating year against punishment category where verdict category is guilty, between 1783 and 1804. Counting by punishment. The percentage imprisoned was probably somewhat higher as *OBO* does not always count in the "imprisonment" category individuals sentenced to a fine and a prison term or to be whipped and imprisoned.
170 "Report from the Committee on the Penitentiary Houses, First Report, 1810–11," *PP*, iii.567 (199), 8.
171 See Gloucester where the magistrates, in conversation with the government in London, decided to build a penitentiary (opened 1791) to hold prisoners sentenced to transportation and death, but who, if they behaved well, could have their sentences altered to imprisonment. McConville, *Prison Administration*, 98–104.
172 MSP, 22 Feb. 1791, *LL*, LMSMPS508610012; Joanna Innes, "The Role of Transportation in Seventeenth- and Eighteenth-Century English Penal Practice," in *New Perspectives in Australian History*, ed. Carl Bridge (London: University of London, 1990), 1–24.
173 *The Parliamentary Register*, vol. 28 (London, 1791), 327.
174 *LL*, LMSMPS508610012.
175 Sue Brown, "Policing and Privilege: Resistance to Penal Reform in Eighteenth-Century London," in *Institutional Culture in Early Modern Society*, ed. Anne Goldgar and Robert Frost (Leiden, Netherlands: Brill, 2004), 114.
176 Quoted in Devereaux, "Convicts," 140.
177 Chalklin, "Reconstruction," 27–8.

178 Ibid., 28.
179 See table 4.3.
180 Beattie, *Crime*, 561.
181 Ibid. For bridewell size, see William Smith, *State of the Gaols in London, Westminster, and Borough of Southwark* (London, 1776), 36. For inmate population, see "Bread Bills," SSP, SHC, QS2/6/1777–84.
182 Beattie, *Crime and Courts*, 562, 580.
183 Ibid., 581.
184 The Corporation played an important role in Bridewell's governance, with all aldermen appointed *ex officio* as governors and, after 1782, twelve common councilmen reserved a place on the board. Still, Bridewell was not a public institution and the Corporation shared governance with other governors who were not magistrates. Copeland, *Bridewell*, 116; Susan Brown, "Politics, Commerce and Social Policy in the City of London, 1782–1802" (DPhil diss., University of Oxford, 1992), 254–5.
185 Hitchcock and Shoemaker, *Lives*, 67.
186 Beattie, *Crime*, 498. See also "Petitions Relating to Detained Criminals, 1706–19," BL, Add MS 61618.
187 Copeland, *Bridewell*, 64.
188 *PP*, 1810–11, iii.567, 50, 8.
189 Ibid.
190 *PP*, 1813–14, iv.249, 93.
191 Assessing the number of offenders sentenced to the hulks or sentenced to death and pardoned on condition that they be imprisoned on the hulks is made difficult by the frequent failure of the Old Bailey Proceedings to specify where a prisoner was confined if sentenced to "imprisonment" or "hard labour." The Middlesex statistics are available only because the magistrates kept their own separate records, which kept track of such numbers. Hulk registers, held by the National Archives, date from only 1811.
192 To defray the costs of buying land and building the prisons, the City was authorized to charge expenses to the Orphan's Fund. 52 Geo III c. 209.
193 "Select Committee on State of the Prisons within the City of London and Southwark, 1818," *PP*, viii.545 (392), 247.
194 Sheehan, "System," 390–7; Chalklin, "Reconstruction," 23–4.
195 Chalklin, "Reconstruction."
196 Sheehan, "System," 398.
197 Ibid., 24–5.
198 Chalklin, "Reconstruction," 31.
199 For a breakdown of expenditure on prison building see Tables 4.1–4.4.
200 *General Regulations for Inspection and Controul of all the Prisons, together with Rules, Order and Bye Laws for government of the Gaol and Penitentiary House of the County of Gloucester* (Gloucester, UK, 1790), 3–4.
201 *Rules, Order and Regulations for the Government of the Gaol for the County of Stafford* (Stafford, UK, 1792), iii–v.
202 Many magistrates paid close attention to what other benches were doing and actively sought to learn from the experience of one another. See for example "Printed Papers Concerning Gaol Administration in Other Counties, 1807–24," Wiltshire and Swindon History Centre, A1/516/4; "Draft Rules for Aylesbury Gaol and House of Correction," Buckinghamshire Archives, Q/AG/11/47; "Rules, Orders, and Regulations for Bury St Edmunds Gaol and House of Correction, 1805," ibid., Q/AG/11/48.

CHAPTER TWO

1 Howard, *The State of the Prisons*, 8.

2 Smith, *Gaols*, 37.

3 *Report of the Committee of the Society for the Imprisonment of Prison Discipline and the Reformation of Juvenile Offenders* (London, 1818), 18–19.

4 Ibid.

5 George Laval Chesterton, *Revelations of Prison Life*, 2nd ed. (London, 1856), 2:18–19.

6 Ibid, 3–4.

7 Quoted from Webbs, *Prisons*, 25. See also McConville, *Administration*, 42.

8 In addition to works cited below see Innes, "Bridewells"; David Eastwood, *Governing Rural England: Tradition and Transformation in Local Government, 1780–1840* (Oxford, UK: Clarendon, 1994), 242–9.

9 DeLacy, *Lancashire*, 102–3, 205–6.

10 Beattie, *Crime*, 492–3.

11 A selection of work, among many others, includes Clare Anderson, *Convicts: A Global History* (Cambridge: Cambridge University Press, 2022); Anderson, ed., *Convicts and Penal Colonies*; David Arnold, "Labouring for the Raj: Convict Work Regimes in Colonial India," in Christian Giuseppe de Vito and Alex Lichtenstein, eds, *Global Convict Labour* (Leiden, Netherlands: Brill, 2015), 197–221; Jared Davidson, *Blood and Dirt: Prison Labour and the Making of New Zealand* (Wellington, NZ: Bridget Williams Books, 2023); Stacey Hynd, "'... a Weapon of Immense Value?' Convict Labour in British Colonial Africa, c. 1850–1950s," in Christian Giuseppe de Vito and Alex Lichtenstein, eds, *Global Convict Labour* (Leiden, Netherlands: Brill, 2015), 249–72; Stephen Nicholas, *Convict Workers* (Cambridge: Cambridge University Press, 1988); Deborah Oxley, *Convict Maids* (Cambridge: Cambridge University Press, 1996); Diana Paton, *No Bond but the Law* (Durham, NC: Duke University Press, 2004); Anoma Pieris, *Hidden Hands and Divided Landscapes* (Honolulu: University of Hawai'i Press, 2009); Richard Tuffin et al., "Landscapes of Production and Punishment: Convict Labour in the Australian Context," *Journal of Social Archaeology* 18, no. 1 (2018): 50–75; Anand Yang, *Empire of Convicts: Indian Penal Labour in Colonial Southeast Asia* (Oakland, CA: California University Press, 2021).

12 "16 December 1656," *Diary of Thomas Burton Esq, Volume 1, July 1653–April 1657*, ed. John Towill Rutt (London: H. Colburn, 1828), 148–59, BHO.

13 7 Jac I c. 4.

14 Ibid.

15 "Rules for the Government of Bridewell, 1552," BL, Sloane MS 2722.

16 "Commissioners of Inquiry into Charities in England and Wales, Thirty-Second Report, part vi, 1840," PP, 219, 390–3; Copeland, *Bridewell*, 50–1; McConville, *Administration*, 33.

17 *Report of Special Committee of Governors of Bridewell* (London, 1819), 4.

18 "Southwark Prisons," in *Survey of London*, 9–21.

19 "Letter from Privy Council to Surrey Justices, June 1605," SHC, LM/COR/4/14.

20 "Southwark Prisons," in *Survey of London*, 9–21.

21 Ibid.

22 "Carpenter's Account for Blocks and Bittles [Beetles]," SHC, QS2/6/1728/Mid/46; "Carpenter's Account for Elm Blocks," SHC, QS2/6/1732/Xmas/66 and QS2/6/1733/Xmas/17.

23 "Middlesex Sessions Rolls: 11 January 1616," in *Middlesex County Records, vol. 2, 1603–1625*, ed. J.C. Jeafferson (London: Middlesex County Record Society, 1887), 119–26, *BHO*.
24 "Petition of Jacob Stoit for Setting the Poor at Work," BL, Add MS 12496, document no. 236. The BL catalogue dates this to 1626, but given that it reads like a contract or a proposal for services, it is more likely that it was written before his appointment in 1616.
25 "Sessions Rolls: 14 February 1626 and 26 July 1632," in *Middlesex Records, vol. 3, 1625–67* (1888), *BHO*.
26 MGOC, 15 Oct. 1741, *LL*, LMSMGO556010464.
27 Ibid.
28 MGOC, 29 Aug. 1723, *LL*, LMSMGO400010181–2.
29 "Petition of Keeper," SHC, QS2/6/1701/61.
30 "Petition of Keeper," SHC, QS2/6/1725/Xmas/28.
31 BPSCM, 1792–1805, LMA, CLC/275/MS33132/001–002.
32 Ned Ward, *The London Spy* (London, 1703), 138; Peter D'Sena, "Perquisites and Pilfering in London Docks, 1700–1795" (MPhil diss., Open University, 1986), 52.
33 Howard, *The State of the Prisons*, 179.
34 MGOC, 15 Oct. 1741, *LL*, LMSMGO556010461.
35 Ibid.
36 Jacob Ilive, *Reasons Offered for the Reformation of the House of Correction in Clerkenwell* (London, 1757), 37. After his first day, Ilive was assigned the women's amount because of his age (over 50).
37 "Hemp Accounts – House of Correction, County Treasurer," LMA, MF/416–422, 424–439. Earliest records (416–422) are all unfit, so they could not be consulted.
38 "Matters for County Day, Apr. 1760," *LL*, LMSMPS504820043; ibid., 22 May 1760, *LL*, LMSMPS504830047.
39 See for example "Churchwardens and Overseers of the Poor Account Books, St Botolph Aldgate Parish, 1744, 1746," *LL*, GLBAAC100040174, GLBAAC100040196.
40 Priestly, *Lives*, 121.
41 *LL*, LMSMPS506520136–143.
42 LMA, MF/426–8; MGOC, July 1778, *LL*, LMSMGO556070213.
43 "Petition by George Winter," SHC, QS2/6/1738/Eas/2a–b; "Certificate of Completion of Work," SHC, QS/2/1732/Eas/31a–b; Beattie, *Crime*, 493n112.
44 "Fourth Schedule. Extracts of Returns concerning Vagrants and Houses of Correction," in "Abstract of Returns made by Overseers of the Poor, 1776," *PP*, xxxi, 292.
45 The keeper purchased additional elm block and mallets for hemp-beating in 1781. "Account of Disbursements," SHC, QS2/6/1781/Mic/15; "Report on Kingston House of Correction," SHC, QS2/6/1782/Mid/22. See also "Committee Report on Southwark House of Correction," SHC, QS2/6/1782/Mid/25.
46 *LL*, LMSMPS506520136–143.
47 QS2/6/1738/Eas/2a, b. There is some reason to doubt these claims, as the previous keeper had been an artsmaster at Bridewell, a role which surely prepared him for the governorship in Southwark. "Petition of George Hooker," SHC, QS2/6/1733/Eas/14a–b.
48 *LL*, LMSMGO400010181–2.
49 BPCM, 23 Nov. 1797, LMA, CLC/275/MS33131/002.
50 MPCM, 19 Apr. 1797, 22 May 1797, LMA, MA/G/GEN/0002.
51 BPCM, 14 Jan. 1795, LMA, CLC/275/MS33131/001.
52 *LL*, LMSMPS506520136–143.

53 BCGM, 25 Feb. 1796, LMA, CLC/275/MS33011/25; BPCM, 21 Jan. 1796, 23 Nov. 1797, LMA, CLC/275/MS33131/001.
54 "Letter from Gibbs, Apothecary, 1783," LMA, CLA/032/01/0034.
55 "Draft Orders, County Day, Feb. 1783," LMA, MJ/SP/1782/02/038.
56 MSP, *LL*, LMSMPS504850056–7; Howard, *The State of the Prisons*, 186.
57 MGOC, *LL*, LMSMGO556070214–LMSMGO556070215.
58 Chalklin, "Reconstruction," 28; Howard, *The State of the Prisons*, 236; BPCM, 18 Oct. 1775, 6 Nov. 1783, LMA, CLC/275/MS33131/001.
59 *PP*, Dec. 1800, 132, 33; Humphries and Weisdorf, "Wages," 428, 432.
60 "King against Bridges, Nov. 1806," 103 "English Reports," 264.
61 Sonia Tycko, "The Legality of Prisoner of War Labour in England, 1648–1655," *Past and Present* 246, no. 1 (2020): 39, 43.
62 Richard Bell, "Charity, Debt and Social Control in England's Early Modern Prisons," *Social History* 41, no. 1 (2022): 28. The quote is from Anon., A *Provocation to Good Works* (London, 1685), 90–1.
63 18 & 19 Car II c. 9.
64 11 Will III c. 19; 6 Geo I c. 19.
65 "Royal Commission on Condition and Treatment of Prisoners in Ilchester Gaol, 1822," *PP*, xi.313 (54), 84, 112.
66 *Regulations for Gloucester*, 38–9; G.O. Paul, *Considerations on the Defects of Prisons, and their Present System of Regulation* (London, 1784), 33; *Rules for Gaol of Stafford*, 5, 19; *General Rules, Orders, Regulations, and Bye-Laws for the Inspection and Government of the Gaol and House of Correction for the County of Salop* (Shrewsbury, UK, 1797), 2–3, 46–8; "Rules of Ipswich Gaol," Norfolk Record Office, C/SAA 1/1, 12–13; "Rules for Gaol and Houses of Correction for County of Norfolk, 1824," Norfolk Record Office, C/SAA 1/10. For early-eighteenth-century experiments see DeLacy, *Lancashire*, 47.
67 Sheehan, "System," 157.
68 "A Plan for Employing Newgate Prisoners," LMA, COL/CA/PCA/01/001.
69 Ibid.
70 *PP*, 1810–11, iii.567, 7, 83. The Surrey gaol keeper testified to sometimes providing knitting for his prisoners.
71 For these orders, passed in 1606 and 1621, see Sheehan, "System," Appendix I and II.c.
72 Joanna Innes, *Inferior Politics: Social Problems and Social Policies in Eighteenth-Century Britain* (Oxford, UK: Oxford University Press, 2009), 228–78.
73 Ibid., 256.
74 Bell, "Charity," 8, 13; Jerry White, "Pain and Degradation in Georgian London: Life in the Marshalsea Prison," *History Workshop Journal* 68 (2009): 86.
75 *PP*, 1810–11, iii.567, 55; "Answers of William Pentlow, Dec. 1772," LMA, MA/G/GEN/0176.
76 "Account of Persons convicted of Felonies or Misdemeanours and now under Sentence of Imprisonment," *PP*, 1779, xxxi, 6–8.
77 Innes, *Inferior Politics*, 256–8.
78 LMA, MA/G/GEN/0176.
79 *PP*, 1779, xxxi, 8.
80 *PP*, 1810–11, iii.567, 51.
81 I plan to explore these debates in greater detail in future work. See *The Parliamentary Debates*, 2nd series, vol. 10 (London, 1824), 139, 226.

82 6 Geo IV c. 40. The controversy remained unresolved, however, so additional legislation (5 Geo IV c. 85) specified that no prisoner before conviction could be employed on the wheels "either with or without his consent."

83 The act gave the divisional justices in Dublin, the Grand Jury, or any three justices the authority to decide the type of labour that prisoners would be required to perform.

84 "Abstracts about Prisons, Oct. 1763," MSP, *LL*, LMSMPS505270158.

85 For thinking about the position of fear in history see Joanna Bourke, "Fear and Anxiety: Writing about Emotion in Modern History," *History Workshop Journal* 55 (2003): 111–33.

86 *PP*, 1813–14, iv.249, 7; *PP*, 1779, xxxi, 4–5.

87 *PP*, 1818, viii.1, 71.

88 For magistrates see Hitchcock and Shoemaker, *Lives*, 327.

89 *PP*, 1818, viii.1, 71–2.

90 Indeed, the court process was supposed to inspire terror: Doug Hay, "Property, Authority, and the Criminal Law," in *Albion's Fatal Tree: Crime and Society in Eighteenth-Century England*, ed. Doug Hay et al. (London: Allen Lane, 1975); Amy Milka and David Lemmings, "Narratives of Feeling and Majesty: Mediated Emotions in the Eighteenth-Century Criminal Courtroom," *The Journal of Legal History* 38, no. 2 (2017): 155–78.

91 DeLacy, *Lancashire*, 36.

92 "Order to Apprehend Keeper, 30 June 1711," *LL*, LMSMPS501230084.

93 "Notice of Intention to Plead Guilty, Aug. 1733," *LL*, LMSMPS502940008. Holding gaol keepers responsible in this way may have been an extension of the sheriff's responsibility to keep debtors in safe custody. See 1 Ann 2 c. 6 and 6 Ann c. 12. For early examples of City of London authorities holding prison offices, especially porters, responsible for escapes see Jonathan McGovern, "Compters at Poultry and Wood Street in Early Modern London," *London Journal* 46, no. 3 (2021): 255–6.

94 MPS, Oct. 1763, *LL*, LMSMPS505270161.

95 Sheehan, "System," 351.

96 Beattie, *Crime*, 296–7.

97 Hitchcock and Shoemaker, *Lives*, 339, 367, 369–70. In 1776 and 1777, Hitchcock and Shoemaker counted fewer than fifty escapes in each year, but in 1778 there were slightly over 150. In 1780, during the Gordon Riots, around 1,600 prisoners escaped. Surrey justices faced similar issues: Ignatieff, *Just Measure*, 85.

98 LMA, MA/G/GEN/0176.

99 Norfolk magistrates appear to have employed prisoners in their gaol and bridewells, for example. "Great Yarmouth Gaol Keeper's Journals, 1825–35," Norfolk Record Office, Y/L 2/46; "Norfolk County Gaol, Keeper's Daily Journal, 1822–35," ibid., MF/RO 576.

100 *PP*, 1776, xxxi, 289–96.

101 Ibid., 294, 289.

102 "Account of Labour and Earnings in Norfolk, Oxfordshire and Dorset," LMA, MA/G/GEN/0432.

103 DeLacy, *Lancashire*, 36; Morgan and Rushton, *Rogues*, 183–5; McConville, *Prison Administration*, 94.

104 Innes, *Inferior Politics*, 180–1; Donna Andrew, *Philanthropy and Police: London Charity in the Eighteenth Century* (Princeton, NJ: Princeton University Press, 1989), 163–4. For anxious writings on the state of the nation's morals by a London alderman see Josiah Dornford, *Nine Letters on the State of the City Prisons* (London, 1786).

105 Samuel Glasse, *National Liberality and National Reform Recommended, A sermon, Preached in the Parish Church of St. George, Bloomsbury, on Sunday, February 4, 1798* (London, 1798), 10–12.

106 Patrick Colquhoun, *Observations and Facts relative to Public Houses in the City of London and its Environs* (London, 1794), 11.

107 Innes, *Inferior Politics*, 180–5, 190–2; M.J.D. Roberts, *Making English Morals: Voluntary Association and Morals Reform in England, 1787–1886* (Cambridge: Cambridge University Press, 2004), ch. 1; M.J.D. Roberts, "Making Victorian Morals? The Society for the Suppression of Vice and Its Critics, 1802–1886," *The Historical Journal* 26, no. 1 (1983): 159–76; Andrew, *Philanthropy*, ch. 6; Simon Devereaux, "Inexperienced Humanitarians? William Wilberforce, William Pitt, and the Execution Crisis of the 1780s," *Law and History Review* 33, no. 4 (2015): 839–85; Faramerz Dabhoiwala, "Sex and Societies for Moral Reform, 1688–1800," *Journal of British Studies* 46, no. 2 (2007): 290–319.

108 Innes, *Inferior Politics*, 216.

109 Ibid., 192–9. Another way for the less elite to get involved with the Proclamation Society was to buy or read their publications. Patrick Colquhoun for example owned *Statement and Propositions from the Society for Giving Effect to His Majesty's Proclamation* (London, 1790). See *The Making of the Modern World*, Gale, U0102308795.

110 Innes, *Inferior Politics*, 189–90n31; Wilberforce, *Life*, 393–4.

111 *Society for the Suppression of Vice. Brief Abstract of their Proceedings, during the First Year of their Establishment* (London, 1803), 3, 5. On the nature of the membership see Innes, *Inferior Politics*, 202; Roberts, "Society for Suppression of Vice," 163.

112 William Mainwaring, *An Address to the Grand Jury of the County of Middlesex* (London, 1785), 1–7, 8–9. Here, Mainwaring's main aim was to forestall police reform in Parliament.

113 "County Day Minutes, 13 Mar. 1787," MSP, *LL*, LMSMPS508200015. Samuel Glasse, *A Narrative of Proceedings, Tending towards a National Reformation, previous to, and consequent upon, His Majesty's Royal Proclamation* (London, 1787), 25–7.

114 Innes, *Inferior Politics*, 190. Glasse, Mainwaring, and Thomas Boddington were all jury members and early Proclamation Society members.

115 MGOC, 24 May 1787, *LL*, LMSMG0556090324, LMSMG0556090330–9; *LL*, LMSMPS508240154–67; *Letter to a Member of Parliament containing a Narrative of Proceedings relative to His Majesty's Proclamation*, 2nd ed. (London, 1788), 40–3.

116 Jean Baker, "The Proclamation Society, William Mainwaring and the Theatrical Representations Act of 1788," *Historical Research* 76, no. 193 (2003): 350.

117 *Proceedings relative to Majesty's Proclamation*, 43.

118 *Resolutions of the Magistrates for Giving Effect to His Majesty's Proclamation* (London, 1790), 12–13; *Statement and Propositions from Society*, 19–22, 25–7.

119 For example, *An Account of the Present State of Prisons and Houses of Correction in the Western Circuit* (London, 1789). Relevant extracts from Howard's *State of the Prisons* were included.

120 *Report of the Sub-Committee Respecting the Improvements Made in the Prisons* (London, 1790); Ignatieff, *Just Measure*, 95.

121 Samuel Glasse, *A Sermon Preached in the Chapel of Magdalen-Hospital* (London, 1777), 6. See also Jonas Hanway, *Letter to Robert Dingley, Esq; Being a Proposal for the Relief and Employment of Friendless Girls and Repenting Prostitutes* (London, 1758), 6–7, 10–11, 20–1.

122 M.G. Jones, *The Charity School Movement* (Cambridge: Cambridge University Press, 1938); M.M. Dick, "English Conservatives and Schools for the Poor c. 1780–1833" (PhD

diss., University of Leicester, 1979); Jeremy Schmidt, "Charity and the Government of the Poor in the English Charity School Movement, circa 1700–1730," *Journal of British Studies* 49, no. 4 (2010): 774–800. Other schools emphasized religion. See Thomas Lacquer, *Religion and Respectability: Sunday Schools and English Working-Class Culture, 1780–1850* (New Haven, CT: Yale University Press, 1976); K.D. Snell, "The Sunday School Movement in England and Wales," *Past and Present* 164 (1999): 122–68.

123 Jones, *Charity*, 155, 159.

124 Dick, "Conservatives," 193–4. Quoting Catharine Cappe, *An Account of Two Charity Schools for the Education of Girls* (York, 1800), and Clara Reeve, *Plans of Education with Remarks on the Systems of other Writers* (London, 1792).

125 Dick, "Conservatives"; *A Brief Statement of the Saint Mary-le-Bone Day School of Industry* (London, 1799).

126 Dick, "Conservatives," 196; *Society for Bettering the Condition and Increasing the Comforts of the Poor* (London, 1797), 1–3; *The Reports of the Society for Bettering the Condition of the Poor and Increasing the Comforts of the Poor, vol. 1*, (London, 1798), 272–86.

127 *List of the Members of the Philanthropic Society* (1791), ii, v; *A Short Account of the Philanthropic Society* (London, 1791), 3. For magistrate membership see also *A List of the Members of the Philanthropic Society, March 31, 1793* (London, 1793); *A List of the Members of the Philanthropic to 31 March 1809* (London, 1809).

128 *An Account of the Institution and Proceedings of the Guardian Asylum* (London, 1789); BCGM, LL, BBBRMG202080584, BBBRMG202090305; *Surrey Gaol and Session House, 1791–1824*, ed. C.W. Chalklin (Surrey, UK: Surrey Recond Society, 2009), 1; "Will of Nicholas Nixon, 5 May 1790," TNA, PROB 11/1192/24. He also donated £500 to the Tower Ward charity school.

129 *An Account of the Asylum, or House of Refuge for the Reception of Orphan Girls* (London, 1769), 1.

130 Jonas Hanway, *Observations on the Causes of the Dissoluteness* (London, 1772), 61; *A Short Account of the Magdalen Hospital* (London, 1807), 4, 7.

131 *A List of the Governors of the Magdalen hospital* (London, 1790); *A List of the Governors of the Magdalen Hospital* (London, 1798).

132 Hanway, *Letter to Robert Dingley*, 12.

133 *Rules and Regulations of the Society for Bettering the Condition of the Poor, at Clapham, Surrey* (London, 1800), 8, 10.

134 Patrick Colquhoun, *An Account of a Meat and Soup Charity* (London, 1797), 10.

135 Hanway, *Letter to Robert Dingley*, 17.

136 Melossi and Pavarini, *Prison and the Factory*, esp. 33.

137 See for example "Petition of Edmund Grove, 1635," LMA, WJ/SR/SN/041/25, available on BHO.

138 "Report of Committee on Officers and Regulations, Apr. 1794," LMA, MA/G/CBF/084.

139 "Sketch of Rules and Regulations, 1794," LMA, MA/G/CBF/202.

140 "Rough Minutes and Reports, 27 Jan. 1796," LMA, MA/G/GEN/0298.

141 "New bridewell," *Whitehall Evening Post* (London), 7–9 Oct. 1794.

142 "Report to Consider Incorporation," SHC, QS2/6/1800/EP/76a; "Report of Magistrates," QS2/6/1800/EPH/81; "Report of Magistrates," QS2/6/1800/MID/17; "Account of William Benton, 9 Apr. 1800," QS2/6/1801/EA/23.

143 *PP*, 1810–11, iii.567, 39.

144 "Report of Magistrates," SHC, QS2/6/1801/MIC/19.

145 "Letter from Lord Middleton," SHC, QS2/6/1801/EPH/47.
146 BPCM, 21 Nov. 1793, LMA, CLC/275/MS33131/002.
147 *Special committee of governors*, 23.
148 BCGM, 31 Jan. 1799, LMA, CLC/275/MS33011/25.
149 BPCM, 21 Nov. 1793, LMA, CLC/275/MS33131/002.
150 BPCM, 30 Apr. 1795, LMA, CLC/275/MS33131/002. See also BCGM, 31 Jan. 1799, CLC/275/MS33011/25.
151 *PP*, 1810–11, iii.567, 84, 86.
152 *PP*, Dec. 1800, appendix 8, 95.
153 *PP*, 1818, viii.1, 282, 285.
154 Philippa Hardman, "Origins of Late Eighteenth-Century Prison Reform in England" (PhD diss.; Sheffield, UK: University of Sheffield, 2007), ch. 3.
155 Patrick Colquhoun, *Treatise on Police of the Metropolis* (London, 1796), 95; William Mainwaring, *An Address to the Grand Jury of the County of Middlesex* (London, 1785), 5–6: "the high price we pay for labour is one of the misfortunes of this country … if labouring men were not suffered to spend their time in ale-houses, they would be at their work; they would have no where else to go."
156 "To the Printer … [from] A Lover of Justice, but an Enemy to Cruelty," *Gazeteer and New Daily Advertiser* (London), 18 May 1770.
157 Hardman, "Prison Reform," 167–8; George Fisher, "Birth of the Prison Retold," *Yale Law Journal* 104, no. 6 (1995), 1259–61.
158 Chalklin, *Public Buildings*, 167; *St James's Chronicle* (London), 28–31 July 1787.
159 PP, 1811, 37–8. See also G.O. Paul's comments, 30.
160 Russel Dobash, "Labour and Discipline in Scottish and English Prisons: Moral Correction, Punishment, and Useful Toil," *Sociology* 17, no. 1 (1983): 1–27, here 2.
161 Innes, "Bridewells," 97; Evans, *Fabrication*, 56–7.
162 Ursula Henriques, "The Rise and Decline of the Separate System of Prison Discipline," *Past and Present* 54 (1972): 61–93; William Forsythe, *The Reform of Prisoners, 1830–1900* (New York: St Martin's Press, 1987), 15–35; Miles Ogborn, "Discipline, Government and Law: Separate Confinement in the Prisons of England and Wales, 1830–1877," *Transactions of the Institute of British Geographers* 20, no. 3 (1995): 295–311.
163 *PP*, 1810–11, iii.567, 4.

CHAPTER THREE

1 Howard, *The State of the Prisons*, 1–2. See also "Notebook containing notes by Howard on visits to prisons and hospitals, 1786–87," Bodleian Archives and Manuscripts, MS. Eng. misc. e. 400.
2 Webbs, *Prisons*, 24–32: "how long this state of unconcern in the many, and of mingled acquiescence and hopelessness in the few, would have persisted, if there had not intervened an exceptional personality, it is useless to discuss." In many accounts of the prison, which tend to centre on the late eighteenth and early nineteenth centuries, the "pre-reform" prison is typically dealt with in a handful of pages. The research leans heavily on contemporary reports by reformers rather than archival research. For scholarly accounts which take this position see Ignatieff, *Just Measure*, ch. 2; James Willis, "Transportation versus Imprisonment in Eighteenth- and Nineteenth-Century Britain: Penal Power, Liberty, and the State," *Law & Society Review* 39, no. 1 (2005): 171–210.

3 Beattie, *Crime and Courts*; Beattie, *Policing and Punishment*; Innes, "Bridewells"; Rod Morgan, "Divine Philanthropy: John Howard Reconsidered," *History* 62, no. 206 (1977): 388–410; Randall McGowen, "The Well-Ordered Prison: England, 1780–1865," in *Oxford History of the Prison*, 77–80. Evidence for such efforts can also be found in county studies, though these works generally do not articulate this wider point.

4 Joanna Innes, "'Reform' in English Public Life: The Fortunes of a Word," in *Rethinking the Age of Reform: Britain 1780–1850*, ed. Arthur Burns and Joanna Innes (London: Cambridge University Press, 2003), 85–6. See also Beattie, *Crime*, 307.

5 For an example of someone becoming interested in his local prison after reading what Howard wrote, see Basil Cozens-Hardy, ed., *Diary of Sylas Neville, 1767–1778* (London: Oxford University Press, 1950).

6 Paul, *Defects of Prisons*, 6. Through the 1780s and 1790s, public figures interested in reforming prisons consistently praised Howard and his contribution to the movement. See also John Brewster, *On the Prevention of Crimes and the Advantages of Solitary Imprisonment* (London, 1792).

7 Howard, *The State of the Prisons*, 21.

8 In a similar vein, Louise Falcini recently argued that the middle decades of the eighteenth century saw London authorities articulate a "coherent policy towards cleanliness and personal hygiene," which transformed the cleanliness of prisons and prisoners. She also stresses that Middlesex authorities introduced pragmatic reforms before Howard's criticisms. Louise Falcini, "Cleanliness and the Poor in Eighteenth-Century London" (PhD diss., University of Reading, 2018), 260.

9 For example, "Accounts of the Nightman," SHC, QS2/6/1765/Eas/14–15, QS2/6/1772/Mic/1; MGOC, 6 Dec. 1750, *LL*, LMSMGO556020436.

10 Prisoners usually pushed these responsibilities onto the newest inmate. Ilive, *Reasons*, 36; Batty Langley, *An Accurate Description of Newgate* (London, 1724), 6.

11 Ilive, *Reasons*, 13.

12 Gary Kelly, ed., *Newgate Narratives*, vol. 1 (London: Routledge, 2008), xiii; "Committee upon Petition Relating to Newgate, 22 Mar. 1765," *LL*, LMSMPS505470059; Falcini, "Cleanliness," 270.

13 Kevin Sienna has argued that attempts to safeguard the public against gaol fever played a "more essential component of penal debates than is often allowed." He emphasizes prisoners' threat to "propertied Englishmen" rather than to themselves. Kevin Sienna, *Rotten Bodies: Class and Contagion in Eighteenth-Century Britain* (New Haven, CT: Yale, 2019), 96–152, here 72.

14 *LL*, LMSMPS505470056; Evans, *Fabrication*, 100–2; Sienna, *Rotten Bodies*, 130.

15 "County Day, 25 Apr. 1754," *LL*, LMSMPS504270130.

16 Winter, *Prisons*, 74.

17 *PP*, 1840, 291, 394.

18 On the ordinary daily diet see BCGM, "Bridewell and Bethlem Hospitals," BCB-09, 309. Cited in Cryar, "The London Bridewell," 161n55; BMCG, 31 Aug. 1694 and 9 June 1699, *LL*, BBBRMG202010405, BBBRMG202020296. The governors paid for most of the food, but the steward also funded part of it.

19 MGOC, 15 Oct. 1741, *LL*, LMSMGO556010456–LMSMGO556010463. See for example the practices of Jeremiah Boreman and his wife when he was keeper of New Prison: "Statement of Susan Bayley, July 1709," *LL*, LMSMPS501070007.

20 MSP, Oct. 1696, *LL*, LMSMPS500450098, LMSMPS500450102; W.J. Hardy, ed., *Middlesex County Records, Calendar of Sessions Books 1689–1709* (London, 1905), iii–xxvi, BHO.

21 *LL*, LMSMGO556010461.

22 Beattie, *Crime*, 301. Baker's accounts (QS2/6, SHC) begin in 1701.

23 For the City, see Sheehan, "System," 306. For Middlesex, see MGOC, 12 Jan. 1764, *LL*, LMSMGO556050027–30; MSP, Apr. 1765 and Dec. 1766, *LL*, LMSMPS505470025–6, LMSMPS505660131.

24 There, using funds arising from a life donation, the chamberlain sent sixty-five penny loaves to prisoners every eight weeks. Otherwise, inmates fended for themselves. Smith, *Gaols*, 38; *PP*, 1813–14, iv, 103.

25 "Petition of Eliz Galaway, Apr. 1708," *LL*, LMSMPS507010081.

26 LL, LMSMGO556010462. See also the burials at Surrey County Gaol in Beattie, *Crime*, 302.

27 Sheehan, "System," 322–4; "Petition by Surgeon," SHC, QS2/6/1750/Xmas/10; "Accounts for Medical Attendance," SHC, QS2/6/1771/Mid/22, QS2/6/1772/Mic/4.

28 "February 1691," in *Sessions Books*, BHO.

29 Copeland, *Bridewell*, 48.

30 14 Geo III c. 59.

31 Sheehan, "System," 324–5; Howard, *The State of the Prisons* (1780), 183, 186–9; MGOC, Jan. 1775, LMSMGO556070042–4.

32 "Report of Committee concerning Rules and Orders, 1774," LMA, CLA/066/01/010.

33 BPCM, 22 and 29 Mar. 1776, LMA, CLC/275/MS33131/001.

34 "Account for Bathing Tubs," SHC, QS2/6/1775/Eph/43; "Report on Clothing for Prisoners," ibid., QS2/6/1775/Eph/46, "Report on Work to House of Correction to Supply Soft Water," ibid., QS2/6/1775/Eph/47; "Account for Medicines and Attendance at Prisons," ibid., QS2/6/1775/Eph/34; ibid., QS2/6/1776/Eph/27; Smith, *Gaols*, 36; Howard, *The State of the Prisons*, 232.

35 Howard, *The State of the Prisons*, 59–60.

36 Ibid., 8–9, 60–2. Howard sometimes insinuated that the county allowance should be withheld from who misbehaved in confinement. He proposed that those who abstained from liquor should be allowed bread, and he notes that only those who behaved well should be given a Sunday dinner.

37 Ibid., 12–14, 42, 44–5.

38 For contemporary accounts see Ned Ward, *London Spy*, 79–82; Langly, *Accurate Description*, esp. 4, 33, 39; Howard, *The State of the Prisons*, 208. On fees: "Fees taken at New Prison, July 1720," *LL*, LMSMPS501870088. For scholarly accounts: Sheehan, "London System," 28, 47–58; E.D. Pendry, *Elizabethan Prisons and Prison Scenes*, vol. 1 (Salzburg, Austria: Universitat Salzburg, 1974), 77, 94–5, 320. On European prisons: Guy Geltner, *The Medieval Prison: A Social History* (Princeton, NJ: Princeton University Press, 2008).

39 22 & 23 Car II c. 20. The act was driven by debtors who sought to improve their incarceration by distancing themselves from the "lewd and prophane language" of felons.

40 Howard, *The State of the Prisons*, 46–7.

41 For earlier attempts, Winter, "Prisons," 75; Pendry, *Scenes*, 112–16; Ilive, *Reasons*, 10–11, 39. The mixing of men and women at night was a source of great scandal, as furour around the Newgate "partners" highlights: "City Sessions Papers, 28 July 1707," *LL*, LMSLPS150180051.

42 "Newgate plans, c. 1750–1790," LMA, COL/CCS/PL/02/095/A–C, 325A–B, COL/SVD/PL/08/0001–0085.
43 *LL*, LMSMPS504850056–9; *LL*, LMSMGO556040120; 19 Jan. 1762, *LL*, LMSMPS505060104; *LL*, LMSMPS505130021.
44 Smith, *Gaols*, 27, 36.
45 Howard, *The State of the Prisons*, 178.
46 Sheehan, "System," 181, no. 3; Bassett, "Newgate," 244–5, shows this order was periodically re-affirmed.
47 Sheehan, "System," 78.
48 MGOC, 24 Feb. 1731, 6 July 1732, *LL*, LMSMGO556000613, LMSMGO556000632.
49 25 Geo II c. 37. Local and royal authorities also sought to silo disorderly or hardened prisoners by sending them to particular prisons. Newgate was often used in this way. Bassett, "Newgate," n2, 6.
50 Sheehan, "System," 81; Howard, *The State of the Prisons*, 181.
51 "Rules: New Prison, 1819," LMA, MA/G/GEN/1186.
52 Evans, *Fabrication*, 175; Smith, *Gaols*, 33.
53 Chalklin, "Reconstruction," 28.
54 BPCM, 8 July 1779, LMA, CLC/275/MS33131/001.
55 18 Oct. 1775, ibid.
56 Howard, *The State of the Prisons*, 42–8, 68–72. His plan is printed between 48–9.
57 Ibid., 43.
58 Ibid.
59 Ibid., 43–4.
60 "An Essay towards ye Reformation of Newgate and other Prisons in and about London," in *Two Hundred Years: The History of the Society for Promoting Christian Knowledge, 1698–1898*, W.O. Allen and E. McClure (London: SPCK, 1898), 54–7; Jonas Hanway, *Solitude in Imprisonment* (London, 1776). For Europe, Spencer J. Weinreich, "Why Early Modern Mass Incarceration Matters: The Bamberg Malefizhaus, 1627–31," *Journal of Social History* 56, no. 4 (2023): 719–52.
61 The City devised orders for its prisons in 1393, 1430–31, 1436, 1488, and 1606 and created additional rules for compters specifically in 1546–47 and 1630 and for Newgate in 1617, 1633, 1643, 1702, 1732, and 1744. Sheehan, "System," 24, 144.
62 Ilive, *Reasons*, 11–12, 15; Langley, *Description*, 6, 12.
63 Howard, *The State of the Prisons*, 153.
64 Ilive, *Reasons*, 37–8.
65 Sheehan, "System," 423–7.
66 Ibid., 175.
67 Ilive, *Reasons*, 24.
68 Ibid., 15, 22–3.
69 Howard, *The State of the Prisons*, 65.
70 Ibid., 70–1.
71 Ibid., 47. There is some archival support for his view. Clerkenwell debtors, for instance, petitioned magistrates for the right to work at their respective trades to support their families in 1780: LMA, MJ/SP/1780/10/005.
72 13 Geo III c. 58; 55 Geo III c. 48.
73 Cryar, "Bridewell," 39n58.
74 Howard, *The State of the Prisons*, 55.

75 Ibid.

76 Ibid., 49.

77 For this paragraph and the administration of early modern prisons generally see Dobb, "Prisons," 93–5; McConville, *Administration*, 1–77.

78 Sheehan, "System," 244.

79 The power to build and repair gaols originated in 1531 and was made perpetual in 1719. 23 Hen VIII c. 2; 33 Hen VIII c. 17; 37 Hen VIII c. 23; 5 Eliz I c. 24; 13 Eliz I c. 25; 11 Will III c. 19; 10 Ann c. 14; 6 Geo I c. 19; 24 Geo III s2 c. 54.

80 Dorothy Powell and Hilary Jenkinson, eds, *Surrey Quarter Sessions, Order-Book and Rolls, 1661–1663* (Kingston on Thames, UK, 1935), 79.

81 MGOC, 18 Jan. 1719, 13 Jan. 1720, *LL*, LMSMGO400000197–9, LMSMGO400000190.

82 Sheehan, "System," 245; "Petition by Keeper," SHC, QS2/6/1757/Misc[II]/41.

83 See ch. 6.

84 7 Jac I c. 4. See, for example, Norwich, where city authorities settled a salary of £28 per annum on the keeper and 40*s.* for a priest from June 1571. "Papers relating to the Bridewell," Norwich Record Office, NCR 12d/17.

85 *Surrey Quarter Sessions*, 10, 37, 49; "Order for Preventing Commitments only for Debt, Jan. 1689," *LL*, LMSMPS500000043; BCGM, 11 May 1694, *LL*, BBBRMG202010375. At Middlesex, responsibility for the matron's salary was pushed first onto the gaol keeper and later the bridewell governor. "Petition of Jones, Keeper of New Prison and Governor of Clerkenwell Bridewell, Jan. 1691," *LL*, LMSMPS5000800389; "Dec. 1750," *LL*, LMSMPS504070058.

86 "Bond given by Governor, 19 Jan. 1720," *LL*, LMSMGO400000201–2; SHC, QS2/6/1724/Mic/6.

87 13 Oct. 1778, LMA, MA/G/GEN/0001; McConville, *Administration*, 43.

88 Sheehan, "System," 19–23. Those appointed to inspect the prisons regularly refused to go for fear of gaol fever.

89 This is a tentative conclusion for Middlesex and Surrey, as there are considerably more surviving records from the early eighteenth century than before. For the City, however, Sheehan has argued convincingly that, from 1732, the City's prisons were much better regulated and more closely supervised. Sheehan, "System." For Middlesex, see July 1709, *Sessions Books*, 335–53, BHO.

90 Howard, *The State of the Prisons*, 66.

91 Daniel Layard, *Directions to Prevent the Contagion of Gaol Fever* (London, 1772); Smith, *Gaols*; Jeremiah Fitzpatrick, *An essay on Gaol-Abuses* (Dublin, 1784); John Jebb, *Thoughts on the Construction and Polity of Prisons* (Bury St. Edmonds, UK, 1785); J.C. Lettsom, *Hints Respecting the Prison of Newgate* (London, 1794). For more on these authors and their recommendations, see Cooper, "English Prison Reform," 53–6.

92 John Brewster, *Sermons for prisons. To which are added prayers for the use of prisoners in solitary confinement* (Stockton, UK, 1790).

93 Francis Burdett, *An Impartial Statement of the Inhuman Cruelties Discovered! In the Coldbath-Fields Prison* (London, 1800). On Burdett see Christina Parolin, *Radical Spaces: Venues of Popular Politics in London, 1790– c. 1845* (Canberra: Australian National University E Press, 2010), 49–82; J.R. Dinwiddy, "Sir Francis Burdett and Burdettite Radicalism," *History* 65 (1980): 17–31.

94 Evans, *Fabrication*, 142–3, 181; Cooper, "English Prison Reform."

95 *Improvements in Prisons* (London, 1790), 5, 23–4, 35–6.

96 Jonas Hanway, *Solitude*, 4, 31.
97 Hanway, *The Defects of Police, the Cause of Immorality, and the Continual Robberies Committed, Particularly in and around the Metropolis* (London, 1775), 213.
98 *Improvements in Prisons*, 5, 35–6.
99 Josiah Dornford, *An Answer to the Report from the Committee Appointed by the Court of Common Council* (London, 1785), 75.
100 Paul, *Defects of Prisons*, 31.
101 Whitling, *Gloucestershire*, 11, 18, 209.
102 Howard, *The State of the Prisons*, 43, 264.
103 Ibid., 71.
104 Brewster, *Sermons*, 33, v–xvii.
105 William Morton Pitt, *A Plan for the Improvement of the Internal Police of Prisons* (London: W. Bulmer, 1804), 14.
106 Paul, *Defects*, 72.

CHAPTER FOUR

1 C.W. Chalkin, *English Counties and Public Building 1650–1830* (London: Hambledon Press, 1998), 163–4, 167–8.
2 Ibid., 4, 16. 141.
3 Quoted from Ignatieff, *Just Measure*, 157. See also R.A. Cooper, "Ideas and Their Execution: English Prison Reform," *Eighteenth-Century Studies* 10, no. 1 (1976): 73–93; Evans, *Fabrication*; Forsythe, *Reform*, 1–14; Sienna, *Rotten Bodies*, ch. 5; DeLacy, *Lancashire*, ch. 3; Philippa Hardman, "Fear of Fever and the Limits of the Enlightenment," *Cultural and Social History* 10, no. 4 (2013): 511–32; Hitchcock and Shoemaker, *Lives*, 235–30; Chalklin, *Buildings*, 171–2.
4 "Grand Jury Presentment, May 1772," *LL*, LMSMPS506190007.
5 Sheehan, "System," 398–9.
6 LMA, MJ/SP/1781/PC/003i.
7 Evans, *Fabrication*, 95.
8 "Legal Case for New House of Correction, Jan. 1786," LMA, MJ/SP/1786/01/105. For Surrey, see 12 Geo III c. 65.
9 *LL*, LMSMPS506240141–43.
10 7 Geo III c. 37.
11 "Committee relating to Newgate, 1765," *LL*, LMSMPS505470057.
12 "Resolution following Report of Prisons Committee, May 1782," *LL*, LMSMPS507400050.
13 "Committee for Repair of Prisons, 5 Mar. 1784," LMA, MA/G/GEN/0035; LMA, MJ/SP/1781/PC/003i; "Apothecary reports, Jan. 1777–Oct. 1783," *LL*, LMSMPS506690041, LMSMPS506800086, LMSMPS507100024, LMSMPS507240033, LMSMPS507730251; ibid., LMA, MA/G/GEN/0231–0232; "Report of Visiting Justices," LMA, MA/G/GEN/0007–0018; "Bill for bread delivered," LMA, MJ/SP/1782/01/027, MJ/SP/1784/02/037; ibid., LL, LMSMPS507540046, LMSMPS507730291, LMSMPS507770340.
14 "Committee for Rebuilding Compters, 6 Jan. 1786," LMA, CLA/032/02/004; Howard, *The State of the Prisons*, 174; Howard, *Lazarettos*, 126.
15 Mar. 1786, LMA, CLA/032/02/006.
16 Neild, *Prisons*, 229; "Giltspur Compter Contract drawings 1787," Sir John Soane Collections, D4/3/4/35; "Returns as to the State of Prisons, 1814," LMA, CLA/032/01/037.

17 *Surrey Gaol and Session House, 1791–1824*, ed. C.W. Chalklin (Surrey, UK: Surrey Record Society, 2009), x.
18 Ibid., xvii.
19 *Thoughts on the Construction and Management of prisons* (London, 1786), 10.
20 Ibid., 11.
21 MPCR, 1784, LMA, MA/G/CBF/080.
22 *PP*, 1813–14, iv, 93.
23 "Report of Aldermen Visiting Gaols in England, 1815," LMA, CLA/032/01/041b.
24 Evans, *Fabrication*, 104, 145. Reformers, though, criticized Newgate for the smallness of the courtyards, and for the City's refusal to build large windows, grates, or slots into the prison walls to allow greater air flow.
25 "Descriptions of plans and estimates, 1784," LMA, MA/G/CBF/206; PP (Dec. 1800), 132, 9.
26 Ibid.; Dorothy Stroud, *George Dance, Architect, 1741–1825* (London: Faber and Faber, 1791), 99; Neild, *Prisons*, 425, 548–9.
27 Ibid., 136.
28 "Rules for House of Correction, 1794," LMA, MA/G/CBF/084C; BPCM, 6 June 1787, LMA, CLC/275/MS33131/001; BPSCM, 14 Nov. 1792, 30 Apr. 1795, LMA, CLC/275/MS33132/001.
29 *Rules and Orders for the Management of House of Correction for Middlesex* (London, 1802), 13–14; "Rules and Orders for Newington House of Correction," SHC, QS5/4/7/3.
30 Neild, *Prisons*, 547; *PP*, 1813–14, iv, 4, 10. At Giltspur, prisoners were given bread every alternate day, but each also received six pounds of potatoes a week.
31 14 Jan. 1785, LMA, CLA/032/02/004.
32 Sarah wrote repeatedly to the Bank of England, with increasing desperation, asking for some assistance. See "Letter 256, F25/4/31," in *Prisoners' Letters to the Bank of England, 1781–1827*, ed. Deirdre Palk (London: London Record Society, 2007), BHO.
33 *PP*, 1813–14, iv.249, 47, 4, 43. For food donations, 10, 83, 103.
34 BPCM, 19 Jan. 1801, LMA, CLC/275/MS33131/001.
35 LMA, MA/G/CBF/084C; *PP*, Dec. 1800, 23–26.
36 *PP*, Dec. 1800, 132, 29; BCPM, 10 Oct. 1792, CLC/275/MS33131/001; BCGM, 25 May 1796, LMA, CLC/275/MS33011/25.
37 *Queries Humbly Offered to the Serious Consideration of the Worthy Magistrates and Inhabitants of the County of Middlesex, relative to their House of Correction* (1760[?]), 1.
38 *Report from the Committee on Cold Bath Fields Clerkenwell* (1799), 13.
39 *PP*, Dec. 1800, 132, 23–4; Dec. 1798, *LL*, LMSMPS509540115.
40 *PP*, Dec. 1800, 132, 43.
41 See "George Dance, Newgate Gaol, Contract Drawings," Soane Collections, D4/4/23.
42 Neild, *Prisons*, 426.
43 Neild, *Small Debts*, 3rd ed., 548; *Report Respecting Improvements in Prisons*, 22. See also MPCM, 17 Oct. 1796, MA/G/GEN/0310.
44 *PP*, 1818, viii.297, 32, 72, 198; BPSC, 26 May 1802, LMA, CLA/275/MS33132/002.
45 For one of the elder Dance's earliest designs see "Newgate, 1775, Comptroller's City Lands Plans," LMA, COL/CCS/PL/02/051. The three quadrangles are a feature of every plan produced (by Dance the Elder, his son, and others) from 1755 onwards. Harold Kalman, "Newgate Prison," *Architectural History* 12 (1969): 50–61, 108–12.
46 The female quadrangle had only common and state sides. *PP*, 1813–14, iv.249, 3, 6.
47 "Newgate Gaol Committee Journal, 23 May 1780," LMA, COL/CC/NGC/04/01/001.
48 *PP*, 1813–14, iv.249, 5–6.

49 No account gives a breakdown of the male felon classes, but these are the categories sometimes used in surviving prison records. "Visiting Magistrates' Report," SHC, QS2/6/1800/EP/81, QS2/6/1801/EP/49/1–2.
50 *Report of Aldermen Appointed to Visit Gaols* (London, 1816), 142.
51 Neild, *Small Debts*, 548.
52 MPCM, 5 Feb. 1798, LMA, MA/G/GEN/0002; Neild, *Prisons*, 136–7. No contemporary plans of this prison survive.
53 On the debtor side, male and female prisoners were given distinct day rooms and sleeping quarters, but in practice, these divisions often broke down. Neild, *Small Debts*, 1st ed., 63–4. See also PP, 1813–14, iv.249, 60.
54 29 Mar. 1787, LMA, CLA/029/02/001; "Committee on Compters, 29 Mar. 1787," LMA, CLA/032/02/004. For the plan see Stroud, "Giltspur," Plate 1; PP, 1813–14, iv.249, 46, 9. The system was further complicated after 1804 when City authorities declared the Poultry unfit. Night charges were thenceforth directed to the Poultry while those others arrested at other times were sent to Giltspur. Those arrested in the City's eastern district remained under the authority of the Poultry keeper, however. For the two keepers' convenience, inmates in Giltspur were separated according to whether they were 'Poultry' or 'Giltspur' inmates.
55 PP, 1813–14, iv.249, 6; Neild, *Prisons*, 136–7.
56 "Design of Borough Compter, 1785," LMA, COL/CCS/PL/02/058/A; "Giltspur Street Compter, Surveyor Department Plans," LMA, COL/SVD/PL/08/0112.
57 PP, 1813–14, iv.249, 46.
58 Ibid., 5.
59 Ibid., 68.
60 "Giltspur Compter, Plan for Convict Cells, 1787," Soane Collections, D4/3/32.
61 Evans, *Fabrication*, 177.
62 On the cost of constructing cells see Mehta, "Courts and Prisons," 191–6.
63 Neild, *Prisons*, 549–8.
64 PP, 1813–14, iv.249, 7, 31–2, 48. See also LMA, CLA/032/01/041b.
65 PP, 1813–14, iv.249, 56.
66 Ibid., 61, 90.
67 Ibid., 8, 58.
68 Ibid., 26; "Journal of the Borough Compter Keeper, 24 Mar. 1818," LMA, CLA/031/02/019.
69 PP, 1839, xxi, 276; Sheehan, "System," 169.
70 W.J. Sheehan, "Finding Solace in Eighteenth-Century Newgate," in *Crime in England: 1550–1800*, ed. J. Cockburn (London: Methuen, 1977), 239–41.
71 "Petition from Newgate's Keeper, 1813," CAGCP, LMA, COL/CA/GAC/03/001.
72 PP, 1813–14, iv.249, 32.
73 Ibid., 4, 82–84. In principle, but often not in practice, visitors had to enter and exit at designated times.
74 Richard Philips, *A Letter to the Livery of London* (London, 1808), 35.
75 CLA/031/02/019. See also PP, 1818, viii.297, 39.
76 Parolin, *Radical Spaces*, 30.
77 "Rebuilding Committee Minutes," LMA, MA/G/CBF/031, 79, 82a, 83. Sometimes they only noted three classes (excluding the fourth), e.g. in PP, Dec. 1800, 132, 70.
78 PP, Dec. 1800, 132, 10–11.
79 *Rules and orders* (London, 1802), 5.

80 MPCR, 7 Jan. 1808, LMA, MA/G/GEN/0003.
81 "Rules at Newington," SHC, QS5/4/7/3.
82 LMA, CLA/032/01/041b, 143.
83 BPSCM, 19 Dec. 1793, 26 July 1798, LMA, CLC/275/MS33132/001; *PP*, Dec. 1800, 132, 15. Lottery vagrants were individuals found guilty of infringing the lottery laws. See Audrey Eccles, "A Superior Kind of Vagrant: Middlesex Lottery Vagrants in the 1790s," *Transactions of the London and Middlesex Archaeological Society* 60 (2008): 213–20.
84 *Rules and orders*, 11.
85 *PP*, Dec. 1800, 132, 36–7.
86 BPCM, 11 Oct. 1775, 22 and 29 Mar. 1785, LMA, CLC/275/MS33131/001. O'Donoghue, *Bridewell*, 201–3.
87 BPCM, 9 Jan. 1793, 5 Nov. 1793, 25 Nov. 1794, LMA, CLC/275/MS33131/002. Work at the men's prison was delayed by building accidents and the decision to move the prison to a different location, within the Bridewell complex, which could be "converted more commodiously with respect to air[,] space and other advantages."
88 Neild, *Prisons*, 551.
89 MSP, LMA, MJ/SP/1786/02; MPCR, Feb. 1784, LMA, MA/G/CBF/079; MPCM, 27 Jan. 1796, LMA, MA/G/GEN/0298; *PP*, Dec. 1800, 132, 9, 85.
90 *PP*, Dec. 1800, 132, 102.
91 Ibid., 15, 17.
92 *PP*, 1809, iv.215 (216), 9.
93 *PP*, Dec. 1800, 132, 11, 26, 61, 101.
94 "Report of Committee, 6 Dec. 1798," *LL*, LMSMGO556110237–44. These prisoners were given a double allowance of bread and a pint of porter each day.
95 *PP*, Dec. 1800, 132, 33.
96 MPCM, 7 Jan. 1804, LMA, MA/G/GEN/0002.
97 *PP*, Dec. 1800, 12, 86, 99.
98 LMA, MA/G/CBF/202.
99 Power to employ all prisoners was authorized by 22 Geo III c. 64. At Bridewell, this meant pass vagrants, though exempted from separate confinement, had to work. BPCM, 9 Jan. 1793, LMA, CLC/275/MS33131/002.
100 "Visitors' Report," SHC, QS2/6/1800/Mid/17.
101 BCGM, 17 Oct. 1777, LMA, CLC/275/MS33011/023; BPCM, 10 Oct. 1792, LMA, CLC/275/MS33131/002.
102 MPCR, 18 Feb. 1796, LMA, MJ/SP/1796/02/024.
103 "Visitors' Reports," SHC, QS2/6/1802/Mid/22, QS/2/6/1814.
104 "Newington Rules," SHC, QS5/4/7/3; "Visitors' report," SHC, QS2/6/1802/Eas/28; LMA, MA/G/CBF/202.
105 Prisoners' profits also went towards paying their discharge fees, where those still existed. *PP*, Dec. 1800, 33; BPSCM, 14 Nov. 1792, LMA, CLC/275/MS33132/001.
106 *PP*, Dec. 1800, 75.
107 Ibid., 75, 95; "Minutes of Committee to Inspect Prisoners' Concerns, 5 Mar. 1796," LMA, MJ/SP/1796/03/001. For Bridewell, see BPCM, 8 July 1795, LMA, CLC/275/MS33131/001; BCGM, 4 Mar. 1802, LMA, CLC/275/MS33011/025. For Surrey see "Memorial of Rev William Mann," SHC, QS2/6/1814/Mid/101.
108 MJ/SP/1796/03/001.

109 MPCR, 7 Jan. 1808, LMA, MA/G/GEN/0003. Examples of later reports: 1 June 1810, LMA, MA/G/GEN/0003; MPCM, 27 Mar. 1813, MA/G/GEN/0383; "Report of Visiting Justices, 20 Dec. 1821," LMA, MA/G/GEN/0418.
110 "Report of Visiting Justices," LMA, MJ/SP/1816/10/45.
111 "Draft rules, 1794," LMA, MA/G/GEN/1268.
112 SHC, QS5/4/7/3; LMA, CLA/032/01/041b, 111.
113 "Rough Minutes and Reports," LMA, MA/G/GEN/0308.
114 BPCM, 6 Nov. 1783, LMA, CLC/275/MS33131/001.
115 LMA, MA/G/GEN/1266.
116 SHC, QS5/4/7/3.
117 BPSCM, 13 Dec. 1792, LMA, CLC/275/MS33132/001.
118 *PP*, Dec. 1800, 132, 25–6, 87, 94; "Additional rules, 1823," LMA, MA/G/GEN/1270; MPCR, 28 Nov. 1807, MA/G/GEN/0002.
119 BPCM, 23 Dec. 1782, LMA, CLC/275/MS33131/001.
120 LMA, CLA/032/01/041b, 144.
121 *PP*, Dec. 1800, 132, 72. Friends of debtors and King's Bench prisoners secured magisterial approval easily, as magistrates did not believe they could ban visitors to these prisoners. Visitors were excluded as a punishment. "Admin correspondence, 19 Apr. 1821," MJ/SP/1821/04/073; MPCR, 30 Nov. 1810, MA/G/GEN/0003.
122 LMA, MJ/SP/1796/02/03; MPCR, 26 Jan. 1810, LMA, MA/G/GEN/0003.
123 Since many prisoners were too poor to supply themselves, the effect was the same for most inmates. MSP, *LL*, LMSMGO556110237–LMSMGO556110244; *PP*, 1798–99, 122, "Report from Committee Appointed to Enquire into Cold Bath Fields," 13; *PP*, Dec. 1800, 23–5.
124 MPCR, 26 Jan. 1810, MA/G/GEN/0003.
125 *PP*, 1818, viii.545 (392), 249. This policy contrasted clearly with the Bridewell governors' tighter one. One possible explanation for the difference might be the fact that City magistrates exercised considerably less oversight over Giltspur than the Bridewell governors exercised over their institution.
126 *PP*, 1813–14, iv.249, 7. These sums are his net profit – what he made after paying his staff. For Middlesex, see MGOC, Sept. 1785, *LL*, LMSMGO556090163.
127 "Committee for Rebuilding the Compters, Minute Book, no. 3, 3 Apr. 1787," LMA, CLA/032/02/004.
128 "Visitors' report," QS2/6/1800/Mid/17. They still took fees from debtors.
129 On the magistrates' deliberations over salaries see "Compter Rebuilding Committee, 3 Apr. 1787," LMA, CLA/032/02/004; MGOC, 12 Sept. 1785, *LL*, LMSMGO556090163; 27 Apr. 1797, ibid.
130 *PP*, 1813–14, iv.249, p.51.
131 "Account of Fees Payable to the Newgate Keeper, Michaelmas 1810 to Michaelmas 1813," CAGCP, LMA, COL/CA/GAC/03/001.
132 MGOC, 1795, *LL*, LMSMGO556100397. Some fees still remained but these were paid into the county fund rather than to the individual officers.
133 LMA, MA/G/GEN/1266.
134 SHC, QS2/6/1798/Mid/7a–c, QS5/4/7/1.
135 Sheehan, "Solace," 233.
136 *PP*, 1813–14, iv.249, 4–5, 36, 47–8, 61–4; *PP*, 1818, viii.297, p. 24; *PP*, 1818, viii.1, 14.
137 22 Geo III c. 64; 24 Geo III s.2 c. 54. Eric Stockdale, "Short History of Prison Inspection in England," *British Journal of Criminology* 23, no. 3 (1983): 209–23.

138 The first experiment lasted only a year, and the second, two years. "Reports of Visiting Justices," LMA, MA/G/GEN/0007–18; PP, Dec. 1800, 132, 103.

139 MPCM, 1 June 1809, LMA, MA/G/GEN/0003.

140 LMA, MA/G/GEN/0298.

141 *Bridewell and Bethlem Hospitals, London. At a court held at Bridewell Hospital, on Monday the 29th day of May, 1776* (London, 1776), 3.

142 BPSCM, 27 July 1792, LMA, CLC/275/MS33132/001.

143 "Court of Aldermen, Prisons Committees," LMA, COL/CA/PCA/01/001–003.

144 "Report of a Committee Appointed to View the Gaol," SHC, QS2/6/1799/Eas/7a–c; "Report of Visiting Magistrates," SHC, QS2/6/1799/Eas/18.

145 For the concept's early history see Barbara Shapiro, "Beyond Reasonable Doubt: The Evolution of a Concept," in *Fictions of Knowledge*, ed. Yota Batsaki et al. (Basingstoke, UK: Palgrave MacMillan, 2012), 19–39; Barbara Shapiro, *Beyond Reasonable Doubt and Probable Cause: Historical Perspectives in the Anglo-American Law of Evidence* (Berkeley, CA: California University Press, 1991).

146 Beattie, *Crime and Courts*, 341–75; John Langbein, *The Origins of the Adversary Criminal Trial* (Oxford, UK: Oxford University Press, 2003), ch. 3–5; Allyson May, *The Bar and the Old Bailey, 1750–1850* (Chapel Hill, NC: University of North Carolina Press, 2003), 233–6. See also Bruce Smith, "The Presumption of Guilt and the English Law of Theft, 1750–1850," *Law and History Review* 23, no. 1 (2005): 133–71.

147 Paul, *Defects of Prisons*, Advertisement.

148 David Steuart and Archibald Cockburn, *General Heads of a Plan for Erecting a New Prison and Bridewell in the City of Edinburgh* (Edinburgh, 1782), 4.

149 "Observations on the bill," *Morning Chronicle* (London), 19 June 1778.

150 Paul, *Defects of Prisons*, 35.

151 Thomas Buxton, *An Inquiry into Whether Crime be Produced or Prevented by our Present System of Prison Discipline* (London, 1818), 1–4.

152 "Inspectors of Prisons, Home District, Third Report, 1837–38," PP, XXX.1 (141), 1–2.

153 "Letter III," *Three Letters on Prison Discipline, Addressed to the Editor of the Norwich Mercury in the Month of September 1819* (Blandford, 1819), 23–4. I read the copy held by the Norfolk Record Office, c/saa 1/3.

154 Jonas Hanway, *Defects of Police*, 213.

155 *Improvements Made in the Prisons*, 5.

156 Buxton, *Prison Discipline*, 11.

157 PP, 1837–38, XXX.1, 1–2. See also "Reply of Inspectors with regard to Court of Aldermen on Newgate, 1836," PP, xlii.283 (486); "Inspectors of Prisons, Home District, Seventh Report, 1842," PP, XX.1 (422), 185–90.

158 PP, Dec. 1800, 132, 77.

159 PP, 1798–99, 122, 5.

160 PP, Dec. 1800, 132, 77. I have written more extensively on these disputes in an article I am preparing for publication entitled "Prison Reform from Below."

161 PP, Dec. 1800, 132, 77–9.

162 Francis Burdett, *An Impartial Statement of the Inhuman Cruelties Discovered! in the Coldbath-Fields Prison* (London, 1800); ibid., *A Further Account (being Part II) of the Cruelties Discovered in the Coldbath-Fields Prison* (London, 1800); PP, Dec. 1800, 132. For Burdett's correspondence and collaboration with inmates see "Observations on Treatment of Prisoners in Cold Bath Fields," Burdett-Coutts Papers, 1798–99, Bodleian

Libraries, MS. Eng. hist. c. 295; "Papers of Burdett relating to Treatment of Political Prisoners, 1798–1833," ibid., MS. Eng. hist. c. 296. Some of these disputes were discussed in Parolin, *Radical Spaces*, 49–82.

163 LMA, MA/G/GEN/0471.

164 MPCR, 3 Mar. 1808, MA/G/GEN/0003.

165 PP, Dec. 1800, 132, 35–7.

166 "Suggestions for Rules," CAGCP, 1812–16, LMA, COL/CA/GAC/03/001.

167 PP, 1810–11, iii.567, 7.

CHAPTER FIVE

1 Douglas Hay, "War, Dearth and Theft in the Eighteenth Century: The Record of the English Courts," *Past and Present* 95 (1982): 117–60.

2 For studies on London and its population see Jacob Field, "Economic Change in a London Suburb: Southwark, c. 1601–1881," *London Journal* 43, no. 3 (2018): 243–66; L.D. Schwartz, *London in the Age of Industrialisation: Entrepreneurs, Labour Force and Living Conditions, 1700–1850* (Cambridge: Cambridge University Press, 1992); John Landers, *Death and the Metropolis: Studies in the Demographic History of London 1670–1830* (Cambridge: Cambridge University Press, 1993); E.A. Wrigley, "English County Populations in the Later Eighteenth Century," *Economic History Review* 60 (2007): 35–69.

3 Harris, *Policing*, ch. 1–3; Ruth Paley, "'An imperfect, inadequate and wretched system'? Policing in London before Peel," *Criminal Justice History* 10 (1989): 95–130; Reynolds, *Bobbies*, esp. ch. 1–6; Jonah Miller, *Gender and Policing in Early Modern England* (Cambridge: Cambridge University Press, 2023), ch. 4–5; Beattie, *Runners*.

4 Harris, *Policing*, ch. 4–5; Reynolds, ch. 7–8.

5 10 Geo 4 c. 44.

6 2 & 3 Vic c. 94.

7 In addition to the works on policing cited above see Inwood, "Policing Morals," 129–46; Jennifer Davis, "Law Breaking and Law Enforcement: The Creation of a Criminal Class in Mid-Victorian London" (PhD diss.; Boston: Boston College, 1985), 180–1; Churchill, *Crime Control and Everyday Life in the Victorian City* (Oxford, UK: Oxford University Press, 2018), esp. part 1; Eleanor Bland, *Policing Suspicion: Proactive Policing in London* (London: Routledge, 2021); Paul Lawrence, "The Vagrancy Act (1824) and the Persistence of Pre-emptive Policing in England since 1750," *British Journal of Criminology* 57, no. 3 (2017): 513–31.

8 PP, 1833, xxxii.387; "Tables of Revenue, Population and Commerce, Part XII, 1844," PP, xlvi.1 (591), 157; "Return of Metropolitan and City Police, 1849," PP, xliv.501 (133); "Return of Metropolitan and City Police, 1852–53," PP, lxxviii.499 (544).

9 Bland, *Policing Suspicion*, figures 4.3–4.6. She looked at arrests of offenders tried at the Old Bailey between 1780 and 1850.

10 Exact numbers of charges committed to prisons are hard to come by since only a handful of prison commitment books have survived, and neither Parliament, local authorities, nor prison inspectors systematically collected information on charges. Still, comments made by authorities when interviewed by parliamentary committees and some surviving archival material provide a guide. PP, 1818, viii.1 (423), 145; "Report of Committee on Police of the Metropolis, 1822," PP, iv.91 (440), 109–10, 118–19, 134; "Watch and Police Committee Returns, 1827–31," LMA, COL/CC/WPC/02/001; "Select Committee on

Police of Metropolis, 1828," *PP*, xvi.1 (600), 125–7, 337; "Select Committee on Police of Metropolis, 1834," *PP*, xvi.1 (600), 51, 155.

11 "Inspectors of Prisons, Fifth Report, 1840," *PP*, xxv.1 (283), 289; *PP*, xx.1 (422), 195.

12 Gray, *Crime*, 20; "Select Committee on Metropolitan Police Offices, 1837–38," *PP*, xv.321 (578), 121. See also Mehta, "Summary Justice," 77.

13 *PP*, 1833, xxxii.387; Jennifer Davis, "A Poor Man's System of Justice: The London Police Courts in the Second Half of the Nineteenth Century," *Historical Journal* 27, no. 2 (1984): 312.

14 Barry Godfrey, "Changing Prosecution Practices and Their Impact on Crime Figures, 1857–1940," *British Journal of Criminology* 48, no. 2 (2008): 172; Douglas Hay and Francis Snyder, "Using the Criminal Law, 1750–1850: Policing, Private Prosecution and the State," in *Policing and Prosecution in Britain 1750–1850*, ed. Hay and Snyder (Oxford, UK: Clarendon Press, 1989), 3–52; David Lemmings, *Law and Government in England during the Long Eighteenth Century* (Basingstoke, UK: Palgrave MacMillan, 2011). For a review of this debate see David Churchill, "Rethinking the State Monopolisation Thesis: The Historiography of Policing and Criminal Justice in Nineteenth-Century England," *Crime, History & Societies* 18 (2014): 131–52. The most recent and fullest treatment of victims' role in the criminal justice system is Cox, Shoemaker, and Shore, *Victims*.

15 Bruce Smith, "The Myth of Private Prosecution in England, 1750–1850," in *Modern Histories of Crime and Punishment*, ed. Markus Dubber and Lindsay Farmer (Stanford, CA: Stanford University Press, 2007), 151–74; Godfrey, "Prosecution," 172; Churchill, *Crime Control*, 200–10.

16 Mehta, "Summary Justice," 81.

17 "Inspectors of Prisons, Home District, Second to Fourteenth Report," *PP*, 1837–50.

18 The numbers held for examination (which also included charges) were reported only in 1833, 1836, and 1840–41. "Return of Committals in London, Westminster, and Southwark, 1834," *PP*, xlvii.27 (52); "Inspectors of Prisons, Home District, Second to Fourteenth Reports, 1837–50," *PP*.

19 "Inspectors of Prisons," ibid.

20 *PP*, 1833, xxxii.387; "Tables of Revenue, Population, and Commerce, Part XII, 1844," *PP*, xlvi.1 (591), 139–47.

21 Other scholars have noted this increased willingness to prosecute: Harris, *Policing*, 127; Emsley, *Crime*, 35; Davis, "Criminal Class," ch. 5.

22 David Bentley, *English Criminal Justice in the Nineteenth Century* (London: Hambledon, 1998), 32–3.

23 Cox, Shoemaker, and Shore, *Victims*, 181–2.

24 Simon Devereaux, "In Place of Death: Transportation, Penal Practices, and the English State, 1770–1830," in *Qualities of Mercy: Justice, Punishment, and Discretion*, ed. Carolyn Strange (Vancouver: University of British Columbia Press, 1996), 67.

25 On attitudes towards crime and how perceptions were shaped, see Peter King, "Newspaper Reporting and Attitudes to Crime and Justice in Late-Eighteenth and Early-Nineteenth Century London," *Continuity and Change* 22 (2007): 73–112.

26 Mainwaring wrote this in a letter to the Sessions' Chairman. He still thought it worthwhile to try reforming offenders through prison discipline. The letter was published in *Second Report SIPD* (London, 1820), 69.

27 "Select Committee of House of Lords on Execution of Criminal Law, Second Report, 1847," PP, vii.5 (534), 33, 259. Metropolitan authorities (in contrast to those who worked at Pentonville) uniformly expressed faith in transportation for these reasons. See also 6, 202.

28 Quote from Middlesex bridewell governor, ibid., 289–90.

29 Quoted in Philip Harling, "The Trouble with Convicts: From Transportation to Penal Servitude, 1840–67," *Journal of British Studies* 53 (2014): 88.

30 Devereaux, "Penal Practices," 68. G.O. Paul did accept that some reprieved convicts might be fit for imprisonment, but he thought potential inmates should undergo a trial period first.

31 *The Parliamentary Register*, vol. 28 (London, 1791), 328. On Powney, see David Fisher, "Powney, Peniston Portlock," in *The History of Parliament: The House of Commons 1790–1820*, ed. R. Thorne (London, 1986), https://www.historyofparliamentonline.org/.

32 *Parliamentary Register*, 327. Mainwaring was especially concerned that Parliament might grant sheriffs and gaolers the authority to remove convicts sentenced to transportation to the Middlesex house of correction, which would be a serious economic burden on the county's ratepayers.

33 PP, 1847, vii.5, 295.

34 PP, 1816, xviii.361; PP, 1817, xvi.161; PP, 1818, xvi.3; "Return of Persons Committed to Gaols," LMA, MJ/SP/1829/01/008.

35 Harling, "Trouble with Convicts," 81–2. On the end of transportation see Hilary Carey, *Empire of Hell: Religion and the Campaign to End Convict Transportation in the British Empire, 1788–1875* (Cambridge: Cambridge University Press, 2019).

36 Hamish Maxwell-Stewart, "Convict Transportation from Britain and Ireland 1615–1870," *History Compass* 8, no. 11 (2010): 1232.

37 McConville, *Administration*, 139.

38 On the regime at Pentonville see Ignatieff, *Just Measure*; Catherine Cox and Hilary Marland, *Disorder Contained: Mental Breakdown and the Modern Prison in England and Ireland, 1840–1900* (Cambridge: Cambridge University Press, 2022), ch. 2.

39 For figures see Brett Diehl, "The English Prison Estate: Role of Local Carceral Institutions in the First Half of the Nineteenth Century" (MPhil diss.; Oxford, UK: University of Oxford, 2017), table 4.3.

40 Ignatieff, *Just Measure*, 185; Churchill, *Crime Control*, 71–5; Roger Swift, *Provincial Police Reform in Early Victorian England* (London: Routledge, 2021), 29; Chris Williams, "Counting Crimes or Counting People," *Crime, History & Societies* 4, no. 2 (2000): 81–3.

41 1 Geo IV c. 56; 7 & 8 Geo IV c. 29; 18 & 19 Vict c. 126; 9 Geo IV c. 31.

42 By 1858, 95.7 per cent of prosecutions were summary. Sweeney, "Extension," 5.

43 "Tables of Revenue, 1844," PP, xlvi.1 (591), 157; "Returns of Police, 1844," PP, xxxix.665 (238); "Return of Persons Taken into Custody, 1849," PP, xliv.501 (133); ibid., 1852–53, PP, lxxviii.499 (544). Before 1831, outcomes at the stipendiary offices were not collated and printed by Parliament. Some records survive for some of the offices, but not many. For outside London: Williams, "Counting Crimes," 81; Michelle Abraham, "The Summary Courts and the Prosecution of Assault in Northampton and Nottingham, 1886–1931" (PhD diss., University of Leicester, 2012), 78.

44 On the decline of magisterial discretion generally see King, *Crime and Justice*; Smith, "Circumventing," 442; Mehta, "Summary Justice," 75–6.

45 "Mansion House Court Register, 1825–29," LMA, CLA/004/04/002; "Guildhall Court Register, 1825–26," LMA, CLA/005/02/001; LMA, CLA/031/03/004.

46 Ibid.

47 For earlier patterns see Paul, *Poverty of Disaster*; Haagen, "Imprisonment," 56.

48 Margot Finn, "Debt and Credit in Bath's Court of Requests," *Urban History* 21, no. 2 (1994): 213.

49 There was a burst of foundations of courts in 1805–11 too. C.W. Brooks, *Lawyers, Litigation and English Society since 1450* (London: Hambledon, 1998), 41, 72.

50 James Grant, *Sketches in London* (London, 1838), 321. Other courts were based in Brentford and Uxbridge, both in Middlesex, and there was a court of record at Hackney and Stephney, which also acted as a court of recovery for small debts. In the City, small debt cases could be heard at the mayor's court at Mansion House and the sheriff's court in Guildhall. "Abstract Return of Courts for Recovery of Small Debts, 1823," PP, xv.275 (576), 10–11.

51 Grant, *Sketches*, 323–5; Finn, "Debt," 214.

52 Finn, "Debt," 213.

53 Because Parliament collected figures from only a handful of prisons, these calculations include only the following prisons: Fleet, Whitecross Street, King's Bench, Marshalsea, Surrey gaol, Borough Compter (from 1809), Newgate, and Giltspur. In 1842 an act of Parliament (5 & 6 Vic c. 22) closed two debtors' prisons, Fleet and Marshalsea. "Account of the Number Committed to Prisons for Debt, 1819," PP, xvii.145 (237), 18–19, 27–8; "Return of Prisoners for Debt Committed to Gaols in London, 1828," PP, xx.181 (76); ibid., 1829, PP, xviii.275 (69); ibid., 1830, PP, xxii. 189 (632).

54 7 & 8 Vic c. 96.

55 "Extracts from Commissioners' Report," LMA, MA/G/GEN/0471.

56 PP, 1809, iv.215, 19.

57 Grant, *Sketches*, 326; Neild, *Prisons*, 142–3.

58 Sanford Neville and William Manning, *Reports of Cases Argued and Determined in Court of King's Bench*, vol. 2 (London, 1834), 138–46. The ruling did not ban the commitment of debtors to New Prison, but the magistrates nonetheless managed to stop this practice.

59 MPCM, 29 Mar. 1821, LMA, MJ/SP/1821/04/072.

60 See Mehta, "Courts and Prisons," 241.

61 7 Will 4 & 1 Vic c. 77.

62 MCVJNP, 24 Nov. and 1 Dec. 1837, LMA, MA/G/CLE/0001.

63 15 Dec. 1837, ibid.

64 11 Jan. and 1 Feb. 1839, ibid.

65 "Reports Pursuant to Gaol Acts, 1830–31," PP, xii.1 (41), 155; "Persons Committed to Prisons under Summary Process, 1831," PP, xv.101 (131); "Inspectors of Prisons, Home District, First to Fourteenth Reports, 1836–50," PP. For a full breakdown see Mehta, "Confined," 242–3, tables 4.3 and 4.4.

66 MPCM, 1796–1812, MA/G/GEN0002–0003; MPCM, 1824–35, MA/G/GEN/0012; "Reports to Gaol Act, 1830–47," PP.

67 For the 1780s, MSP, *LL*, LMSMPS506770085, LMSMPS506820162, LMSMPS507100024, LMSMPS506800086, LMSMPS507110120, LMSMPS507260052, LMSMPS507500016, LMSMPS507360026, LMSMPS507700034, LMSMPS507810062, LMSMPS508000137, LMSMPS507730252, LMSMPS508180008; Howard, *The State of the Prisons*, 181. For the 1810s, PP, 1818, viii.1, 49.

68 PP, 1818, viii.1, 49–51, 54.

69 "New Prison Accounts, 1816–19," LMA, MA/G/GEN/0478; PP, 1818, viii.1, 49. On top of this, the county spent £20,000 on repairs at the gaol between 1801 and 1831: PP, 1831, xv, 26.
70 "New Prison Rules," LMA, MA/G/GEN/1186; PP, 1828, xx.327, 160–2.
71 In 1844, the year the magistrates resolved to rebuild the gaol, the average number of prisoners held was 108 – well below the gaol's official capacity of 240. Most prisoners were held for less than two weeks, and the greatest period held was about three weeks in the mid-1830s. PP, 1845, xxiii, 393; "Select Committee of House of Lords on Gaols and Houses of Correction, First Report," PP, 1835, xi.1 (438), 249.
72 PP, 1837, xxxii, 129.
73 PP, 1845, xxiii, 396.
74 William Hepworth Dixon, *The London Prisons* (London, 1850), 229.
75 PP, Dec. 1800, 132, 81.
76 PP, 1809, iv.215, 17.
77 "Account of Cells, 1 Mar. 1821," LMA, MJ/SP/1822/03/004.
78 MPCR, Dec. 1822, LMA, MJ/SP/1823/01/133.
79 MPCR, 1821–22, LMA, MJ/SP/1821/10/059; MJ/SP/1821/11/001; MJ/SP/1822/01/033; MJ/SP/1822/05/047; MJ/SP/1822/11/001.
80 MPCM, MA/G/GEN/0002–0003, 0012.
81 "Prison Administration, 2 May and 17 Oct. 1822," LMA, MJ/SP/1822/05/047; LMA, MJ/SP/1823/01/133.
82 Ibid.
83 *Seventh Report SIPD* (London, 1827), 101.
84 On the magistrates' decision-making see *Sixth Report SIPD* (London, 1824), appendix, 96; *Eighth Report SIPD* (London, 1832), appendix, 27–8. For the prison design see "Specifications for Architects, 4 May 1824," LMA, MA/G/GEN/0556. On radial prisons, see Norman Johnston, "The Development of Radial Prisons" (PhD diss., University of Pennsylvania, 1958).
85 MGOC, 6 Apr. 1826, LMA, MJ/O/C/021. *Sixth Report SIPD*, appendix, 17, 96; *Seventh Report SIPD* (London, 1827), appendix, 100.
86 "Committee Report," LMA, MJ/SP/1827/05/139.
87 Smaller works went ahead while the boundary wall was being built. In 1825–26, for example, the chapel was altered for a little under £500 to allow all prisoners to fit. "Draft Minutes, 20 Oct. 1825," LMA, MA/G/CBF/011; *Seventh Report SIPD*, appendix, 100.
88 PP, 1830, xxiv.1, 161; PP, 1830–31, xii.1, 154; "Return of Amount Expended by Middlesex, Surrey and Essex, for Erection and Repairs of Prisons, 1815–36," PP, xlii.293 (569).
89 PP, 1818, viii, 290; *Third Report SIPD* (London, 1821), appendix, 45; *Fourth Report SIPD* (London, 1822), appendix, 56.
90 MPCR, LMA, MJ/SP/1823/01/133, MJ/SP/1823/04/112. It is not clear from the reports whether this just includes vagrants to be passed or all vagrants.
91 "Return of Classes of Prisoners in Middlesex, Surrey and City of London, 1835," PP, xlv.165 (86).
92 "Account of Persons Committed Under Summary Process, 1831," PP, xv.101 (131); "Inspectors of Prisons, Home District, First to Tenth Report," PP, 1836–45.
93 PP, 1840, xxv.1, 22; PP, 1847–48, xxxv.461 (1006), 64–5.
94 The proportion of felons did not grow consistently over the period, but on trend, it did. The female population became especially dominated by felons. PP, 1823–47, "Reports and Schedules to Gaol Acts."

95 "Reports to Gaol Act," PP, 1824–47.
96 7 & 8 Vic c. 96.
97 PP, 1835, xi.1 (438), 226.
98 4 & 5 Will IV c. 36.
99 Based on the twelve days for which population records survive. Neild, *State*, 547.
100 PP, 1819, xvii.371, 44.
101 PP, 1839, xxi.1, 365.
102 PP, 1835, xlv.165, 101.
103 Though no records of the prison population survive, Surrey provided each prisoner with a 1*lb* loaf of bread each day, and records of loaves delivered survive. I have equated the number of loaves with the number of prisoners – an imprecise approach, but one that should give us a rough indication of prisoners held daily. SHC, QS2/6/1795/Eas/11; QS2/6/1796/Mid/19; QS2/6/1795/Mich/33; QS2/6/1796/Eph/47; QS2/6/1796/Eas/9; QS2/6/1797/Mid/63; QS2/6/1796/Mic/39.
104 PP, 1819, xvii.371, 39.
105 *Second Report SIPD*, appendix, 25. On polygonal prisons, see Evans, *Fabrication*, 276–95.
106 *Third Report SIPD*, appendix, 74; *Fourth Report SIPD*, appendix, 58.
107 *Fourth Report SIPD*, appendix, 58.
108 PP, 1835, xlv.165, 101.
109 "New Prison Committee Minute Book, Wandsworth, 1847–52," LMA, ACC/3444/AD/01; "Wandsworth, 1849–50," SHC, QS5/4/5/29–30, QS5/4/6/153–164.
110 "Report on Discipline and Management of Convict Prisons, 1852–53," PP, li.247 (1659), 37, 58. For Brixton, see Neil Davie, "'Business as Usual?' Britain's First Women's Convict Prison, Brixton, 1853–1869," *Crimes and Misdemeanours* 4 (2012): 37–52.
111 For all figures in this paragraph, see PP, 1824, xix.215; "Inspectors of Prisons," PP, 1836–46.
112 "Reports to Gaol Acts," PP, 1824–47; PP, 1837–8, xxx.1; PP, 1845, xxiii.1.
113 By this point, Ludgate Prison was part of Giltspur Prison, and one keeper managed both. Nevertheless, Ludgate was still considered a distinct institution, and the prisoners were kept in separate quarters. PP, 1813–14, iv.249, 9.
114 "Prisoners Committed to Newgate," CAGCP, LMA, COL/CA/GAC/03/001.
115 Sheehan, "System," 101.
116 Neild, *Prisons*, 229.
117 52 Geo III c. 209.
118 Ibid.
119 52 Geo III c. 209.
120 PP, 1818, viii.545, 247; "Select Committee on State of Gaols, 1819," PP, vii.1 (579), 256, 268. For Newgate, PP, 1842, xx.1, 190.
121 The Newgate keeper claimed in 1836 that those convicts sent to Newgate for a period of imprisonment were sent "because they cannot pass the sentence of imprisonment in any other place—it must be in the common gaol." Such an explanation suggests committing bodies had little choice regarding the prison in which offenders were incarcerated. "Minutes of Evidence as to Treatment of Prisoners, 1836," LMA, CLA/035/02/047, no. 2.
122 "Inspectors of Prisons, Third Report, 1837–38," PP, xxx.1 (141), 153.
123 See for example Smith, "Violence," 322.
124 LMA, CLC/275/MS33138/001–006.
125 PP, 1837, xxxii.1, 199; PP, 1842, xx.1, 202–4. The total number includes prisoners committed to the house of correction as well as to the prison side since official figures did not

distinguish between the two. If we had figures only for the prison side of Giltspur, the dominance of night charges and remand prisoners would be even larger.

126 Inspectors' reports show that no felons were committed to await trial in Giltspur. "Inspector of Prisons, Home District, Second to Fourteenth Report," PP, 1837–50.

127 Howard, *The State of the Prisons*, 208; Neild, *Prisons*, 60, 67; LMA, CLA/031/01/003; *Fifth Report SIPD* (London, 1823), appendix, III.

128 A committee considering the compter's enlargement set up in October 1816, but plans were delayed after the Bridgehouse Committee refused to use their funds to pay for the work. "Letter to Sir John Eamer, Lord Mayor, from John Law, 30 Sept. 1816," LMA, COL/CA/GAC/03/002; CAGCP, 15 Oct. 1816, 21 Jan. 1817, LMA, COL/CA/GAC/03/002; PP, 1818, viii.297, 118–23.

129 PP, 1837, xxxii.1, 178. For the cost: PP, 1831, xv.491, 36.

130 For example PP, 1837–38, xxx.1, 278–81. Surrey started requiring such inmates to pick oakum from the 1830s, probably under pressure from the Home Office. Across England, different counties took distinct approaches. See also *Rules and Regulations for Gaol and House of Correction of the County of Worcester* (1844).

CHAPTER SIX

1 Norman Gash, "After Waterloo: British Society and the Legacy of the Napoleonic Wars," *Transactions of the Royal Historical Society* 28 (1978): 147, 152–4.

2 David Green, *Pauper Capital: London and the Poor Law, 1790–1870* (Farnham, UK: Ashgate, 2010), 26, 30–6; Eastwood, *Governing*, ch. 5–7.

3 E.P. Thompson, *The Making of the English Working Class* (London: Victor Gollancz, 1963); John Belchem, *Popular Radicalism in Nineteenth-Century Britain* (Basingtoke, UK: Macmillan, 1996); Philip Harling, "Rethinking Old Corruption," *Past and Present* 147 (1995): 127–58.

4 "Prisons and Penitentiaries," *Quarterly Review* 30 (1823–24): 425, 440. Quoted in Randall McGowen, "Penal Reform and Politics in Early Nineteenth-Century England," in *Imagining the British Atlantic after the American Revolution*, ed. Michael Meranze and Saree Makdisi (Toronto: University of Toronto Press, 2015), 200.

5 William Allen quoted in Randall McGowen, "A Powerful Sympathy: Terror, the Prison, and Humanitarian Reform in Early Nineteenth-Century Britain," *Journal of British Studies* 25, no. 3 (1996): 312–34, here 326–7.

6 SIPD was created by the merging of two older societies, the Society for the Diffusion of Knowledge on the Punishment of Death and Imprisonment of Prison Discipline (1801) and the Society for Investigating the Cause of Increase of Juvenile Delinquency (1815).

7 McGowen, "Sympathy," 313, 326–7; Forsythe, *Reform*, 16; R.A. Cooper, "The English Quakers and Prison Reform, 1809–23," *Quaker History* 68 (1979): 3–19; Elizabeth Fry, *Memoir of the Life of Elizabeth Fry*, vol. 1, ed. Katharine Fry and Rachel Elizabeth Cresswell (London, 1847), 384.

8 For example see the ideas of Jeremy Bentham in Janet Semple, *Bentham's Prison: A Study of the Panopticon Penitentiary* (Oxford, UK: Clarendon, 1993).

9 Crone, *Illiterate Inmates*, 12–13.

10 Ignatieff, *Just Measure*, 174.

11 R.A. Cooper, "Jeremy Bentham, Elizabeth Fry, and English Prison Reform," *Journal of the History of Ideas* 42, no. 4 (1981): 675–90, here 687–90.

12 Quoted in McGowen, "Well-Ordered Prison," 98.
13 Ibid., 88; Ignatieff, *Just Measure*, 174–5.
14 Cooper, "Bentham, Fry, and Reform," 688–9. Cooper may take this point too far. In 1823 the PDS published a new set of rules for prisons. In the appendix, in a section on tread-wheel labour, they note that in "some prisons by far too much dependence has been placed on the deterring influence of tread-wheel labour, while but little earnestness had been evinced to take advantage of that subjection of mind which the punishment has a tendency to produce, and which might be available for the purposes of religious impressions and permanent improvement." They stressed that tread-wheel labour should be used in combination with religious instruction; if hard labour was "considered as superseding or weakening the necessity for [ministers'] labours," this should be "deplored." See "Rules for the Government of Gaols (London, 1823)," LMA, MA/G/GEN/1242, here 96.
15 Finn, *Credit*, 160; Finn, "Henry Hunt's Peep into a Prison," in *English Radicalism 1550–1850*, ed. Glenn Burgess and Matthew Festenstein (Cambridge, 2007), 191–216, here 200.
16 On attitudes towards the poor and poor law policy, see Green, *Pauper Capital*, 5–12, 48–50; Eastwood, *Governing*, 101–32, 146–5; John Broad, "Parish Economies of Welfare, 1650–1834," *Historical Journal* 42, no. 4 (1999): 985–1006.
17 Evans, *Fabrication*, 250.
18 Henriques, "Separate," 67; Henriques, *Welfare*, 164; DeLacy, *Lancashire*, 211.
19 Cooper, "English Prison Reform," 268–9; for such views amongst London magistracy: *PP*, 1819, vii.1 (579), 285.
20 CLA/032/01/041b, 22.
21 McGowen, "Well-Ordered," 89–90; R.A. Cooper, "English Prison Reform"; DeLacy, "Grinding Men Good? Lancashire's Prisons at Mid-Century," in *Policing and Punishment in Nineteenth-Century Britain*, ed. V. Bailey (London: Routledge, 1981), 201.
22 Henriques, "Separate," 67; Ignatieff, *Just Measure*, 179; McGowen, "Well-Ordered," 90.
23 Finn, "Peep," 200.
24 For this period see Carey, *Empire of Hell*; Devereaux, *Execution*, ch. 7–9.
25 One tactic of the anti-transportation movement was to suggest that the punishment bred vice – in particular, campaigners focused on allegations of bestiality and homosexuality. Tim Causer, "Anti-Transportation, 'Unnatural Crime' and the Horrors of Norfolk Island," *Journal of Australian Colonial History* 14 (2012): 230–40; Kirsty Reid, *Gender, Crime and Empire* (Manchester, UK: Manchester University Press, 2007).
26 For these committees and the effect of changing laws see M.J.D. Roberts, "Public and Private in Early Nineteenth-Century London," *Social History* 13, no. 3 (1988): 273–94; M.J.D. Roberts, "Reshaping the Gift Relationship," *International Review of Social History* 36, no. 2 (1991): 201–31; Lawrence, "Pre-emptive Policing," 513–31.
27 "Report of the Committee on Mendicity, 1814–15," *PP*, iii.231 (473), 5.
28 "Select Committee on Metropolis' Police Offices, 1837–38," *PP*, xv.321 (578), 35.
29 "Report from Committee on Existing Laws relating to Vagrants, 1821," *PP*, iv.121 (543), 4.
30 *PP*, 1837–38, xv, 35. See also comments made to 1834 Parliamentary Committee on Poor Laws by those who claimed that paupers were "too much protected" at the magistrate courts. Cited in Green, *Pauper Capital*, 170–6, here 173.
31 For distress as justification see comments made by Middlesex magistrates, an officer attached to a magistrate office, and a prison clerk: *PP*, 1821, iv, 35, 60–1, 69, 88.
32 Ibid., 62.
33 Ibid.

34 Ibid., 58, 60. As Hobler notes, the Lord Mayor formerly gave such individuals a walking pass, rather than punishing them by imprisonment, but this practice was banned.

35 PP, Dec. 1800, 132, 15, 17, 111; PP, 1809, iv, 13, 16, 35; CLA/032/01/041b.

36 PP, 1821, iv.121, 64.

37 "Select Committee on Prison Discipline, 1850," PP, xvii.1 (632), 20, q241; Eric Stockdale, "The Rise of Joshua Jebb, 1837–1850," *British Journal of Criminology* 16, no. 2 (1976): 164–70.

38 BPCM, 14 Jan. 1795, LMA, CLC/275/MS33131/001; BCGM, 25 Feb. 1796, LMA, CLC/275/MS33011/25.

39 LMA, CLC/275/MS33011/25.

40 3 Geo IV c. 40.

41 LMA, CLC/275/MS33138/001–003; *Report of Bridewell*, 23.

42 For early evidence for organized resistance to the treadmills by the prisoners see BPSCM, 19 Nov. 1823, CLC/275/MS33132/006.

43 "Agreement between Prison Committee and Fletcher, 3 May 1817," CAGCP, LMA, COL/CA/GAC/03/002; "Remarks made on Fletcher's Bill," ibid.; "Contract for a Mill," ibid.; *Fourth Report SIPD*, 58.

44 "1823 Rules," LMA, MA/G/GEN/1270; "Report of Visiting Justices," LMA, MJ/SP/1823/01/033.

45 MPCM, MJ/SP/1821/04/072; MJ/SP/1821/06/003.

46 "Duty and Power of Visiting Justices and Proposed Rules," LMA, MJ/SP/1829/A/001.

47 "Draft Minutes, 17 Oct. 1835, 5 Dec. 1835," LMA, MA/G/CBF/013.

48 MA/G/GEN 1230; "Report Book, 12 May 1843 and 9 June 1843," LMA, MA/G/CBF/006.

49 "Select Committee on T. Croggon's Imprisonment in Newgate, 1812–13," PP, iii.247 (312); PP, 1813–14, iv.249; PP, 1818, viii.1; PP, 1818, viii.297; "Royal commission on Fleet, Westminster and Marshalsea, 1819," PP, xi.325 (109).

50 Alex Pitofsky, "The Warden's Court Martial: James Oglethorpe and the Politics of Eighteenth-Century Prison Reform," *Eighteenth-Century Life* 24 (2000): 88–102; Jerry White, "Pain and Degradation in Georgian London," *History Workshop Journal* 68 (2009): 69–98.

51 Legislation passed includes 55 Geo III c. 50; 56 Geo III c. 116; 4 Geo IV c. 64; 5 Geo IV c. 85; 5 & 6 Will IV c. 38. See also Devereaux, "Convicts and the State," ch. 4–7; Cooper, "Reform," ch. 12.

52 Eastwood, *Governing*, 251–3.

53 I plan to discuss these events in greater detail in a forthcoming article on the politics of prison reform in the City, but more information can also be found in Mehta, "Courts and Prisons," 289–94.

54 CAGCP, 3 Apr. 1816, LMA, COL/CA/GAC/03/001; "Newgate Rules, 1817," LMA, CLA/035/02/034; PP, 1818, viii, 48; LMA, MA/G/GEN/1186.

55 LMA, CLA/035/02/034; LMA, MA/G/GEN/1186.

56 PP, 1818, viii.1, 9; MA/G/GEN/1186.

57 "Reports and Schedules pursuant to Gaol Acts, 1828," PP, xix.1, 401 (24), 297.

58 PP, 1837–38, xxx.1, 261, 276; PP, 1837, xxxii.1, 152, 179, 189, 203.

59 LMA, MA/G/GEN/1186; LMA, CLA/035/02/034.

60 "Additional Rules: New Prison, 1823," LMA, MA/G/GEN/1187; "Proposed Rules and Regulations for Giltspur, 1835," LMA, CLA/029/01/003; "Report of Gaol Committee to Court of Alderman with draft of Proposed Regulations, 1847," LMA, CLA/032/01/029/A.

61 PP, 1836, xxxv.1, 6.

62 "Rules and Orders for Management of Clerkenwell New Prison, 1818," LMA, MJ/SP/1818/11/057; PP, 1837, xxxii.1, 178–9.

63 LMA, MA/G/GEN/1186.
64 "Journal of Borough Compter, 16 Dec. 1817, 24 Mar. 1818," LMA, CLA/031/02/019; "Statement of Ordinary, 1823–24," COL/CA/GAC/005; "Reply of inspectors regarding Aldermen's report on Newgate, 1836," *PP*, xlii.283 (486), 1; *PP*, 1837, xxxii.1, 131–2, 178, 186–7.
65 Buxton, *Inquiry*, 11–12; *Rules Proposed for Government of Gaols*, 25; *PP*, 1857, session 1, vii.1 (2169), 188; *PP*, 1829, xx.327, 297.
66 *Journals of the House of Commons*, vol. 78 (London, 1824), 320; *JHC*, vol. 29 (London, 1824), 139.
67 Helen Johnston, *Crime in England, 1815–1880* (Abingdon, UK: Routledge, 2015), ch. 9; King, *Crime and Law*, part i; Heather Shore, *Artful Dodgers: Youth and Crime in Early Nineteenth-Century London* (Woodbridge, UK: Boydell, 2002).
68 Crone, *Illiterate Inmates*, 38–9; "Statement of Ordinary, Papers 1823–24," COL/CA/GAC/005. It is possible that Cotton established the school at the instruction of the aldermen, as an 1815 report had recommended the chaplain found a school for the instruction of children.
69 *Sketch of the Origins and Results of Ladies' Prison Associations, with Hints for the Formation of Local Associations* (London, 1827), 7; *Third Report SIPD*, 50.
70 "Sundry Rules suggested by Ladies appointed for the Employment and Better Management of female Prisoners in Newgate, 1817," COL/CA/GAC/03/002.
71 *Origins of Ladies' Associations*, 7.
72 *Third Report SIPD*, Appendix, 48.
73 *PP*, 1829, xix.1, 401 (24), 229.
74 *PP*, 1839, xxxviii.17 (36), 198.
75 27 Sept. 1821, MJ/O/C/021.
76 *PP*, 1826–27, xix.365 (46), 224; "Reports of Visiting Justices, 14 Mar. 1833," LMA, MJ/SP/XX/549.
77 Forsythe, *Reform*, 18, loosely quoting Joseph Gurney, *Notes on a Visit Made to Some Prisons* (London, 1819).
78 14 Mar. 1833, LMA, MJ/SP/XX/549; *PP*, 1834, xlvi.1 (1), 154.
79 Evans, *Fabrication*, 297–9, 303; Forsythe, *Reform*, 21; DeLacy, *Lancashire*, 203–13; Henriques, "Separate," 67.
80 The SIPD recommended each male prisoner step 12,000 feet a day. *Description of the Tread Mill, for the Employment of Prisoners* (London, 1823).
81 6 Oct. 1825, LMA, MA/G/CBF/011; "Verdict of Inquisition into Death of Jeremiah Bryan," LMA, MJ/SP/1827/PC/028; "Copy of Letter from Hobhouse asking if Bodily Mischief Had Been Experienced by Prisoners on Treadwheel, 24 Dec. 1823," LMA, MA/G/GEN/500.
82 For contemporary opinions see "The Mill-Treaders' Lament at Brixton," *The Literary and Weekly Review* (London), 28 Sept. 1822, 620, accessed from *British Periodicals*, https://www.proquest.com/historical-periodicals/; "The Tread or Stepping Mill," *Liverpool Mercury* (Liverpool), 6 June 1823; John Cox Hippisley, *Prison Labour &c* (London, 1823); "The Tread-mill," *Chambers's Edinburgh Journal* (Edinburgh), 10 Aug. 1839, *British Periodicals*. See also Priestly, *Victorian Prison Lives*, 124–31.
83 Richard Brown and David Fisher, "Mainwaring, George Boulton," *House of Commons*.
84 *Second Report SIPD*, appendix, 68–71.
85 *Third Report SIPD*, 35.
86 "Letter from William Crawford to Edward Harbord," Norfolk Record Office, GTN 5/9/25/5. Harbord was an active reformer and leading magistrate in Norfolk.
87 "Replies from Gaolers to Questions on Labour and Costs," LMA, MA/G/GEN/0481–9.

88 "Reply from John Orridge, 1820," MA/G/GEN/0493.
89 LMA, MA/G/GEN/0481–9; MJ/SP/1803/019; MA/G/GEN/0432; MA/G/CBF/0201; "Report on gaols," LMA, CLA/032/01/041b.
90 With respect to the treadwheel, Bury St Edmunds took a clear leading position in shaping policy throughout England. For its influence see for instance "Minutes of Committee Relating to Gaol, 10 May 1817," Buckingham Archives, Q/AGI/1. For London's influence see for example Report of Committee for Superintending Gaol of Norfolk, 1819," Norfolk Record Office, C/Saa 1/4; "Printed Papers concerning Gaol Administration in other Counties," Wiltshire and Swindon History Centre, A1/516/4.
91 "Report on Discipline, 1820," LMA, MA/G/GEN/0494.
92 "Letter concerning Cubitt's bills," LMA, MA/G/GEN/0499.
93 This is clear from the sub-committee minute books, which record the prisoners working each day. LMA, CLC/275/MS33132/003–005.
94 Ibid. The male prisoners were sometimes employed in pulverizing oysters in these years, but the committee was not satisfied with this labour. The different types of labour introduced are charted in the sub-committee minutes.
95 *Report of Special Committee of Governors*, 14.
96 "Contract with Thomas Miles Cooper for setting up a mill, Oct. 1817," LMA, CAGCP, COL/CA/GAC/03/001; "Agreement with Samuel Fletcher, 3 May 1817," ibid.; *PP*, 1818, viii.297, 82, 84–5; *PP*, 1828, xx.327, 297; *PP*, 1839, xxi.1, 388.
97 DeLacy, *Lancaster*, 207.
98 Ibid., 207–8; *PP*, 1828, xx.327 (2), 22; *PP*, 1835, xi.1, Appendix, No. 9.
99 MPCR, MJ/SP/1823/02/047.
100 *PP*, 1837, xxxii, 85. To assess the proportion of the prison employed in "menial" labour, I have used the daily average number of prisoners in Coldbath Fields in 1836 (871) rather than the specific day in May 1836 as I do not have the latter figure.
101 This was true in Brixton and Giltspur houses of correction too. See *PP*, 1840, xxv.1, 332; *PP*, 1839, xxi.1, 393.
102 Ibid.; *PP*, 1837–38, xxx.367, 303. On 1 Aug. 1839, eighty-three inmates were engaged as "handicraftsmen" or in working in the store yards and grounds of the prison. Interestingly, a fairly large number (thirteen) were employed as "knifemen" – compared to nine carpenters and four shoemakers, for example.
103 Mayhew, *Prisons*, 315. See Bethell, *Star Men*, 128–33, 161–5, for a discussion of printing in convict prisons in a later period.
104 *PP*, 1818, viii.1, 81; *PP*, 1835, xi. 1, 141; *PP*, 1837, xxxii.1, 170; LMA, MA/G/GEN/1270. The use of the term "monitor" is interesting because it was used in schools too. Under the monitorial system, developed independently by Andrew Bell and Joseph Lancaster, older students were used to teach younger students, which enabled one instructor to teach a large number of students at once. David Komline, *The Common School Awakening* (Oxford, UK: Oxford University Press, 2020), 13–23.
105 *PP*, 1837, xxxii.1, 188–9. Tradesmen outside the prison supplied the wardsmen with these goods to sell.
106 MPCR, 14 Sept. 1810, LMA, MA/G/GEN/0003; MPCM, 8 Sept. 1825, LMA, MA/G/CBF/011. For earlier examples, BPSCM, 20 June 1793, 20 Feb. 1794, LMA, CLC/275/MS33132/001. In one case, a prisoner, Mary Guttage, was given two shillings for her extreme industriousness and her court order to be whipped was cancelled.
107 BPSCM, 28 Oct. 1818, LMA, CLC/275/MS33132/005.

108 "Rules for CBF," LMA, MJ/SP/1823/02/047.

109 *PP*, 1818, viii.1, 81.

110 *PP*, 1835, xi.1, 140.

111 *PP*, 1837, xxxii, 85.

112 "Select Committee of House of Lords on State of Prison Discipline," *PP*, 1863, ix.1 (499), vii.

113 The committee recommended that Parliament define hard labour. The 1865 *Prisons Act* did not go quite this far, but it did provide a list of acceptable employments that constituted hard labour. Before this, only the 1779 *Transportation Act* had included such a list, and those works ("raising Sand, Soil, and Gravel from, and cleansing, the River Thames") were not obviously transferrable to prisons. The 1824 act only mentioned the treadwheel, and the discussion revolved around the unsuitability of treadwheel labour for untried inmates.

114 LMA, MJ/SP/1823/02/047, MJ/SP/1823/01/133.

115 *Fourth Report SIPD*, Appendix, 58; CAGCP, 1816–17, COL/CA/GAC/03/002; *PP*, 1818, viii.297, 82.

116 See for example "Mr Penn's Report on Tread Wheel, 1826," Wiltshire and Swindon History Centre, A1/509/10; "Letters from Timothy Bramwell, September to November 1825," Norfolk Record Office, c/saa 1/9.

117 *PP*, 1818, viii.297, 82.

118 "Visiting Magistrates' Report," SHC, QS2/6/1820/Eas/12.

119 *PP*, 1837–88, xxx.1, 296. See also *PP*, 1845, xxiii.1, 407–8.

120 *PP*, 1818, viii.297, 81–2; *Seventh Report SIPD*, Appendix, 87–8.

121 *PP*, 1840, xxv.1, 281. On women's role in laundry work in London see Falcini, "Cleanliness," ch. 4.

122 MPCM, 18 Aug. 1831, LMA, MA/G/GEN/0012; *PP*, 1840, xxv.1, 215; *PP*, 1836, xlii.1, 100; *PP*, 1841 Session 2, iv.1, 250.

123 *PP*, 1850, xxviii.1, 10.

124 There were ten flax-breaking machines in 1826. *Seventh Report SIPD*, Appendix, 86; *PP*, 1837–38, xliii.227, 197.

125 For more on prison uniforms see Vivienne Richmond, *Clothing the Poor in Nineteenth-Century England* (Cambridge: Cambridge University Press, 2013), ch. 10; "Rules for CBF, Oct. 1821," LMA, MJ/SP/1821/10/059; "Teague's report, 4 Nov. 1831," CAGCP, LMA, COL/GAC/03/006.

126 Hanway, *Solitude*, 6.

127 *PP*, 1850, xxviii.1, 14; Mayhew, *Prisons*, 313–14.

128 Mayhew, *Prisons*, 313–14.

129 *PP*, 1836, xlii.1, 101.

130 *PP*, 1850, xxviii.1, 19. See also the Brixton governor's remarks on training prisoners: *PP*, 1835, xi.1, 154.

131 *PP*, 1844, xxxix.403, 196. Richmond, *Clothing*, 40.

132 *PP*, 1839, xxxviii.17, 102.

133 *PP*, 1850, xxviii.1, 19.

134 MPCM, 6 Jan. 1825, LMA, MA/G/CBF/0011; MPCM, 21, 28 July 1831, LMA, MA/G/GEN/0012.

135 "Visiting Justices' Order Book, 26 July 1834," LMA, MA/G/CBF/029.

136 *PP*, 1850, xxviii.1, 14–5.

137 *PP*, 1840, xxv.1, 216.

138 Ibid.; *PP*, 1850, xxviii.1. There does not seem to have been wide popular or trade opposition to these plans at this point, in contrast to what happened after the prison system was nationalized and attempts were made to introduce mat-making: Sean McConville, *English Local Prisons, 1860–1900: Next Only to Death* (London: Routledge, 1995), 254–63.

139 PP, 1842, xxxii.1, 118.
140 PP, 1847–48, lii.465 (96), 147.
141 MPCM, 4 Feb. 1848, LMA, MA/G/CBF/018; PP, 1851, xxvii.1 (1384), 204. For Dagnall see *Post Office London Directory* (London, 1843), 150.
142 PP, 1863, ix.1, 447.
143 Leonore Davidoff and Catherine Hall, *Family Fortunes: Men and Women of the English Middle Class, 1780–1850* (Chicago: Chicago University Press, 1987); Anna Clark, *The Struggle for the Breaches: Gender and the Making of the British Working Class* (Berkeley, CA: University of California Press, 1997); Kathryn Gleadle, *British Women in the Nineteenth Century* (Basingstoke, UK: Palgrave, 2001).
144 PP, 1863, ix.1, vii. The witness evidence from this report broadly highlights the divergence of opinion by officials on productive labour.
145 McConville, *Local Prisons*, 249n58.
146 *Fourth Report* SIPD, 36–7. See also comments made by Hoare, the SIPD chairman and Middlesex magistrate, in PP, 1835, xi.1, 20.
147 PP, 1829, xix.1, 401, 301.
148 PP, 1826–27, xix.365 (46), 231; PP, 1834, xlvi.1, 231. *Sixth Report* SIPD, Appendix, 134–5.
149 SHC, QS2/6/1820/Eas/12.
150 MGOC, 16 Feb., 13 Apr. 1826, LMA, MJ/O/C/021.
151 PP, 1826, xxiv.1, 169.
152 LMA, CLC/275/MS33011/25.
153 BPSCM, 28 Apr. 1819, 18 Mar. 1818, LMA, CLC/275/MS33132/006.
154 For example BPSCM, 1 Nov. 1820, LMA, CLC/275/MS33132/007.
155 PP, 1826–27, xix.365, 226.
156 Ibid.; see also PP, 1836, xlii.1 (31), 99; PP, 1846, xxxiv.187 (53), 151.
157 PP, 1843, xliii.1 (43), 118.
158 For such evidence see "Gaol Reports," PP, 1826–47; BPSCM, 17 May 1826, CLC/275/MS33132/007; "Chaplain's Report, 1844," LMA, MJ/SP/1844/10/008.
159 Evans, *Fabrication*, 388–9.
160 "Select Committee House of Lords on Gaols and Houses of Correction, Second Report," PP, 1835, xii.1, 57 (439), iv–v, viii.

CONCLUSION

1 4 Geo IV c. 64. The act was initially brought by Peel's predecessor, Sidmouth, but his bill was defeated twice. Peel's measure passed on the second attempt. Gash, Devereaux, and Cooper, in contrast to early-twentieth-century historians such as the Webbs, have played down Peel's role in the passage of this bill. Devereaux, for example, notes that Peel was either trying to intercept a policy "before more extensive concessions could be demanded" or "following an opinion that was becoming increasingly difficult to resist": Deveraux, "Convicts," 458; Norman Gash, *Mr. Secretary Peel: The Life of Sir Robert Peel to 1830* (London: Longmans, 1985), 315–17. For the act's passage see Richard Butler, "Rethinking the Origins of the British Prisons Act of 1835: Ireland the Development of Central-Government Prison Inspection, 1820–35," *Historical Journal* 59, no. 3 (2016): 721–46, here 731–6; Cooper, "Reform," 237–42. On the growing culture of audit and the flow of information see David Eastwood, "Amplifying the Province of Legislature: The

Flow of Information and the English State in the Early Nineteenth Century," *Historical Research* 62, no. 149 (1989): 276–94.

2 PP, 1831–32, vii.559 (547); PP (1835), xi.1 (438).

3 Cooper, "Reform," 284–92.

4 5 & 6 Will 4 c. 38. McConville, *Administration*, 170–1; Forsythe, "Centralisation and Local Autonomy: The Experience of English Prisons, 1820–1877," *Journal of Historical Sociology* 4, no. 3 (1991): 317–45; Stockdale, "Prison Inspection," 209–23.

5 Henriques, "Separate," 74–7; William Forsythe, "William Crawford (1788–1847)," ODNB (last updated 3 Jan. 2008), https://doi.org/10.1093/ref:odnb/6646.

6 The act was drafted by Russel and Crawford and introduced into Parliament by Lord John Russel, the Home Secretary. William Forsythe, "The Beginnings of the Separate System of Imprisonment, 1835–1840," *Social Policy and Administration* 13, no. 2 (1979): 109.

7 Tim Crook, "Model Institutions and the Geography of Social Reform in Early Victorian Britain," *Historical Journal* 62, no. 3 (2019): 798.

8 Ibid., 808; Henriques, "Separate," 78.

9 "Report of Aldermen on Report of Inspectors on Newgate, 1836," PP, xlii.231 (414); "Minutes of Evidence on Treatment of Prisoners in Newgate," LMA, CLA/035/02/047.

10 "Rules for New Prison, Dec. 1837," LMA, MA/G/GEN/1205; "Proposed Rules for Giltspur, 1835," LMA, CLA/029/01/003.

11 PP, 1835, xi.1, 225.

12 Ibid., 203; "Regulations for House of Correction and New Prison, 1842," LMA, MA/G/GEN/1243.

13 MCVJNP, 6 and 20 Oct. 1837, 15 Dec. 1837, 11 Jan. 1838, LMA, MA/G/CLE/0001; PP, 1845, xxiii.1, 397.

14 MCVJNP, 13 and 26 Oct. 1837, 19 Dec. 1837, LMA, MA/G/CLE/0001.

15 19 and 24 Jan. 1838, 2 Feb. 1838, ibid.

16 "Inspectors of Prisons, Home District, Twenty-Third Report, 1857–58," PP, xxix.69 (2411), 108.

17 PP, 1837, xlv.1 (108), 99.

18 James J. Willis, "Transportation versus Imprisonment in Eighteenth- and Nineteenth-Century Britain: Penal Power, Liberty, and the State," *Law and Society Review* 39 (2005): 171–210, here 172; David Philips, "A Just Measure of Crime, Authority, Hunters and Blue Locusts: The 'Revisionist' Social History of Crime and the Law in Britain 1780–1850," in *Social Control and the State: Historical and Comparative Essays*, ed. S. Cohen and A. Scull (Oxford, UK: Blackwells, 1983), 67. See also Ignatieff, "State, Civil Society, and Total Institutions."

19 Willis, "Transportation," 198.

20 *Parliamentary Register*, vol. 4 (London: J. Debrett, 1776), 104–6; *Parliamentary Register* (London: J. Almon, 1778), 83–4.

21 Nathan, "Letter IX. To my Fellow Subjects," *Public Advertiser* (London), 6 July 1778. See also Jonas Hanway, "Letter IX," *Public Advertiser*, 21 Apr. 1779; "Observations on Bill," *Morning Chronicle* (London), 19 June 1778; "Observations on the Bill Continued," *Morning Chronicle* (London), 23 June 1778.

22 Devereaux, "Inexperienced Humanitarians?," 877.

23 Willis, "Transportation," 172; Foucault, *Discipline and Punish*.

Bibliography of Manuscript and Archival Sources

BODLEIAN ARCHIVES AND MANUSCRIPTS, UNIVERSITY OF OXFORD, UK

MS. Eng. misc. e. 400 "Notebook containing notes by Howard on Visits to Prisons and Hospitals, 1786–87"
MS. Eng. hist. c. 295 "Observations on Treatment of Prisoners in Coldbath Fields," Burdett-Coutts Papers, 1789–99
MS. Eng. hist. c. 296 "Papers of Burdett relating to Treatment of Political Prisoners, 1798–1833"

BRITISH LIBRARY, LONDON, UK

Add MS 12496, document no. 236, "Petition of Jacob Stoit for Setting the Poor at Work"
Add MS 61618, "Petitions to Queen Anne, George I, etc., of and relating to Detained Criminals"
Sloane MS 2722, "Rules for the Government of Bridewell, 1552"

BUCKINGHAMSHIRE ARCHIVES, AYLESBURY, UK

Q/AG/1/1 "Minutes of Committee Relating to Gaol, May 1819"
Q/AG/11/47 "Draft Rules for Aylesbury Gaol and House of Correction"
Q/AG/11/48 "Rules, Orders, and Regulations for Bury St Edmunds Gaol and House of Correction, 1805"

LONDON METROPOLITAN ARCHIVES, LONDON, UK

Bridewell Hospital
CLC/275/MS33011/023–026 "Minutes of the Court of Governors, 1751–1822"
CLC/275/MS33133 "Extracts from Prison Committee Minutes"
CLC/275/MS33138/001–005 "Commitment Books, 1809–25"
CLC/275/MS33132/001–007 "Prison Sub-Committee Minute Books, 1792–1832"
CLC/275/MS33131/001–002 "Prison Committee Minute Books, 1775–1802"
CLC/275/MS33140/001–007 "Weekly Returns of Prisoners in Custody, 1817–23"
CLC/275/MS33141/001 "Character Books, 1841"

City Courts
CLA/004/04/002 "Mansion House, Court Register, 1825–29"
CLA/005/02/001, 003 "Guildhall, Court Registers, 1825–26, 1836–37"
CLA/031/03 "Southwark Compter, Magistracy"
COL/CA/01/01/222–3, 226 "Court of Aldermen Repositories"

City Prisons and Prison Administration

CLA/028/01/027 "Wood Street Compter, lists of prisoners, 1788–91"
CLA/028/03/002 "Wood Street, apothecaries bill, 1675"
CLA/028/03/011 "Wood Street Compter, Rules"
CLA/029/01/002, 004, 007 "Giltspur Street Compter, Administration"
CLA/029/02/001–004 "Giltspur Compter, Rebuilding"
CLA/030/01/014 "Poultry Compter and Giltpsur Street, Charge Book, 1802–04, 1807–09"
CLA/030/01/015 "Giltspur Street, Charge Book, 1809–11"
CLA/030/01/019 "Poultry Charge Book, 1800–04"
CLA/030/01/023 "Giltspur Street, Commitment Book, 1811–23"
CLA/031/01/001 "Southwark Compter, committals for debt, 1811–20"
CLA/031/01/003–007 "Southwark, Charge Books, 1814–42"
CLA/031/01/009 "Southwark, committals for trial, 1814–42"
CLA/031/02/008 "Letter, Lord John Russel, to visiting magistrates, October 1835"
CLA/031/02/009 "Appointment of John Law"
CLA/031/02/010 "Southwark, a short account"
CLA/031/02/013 "Southwark, miscellaneous papers, 1814–42"
CLA/031/02/015 "Southwark, surgeon's visiting book, 1814–23"
CLA/031/02/016 "Southwark, visiting book, 1823–36"
CLA/031/02/017 "Southwark, weekly return of prisoners"
CLA/031/02/018 "Return of Borough Compter, 1822–34"
CLA/031/02/019 "Journal of Borough Compter, 1817–23"
CLA/032/01/012 "Extracts relating to Foundation of Prisons"
CLA/032/01/034 "Thomas Gibbs, apothecary: papers"
CLA/032/01/035 "An address to the livery and citizens re Alderman Clarke and Mr. Dornford"
CLA/032/01/037, 044 "Prison Returns, 1808–19, 1823–44"
CLA/032/01/038 "Report from the Committee on Gaols of London, 1814"
CLA/032/01/039 "Report on Gaols in England"
CLA/032/01/040 "Particulars of various prisons, being data for reports"
CLA/032/01/041/A–B "Committee of Aldermen Report, 1815"
CLA/032/01/042 "Rough minute book, 1814"
CLA/032/01/045 "Minutes of Committee on Newgate and Compters, 1719"
CLA/032/02/004–006 "Committee for Rebuilding Compters"
CLA/035/02/030–036 "Newgate Prison, Rules and Orders"
CLA/035/02/047, "Minutes of Evidence as to treatment of prisoners in Newgate, 1836"
CLA/035/02/048 "Rough Minutes, Letters, and Papers relative to Prisoners' Grievances"
CLA/035/02/050 "Visiting Justices Minute Books, 1814–23"
COL/CC/NGC/01/01/001 "Common Council Newgate Committee, Minute Book, 1755–66"
COL/CC/NGC/01/04/001 "Common Council Newgate Committee, Journal, 1767–85"
COL/CA/PCA/01/001–003 "Aldermen Prisons Committee, Rough Minutes, c. 1784–97"
COL/CA/GAC/01/001–006 "Aldermen Gaol Committee, Minutes, 1817–33"
COL/CA/GAC/03/001–006 "Aldermen Gaol Committee, Papers, 1812–31"
COL/SVD/PL/08 "Surveyor's Department, Plans, Justice"
COL/CCS/PL/01 "Comptroller's Bridge House Plans"
COL/CCS/PL/02 "Comptroller's City Lands Plans, Prisons"

Other

COL/CC/WPC/02/001 "Watch and Police Committee Returns, 1827–31"

Middlesex: Court in Session

MJ/CC/B "Calendars of Prisoners"
MJ/CC/R "Calendars of Prisoners"
MJ/CC/V/001–002 "Registers of Prisoners, 1747–48, 1778–80"
MJ/CP/P "Lists of Prisoners after Trial"
MJ/O/C/021 "Middlesex General Orders of Court, 1824–26"
MJ/SB/B "Sessions Books, Minutes"
MJ/SP/1700–1840 "Sessions Papers"
MJ/SP/XX/549–553, 558 "Judicial Administrative Papers"
MSJ/C/C "Summary Convictions, 1774–94"

Middlesex: Prison Administration

MA/D/G/005, 007 "Prison Building Contracts"
MA/G/GEN "Prison Administration"
MA/G/CBF/1–456 "House of Correction, Cold Bath Fields"
MA/G/CLE/0001–0002 "New Prison Clerkenwell, Visiting Justices Committee, Minutes, 1837–44"
MA/G/CLE/0032–3 "Cash Book of New Prison Keeper, 1790–98"
MF/416–439 "Hemp Accounts"
ACC/3444/AD/01 "New Prison Committee Minute Book, Wandsworth, 1847–52"

NATIONAL ARCHIVES AT KEW, LONDON, UK

PROB 11/1443/147 "Will of Peter Perchard"
PROB 11/1192/24 "Will of Nicholas Nixon"
HO 77 "Home Office: Newgate Prison Calendars, 1782–1853"
HO 26/1–7 "Home Office: Criminal Registers of Prisoners in Middlesex and the City, 1791–1800"

NORFOLK RECORD OFFICE, NORWICH, UK

C/Saa 1/1 "Rules of Ipswich Gaol"
C/Saa 1/3 "*Three Letters on Prison Discipline, Addressed to the Editor of the Norwich Mercury in the Month of September 1819*"
C/Saa 1/4 "Report of Committee for Superintending Gaol of Norfolk, 1819"
C/Saa 1/9 "Letters from Timothy Bramwell, Sept. to Nov. 1825"
C/Saa 1/10 "Rules for Gaol and Houses of Correction for County of Norfolk, 1824"
GTN 5/9/25/5 "Letter from William Crawford to Edward Harbord"
MF/RO 576 "Norfolk County Gaol, Keeper's Daily Journal, 1822–35"
NCR 12d/17 "Papers Relating to the Bridewell"
Y/L 2/46 "Great Yarmouth Gaol Keeper's Journals, 1825–35"

SIR JOHN SOANE'S MUSEUM COLLECTION, LONDON, UK

D4/4/1–23 "George Dance Office, Prisons"
D4/3/4–35 "Dance, Prisons"

SURREY HISTORY CENTRE, WOKING, UK

LM/COR/4/16 "Letter from Privy Council to Surrey Justices, June 1605"
QS2/6/1701–1825 "Surrey Quarter Session Bundles"
QS2/4/1/1–4 "Minutes and Accounts for New County Gaol, 1791–1824"
QS5/4/5 "Papers relating to Acquisition and Development of Gaols and Session House"
QS5/4/6/83–103 "Brixton: Plans"
QS5/4/6/153–64 "Wandsworth House of Correction"
QS5/4/7 "Rules for Gaols"

WILTSHIRE AND SWINDON HISTORY CENTRE, CHIPPENHAM, UK

A1/516/4 "Printed Papers concerning Gaol Administration in other Counties"
A1/509/10 "Mr Penn's Report on Tread Wheel, 1826"

ONLINE DEPOSITORIES

British History Online, http://www.british-history.ac.uk/
British Library Newspapers, https://www.gale.com/intl/primary-sources/british-library-newspapers
British Newspaper Archive, https://www.britishnewspaperarchive.co.uk/
British Periodicals, https://www.proquest.com/historical-periodicals
Digital Panopticon, https://www.digitalpanopticon.org/
Eighteenth-Century Collections Online, https://www.gale.com/intl/primary-sources/eighteenth-century-collections-online
London Lives, http://www.londonlives.org
Metropolitan Museum of Art, https://www.metmuseum.org/art/collection
Proceedings of the Old Bailey Online, http://www.oldbaileyonline.org
Seventeenth- and Eighteenth-Century Burney Newspapers Collection, British Library, https://www.gale.com/intl/c/17th-and-18th-century-burney-newspapers-collection
UK Parliamentary Papers, https://parlipapers.proquest.com/
University of North Texas Libraries, https://digital.library.unt.edu/
Wellcome Collection, https://wellcomecollection.org

Index